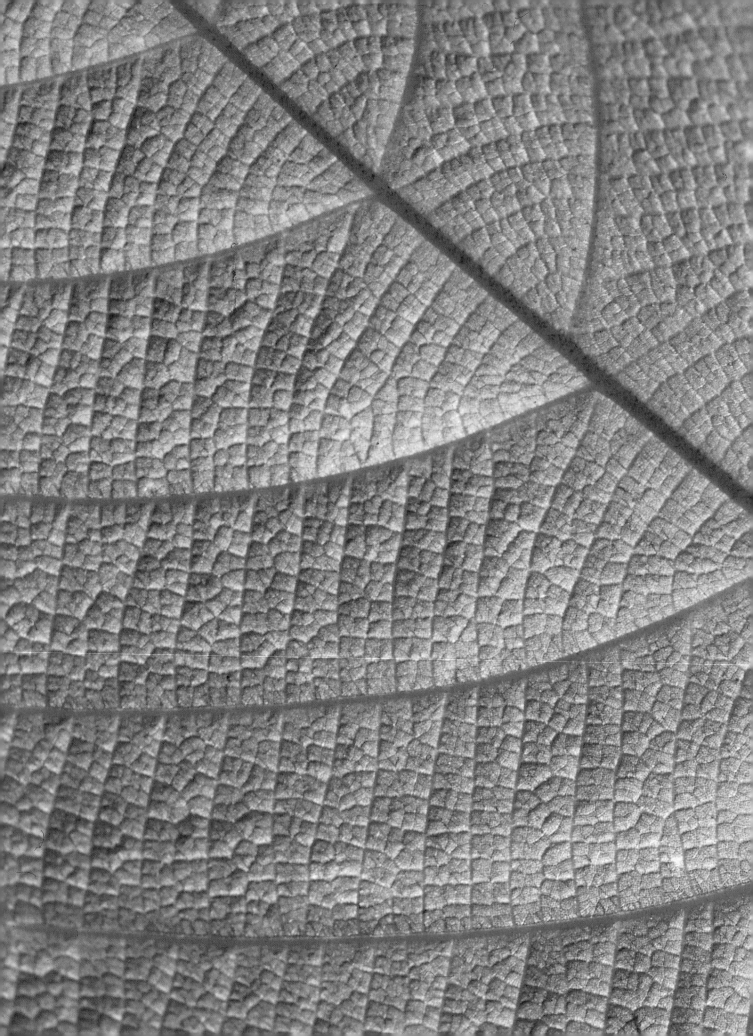

HARCOURT

Science

CALIFORNIA EDITION

Harcourt School Publishers

Orlando • Boston • Dallas • Chicago • San Diego

www.harcourtschool.com

Cover Image
This frog is a reticulated, clown tree frog. It is found in the rain forest surrounding the Amazon river valley in Peru.

Printed in the United States of America

ISBN 0-15-317655-5

14 15 16 17 18 19 20 032 10 09 08 07 06 05

Authors

Marjorie Slavick Frank
Former Adjunct Faculty Member at
    Hunter, Brooklyn, and Manhattan
    Colleges
New York, New York

Robert M. Jones
Professor of Education
University of Houston-Clear Lake
Houston, Texas

Gerald H. Krockover
Professor of Earth and Atmospheric
    Science Education
School Mathematics and Science
    Center
Purdue University
West Lafayette, Indiana

Mozell P. Lang
Science Education Consultant
Michigan Department of Education
Lansing, Michigan

Joyce C. McLeod
Visiting Professor
Rollins College
Winter Park, Florida

Carol J. Valenta
Vice President—Education,
    Exhibits, and Programs
St. Louis Science Center
St. Louis, Missouri
Former teacher, principal, and
    Coordinator of Science Center
    Instructional Programs
Los Angeles Unified School District
Los Angeles, California

Barry A. Van Deman
Science Program Director
Arlington, Virginia

Senior Editorial Advisor

Napoleon Adebola Bryant, Jr.
Professor Emeritus of Education
Xavier University
Cincinnati, Ohio

Program Advisors

George W. Bright
Professor of Mathematics Education
The University of North Carolina at
    Greensboro
Greensboro, North Carolina

Pansy Cowder
Science Specialist
Tampa, Florida

Robert H. Fronk
Head, Science/Mathematics
    Education Department
Florida Institute of Technology
Melbourne, Florida

Gloria R. Guerrero
Education Consultant
Specialist in English as a Second
    Language
San Antonio, Texas

Bernard A. Harris, Jr.
Physician and Former Astronaut
(STS 55—*Space Shuttle Columbia*,
STS 63—*Space Shuttle Discovery*)
Vice President, SPACEHAB Inc.
Houston, Texas

Lois Harrison-Jones
Education and Management
    Consultant
Dallas, Texas

Linda Levine
Educational Consultant
Orlando, Florida

Kenneth R. Mechling
Professor of Biology and Science
    Education
Clarion University of Pennsylvania
Clarion, Pennsylvania

Barbara ten Brink
Science Director
Round Rock Independent School
    District
Round Rock, Texas

Reviewers and Contributors

Jay Bell
K-6 Science Specialist, Curriculum
    Department
Lodi Unified School District
Lodi, California

Roland Boucher
Principal, Fox and Burnham Schools
Haverhill, Massachussetts

Kathy Jo Graley
Teacher, Kenna Elementary
Charleston, West Virginia

Gary D. Gray
Teacher, Eastern Hills Elementary
Fort Worth ISD
Fort Worth, Texas

Clyde Partner
Science/Health Curriculum
    Coordinator
Evanston S.D. #65
Evanston, Illinois

Michael F. Ryan
Educational Technology Specialist
Lake County Schools
Tavares, Florida

Judy Taylor
Teacher, Silvestri Junior High School
Las Vegas, Nevada

UNIT A

L I F E   S C I E N C E
Systems of Living Things

Chapter 1

From Single Cells To Body Systems	**A2**
Lesson 1—What Are Cells, and What Do They Do?	A4
Lesson 2—How Do Body Systems Transport Materials?	A14
Lesson 3—How Do Bones, Muscles, and Nerves Work Together?	A22
Science Through Time • Discovering Cells	A28
People in Science • Bernard A. Harris Jr.	A30
Activities for Home or School	A31
Chapter Review and Test Preparation	A32

Chapter 2

Classifying Living Things	**A34**
Lesson 1—How Do Scientists Classify Living Things?	A36
Lesson 2—How Are Animals Classified?	A42
Lesson 3—How Are Plants Classified?	A48
Science Through Time • Naming Living Things	A54
People in Science • Ynes Enriquetta Julietta Mexia	A56
Activities for Home or School	A57
Chapter Review and Test Preparation	A58

Chapter 3

Plants and Their Adaptations	**A60**
Lesson 1—What Are the Functions of Roots, Stems, and Leaves?	A62
Lesson 2—How Do Plants Recycle Materials?	A70
Lesson 3—How Do Plants Reproduce?	A78
Lesson 4—How Do People Use Plants?	A86
Science and Technology • Potato Vaccines	A92
People in Science • Alice Eastwood	A94
Activities for Home or School	A95
Chapter Review and Test Preparation	A96

Chapter 4

Plant Processes	**A98**
Lesson 1—How Do Plants Make Food?	A100
Lesson 2—How Do Plants Respond To Light and Gravity?	A108
Lesson 3—How Do Vascular Plants Reproduce Sexually?	A114
Lesson 4—How Do Plants Grow?	A120
Science and Technology • Corn Cards and Super Slurpers	A128
People in Science • Shirley Mah Kooyman	A130
Activities for Home or School	A131
Chapter Review and Test Preparation	A134
Unit Project Wrap Up	A136

UNIT B

EARTH SCIENCE
Weather and Space

Chapter 1 — Earth's Air and Water — B2

Lesson 1—What Makes Up Earth's Atmosphere?	B4
Lesson 2—How Are Atmospheric Conditions Measured?	B10
Lesson 3—What Role Do Oceans Play in the Water Cycle?	B18
Lesson 4—Why Is the Water Cycle Important?	B24
Science and Technology • Wetlands with a Purpose	B30
People in Science • Denise Stephenson-Hawk	B32
Activities for Home or School	B33
Chapter Review and Test Preparation	B34

Chapter 2 — Earth's Weather — B36

Lesson 1—What Causes Wind?	B38
Lesson 2—How Do Air Masses Affect Weather?	B44
Lesson 3—What Causes Severe Storms?	B50
Science Through Time • Major Events in Weather Forecasting	B58
People in Science • Carolyn Kloth	B60
Activities for Home or School	B61
Chapter Review and Test Preparation	B62

Chapter 3 — Weather Prediction and Climate — B64

Lesson 1—How Can Weather Be Predicted?	B66
Lesson 2—What Is Climate and How Does it Change?	B74
Science and Technology • Tracking El Niño	B82
People in Science • Edward Lorenz	B84
Activities for Home or School	B85
Chapter Review and Test Preparation	B86

Chapter 4 — Earth and the Moon — B88

Lesson 1—How Do Earth and the Moon Compare? — B90
Lesson 2—How Have People Explored Space? — B98
   Science Through Time • The History of Rockets and Spaceflight — B106
   People in Science • Harrison Schmitt — B108
   Activities for Home or School — B109
Chapter Review and Test Preparation — B110

Chapter 5 — The Solar System — B112

Lesson 1—What Are the Features of the Sun? — B114
Lesson 2—What Are the Planets Like? — B122
Lesson 3—Why Do the Planets Stay in Orbit? — B130
   Science and Technology • Magnetars — B136
   People in Science • Julio Navaro — B138
   Activities for Home or School — B139
Chapter Review and Test Preparation — B142

Unit Project Wrap Up — B144

PHYSICAL SCIENCE

Matter and Energy

Chapter 1   **Matter and Its Properties**   **C2**

Lesson 1—How Can Physical Properties Be Used to Identify Matter?   C4
Lesson 2—How Does Matter Change from One State to Another?   C12
Lesson 3—How Does Matter React Chemically?   C20
     Science and Technology • Self-Healing Asphalt   C28
     People in Science • Theophilus Leapheart   C30
     Activities for Home or School   C31
Chapter Review and Test Preparation   C34

Chapter 2   **Atoms and Elements**   **C36**

Lesson 1—What Are Atoms and Elements?   C38
Lesson 2—What Are Compounds?   C46
     Science Through Time • Discovering Elements   C52
     People in Science • Glenn Seaborg   C54
     Activities for Home or School   C55
Chapter Review and Test Preparation   C58

Chapter 3   **Energy**   **C60**

Lesson 1—What Are Kinetic and Potential Energy?   C62
Lesson 2—What Is Electric Energy?   C68
Lesson 3—What Are Light and Sound Energy?   C76
Lesson 4—What Are Thermal and Chemical Energy?   C84
     Science Through Time • Developing Sources of Energy   C90
     People in Science • Jean M. Bennett   C92
     Activities for Home or School   C93
Chapter Review and Test Preparation   C94

Unit Project Wrap Up   C96

Extension Chapters

Chapter 1 | **Renewable and Nonrenewable Resources** **E2**

Lesson 1—What Are Natural Resources?   E4
Lesson 2—How Do Fossil Fuels Form?   E10
Lesson 3—How Are Natural Resources Conserved?   E18
    Science and Technology • Getting More Oil from Wells   E24
    People in Science • Paul D. MacCready   E26
    Activities for Home or School   E27
Chapter Review and Test Preparation   E28

Chapter 2 | **How People Use Energy** **E30**

Lesson 1—How Do People Use Fossil Fuels?   E32
Lesson 2—How Can Moving Water Generate Electricity?   E38
Lesson 3—What Other Sources of Energy Do People Use?   E44
    Science and Technology • Canola Motor Oil   E50
    People in Science • Meredith Gourdine   E52
    Activities for Home or School   E53
Chapter Review and Test Preparation   E54

Introduction and References

Introduction

Using Science Process Skills	x
Science Safety	xvi

References

Science Handbook	R2
Health Handbook	R11
Glossary	R42
Index	R52

Using Science Process Skills

When scientists try to find an answer to a question or do an experiment, they use thinking tools called process skills. You use many of the process skills whenever you think, listen, read, and write. Think about how these students used process skills to help them answer questions and do experiments.

Greg is finding leaves for his leaf collection. He carefully **observes** the leaves and **compares** their shapes, sizes, and colors. He **measures** each leaf with a ruler. Then he **classifies** the leaves into groups by their sizes.

Try This Use the process skills of observing, comparing, measuring, and classifying to organize your own collection of nature objects.

Talk About It By what other characteristics could Greg classify the leaves in his collection?

Process Skills

Observe—use the senses to learn about objects and events

Compare—identify characteristics of things or events to find out how they are alike and different

Measure—compare an attribute of an object, such as its mass, length, or volume, to a standard unit such as a gram, a centimeter, or a liter

Classify—group or organize objects or events in categories based on specific characteristics

It is a rainy Monday. Pilar wants to know if it will rain during the coming weekend. She **gathers** and **records** data to make a prediction about the weather. She observes the weather each day of the week and records it. She **displays** the data on a chart. On Friday, she **predicts**, based on her observations, that it will rain during the weekend.

Try This Beginning on a Monday, gather data about the temperature at noon. Record your data. Repeat this for four more days. Find a way to display your data. Then predict what the temperature will be at noon on Saturday.

Talk About It Why do you think Pilar predicted it would rain during the weekend?

Process Skills

Gather Data— make observations and use them to make inferences or predictions

Record Data— write down observations

Display Data— make tables, charts, or graphs

Predict— form an idea of an expected outcome based on observations or experience

Kim is interested in knowing how the size of a magnet is related to its strength. He **hypothesizes** that larger magnets are stronger than smaller magnets. He **plans and conducts a simple investigation** to see if his hypothesis is correct. He gathers magnets of different sizes. He finds items of different weights that the magnets will attract. He tests each item on each magnet, and records his findings. His hypothesis is correct until he tests the last item, a toy truck. When the largest horseshoe magnet cannot pick up the truck, but a smaller bar magnet can, he **infers** that the largest magnet is usually the strongest, but not always.

Try This Make a hypothesis about something you are interested in. Plan and conduct an investigation to test your hypothesis.

Talk About It Kim used different shapes of magnets as well as different sizes in his investigation. Do you think this could make a difference in the results? Why or why not?

Process Skills

Hypothesize — make a statement about the expected outcome based on observation, knowledge, and experience

Plan and Conduct Simple Investigations — identify and perform the steps necessary to find the answer to a question, using appropriate tools and recording and analyzing the data collected

Infer — use logical reasoning to explain events and draw conclusions based on observations

Emily sees an ad about food wrap. The people in the ad claim that Tight-Right food wrap seals containers better than other food wraps. She plans a simple investigation to find out if this claim is true.

Emily **identifies and controls the variables** by choosing three bowls that are exactly the same. She labels the bowls A, B, and C. She places the bowls on a tray, and puts exactly 250 mL of water in each bowl. She cuts a 25-cm piece of Tight-Right wrap and places it on top of bowl A. She places 25-cm pieces of other brands of wrap on bowls B and C. She seals the wrap to the top of all three bowls as tightly as she can.

Emily **experiments** with the seals by pulling sharply on the tray. The water sloshes up the sides of the bowls. Water does not leak out the top of bowl A. On bowls B and C, the seals are broken, and water has spilled over onto the tray. From her observations, Emily infers that the claim for Tight-Right wrap is true.

Try This Plan an experiment to test different brands of a product your family uses. Identify the variables that you will control.

Talk About It Why did Emily use the tray in her experiment?

Process Skills

Identify and Control Variables — identify and control factors that affect the outcome of an experiment

Experiment — design ways to collect data to test hypotheses under controlled conditions

You will have many opportunities to practice and apply these and other process skills in *Harcourt Science.* An exciting year of science discoveries lies ahead!

Safety in Science

Doing investigations in science can be fun, but you need to be sure you do them safely. Here are some rules to follow.

 Think ahead. Study the steps of the investigation so you know what to expect. If you have any questions, ask your teacher. Be sure you understand any safety symbols that are shown.

 Be neat. Keep your work area clean. If you have long hair, pull it back so it doesn't get in the way. Roll or push up long sleeves to keep them away from your experiment.

3 Oops! If you should spill or break something, or get cut, tell your teacher right away.

 Watch your eyes. Wear safety goggles anytime you are directed to do so. If you get anything in your eyes, tell your teacher right away.

5 Yuck! Never eat or drink anything during a science activity.

6 Don't get shocked. Be especially careful if an electric appliance is used. Be sure that electric cords are in a safe place where you can't trip over them. Don't ever pull a plug out of an outlet by pulling on the cord.

7 Keep it clean. Always clean up when you have finished. Put everything away and wipe your work area. Wash your hands.

In some activities you will see these symbols. They are signs for what you need to be safe.

CAUTION
Be especially careful.

CAUTION
Wear safety goggles.

CAUTION
Be careful with sharp objects.

CAUTION
Don't get burned.

CAUTION
Protect your clothes.

CAUTION
Protect your hands with mitts.

CAUTION
Be careful with electricity.

Systems of Living Things

UNIT A

LIFE SCIENCE

Systems of Living Things

Chapter 1 From Single Cells to Body Systems   **A2**

Chapter 2 Classifying Living Things   **A34**

Chapter 3 Plants and Their Adaptations   **A60**

Chapter 4 Plant Processes   **A98**

Unit Project

Animal and Plant Fold-Outs

Make fold-outs that show the growth of living things. Choose two plants and two animals to investigate. Fold four large sheets of paper into three parts each. Label the parts of each sheet *Young, Growing and Changing,* and *Mature*. Research how the plants and animals you've chosen grow and change. Draw a picture showing the growth process on each section of the fold-outs. Make notes on the back of the fold-outs that describe your pictures.

Chapter

LESSON **1**
**What Are Cells, and
What Do They Do?**   **A4**

LESSON **2**
**How Do Body Systems
Transport Materials?** **A14**

LESSON **3**
**How Do Bones, Muscles,
and Nerves Work
Together?**   **A22**

SCIENCE THROUGH TIME   **A28**

PEOPLE IN SCIENCE   **A30**

ACTIVITIES FOR HOME
OR SCHOOL   **A31**

CHAPTER REVIEW AND
TEST PREPARATION   **A32**

From Single Cells to Body Systems

Do you know what a fish, a tree, and a human being have in common? They are all made of tiny cells that carry on the processes of life.

Vocabulary Preview

cell	villi
cell membrane	nephrons
	bone marrow
nucleus	joints
cytoplasm	tendons
diffusion	ligaments
osmosis	neuron
tissue	receptors
organ	
system	
capillaries	
alveoli	

☷FAST FACT

**Your body contains about
40,000 miles of blood vessels.
Within the blood vessel shown
here are disk-shaped red
blood cells and round white
blood cells.**

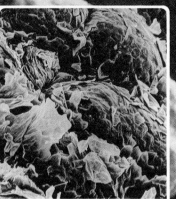

A scanning electron microscope (SEM) can magnify objects as much as 900,000 times. This electron micrograph shows human face cells magnified 100,000 times.

A single square inch of human skin has more than 19 million cells.

What Are Cells, and What Do They Do?

In this lesson, you can . . .

 INVESTIGATE what cells look like.

LEARN ABOUT cells.

LINK to math, writing, health, and technology.

 **INVESTIGATE**

Observing Cells

Activity Purpose If you're looking at a landscape from far away, you might use a telescope to make the details clearer. Suppose you focus the telescope on a distant farm. You can see crates of freshly harvested onions. Now suppose you use a microscope to magnify the scene more and more. What details about an onion might you **observe**? In this investigation you'll observe a thin layer of an onion skin. Then you will observe and **compare** other plant cells and animal cells.

Materials

- Microslide Viewer
- Microslide of cell structure
- colored pencils

Alternate Materials

- slice of onion
- microscope slide
- coverslip
- dropper
- red food coloring
- microscope
- colored pencils

Activity Procedure

1 Insert the Cell Structure Microslide in the slot on the Microslide Viewer. Turn the focus knob until you can see the cells clearly. (Picture A)

2 **Observe** the onion skin cells and the human cheek cells. **Record** your observations by using the colored pencils to make drawings.

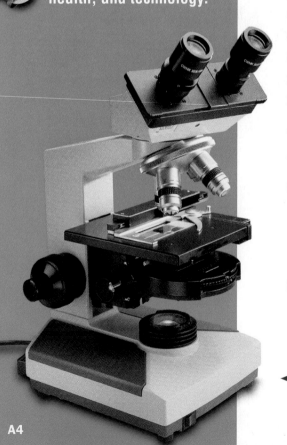

◄ This microscope allows a person to study a thin slice of material under high magnification.

3. Now **observe** the green leaf cells and the nerve cells. Again, **record** your observations by making drawings. (Picture B)

4. Now **compare** your drawings. Make a Venn diagram with two large, overlapping circles. Label the circles *Plant Cells* and *Animal Cells*. Label the area where the circles overlap *Both Cells*. Draw the cell parts that you **observed** in the proper circles. Leave enough room to label the parts as you read about them in this lesson.

Picture A

Draw Conclusions

1. **Compare** the outer layers of plant and animal cells.

2. In the centers of most cells are structures that control the cells' activities. How many of these structures are there in each of the cells you **observed**?

3. **Scientists at Work** Scientists often **infer** characteristics of a group of objects by **observing** just a few of the objects. From your observations, what do you infer about the number of controlling structures in a cell?

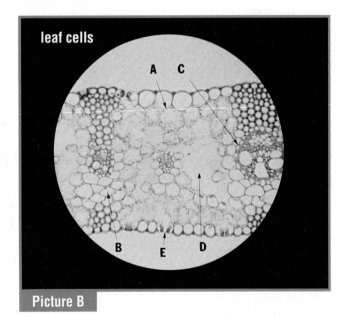
leaf cells
Picture B

Investigate Further Now that you have **observed** photo-micrographs of cells, what questions do you have about living cells? Use the materials in the *Alternate Materials* list to **plan and conduct a simple investigation** based on your questions. Write instructions that others can follow in carrying out the procedure. See page R5 for tips on using a microscope.

Process Skill Tip

You can **infer** based on what you **observe**, or based on other information you have about a subject.

Cells

The Discovery of Cells

FIND OUT

- what cells are
- how cells are organized
- what cells do

VOCABULARY

cell
cell membrane
nucleus
cytoplasm
diffusion
osmosis
tissue
organ
system

The Microslide you used in the investigation allowed you to observe parts of plants and animals under magnification. Without magnification, you couldn't have seen the structures you did. A microscope magnifies objects in a similar way. In fact, the photomicrographs you observed were taken through a microscope. The first microscopes were invented in the early 1600s. One scientist who built and used an early microscope was Robert Hooke.

In 1665 Hooke observed a thin slice of cork through a microscope. The tiny walled spaces he saw in the cork reminded him of tiny rooms. So he called them cells. Over the next 200 years, scientists learned more and more about cells. They learned that the **cell** is the basic unit of structure and function of all living things. The time line below shows some important early discoveries about cells.

✔ **Why were cells not observed before the 1600s?**

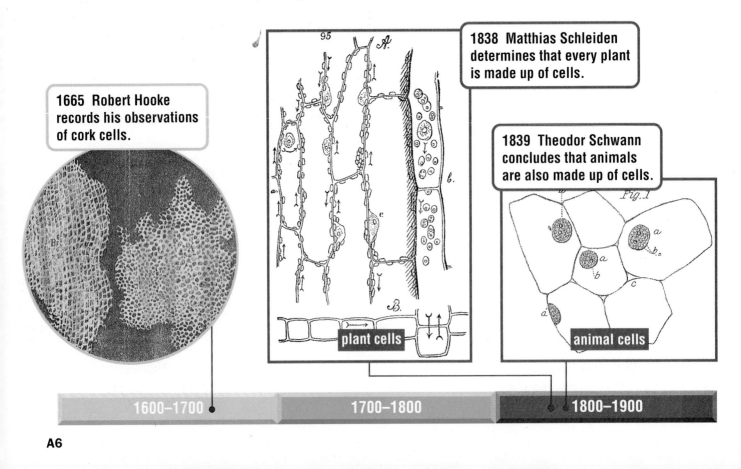

1665 Robert Hooke records his observations of cork cells.

1838 Matthias Schleiden determines that every plant is made up of cells.

1839 Theodor Schwann concludes that animals are also made up of cells.

plant cells

animal cells

1600–1700   1700–1800   1800–1900

Kinds of Cells

Scientists have classified about a million kinds of plants and animals. But as different as those plants and animals seem to be, all of them are made of cells.

The simplest organisms, such as bacteria, are each a single cell. Most plants and animals, however, are made up of many cells. Humans, for example, are made up of *trillions* of cells. An organism with many cells usually has many different kinds of cells. Each kind of cell has a special function for the organism.

The size and shape of a cell depend on its function. Red blood cells, for example, are small and disc-shaped. They can easily fit through the smallest blood vessels. Muscle cells are long and thin. When they contract, or shorten, they produce movement. Nerve cells, which carry signals from the brain to the muscles, are very long.

Plants also have different kinds of cells. Some plant cells take in water from the soil. Others protect the plant. And still others make food.

Cells work together to perform basic life processes that keep organisms alive. These processes include releasing energy from food, getting rid of body wastes, and making new cells for growth and repair. However, every individual cell can perform all of these processes for itself.

✔ **Why might bone cells be different from muscle cells?**

The "skin" cells of this plant's leaves keep it from losing too much water. ▼

◄ The skin cells make a watertight covering of scales that keep this iguana from losing water, too.

Plant and Animal Cells

Although cells are the basic unit of all living organisms, cells contain even smaller structures called *organelles* (awr•guh•NELZ). Each organelle has a particular function in the life processes of a cell.

All cells—except those of bacteria—have similar organelles. For example, every cell is enclosed by a thin covering called the **cell membrane**. The cell membrane holds the parts of the cell together. It also separates the cell from its surroundings.

Most cells have a nucleus (NOO•klee•uhs). The **nucleus** controls the cell's activities. The nucleus is enclosed in its own membrane. One function of the nucleus is cell reproduction. Cells can grow only to a certain size. So in order for plants and animals to grow, the number of cells has to increase.

Inside the nucleus are threadlike structures called *chromosomes* (KROH•muh•sohmz).

THE INSIDE STORY

Comparing Plant and Animal Cells

Plant cells have different shapes and sizes, but they all have the same parts. The diagram shows what you might observe if you could look inside a leaf cell. The organelles you see are working parts of a complete cell. Each organelle has its own specific function.

Plant Cell Structures

Nucleus— ❶ the organelle that controls all of a plant cell's activities and the production of new cells

Chromosomes— ❷ threadlike structures that contain information about the characteristics of the plant

Cell membrane— ❸ a covering that holds the plant cell together and separates it from its surroundings

Cell wall— ❹ a rigid layer that supports and protects the plant cell

Cytoplasm— ❺ a jellylike substance that contains many chemicals to keep the cell functioning

Chloroplasts— ❻ organelles that make food for the plant cell

Vacuole— ❼ an organelle that stores food, water, or wastes

Mitochondria— ❽ organelles that release energy from food

These contain information about the characteristics of the organism. When a cell reproduces, identical chromosomes go into each new cell.

Between the cell membrane and the nucleus is the cytoplasm (SYT•oh•plaz•uhm). **Cytoplasm** is a jellylike substance containing many chemicals to keep the cell functioning.

There are several kinds of organelles in the cytoplasm. Each is enclosed in a membrane. *Mitochondria* (myt•oh•KAHN•dree•uh)

release energy from food. *Vacuoles* (VAK•yoo•ohlz) are storage organelles. They store food, water, or waste materials.

Two organelles make plant cells different from animal cells. In addition to a cell membrane, a plant cell is surrounded by a rigid *cell wall*, which gives it strength. Plant cells also have *chloroplasts*, which make food.

✔ **How do plant cells and animal cells differ?**

The functions that allow an animal to live and grow are also carried out in its cells. Although the iguana's skin cells are a different shape and size from its blood cells, each cell typically contains the same parts. As you look at the diagram of an animal cell, notice how it differs from the plant cell.

Animal Cell Structures

Nucleus— ❶	the organelle that controls all of an animal cell's activities and the production of new cells
Chromosomes— ❷	threadlike structures that contain information about the characteristics of the animal
Cell membrane— ❸	a covering that holds the animal cell together and separates it from its surroundings
Cytoplasm— ❹	a jellylike substance that contains many chemicals to keep the cell functioning
Vacuoles— ❺	organelles that store food, wastes, or water
Mitochondria— ❻	organelles that release energy from food

Cell Transport

All the activities of a cell require energy. That energy is supplied by the mitochondria. Mitochondria need food, oxygen, and water to produce energy. This process produces carbon dioxide as a waste. How do cells get needed materials like food, water, and oxygen? And how do they get rid of wastes, like carbon dioxide?

Most materials move into and out of cells by diffusion. In the process of **diffusion**, particles of a substance move from an area where there are a lot of particles of the substance to an area where there are fewer particles of the substance.

For example, red blood cells carry oxygen from the lungs to all parts of the body. There is a lot of oxygen in red blood cells and very little in other body cells. So oxygen diffuses out of red blood cells and into body cells. At the same time, there is a lot of carbon dioxide in body cells and very little in the blood. So carbon dioxide diffuses out of body cells and into the blood.

Diffusion of materials into and out of cells takes place through the cell membrane. You might think of a cell membrane as a filter. It allows some particles to pass through, but it keeps other particles out.

Water and materials dissolved in water—such as oxygen or sugar—diffuse easily through cell membranes. Diffusion doesn't need energy from the cell. This energy-free movement of materials through a cell membrane is called *passive transport.*

The movement of water and dissolved materials through cell membranes is so important to living organisms that it is given a special name— **osmosis**. Cells get most of their water by osmosis.

Osmosis keeps plants from wilting. There is usually more water in the soil than in the

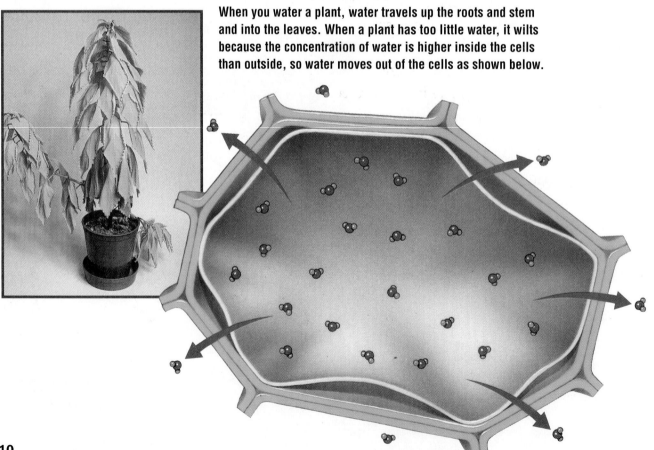

When you water a plant, water travels up the roots and stem and into the leaves. When a plant has too little water, it wilts because the concentration of water is higher inside the cells than outside, so water moves out of the cells as shown below.

Passive Transport

This diagram of a cell membrane shows how substances enter a cell during passive transport. Notice how water can diffuse through any part of the cell membrane. Passive transport is like traveling downstream in a canoe. The current carries the canoe, and you don't need to use any energy to paddle.

Active Transport

energy

This diagram shows how substances move through a cell membrane during active transport. Cell energy "pushes" the carrier proteins through channels in the cell membrane. Active transport is like traveling upstream in a canoe. You must use energy to paddle the canoe to make it move.

roots of plants. So water flows into plant cells. Water flowing into plant cells fills the vacuoles, which pushes the cytoplasm tightly against the cell walls. This causes plant stems and leaves to stand straight.

If the soil is very dry, there is more water in the plant than in the soil. Water leaves the plant by osmosis. The loss of water from the plant's vacuoles causes cytoplasm to shrink away from cell walls. The plant wilts and may die if it loses too much water.

Not all of the materials a cell needs are small enough to simply diffuse into the cell. And cells often need more of a substance than they can get through diffusion. For example, if a swimmer's muscle cells already have more sugar in them than there is in the blood, sugar won't diffuse into those cells. Mitochondria in the muscle cells might not

be able to produce the energy the swimmer needs.

However, there is another way for cells to get the materials they need. Cells can use a carrier either to transport materials that are too large to pass through the cell membrane or to transport materials against diffusion. This type of transport is called *active transport.*

A carrier transports materials into and out of a cell through a channel in the cell membrane. To do this, the carrier needs energy from the cell. In fact, one-third of the energy made by a cell is used to transport substances through the cell membrane in this way.

✔ **How does active transport differ from passive transport?**

Tissues, Organs, and Systems

In an organism made up of many cells, similar cells work together. Cells that work together to perform a specific function form a **tissue**. There are four kinds of tissues in humans and most other animals.

Most of the mass of an animal is *muscle tissue*. Muscle tissue is made up of cells that contract when they receive signals from the brain. The contraction and relaxation of muscle tissue move the skeleton. The signals that cause muscle tissue to contract travel through another kind of tissue—*nervous tissue*. The brain and spinal cord, as well as the places where sight, hearing, taste, smell, and touch begin, are all nervous tissue.

Connective tissue is the third kind of tissue. It includes the tissue in bones, cartilage, and tendons. Blood is also a connective tissue.

The final kind of tissue is *epithelial* (ep•ih•THEE•lee•uhl) *tissue.* Epithelial tissue includes the body covering of an animal. It also lines most internal organs.

Just as cells that work together form a tissue, tissues that work together form an **organ**. Each organ in an animal's body is made of several kinds of tissues. Skin, for example, is an organ. It is made of many layers of epithelial tissue, as well as muscle tissue, nervous tissue, and a cushioning layer of connective tissue.

Each organ in an animal's body performs a major function that keeps the animal alive. The heart, for example, is an organ that pumps blood throughout the animal's body.

Organs that work together to perform a function form a **system**. A human has ten

In this diagram, you can see the four levels of organization in the digestive system. ▼

Body Organization

❶ This is a specialized cell.

❷ Similar cells form a tissue.

❸ This tissue forms part of an organ—the stomach.

❹ The stomach is part of a system that digests food, transfers digested food into the blood, and removes wastes.

major body systems. You will learn about some of those systems in the next two lessons.

Plant cells also form tissues, such as the bark of a tree. And plant tissues work together, forming organs, such as roots and leaves. You will learn more about plants in Chapters 3 and 4.

✔ **What kind of tissue gives an organism the ability to move?**

Summary

All living things are made up of one or more cells. Each cell is able to perform the functions that support life. Plant cells differ from animal cells in that they have cell walls and chloroplasts. Cells obtain the materials they need by passive or active transport through the cell membrane. Cells with similar functions form tissues. Tissues that function together make up an organ. Organs working together form a body system.

Review

1. What is the function of a cell's nucleus?
2. How do vacuoles in plant cells help keep the plant upright?
3. What is the difference between diffusion and osmosis?
4. **Critical Thinking** If you stand at one end of a room and spray perfume into the air, a person at the other end of the room will soon smell the perfume. Explain.
5. **Test Prep** One example of a tissue is —
   - **A** heart
   - **B** nucleus
   - **C** muscle
   - **D** mitochondria

LINKS

MATH LINK

Problem Solving Suppose a single cell divides into two cells every 15 min. If each of those also divides into two, and so on, how long will it take for a single cell to produce 500 cells?

WRITING LINK

Informative Writing—Compare and Contrast Write two or three paragraphs for your teacher comparing plant cells and animal cells.

HEALTH LINK

Interview a Doctor Find out how studying cells helps doctors understand the human body. Brainstorm with a family member to come up with questions you can ask your doctor the next time you have an appointment.

TECHNOLOGY LINK

Learn more about cells and body systems by using the activities and information provided on the Harcourt Learning Site.
www.harcourtschool.com/ca

WELCOME TO THE LEARNING SITE

Cells and Tissues

How Do Body Systems Transport Materials?

In this lesson, you can . . .

INVESTIGATE cells and tissues.

LEARN ABOUT four human body systems.

LINK to math, writing, social studies, and technology.

Activity Purpose Your body is made up of cells that are organized into tissues, organs, and systems. Cells are highly specialized for the functions they perform for the body. Even cells that make up similar tissues can differ in many ways. In this investigation you will **observe** and **compare** under magnification several kinds of cells and tissues.

Materials

- Microslide Viewer
- Microslide of animal tissues
- colored pencils

Alternate Materials

- prepared slides of epithelial, connective, and nervous tissues
- microscope

Activity Procedure

1 Insert the Animal Tissues Microslide in the slot of the Microslide Viewer. Turn the focus knob until you can see the cells and tissues clearly. (Picture A)

2 **Observe** the voluntary muscle cells. **Record** your observations by using the colored pencils to make a drawing. Label your drawing with the name of the tissue. Then describe the tissue. You may use the Microslide text folder to help you write your description. (Picture B)

◀ The materials your body uses to produce energy must be replaced.

A14

Picture A

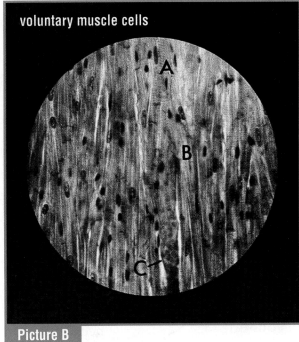

voluntary muscle cells

Picture B

3 Repeat Step 2 for the smooth muscle cells and the heart muscle.

4 **Compare** the three kinds of muscle tissue.

Draw Conclusions

1. How are the three kinds of muscle tissue alike? How are they different?

2. The dark-stained organelles you **observed** in the muscle tissues are mitochondria. Which kind of muscle tissue has the most mitochondria?

3. **Scientists at Work** When scientists **compare** objects, they often **infer** reasons for any differences. What do you infer about why one kind of muscle tissue has more mitochondria than the others?

Investigate Further Now that you have **observed** several kinds of tissues, develop a testable question about differences among tissues. Use the materials in the *Alternate Materials* list to study other kinds of tissues. Observe the tissues under the microscope, and draw and label any differences you see. **Infer** how these tissues are different from the muscle tissues you observed. See page R5 for tips on using a microscope.

> **Process Skill Tip**
>
> Making drawings of objects allows you to **compare** them and **infer** reasons for differences between them.

A15

Human Body Systems

From Cells to Systems

FIND OUT

- about the circulatory, respiratory, digestive, and excretory systems
- which organs make up each system
- how the systems work together

VOCABULARY

capillaries
alveoli
villi
nephrons

The tissues you observed in the investigation combine in various ways to form body organs. Certain organs work together to form body systems. Each body system has a specific task that helps keep you alive. But your body systems also work together. On its own, a single body system cannot keep you alive.

The digestive system, for example, breaks down food into nutrients the body needs for energy. But without the circulatory system, the nutrients couldn't travel to the parts of the body that need them. The circulatory system also delivers the oxygen needed to release energy from food. However, without the respiratory system, oxygen couldn't get into the circulatory system. And all body processes produce wastes that must be removed. The excretory and respiratory systems share this function, with transportation provided by the circulatory system.

As you can see, working together is important for living organisms. Cells work together to form tissues. Tissues work together to form organs. Organs work together to form systems. And systems work together to keep you alive.

✔ **How do body systems depend on each other?**

These red blood cells are part of a tissue—blood. ▼

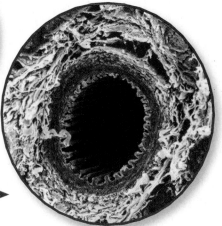

Blood vessels are another kind of tissue in the circulatory system. ▶

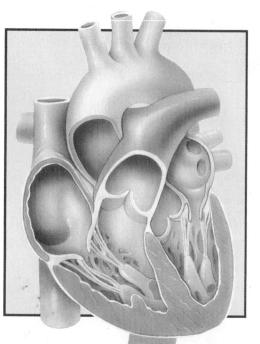

The heart is an organ of the circulatory system. It is made of muscle tissue. ▶

The Circulatory System

The circulatory system transports oxygen, nutrients, and wastes through the body in the blood. The liquid part of blood, called *plasma*, is mostly water. It also contains dissolved nutrients and waste products, such as carbon dioxide. The solid part of blood includes red blood cells and white blood cells. Red blood cells absorb oxygen from air in the lungs and transport it to every cell in the body. White blood cells help the body fight infection. They attack and destroy viruses and bacteria that enter the body.

Blood also contains *platelets*—tiny pieces of blood cells inside membranes. Platelets cause blood to clot when a blood vessel is cut. They also help repair damage to blood vessels.

The heart, an organ made of muscle tissue, pumps blood through blood vessels. The heart has four chambers, or parts. Oxygen-rich blood from the lungs enters one chamber. It moves to the next chamber, from which it is pumped to the body. Oxygen-poor blood from the body enters the third chamber. It moves to the fourth chamber, from which it is pumped to the lungs.

Blood leaves the heart through blood vessels called *arteries*. Arteries lead to capillaries. **Capillaries** are blood vessels so small that blood cells have to move through them in single file. There are capillaries throughout the body, so nutrients and oxygen can reach every cell. Waste products from cells are picked up by plasma in the capillaries. Capillaries lead to larger vessels, called *veins*, which return blood to the heart.

✔ **Why are platelets important?**

Capillaries

▲ Oxygen and nutrients diffuse from the blood into cells through capillary walls. The total length of capillaries in an adult human is more than 80,000 km (about 50,000 mi).

The heart beats all the time, pushing the blood into arteries. You can feel the push as a pulse in the artery in your wrist. ▼

blood

heart

veins

arteries

The Respiratory System

Your body uses a lot of energy. So your cells need a lot of food and oxygen. You get the oxygen your cells need by breathing. When you inhale, several liters of air are pulled into your body. The air is filtered by tiny hairs in your nose and warmed by capillaries that line the nasal passages. Warm, clean air then travels down your *trachea*, or windpipe.

In your chest, the trachea branches into two tubes called *bronchi* (BRAHNG•kee). Each tube leads into a lung. In the lungs, the bronchi divide into smaller and smaller tubes. At the end of the smallest tubes are tiny air sacs called **alveoli** (al•VEE•oh•lee). The walls of the alveoli are only one cell thick and are surrounded by capillaries.

The capillaries surrounding the alveoli get blood from the *pulmonary arteries* coming from the heart. This blood contains a lot of carbon dioxide. Carbon dioxide is a waste produced by the process that releases energy in cells. Carbon dioxide diffuses through the thin walls of the alveoli and into air that will be exhaled. At the same time, oxygen from inhaled air diffuses through the alveoli and into red blood cells in the capillaries. The oxygen-rich blood then flows from the capillaries into the *pulmonary veins* and back to the heart. From the heart, oxygen-rich blood is pumped to other parts of the body.

✔ **What happens in the alveoli?**

The lungs are the major organs of the respiratory system. ▼

trachea

bronchi

▲ The gas exchange of oxygen and carbon dioxide takes place in the alveoli.

The lungs are on a separate circuit of the circulatory system. The heart pumps oxygen-poor blood through the pulmonary arteries to the lungs. The oxygen-rich blood travels through the pulmonary veins back to the heart. ▼

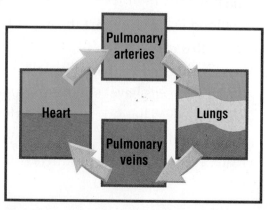

Pulmonary arteries

Heart

Lungs

Pulmonary veins

The Digestive System

Your digestive system provides the nutrients your cells need to produce energy. To provide nutrients, the digestive system performs two functions. The first is to break food into nutrients. The second is to get the nutrients into the blood. Then the circulatory system transports them to your cells.

Digestion begins as you chew food, breaking it into smaller pieces so that you can swallow it. Glands in your mouth produce saliva. Saliva moistens food and begins to break down starchy foods, such as pasta, into sugars. (If you chew an unsalted cracker for a while, it will begin to taste sweet.)

When you swallow, food passes through the *esophagus* (ih•SAHF•uh•guhs), a long tube that leads to the stomach. Gastric juice, produced by the stomach, contains acid and chemicals that break down proteins.

After several hours in the stomach, partly digested food moves into the small intestine. Digestion of food into nutrients is completed by chemicals produced in the small intestine. Nutrients diffuse through the **villi**, projections sticking out of the walls of the small intestine, into the blood. From the small intestine, undigested food passes into the large intestine. There, water and minerals diffuse into the blood, and wastes are removed from the body.

Two other organs have a role in digestion. The *liver* produces bile, which is stored in the *gallbladder* until it's needed. Bile breaks down fats into smaller particles that can be more easily digested. The *pancreas* produces a fluid that neutralizes stomach acid and chemicals that help finish digestion.

✔ **In what organ of the digestive system do nutrients enter the blood?**

As food passes through the digestive system, chemicals break it down into nutrients the body cells need. ▼

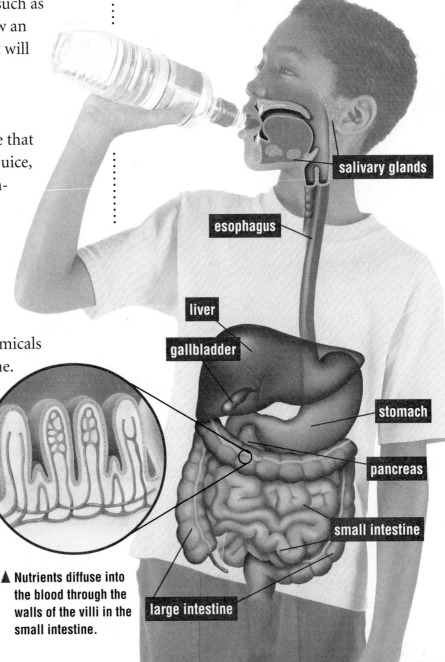

salivary glands

esophagus

liver

gallbladder

stomach

pancreas

small intestine

large intestine

▲ Nutrients diffuse into the blood through the walls of the villi in the small intestine.

The Excretory System

The circulatory system supplies food and oxygen to the body's cells. It carries away waste products from the production of energy. The wastes must then be removed from the blood. This is the function of the excretory system.

Cell wastes include carbon dioxide and ammonia. As you learned, the respiratory system gets rid of carbon dioxide. Ammonia is carried by the blood to the liver, where it is changed to urea.

From the liver, urea is carried by the blood to the kidneys. These organs are located behind the liver and stomach. As blood flows through capillaries in the kidneys, urea and water diffuse into tubes called **nephrons**.

Urine, which is urea and water, flows from the kidneys through tubes called *ureters*. The ureters empty into a muscular organ called the bladder. When the bladder is full, urine leaves the body through a channel called the *urethra*.

The kidneys, ureters, bladder, and urethra make up the excretory system. This system takes wastes from the blood and removes them from the body as urine. ▼

▲ Wastes and water are removed from the capillaries that run through the kidneys. Materials that the body needs are returned to the capillaries.

The excretory system keeps the amount of water in the body fairly constant.

Daily Water Gain and Water Loss in Adults

Water Gain		Water Loss	
From cell activities	400 mL	In solid wastes	100 mL
From eating	900 mL	From skin and lungs	1000 mL
From drinking	1300 mL	As urine	1500 mL
Total	2600 mL	Total	2600 mL

Cell wastes aren't the only wastes the body needs to get rid of. When you exercise, your body gets warm. Excess heat is eliminated by sweating. Sweat is a salty liquid that evaporates from the skin. Evaporation pulls heat from capillaries just below the skin. The blood and the entire body are cooled.

✔ **How do cell wastes get to the kidneys?**

Summary

Body cells are organized into tissues, organs, and systems that work together to keep the body alive. The circulatory system transports materials throughout the body. In the respiratory system, oxygen diffuses into the blood and carbon dioxide diffuses out of the blood. The digestive system breaks down food into nutrients that can be used by cells. The excretory system removes cell wastes from the blood.

Review

1. How do the functions of red blood cells and white blood cells differ?
2. In what way do the respiratory and circulatory systems work together?
3. What does the pancreas do?
4. **Critical Thinking** Between the trachea and the esophagus is a flap of skin called the *epiglottis*. What do you think its function is?
5. **Test Prep** Inhaled oxygen diffuses through the walls of the —
   A ureters
   B bronchioles
   C pulmonary arteries
   D alveoli

LINKS

MATH LINK

Heartbeat Rate Count the number of times your heart beats in 15 sec. Then multiply the number by 4 to find your approximate heartbeat rate per minute. At that rate, how many times would your heart beat in one year?

WRITING LINK

Informative Writing—Report Find out more about one of the body systems. Write a brief report for your teacher. Describe in detail the organs of the system. Also explain how the system functions.

SOCIAL STUDIES LINK

Early Physicians Some of the first recorded information about physicians described Imhotep, who lived in Egypt during the Third Dynasty (about 2700–2500 B.C.). Find out about Imhotep and his contributions to ancient medicine.

TECHNOLOGY LINK

Learn more about the functioning of the heart by investigating *One Heart— Two Amazing Pumps* on the **Harcourt Science Explorations CD-ROM.**

How Do Bones, Muscles, and Nerves Work Together?

In this lesson, you can . . .

INVESTIGATE how muscles cause movement.

LEARN ABOUT the skeletal, muscular, and nervous systems.

LINK to math, writing, art, and technology.

INVESTIGATE

How Muscles Cause Movement

Activity Purpose Your respiratory, circulatory, digestive, and excretory systems function automatically, without the need for you to give them directions. Other systems in your body are under your control, at least some of the time. When you run for a bus, for example, you direct your skeleton, muscles, and nerves to work together. In this investigation you'll **observe** what your muscles do when you bend your arm.

Materials

- tape measure

Activity Procedure

1 Place your left hand on top of your right arm, between the shoulder and elbow. Bend and straighten your right arm at the elbow. **Observe** the movement by feeling the muscles in your right arm. (Picture A)

2 The muscle on the front of the upper arm is called the *biceps*. The muscle on the back of the upper arm is called the *triceps*. **Compare** the biceps and the triceps as you bend and straighten your arm. **Infer** which muscle controls the bending movement and which controls the straightening movement.

◀ In-line skating requires the coordination of your skeletal system, muscular system, and nervous system.

Picture A

Picture B

3 Have a partner use the tape measure to **measure** the distance around your upper arm when it is straight and when it is bent. **Record** the measurements. (Picture B)

4 Repeat Steps 2 and 3, using your right hand and your left arm.

5 **Compare** the sets of measurements.

Draw Conclusions

1. What did you **infer** about the muscles controlling the bending and the straightening of your upper arm?

2. Why are two muscles needed to bend and straighten your arm? Why can't one muscle do it?

3. **Scientists at Work** Scientists often **hypothesize** about things they **observe**. Hypothesize about any differences between the measurements of your right arm and the measurements of your left arm.

Investigate Further Repeat the investigation with different pairs of muscles. For example, try bending your leg at the knee while **observing** the muscles in your thigh. See if these measurements also support your hypothesis. **Draw conclusions** about differences in muscle sizes from the data you collected. Decide whether more data is needed to support your conclusions.

Process Skill Tip

When you **hypothesize**, you tell what you think will happen based on what you **observe**. A hypothesis can be tested by doing an experiment.

A23

Systems Working Together

Bones and Joints

The bones of your body are living organs made up of connective tissues. The tissues include an outer protective membrane, a layer of hard material, and a soft center containing bone marrow. **Bone marrow** is a connective tissue that produces red blood cells and white blood cells.

Bone cells form canals throughout the hard layer. The cells are connected to each other and to blood vessels. Bone cells secrete the rocklike material, made of calcium, that gives bones their strength and hardness. The protective membrane surrounding bones repairs them if they are broken.

Your body contains several kinds of bones. These include long bones in your arms and legs, flat bones in your shoulders and hips, and short bones in your fingers and toes. Other kinds of bones include the irregular bones in your wrists and ankles.

Bones meet at **joints**, where they are attached to each other and to muscles. Different kinds of joints allow different kinds of movement. Hinge joints, for example, allow back-and-forth movement, like the movement of a door hinge. Ball-and-socket joints allow circular motion, like the motion of a joystick. Some joints, such as the ones in your skull, don't allow any movement.

✔ **What kind of tissue are bones made of?**

FIND OUT

• what the structure and function of bones are

• how the skeletal, muscular, and nervous systems work together

VOCABULARY

bone marrow
joints
tendons
ligaments
neuron
receptors

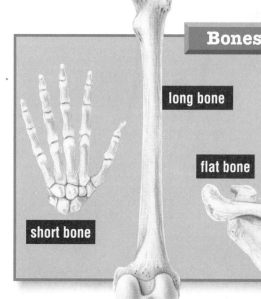

Bones

short bone

long bone

flat bone

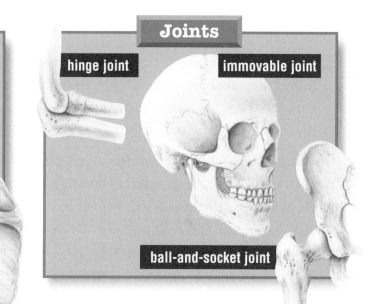

Joints

hinge joint

immovable joint

ball-and-socket joint

The Skeletal System

Bones are organized into a skeleton, which provides support for your body. Your skeleton also protects many of your internal organs. For example, your skull completely encloses your brain.

The outer layer of a bone provides a surface for the attachment of muscles. On each side of a joint, muscles are attached to bones by **tendons**, tough bands of connective tissue. Bones are attached to each other by **ligaments**, bands of connective tissue that hold the skeleton together.

An adult human skeleton has 206 bones. Each hand has 27 bones and each foot has 26 bones. The skull is made up of 23 bones. Not all of the skeleton is bone. Your outer ears and the tip of your nose are *cartilage*—another type of connective tissue. Cartilage also coats the ends of bones where they meet at a joint. This allows smooth movement between bones.

✔ **How are muscles attached to bones?**

The Muscular System

There are three kinds of muscles—voluntary muscles, smooth muscles, and cardiac muscles. *Voluntary muscles* move bones and hold your skeleton upright. These muscles are made up of groups of muscle tissues bound together by connective tissue. They are generally attached to two or more bones, either directly or through tendons. Where muscles attach to bones at a joint, they work in opposing pairs. As you observed in the investigation, one muscle contracts to bend a joint. Another contracts to straighten it.

Smooth muscles contract slowly and move substances through the organs they surround. These muscles run in bands around the walls of blood vessels and digestive organs.

Cardiac muscles make up the walls of the heart. Their function is to pump blood. Some cardiac muscles work together to set the heartbeat rate. They ensure that all the cardiac muscles beat at the same time.

✔ **Why must voluntary muscles work in pairs?**

The bones of the elbow are held together by ligaments.

Long tendons connect the wrist bones with the muscles in the forearm.

The rib cage protects the heart and lungs.

The Nervous System

Your nervous system allows you to experience things and to react to your environment. It connects all the tissues and organs of your body to your brain. The nervous system consists of two parts—the central nervous system and the peripheral nervous system. The central nervous system is made up of the brain and the spinal cord. The spinal cord is a bundle of nerves, about as thick as a pencil. It runs from the base of the brain to the hips.

The peripheral nervous system consists of sensory organs, such as the eyes and ears, and body nerves. Nerves are bundles of nerve cells, or neurons. A **neuron** is a specialized cell that can receive signals and transmit them to other neurons.

Signals traveling along nerves jump the gap between neurons. This gap is called a *synapse.* The signal is carried across the synapse by chemicals produced in the sending neuron.

Sensory organs contain neurons called receptors. **Receptors** are nerve cells that detect conditions in the body's environment. Receptors in the ears detect sound waves. Those in the skin detect heat and cold, pressure,

spinal cord

Nerves are clusters of neurons that stretch between the central nervous system—the brain and the spinal cord—and every other part of the body. ▶

touch, and pain. Receptors in the eyes detect light and color. Those in the mouth and nose detect tastes and smells. Each receptor sends a signal through nerves to the central nervous system.

The central nervous system interprets signals it receives from nerves and determines what response is needed. Signals sent by the brain travel through nerves and direct all of the body's muscles. The brain also controls the body's automatic functions, such as respiration, circulation, and digestion.

Some muscle actions are automatic responses to situations. These are called *reflexes.* For example, when a pain signal from a skin receptor reaches the spinal cord, the nerve carrying the signal transmits it directly to a nerve that controls muscles, as well as to a nerve traveling to the brain. The reflex action of the muscles to avoid the source of pain happens before the signal reaches the brain. In other words, you react to pain before you even feel pain.

✔**What takes place at a synapse?**

Axons make nerve cells the longest cells in the body. A single axon stretches between the spinal cord and the toes. ▼

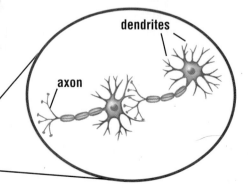

dendrites

axon

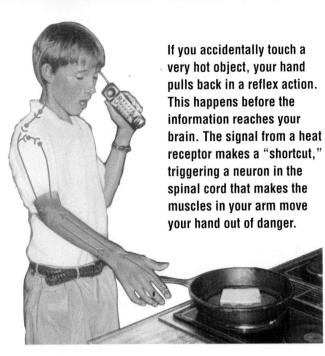

If you accidentally touch a very hot object, your hand pulls back in a reflex action. This happens before the information reaches your brain. The signal from a heat receptor makes a "shortcut," triggering a neuron in the spinal cord that makes the muscles in your arm move your hand out of danger.

Summary

Bones are living organs that make up the skeletal system. Skeletal bones move because of the action of pairs of voluntary muscles. Smooth muscles line the digestive organs and blood vessels. Cardiac muscles make up the walls of the heart. Muscles are controlled by the central nervous system. Nerves are bundles of neurons. They carry signals from sensory organs to the brain and from the brain to the muscles.

Review

1. What is produced in bone marrow?
2. What function do ligaments perform?
3. What kinds of muscles move food through the digestive system?
4. **Critical Thinking** What kind of action is a sneeze caused by pepper in the air? Explain.
5. **Test Prep** Tendons are connective tissue that —
   A makes blood cells
   B carries signals from receptors
   C connects one bone to another
   D connects a bone to a muscle

LINKS

MATH LINK

Comparing Measurements Work with a partner to test your reaction time. Have your partner hold a meterstick vertically so that the lower end is just above the open fingers of your hand. When your partner lets the meterstick go—without warning—catch it between your fingers. Record the measurement where your fingers grasp the stick. Repeat the activity several times, and compare your results.

WRITING LINK

Informative Writing—Description Fill one bowl with ice-cold water, one with hot—but not too hot—water, and one with lukewarm water. Leave one hand in the cold water and one in the hot water for about a minute. Then put both hands into the lukewarm water. Write a paragraph describing the results.

ART LINK

Pointillism Pointillist paintings are composed of small, separate dots of color, like a photograph. The brain interprets the dots as a picture. Try making a pointillist painting of your own.

TECHNOLOGY LINK

Learn more about the benefits of exercise by viewing *The Importance of Exercise* on the **Harcourt Science Newsroom Video** in your classroom video library.

DISCOVERING CELLS

In 1665, English scientist Robert Hooke peered through his homemade microscope. Studying cork tissue, he named the little boxes he saw "cells." Hooke didn't realize it at the time, but his discovery of cells would have a great impact on biology.

Plants and Animals

It was nearly 200 years before scientists began to realize that Hooke's cells were a part of all living things. In 1831 scientists observed the nucleus of a cell and named it "little nut." They had no idea how impor-

tant it was to the cell. In 1838 Matthias Schleiden studied a variety of plant tissues and found that every type was made of many cells. A year later Theodor Schwann found that all animal tissues, too, were made of cells. Schleiden and Schwann are considered to have begun the cell theory—which states that cells are the building blocks of life and that cells come from other cells.

Cells and Germs

Developments in the cell theory produced interest in single-celled organisms. In 1857,

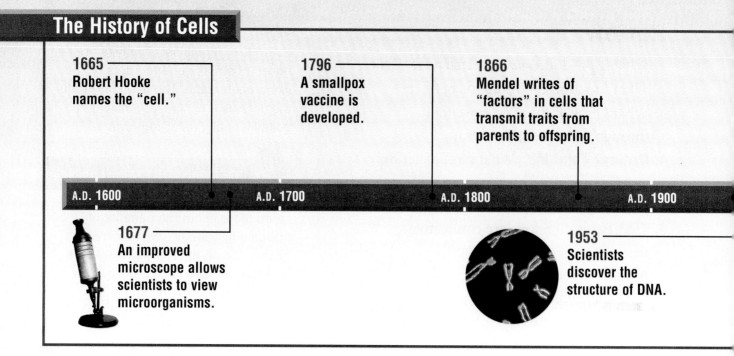

The History of Cells

1665
Robert Hooke names the "cell."

1796
A smallpox vaccine is developed.

1866
Mendel writes of "factors" in cells that transmit traits from parents to offspring.

A.D. 1600 A.D. 1700 A.D. 1800 A.D. 1900

1677
An improved microscope allows scientists to view microorganisms.

1953
Scientists discover the structure of DNA.

after researching single-celled organisms, Louis Pasteur showed that some single-celled microorganisms, such as bacteria, can enter into and infect an organism, causing disease. Pasteur's germ theory changed medicine. Disease-causing organisms could now be identified, and methods could be developed to fight them.

Vaccines and Antibiotics

Pasteur's work also contributed to the development of vaccination—a process in which a killed microorganism is used to prevent infection by similar, but deadly, live microoganisms. Pasteur developed the first vaccine against rabies.

By the turn of the century, many other scientists were studying microorganisms and disease. In 1905 the bacterium that causes tuberculosis was identified. By the 1940s, scientists had developed antibiotics, such as penicillin, to fight bacterial infections.

Mysteries of the Cell Unraveled

Cell research wasn't limited to medicine. Scientists were also researching cell parts and their functions, as well as the factors of heredity carried by cells. In 1953 scientists discovered the structure of DNA—the chemical inside the nucleus that contains all the information a cell needs to function and reproduce.

Today scientists research how certain molecules are used by and affect cells. Scientists are also working to alter or control chemical processes in cells that cause diseases or disorders.

THINK ABOUT IT

1. How did Pasteur's research with single-celled organisms improve people's lives?

2. In addition to Hooke's observations of cells, what other scientific evidence led to the development of the cell theory?

A white blood cell (stained blue) surrounds bacteria (stained orange) and destroys them.

1997 Geneticists clone a living organism—a sheep—by implanting the nucleus from a body cell of an adult sheep into a fertilized egg cell.

A.D. 2000

1980 Molecular biologists identify several genes that can cause cancers in humans.

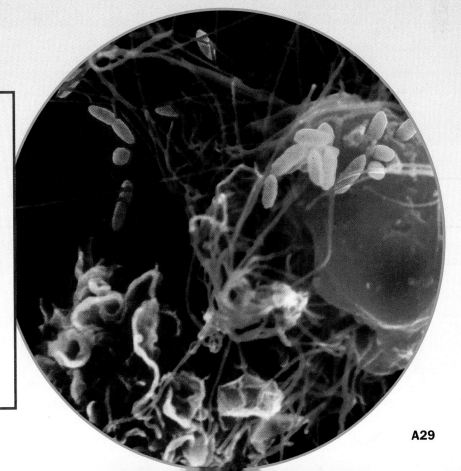

Bernard A. Harris, Jr.

ASTRONAUT, PHYSICIAN

"What a sight . . . the Earth below us, the clouds that look like they're hugging it. It's even more incredible than I imagined."

When Bernard A. Harris, Jr., opened the hatch of the space shuttle *Discovery* and stepped outside, he became the first African American ever to walk in space. It was an amazing moment for a man who, from the age of 13, had dreamed of becoming an astronaut. His dream had been born as, watching on television, he saw Neil Armstrong take that first step on the moon. Although he kept his goal a secret, Dr. Harris worked constantly toward it, studying biology and medicine.

Dr. Harris's first trip in space was aboard the space shuttle *Columbia* in 1993. He and his crewmates experimented to find out the effects of space travel on the human body. The researchers learned that for every month astronauts spend in space, they lose 22.4–44.5 newtons (5–10 lb) of their body weight. In addition, they lose 20 percent of their blood volume because their bone marrow makes less blood.

While in space, Dr. Harris used sound waves to "see" his own heart and discovered that, under the conditions of near weightlessness, it shrank and shifted in his chest. "I had to listen for it in a slightly different place," he recalls.

Today, Dr. Harris is vice-president of SPACE-HAB, Inc., a company that furnishes payloads and experimental modules for NASA's space shuttles. He also is active in a program called Dare to Dream, which he started in a Houston school district.

THINK ABOUT IT

1. Why did Dr. Harris have to listen for his heart in a different place?
2. What physical effects might astronauts experience if they remain in space for many months?

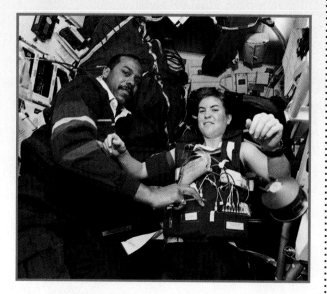

Medical research in space

Balloon Lungs

How do lungs work?

Materials

- 2 balloons
- plastic soda bottle
- scissors

Procedure

1 Remove the cap and cut the bottom off the bottle.

2 Put one balloon into the bottle. Secure the lip of the balloon to the top of the bottle.

3 Cut the lip off the second balloon. Stretch the large part of the second balloon over the bottom of the bottle.

4 With your fingers, pull down on the second balloon and then release it. Observe what happens to the first balloon.

Draw Conclusions

When you pull on the second balloon, what happens inside the bottle? What part of the respiratory system does each part of your model represent?

Skeletal Systems

What adaptations do skeletons show?

Materials

- butcher paper
- meterstick
- 5 people
- marker

Procedure

1 Measure out about 7 m of butcher paper.

2 Have one person lie in the center of the paper. This person should stretch out his or her arms as shown.

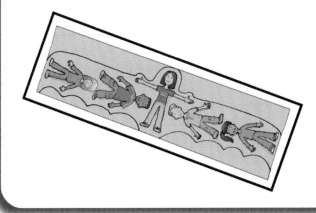

3 Have two other people lie end-to-end on each side of the first person.

4 Use the marker to draw around the first person, including the top edge of his or her outstretched arms and thumbs.

5 To complete the top edge, draw a sloping line the lengths of the people on both sides as shown. Draw the lower edge with four points and four scallops as shown.

Draw Conclusions

While the skeletal systems of all mammals are similar, there are differences due to various adaptations. The skeletons of bats show adaptations for flight. If humans could fly, how many times longer than their bodies would their wings need to be? What other skeletal adaptations of mammals can you think of?

Chapter 1 Review and Test Preparation

Vocabulary Review

Use the terms below to complete the sentences. The page numbers in ( ) tell you where to look in the chapter if you need help.

cell (A6)

cell membrane (A8)

nucleus (A8)

cytoplasm (A9)

diffusion (A10)

osmosis (A10)

tissue (A12)

organ (A12)

system (A12)

capillaries (A17)

alveoli (A18)

villi (A19)

nephron (A20)

bone marrow (A24)

joints (A24)

tendons (A25)

ligaments (A25)

neuron (A26)

receptors (A26)

1. The ____ are projections of the inside wall of the small intestine.

2. The smallest blood vessels are the ____.

3. Similar cells work together in a ____, which is part of an ____, which is part of a ____.

4. Cells that detect conditions in the body's environment are ____.

5. The ____ controls cell activities, and the ____ regulates what enters and leaves the cell.

6. Air sacs in the lungs through which oxygen and carbon dioxide diffuse into and out of the blood are the ____.

7. The ____ is the basic unit of structure of all living things.

8. At ____, bones are connected to each other by ____, while ____ connect bones to muscles.

9. A ____ is made up of a cell body, an axon, and several dendrites.

10. The structure in the kidney that filters urea and water from the blood is a ____.

11. Particles move from areas where there are a lot of them to areas where there are fewer of them by ____. Water and materials dissolved in water pass through a membrane by ____.

12. The jellylike substance between the cell membrane and the nucleus is the ____.

13. Blood cells are produced in ____.

Connect Concepts

Complete the chart by filling in terms from the Word Bank.

smooth muscle

oxygen

small intestine

nutrients

cardiac muscle

lungs

esophagus

alveoli

voluntary muscle

Food
travels down the __14.__ to the stomach and then to the __15.__, where __16.__ diffuse into the blood.

Air
travels down the trachea to the __17.__, where __18.__ diffuses into the blood through the walls of the __19.__.

__16.__ and __18.__
are carried by the blood to muscle cells. The energy they produce in __20.__ tissue is used to move bones. The energy they produce in __21.__ tissue is used to move food through the digestive system. The energy they produce in __22.__ tissue is used to move blood through the circulatory system.

Check Understanding

Write the letter of the best choice.

23. The tissue that makes up bones, tendons, and ligaments is —
    A connective tissue
    B epithelial tissue
    C muscle tissue
    D voluntary tissue

24. Bile, produced by the liver, breaks down —
    F muscle tissue
    G fats
    H stomach acid
    J white blood cells

25. The urea and water that make up urine are removed from the blood in the —
    A bladder
    B kidneys
    C pancreas
    D urethra

26. A plant stands up straight because of water pressure against the —
    F cell walls
    G nucleus
    H cellular membrane
    J chloroplasts

27. A neuron transmits signals from its —
    A synapse
    B dendrites
    C cell body
    D axon

28. The liver is an organ of the —
    F digestive system only
    G excretory and digestive systems
    H circulatory system only
    J circulatory and excretory systems

Critical Thinking

29. A nerve can carry signals both to the brain and from the brain. Why can't an individual neuron do this?

30. Platelets in the blood cause clotting. Why is this important?

31. On each side of the heart, a valve allows blood to travel from the upper chamber to the lower chamber. Why is this important?

Process Skills Review

32. If you are **observing** cells under a microscope, what will lead you to **infer** that the cells are animal cells?

33. How would you test the **hypothesis** that there is never a ball-and-socket joint between a hinged joint and the end of a limb of a skeleton?

Performance Assessment

Body Systems

Use colored pencils to draw the organs and vessels of the excretory system on a human body outline. Label each part. Describe how this system works to eliminate waste from the body cells.

Classifying Living Things

LESSON **1**
How Do Scientists Classify Living Things?   A36

LESSON **2**
How Are Animals Classified?   A42

LESSON **3**
How Are Plants Classified?   A48

SCIENCE THROUGH TIME   A54

PEOPLE IN SCIENCE   A56

ACTIVITIES FOR HOME OR SCHOOL   A57

CHAPTER REVIEW AND TEST PREPARATION   A58

Have you ever noticed how some living things have the same kinds of parts? A cat and a dog each have fur, four legs, and a tail. An ant and a cockroach each have six legs. Scientists look at the similarities among living things and put them into groups.

Vocabulary Preview

classification
kingdom
moneran
protist
fungi
genus
species
vertebrates
mammals
reptiles
amphibians
fish
birds
invertebrates
vascular plants
nonvascular plants

⁝⁝FAST FACT

A kelp may look like a plant, but it's not. The leaf and stem parts of a kelp are different from those of plants. Instead, kelps belong to the protist kingdom. Other protists include microscopic amoebas and paramecia.

A duckbill platypus looks like a mixed-up animal. You might think it's a bird because it has a bill and lays eggs. But scientists say it's a mammal, like a dog or cat, because it has fur and produces milk for its young.

FAST FACT

This Ithaca bog beetle was in an insect collection at Cornell University in Ithaca, New York, for 85 years before anyone realized it had no scientific name. Scientists think there are many more living things to be classified and named. Many haven't even been discovered yet.

Numbers of Living Things

Type of Living Thing	Number of Known Species, or Kinds
Insects	750,000
Fish	25,000
Orchids	20,000

How Do Scientists Classify Living Things?

In this lesson, you can . . .

INVESTIGATE ways to group nonliving objects.

LEARN ABOUT classification.

LINK to math, writing, art, and technology.

INVESTIGATE

Classifying Shoes

Activity Purpose You've probably looked for a certain book in a library. Imagine how hard it would be to find a book in a library full of books if they were not grouped by topic. In this activity you will practice **classifying** some familiar items.

Materials

- shoes
- newspaper or paper towels

Activity Procedure

1 Take off one shoe and put it with your class-mates' shoes. If you put the shoes on a desk or table, cover it first with newspaper or paper towels. (Picture A)

2 Find a way to **classify** the shoes. Begin by find-ing two or three large groups of shoes that are alike. Write a description of each group. (Picture B)

3 **Classify** the large groups of shoes into smaller and smaller groups. Each smaller group should be alike in some way.

◀ This sun bear is a type of animal called a mammal. What other types of animals can you name?

Picture A

Picture B

4 Write a description of each smaller group.

5 Stop classifying when you have sorted all the shoes into groups with two or fewer members.

Draw Conclusions

1. What features did you use to **classify** the shoes?

2. **Compare** your classification system with a classmate's system. How are your systems alike? How are they different?

3. **Scientists at Work** Scientists **classify** living things to show how living things are alike. Why might it be important for scientists to agree on a set of rules for classifying living things?

Investigate Further **Classify** other groups of things such as toys, cars, or pictures of plants and animals. Write a brief explanation of your classification system.

Process Skill Tip

When you **classify** things, you put them into groups based on how they are alike. Things that are not similar are in different groups. Things that have similar characteristics form a group.

Classification

Grouping Living Things

FIND OUT

- why scientists group living things
- the names of the five largest groups of living things

VOCABULARY

classification
kingdom
moneran
protist
fungi
genus
species

If you were asked to go to the grocery store to buy fresh peaches, how would you find them? You know how your grocery store is set up, so you would probably go to the produce department and find the fruit section. There you would look for peaches. If a store put some fruit with the cereal and some with the meat, finding peaches would be much more difficult.

Like grocery shoppers, scientists need to be able to find things easily. Just as you did with shoes in the investigation, scientists look at living things and identify their characteristics. They then group together living things that have similar features. This act of grouping things by using a set of rules is called **classification** (klas•uh•fih•KAY•shuhn).

✔ **How do scientists group living things?**

The living things shown in the forest scene and in the smaller photos belong to different groups.

Bacterium

Paramecium

Water strider

The Five Kingdoms

	Kingdom	Important Characteristics	Examples
	Animals	Many-celled, feed on other living things	Monkeys, birds, frogs, fish, spiders
	Plants	Many-celled, make their own food	Trees, flowers, grasses, ferns, mosses
	Fungi	Most many-celled, absorb food from other living things or dead things such as logs	Mushrooms, yeasts, molds
	Protists	Most one-celled, make their own food or feed on other living things	Algae, amoebas, diatoms
	Monerans	One-celled, no cell nuclei, some make their own food, some feed on other living things	Bacteria

Grouping by Similarities and Differences

Scientists classify for many reasons. Classifying living things makes it easier to find and share information about them. When scientists discover a new living thing, classification can show how the new living thing relates to others that are already classified.

All living things can be classified into one of five kingdoms. A **kingdom** (KING•duhm) is the largest group into which living things can be classified. Every member of a kingdom has some characteristics that are the same as those of other members. For example, bacteria are monerans. Every member of the **moneran** (muh•NER•uhn) kingdom has only one cell. The cell has no nucleus.

Compare the bacterium to the paramecium on page A38. Paramecia are protists. Most members of the **protist** (PROHT•ist) kingdom also have only one cell. However, each cell does have a nucleus.

Fungi make up a third kingdom. **Fungi** (FUHN•jy) have nuclei, and most are many-celled. They look like plants, but they can't make their own food as plants do. You have eaten fungi if you've ever eaten mushrooms.

Plants and animals make up the other two kingdoms. Every day you see members of these two kingdoms, such as grass, flowers, cats, and dogs.

✔ **How are monerans and protists the same? How are they different?**

Forming Smaller Groups

Classification doesn't stop at the kingdom level. Scientists studied the living things in each kingdom to see how they are alike and how they are different. They used characteristics to make smaller and smaller groups, and they gave each smaller group a name. The most specific classification groups have only one type of living thing. The chart below shows how brown bears can be classified by using this method.

Most living things have a common name such as *brown bear*. But common names may be different in different places. It's important to have names that scientists everywhere recognize. For this reason, scientists name animals with the labels of the two smallest classification groups. The name of the second smallest group, the **genus** (JEE•nuhs), is joined with the name of the smallest group, the **species** (SPEE•sheez). For example, the scientific name for a house cat is *Felis domesticus*, and a brown bear is called *Ursus arctos*.

✔ **How do scientists form smaller groups of living things?**

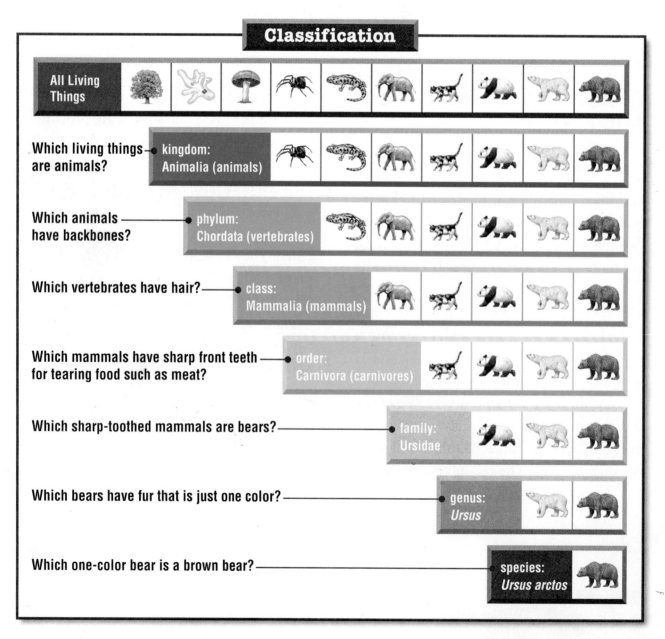

Classification

All Living Things

Which living things are animals? → **kingdom: Animalia (animals)**

Which animals have backbones? → **phylum: Chordata (vertebrates)**

Which vertebrates have hair? → **class: Mammalia (mammals)**

Which mammals have sharp front teeth for tearing food such as meat? → **order: Carnivora (carnivores)**

Which sharp-toothed mammals are bears? → **family: Ursidae**

Which bears have fur that is just one color? → **genus: Ursus**

Which one-color bear is a brown bear? → **species: Ursus arctos**

▲ This bear cub's scientific name is
Ursus (genus) *arctos* (species).

Summary

Scientists organize living things to make studying and discussing them easier. Scientists classify all living things into five kingdoms—monerans, protists, fungi, plants, and animals. The five kingdoms are divided into smaller groups.

Review

1. Why do scientists organize information about living things?

2. What are the five kingdoms of living things?

3. How do scientists name each type of living thing?

4. **Critical Thinking** There are probably millions of living things that scientists haven't discovered yet. If scientists were to find a living thing that didn't fit into any of the five kingdoms, what would they need to do?

5. **Test Prep** Which kingdom contains one-celled living things without nuclei?

   A plants   C fungi

   B monerans   D protists

LINKS

MATH LINK

Graphing Suppose you have found a cave in which animals—three snakes, six bats, and a bear—are living. To report your discovery to your classmates, make a bar graph showing the types and numbers of animals in the cave.

WRITING LINK

Informative Writing—Description Suppose you've discovered a new species of living thing. For your teacher, write two or three paragraphs to describe how you found it, what its characteristics are, and how you decided on its name.

ART LINK

Designing Labels Think about how you could improve the organization of your books, games, or CDs. Classify them and then design picture labels for each group. Put the labels on your books, games, or CDs so that you can more easily find the ones you want.

TECHNOLOGY LINK

Learn more about some bears by viewing *China Panda* on the **Harcourt Science Newsroom Video** in your classroom video library.

How Are Some Animals Classified?

In this lesson, you can . . .

INVESTIGATE a model of a backbone.

LEARN ABOUT vertebrate classification.

LINK to math, writing, health, and technology.

Building a Model Backbone

Activity Purpose Animals are classified into several groups. Animals in one of these groups all have a backbone that protects the spinal cord and helps support the body. In this investigation you will **make and use a model** backbone.

Materials
- chenille stem
- wagon-wheel pasta, uncooked
- candy gelatin rings

Activity Procedure

1 CAUTION **Never eat anything you use in an Investigate.** Bend one end of the chenille stem. Thread six pieces of wagon-wheel pasta onto the stem. Push the pasta down to the bend in the stem. Bend the stem above the pasta to hold the pasta in place.

2 Bend and twist the stem. What do you see and hear?

3 Take all the pasta off the chenille stem except one. Thread a candy gelatin ring onto the stem, and push it down. (Picture A)

◀ Birds have backbones. Worms, like the one the bird is eating, don't.

Picture A

Picture B

4 Add pasta and rings until the stem is almost full. Bend the stem above the pasta and rings to hold them in place. (Picture B)

5 Bend and twist the stem. What do you see and hear?

6 Draw pictures of the model backbones you made. **Compare** your models with that shown in the picture on page A57.

Draw Conclusions

1. A real backbone is made of bones called vertebrae (VER•tuh•bree) and soft discs that surround the spinal cord. What does each part of your final model stand for?

2. How is your final model like a real backbone?

3. Study your final model again. What do the soft discs do?

4. **Scientists at Work** Scientists **use models** to study how things work. Would a piece of dry, uncooked spaghetti or some other material work better than a chenille stem to stand for the spinal cord in your model? Try it and see. Then write a report of your investigation. Be sure to include the results of any tests you conducted with other materials, and any conclusions you drew about using those materials in your model backbone.

Process Skill Tip

Some objects are too big, too small, or too far away to observe directly. You can't observe your backbone directly because it is inside your body. But you can **make a model** to learn more about it.

Vertebrate Classification

Animals with a Backbone

FIND OUT

- **how vertebrates are classified**

- **what groups of animals make up vertebrates**

VOCABULARY

vertebrate

mammal

reptile

amphibian

fish

bird

invertebrate

You are probably familiar with many members of the animal kingdom. An animal is a living thing made up of many cells that have nuclei. Animals can't make their own food. They must eat other living things to survive. Scientists divide the animal kingdom into several large groups. One group of animals has backbones.

Animals that have a backbone are called **vertebrates** (VER•tuh•brits). Most vertebrates have sharp senses and large brains. These characteristics help them survive in their surroundings.

The large group of vertebrates is divided into several smaller groups. **Mammals** (MAM•uhlz) have hair and produce milk for their young. Cats and dogs are mammals that you may have as pets. Lizards, snakes, and turtles are reptiles. **Reptiles** (REP•tylz) have dry, scaly skin. **Amphibians** (am•FIB•ee•uhnz) have moist skin and no scales. Most of them begin life in water, but they live on land as adults. Frogs, toads, and newts are amphibians. Other groups of vertebrates include birds and fish.

Mongoose

Frog

◀ A mongoose and a frog are both vertebrates. What characteristic do they share with a snake?

Snake skeleton

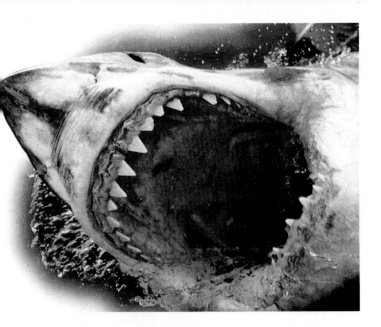

▲ Although a shark's backbone isn't made of bone, a shark is still a vertebrate.

Snail

Tortoiseshell beetle

Sea sponge

Crabs, snails, sea sponges, and beetles are invertebrates. None of these animals has a backbone.

Sharks, eels, bass, and tuna are fish. **Fish** are vertebrates that live their entire lives in water. Most fish have hard scales covering their bodies and gills to take the oxygen they need directly from the water.

Birds are vertebrates with feathers. A bird's feathers keep it warm and help it to fly. Owls, robins, and parrots are birds. Some birds, such as penguins, don't fly.

Not all animals have a backbone. Animals without a backbone are called **invertebrates** (in•VER•tuh•brits). There are many more kinds of invertebrates than there are vertebrates.

Some invertebrates may have a hard outer shell. Snails, clams, and crabs are invertebrates with shells. Invertebrates also include several groups of worms. Worms have no shells, legs, or eyes. Earthworms, tapeworms, and flatworms are all invertebrates. Insects, spiders, and starfish are also invertebrates.

✔ **What characteristic do all vertebrates have in common?**

Only a small part of all the animals in the world have a backbone. ▶

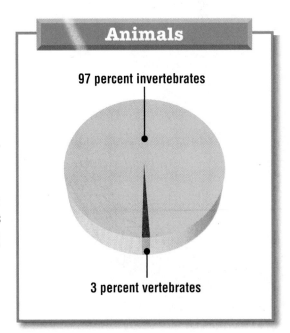

Animals

97 percent invertebrates

3 percent vertebrates

Body Parts for Jumping

Frogs and grasshoppers are in different animal groups. Both animals are known for their ability to jump. Their back legs are different, but they work in much the same way.

1. A frog's thigh muscles attach to its leg bones at the movable hip and knee joints. When the thigh muscles tighten, they pull on the knee joints.

2. The frog's webbed feet are sticky and can grip the ground. With its feet set, its leg muscles lift its body up and forward.

1. A grasshopper's thigh muscles attach to the inside of its skeleton at flexible joints. The other ends of the muscles attach to its knee joints. When the thigh muscles tighten, they pull on the knee joints.

2. The grasshopper's feet have claws and grip the ground. With its feet set, its leg muscles lift its body up and forward.

A Closer Look at Animals

Not all animals have a backbone, but almost all animals have skeletons and muscles that work together to allow the animals to move. The skeletons of vertebrates are made up of bones that support their bodies from the inside. Muscles attach to the bones at movable joints.

Most invertebrates have skeletons that form hard outer coverings. These skeletons are made of a material much like human fingernails. Muscles attach on the inside of these coverings at flexible joints.

✔ **Where do muscles attach to the skeletons of animals?**

Summary

Vertebrates, such as mammals, reptiles, amphibians, birds, and fish, have backbones. Invertebrate animals, such as arthropods, mollusks, and worms, do not have backbones.

Review

1. Which group of vertebrates begins life in water and later lives on land?
2. How is a spider different from an insect?
3. How are the skeletons of vertebrates and invertebrates different?
4. **Critical Thinking** How might having sharp senses and large brains help vertebrates survive?
5. **Test Prep** Which animals are **NOT** vertebrates?
   A reptiles
   B mammals
   C amphibians
   D arthropods

LINKS

MATH LINK

Graphing Vertebrate skeletons are made up of bones. The adult human spine has 33 bones. Find out how many bones the spines of five other vertebrates have. Make a bar graph to show what you learn.

WRITING LINK

Informative Writing—Explanation You've learned that skeletons support animals' bodies and help them move. Skeletons also protect animals' organs. Would you prefer to have a hard outer shell or the skeleton you have now? Write a paragraph to explain your answer to a classmate.

HEALTH LINK

Prevention Calcium helps build strong bones. Eating calcium-rich foods prevents bone problems as you get older. Find out which foods are rich in calcium. Then make a chart to post in your kitchen at home.

TECHNOLOGY LINK

Learn more about vertebrates by investigating *Vertebrate Challenge* on the **Harcourt Science Explorations CD-ROM.**

How Are Plants Classified?

In this lesson, you can . . .

INVESTIGATE plant stems.

LEARN ABOUT plant classification.

LINK to math, writing, literature, and technology.

INVESTIGATE

Plant Stems

Activity Purpose You have learned that animals can be classified by whether they have a backbone. Plants also can be classified by their parts. One of those parts is the stem. In this investigation you will **observe** a stem, or stalk, of celery to help you **infer** what stems do.

Materials
- fresh celery stalk with leaves
- plastic knife
- two containers
- water
- red food coloring
- blue food coloring
- paper towels
- hand lens

Activity Procedure

1. Use the plastic knife to trim the end off the celery stalk. Split the celery from the middle of the stalk to the bottom. Do not cut the stalk completely in half. (Picture A)

2. Make a chart like the one here.

Time	Observations

▼ These flowers and mosses are two different types of plants. They move water in different ways.

Picture A

Picture B

3 Half-fill each container with water. Add 15 drops of red food coloring to one container. Add 15 drops of blue food coloring to the other container.

4 With the containers side by side, place one part of the celery stalk in each container of colored water. You may need to prop the stalk up so the containers don't tip over. (Picture B)

5 **Observe** the celery every 15 minutes for an hour. **Record** your observations on your chart.

6 After you have completed your chart, put a paper towel on your desk. Take the celery out of the water. Cut about 2 cm off the bottom of the stalk. Use the hand lens to **observe** the pieces of stalk and the freshly cut end of the stalk.

Draw Conclusions

1. Where did the water travel? How do you know?

2. How fast did the water travel? How do you know?

3. **Scientists at Work** Scientists **infer** what happens in nature by making careful observations. Based on this investigation, what can you infer about the importance of stems?

Investigate Further How could you change a white carnation into a flower with two colors? Draw and write an explanation of your answer.

Process Skill Tip

When you **infer**, you use what you observe to explain what happened. Inferring is like using clues to solve a mystery. Observing carefully, like finding good clues, can help you infer correctly.

Plant Classification

Plants with Tubes

FIND OUT

- how the plant kingdom is divided
- members of each main group of plants

VOCABULARY

vascular plant
nonvascular plant

All plants are members of the plant kingdom. Plants have many cells, and their cells have nuclei. Unlike animals, plants do not need to eat other living things to survive. Instead, they make their own food. Scientists divide the plant kingdom into two main groups. One group of plants has tubes. The other group does not.

Vascular (VAS•kyuh•ler) **plants** have tubes. These tubes can be found in roots, stems, and leaves. Water and nutrients enter a plant through the roots. The tubes in the roots then carry this mixture to the stems. You observed some stem tubes in the investigation. Tubes in stems carry the water and nutrients to tubes in a plant's leaves. A different set of tubes carries the food the leaves make to the other parts of the plant. Some food tubes run from the leaves to the roots.

Ferns are a type of vascular plant. The tubes of fern stems form a network. They often split apart and rejoin. Cells that make up the tubes are stiff. This helps provide support for the fern as its stems grow.

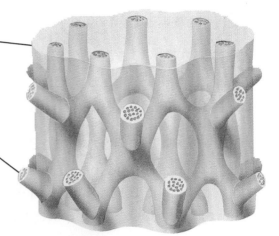

A fern is a vascular plant. Notice the network of tubes that make up the stem.

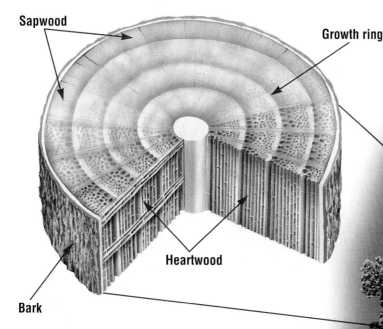

Sapwood

Growth ring

Heartwood

Bark

Trees are another type of vascular plant. The stems of trees contain cells that are woody, or very hard. Some large bushes also have woody stems. The largest woody stem of a tree is called the trunk. Look at the detailed slice of the tree trunk. The center of the trunk is made of hard, dead tubes called *heartwood*. Around the heartwood is a ring of *sapwood*. The living tubes that carry water and food are in the sapwood. Each year, a new set of tubes forms, and an old set dies, adding a growth ring to the trunk. The outside layer of the trunk is called the bark. The bark is made up of dead cells that protect the living sapwood layer.

There are many other types of vascular plants. Any plant that has flowers or cones is a vascular plant.

✔ **What is carried by the tubes of vascular plants?**

The giant sequoia is a conifer. Conifers (KAHN•uh•ferz) are vascular plants that produce cones. As new sapwood is added each year, a new growth ring forms in the trunk. ▶

A51

Plants Without Tubes

Have you ever seen something that looked like a green carpet growing on stones and walkways? If so, you probably saw moss. Moss is a nonvascular plant. **Nonvascular** (nahn•VAS•kyuh•ler) **plants** don't have tubes. Water must soak into the plants and pass slowly from cell to cell. Food made in the plants must travel with the water from cell to cell. For this reason, nonvascular plants live in damp places and don't grow to be large or tall.

Mosses are often the first plants to grow on bare rock. Their rootlike structures help break down the rock into soil. When the mosses die, their dead bodies help to enrich the soil, making it more fertile. Nonvascular plants need fertile, moist soil in which to grow.

Nonvascular plants have no roots, stems, or leaves. The lobes, or rounded parts, of the liverwort may look like leaves, but they are not true leaves because they have no tubes.

✔ **How does water travel through a nonvascular plant?**

Enlarged, these liverworts look like small palm trees with leafy bases. However, liverworts have no tubes. So, they have no true stems or leaves. ▶

▲ **Moss grows in shady, damp places.**

▲ These plants are liverworts. Liverworts also grow in damp places.

Summary

Scientists have classified plants into two main groups. Vascular plants, such as ferns and trees, have tubes. Because they have tubes to carry water and nutrients, vascular plants can grow quite tall.

Nonvascular plants, such as mosses, do not have tubes. So water must move from cell to cell. These plants need to live in a moist place, and they do not grow to be very large.

Review

1. What are the two main groups of plants?
2. Where are the tubes of vascular plants found?
3. Because nonvascular plants do not have tubes, in what kind of place do they need to grow?
4. **Critical Thinking** What probably would happen to a plant if its main stem were crushed or broken?
5. **Test Prep** Which of these is an example of a nonvascular plant?

   A conifer   **C** moss
   B fern   **D** flower

LINKS

MATH LINK

Nature's Weather Record The width of a growth ring depends on the amount of rainfall the tree received that year. Wide rings form in rainy years. Narrow rings form in dry years. Examine a tree stump or the end of a log. Count the growth rings, and then measure the width of each ring. Make a line graph or a bar graph to show what you see. What can you infer from your graph?

WRITING LINK

Informative Writing—Description
Gather several types of plants, and examine their characteristics. Write clues describing each plant. Your clues can be about color, smell, height, size, or the plant's use, or they may tell where it was found. Read your clues to your classmates, and see if they can guess your plant.

LITERATURE LINK

Sugaring Time Would you like to learn how maple syrup is made from sap that flows through the tubes in maple trees? Read *Sugaring Time* by Kathryn Lasky.

TECHNOLOGY LINK

Learn more about plant classification by visiting the Harcourt Learning Site for related links, activities, and resources.
www.harcourtschool.com/ca

WELCOME TO **THE LEARNING SITE**

NAMING Living Things

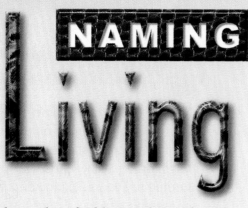

People have classified living things for a long time. Cave people probably sorted animals into groups such as those that were good to eat and those that were likely to eat you. Classification is an important first step in the study of almost anything.

The history of classification shows how ideas in science can change through time. As scientists learn more, they change their ideas about how things work. For example, the first recorded classification system for living things that we know about was developed by Aristotle. Aristotle was a philosopher, teacher, and scientist in ancient Greece. In about 350 B.C. he classified living things into two large groups—plants and animals. He divided animals by how they looked, how they behaved, and where they lived. He divided plants by their size and shape. He said that the three main divisions of the plant kingdom were trees, shrubs, and herbs (small plants such as grasses).

A New System

Aristotle's system didn't work for all plants and animals. However, it was used for more than 2000 years. In 1753, Carolus Linnaeus published the system that is the basis for the system we use today. Linnaeus, like Aristotle, divided living things into two kingdoms. However, for more exact sorting, he then broke the kingdoms into many smaller groups. The smallest group is the *species.* Today, scientists use genus and species names to identify living things.

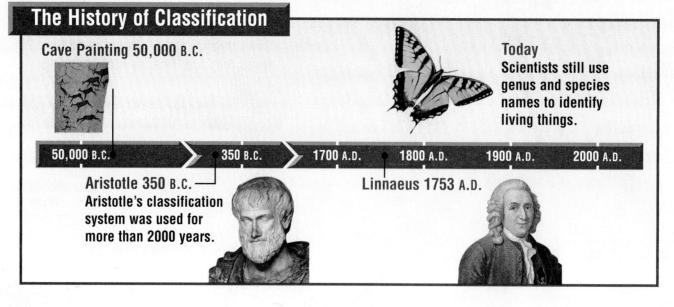

The History of Classification

Cave Painting 50,000 B.C.

Today
Scientists still use genus and species names to identify living things.

| 50,000 B.C. | 350 B.C. | 1700 A.D. | 1800 A.D. | 1900 A.D. | 2000 A.D. |

Aristotle 350 B.C.
Aristotle's classification system was used for more than 2000 years.

Linnaeus 1753 A.D.

Which Cat?

Genus and species names are important because they help scientists and other people talk about exactly the same organisms. For example, people use different names for one kind of large cat—*puma, panther,* and *mountain lion.* However, a scientist uses only the name *Felis concolor.* That way you know exactly which type of cat he or she is talking about.

As microscopes and other instruments for the study of living things became better, people began to realize that there were probably more than two kingdoms. Fungi were the first organisms classified as a new kingdom. After a lot of study, living things were divided into five different kingdoms. Some scientists now suggest that there may be as many as seven kingdoms.

As we learn more, our ideas about how living things are related change. As those ideas change, the way we classify the world of living things also changes. Each change in the classification system is a direct result of more study and better understanding of the relationships of living things.

THINK ABOUT IT

1. Linnaeus classified living things. Give examples of two other classification systems and what they classify.
2. How have changes in technology affected the classification of living things?

In different parts of the United States, both of these animals are called gophers. The scientific name of each helps you know to which animal a scientist is referring.

Gopherus polyphemus (gopher tortoise)

Marmota monax (gopher or woodchuck)

Ynes Enriquetta Julietta Mexia

BOTANICAL EXPLORER

Ynes Mexia spent the last 13 years of her life, from 1925 to 1938, collecting plant specimens outside the United States. She was the daughter of an agent for the Mexican government, so she knew other languages and understood other cultures. This helped her when she traveled. She visited many places, including Mexico, Alaska, Brazil, Ecuador, Argentina, Bolivia, and Peru. During her trips she discovered almost 50 new plant species.

While living in San Francisco, Ms. Mexia traveled with the local Sierra Club. She took classes in natural science at the University of California and became interested in botany (BAHT•uhn•ee). She took a class on flowering plants, and it changed her life.

The botany class led to her first collecting trip, with botanist Roxanna S. Ferris. The trip was cut short when Ms. Mexia fell from a cliff. She broke several ribs and injured her hand. But before her fall, she had already collected 500 species of plants. One new species was named in Ms. Mexia's honor.

Nearly all of Ms. Mexia's trips were to tropical countries. Because of the humid climates, it was

difficult to dry and preserve plant samples. Alice Eastwood, a noted botanist, taught Ms. Mexia how to collect and preserve plants. Later, Ms. Mexia was proud to tell Eastwood that she had been able to preserve every specimen she collected!

Ms. Mexia's samples went to important museums, such as the Field Museum in Chicago and the Gray Herbarium (her•BAIR•ee•uhm) at Harvard University. During 13 years she collected 137,600 plant specimens.

THINK ABOUT IT

1. Do you think it is easier to collect and preserve plants now? Why?

2. How do you think collecting plants helps scientists understand more about plant classification?

Bracken fern

Backbone Construction

How do backbones give vertebrates flexible support?

Materials
- construction paper
- tape
- scissors
- book

Procedure

① Roll the paper into a tube about 5 cm across. Tape all along the edge.

② Stand the tube on one end. Will the tube hold up a pair of scissors? A book? More than one book?

③ Squeeze the tube gently to make an oval. Make slits about 2 cm apart all down the tube. Cut the slits from each side almost to the middle.

④ Experiment to see how much weight the tube will now hold up.

Draw Conclusions

What happened each time the tube gave way? How did the cuts change the tube?

Plants and Water

Why do leaves give off water?

Materials
- pencil
- water
- marker
- scissors
- piece of thin cardboard
- leaf with a long stem
- modeling clay
- 2 clear plastic cups

Procedure

① Carefully use the pencil to poke a hole in the center of the cardboard. Then push the leaf stem through the hole. Use the clay to close up the hole around the stem. Be careful not to pinch the stem.

② Fill one cup about $\frac{2}{3}$ full with water. Mark the water line with the marker.

③ Snip off about 1 cm from the stem end. Place the cut stem into the water, resting the cardboard on the rim of the cup. Place the empty cup over the leaf. Set the cups in the sun.

④ After a few hours, observe both cups and the stem. Record your observations.

Draw Conclusions

What can you infer from your observations?

Chapter **2** Review and Test Preparation

Vocabulary Review

Use the terms below to complete the sentences. The page numbers in ( ) tell you where to look in the chapter if you need help.

classification (A38)　　**reptile** (A44)

kingdom (A39)　　**amphibian** (A44)

monerans (A39)　　**invertebrate** (A45)

protists (A39)　　**birds** (A45)

fungi (A39)　　**fish** (A45)

genus (A40)　　**vascular plants** (A50)

species (A40)　　**nonvascular**

vertebrate (A44)　　　**plants** (A52)

mammal (A44)

1. The largest group into which scientists classify living things is a ____.

2. An animal that does not have a backbone is an ____.

3. Plants are either ____ or ____, depending on the presence of tubes.

4. ____ and ____ are the smallest groups into which living things are classified.

5. An animal with a backbone is a ____.

6. The two kingdoms of microscopic living things are ____ and ____.

7. ____, ____, ____ are vertebrates.

8. ____ and ____ are also vertebrates.

9. Scientists use ____ to organize living things.

10. ____ have many cells with nuclei and absorb food from other living things.

Connect Concepts

Use the terms in the Word Bank to complete the concept map.

animals

classification

fungi

genus

kingdoms

monerans

plants

protists

species

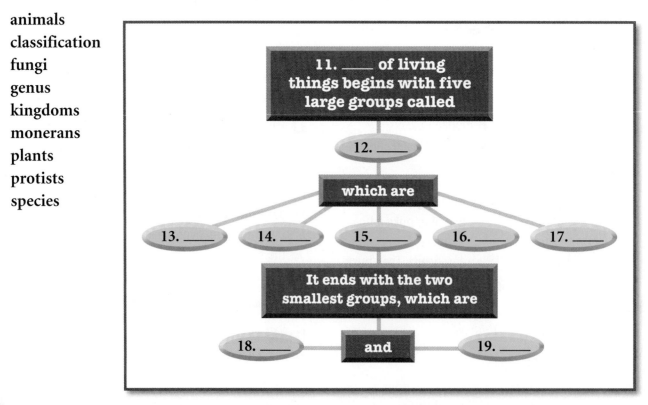

11. ____ of living things begins with five large groups called

12. ____

which are

13. ____　14. ____　15. ____　16. ____　17. ____

It ends with the two smallest groups, which are

18. ____　and　19. ____

Check Understanding

Write the letter of the best choice.

20. Which of the following is a type of moneran?

 A algae   **C** fish

 B bacteria   **D** mushroom

21. Which characteristic makes vertebrates different from invertebrates?

 F Vertebrates have a backbone.

 G Vertebrates do not have a backbone.

 H Vertebrates are monerans.

 J Invertebrates have a backbone.

22. In a nonvascular plant, water travels —

 A through the roots

 B through the sapwood

 C from cell to cell

 D through the flowers

23. Which part of a vascular plant has tubes for carrying water and food?

 F leaves   **H** bark

 G heartwood   **J** seeds

24. Which of the following is **NOT** a kingdom?

 A fungi   **C** plants

 B animals   **D** vertebrates

25. Where do muscles attach to the skeletons of invertebrates?

 F at flexible shell joints

 G at the backbone

 H where bones meet

 J at movable bone joints

26. Which of the following vertebrates have hair and give milk for their young?

 A reptiles   **C** amphibians

 B mammals   **D** birds

27. What makes a moneran different from a protist?

 F A moneran has no nucleus.

 G A moneran has a backbone.

 H A moneran has tubes.

 J A moneran has jointed legs.

Critical Thinking

28. Why is it important that scientists share what they learn from their research?

29. A dog has a backbone and fur. To which kingdom and to which two smaller groups does it belong?

Process Skills Review

30. Which three items would you **classify** in one group? Explain your answer.

 shoelace, stop sign, button, zipper

31. Which would make the better **model** for showing how water is carried inside a tree? Explain your answer.

 a frozen-treat stick and paper

 a cardboard tube and a rubber hose

32. Think about your observations of the feet of ducks and chickens. Which animals would you **infer** are the better swimmers? Explain your answer.

Performance Assessment

Sorting Scheme

Work with a group to make rules for classifying items in your desks or in your classroom. Sort the items into several "kingdoms." Then sort the members of each kingdom into as many smaller groups as you can.

LESSON **1**
What Are the Functions of Roots, Stems, and Leaves?   **A62**

LESSON **2**
How Do Plants Recycle Materials?   **A70**

LESSON **3**
How Do Plants Reproduce?   **A78**

LESSON **4**
How Do People Use Plants?   **A86**

SCIENCE AND TECHNOLOGY   A92
PEOPLE IN SCIENCE   A94
ACTIVITIES FOR HOME OR SCHOOL   A95
CHAPTER REVIEW AND TEST PREPARATION   A96

Plants and Their Adaptations

While animals can search for food and water, plants must meet these needs rooted in one place. But plants have many adaptations that help them survive.

FAST FACT

Part of a rain forest no larger than a city block may have more than 400 different kinds of trees. Most forests in the United States have no more than 20 different kinds of trees in the same area.

Vocabulary Preview

xylem
phloem
chlorophyll
nitrogen cycle
carbon dioxide–oxygen cycle
spore
gymnosperm
pollen
angiosperm
grain
fiber

Have you ever heard the expression "as American as apple pie"? It may surprise you to learn that the apple is not a native American plant and that apple pie was invented in Europe.

Food Origins

Food	Probable Origin
Apple	Southeast Europe
Banana	Southeast Asia
Oats	Western Europe
Pineapple	Latin America
Potato	Peru
Rice	India
Tomato	Mexico

FAST FACT

Buffalo grass has a thick network of roots. These roots and the soil they hold are called *sod*. The roots hold the soil so well that many settlers on the American plains used sod to build their homes.

What Are the Functions of Roots, Stems, and Leaves?

In this lesson, you can . . .

INVESTIGATE the parts of plants.

LEARN ABOUT plant parts and their functions.

LINK to math, writing, social studies, and technology.

The silver sword grows only in Hawai'i. ▶

The Parts of a Vascular Plant

Activity Purpose Towering oak trees and potted geraniums have many parts in common. Vascular plants have roots, stems, and leaves. The sizes and shapes of these parts differ, but each part has a function that helps the plant live. In this investigation you will **observe** a plant and identify its parts.

Materials

- potted plant
- hand lens
- ruler
- newspaper
- plastic knife

Activity Procedure

1 Make a drawing of the plant. List all the parts of the plant that you can name.

2 **Observe** the leaves. What colors are they? Use the ruler to measure the length and width of the leaves. Are they all the same shape and size? Are they wide or narrow? Are they long or short? Do they grow singly or in pairs? Observe them more closely with the hand lens. What more can you say about them? Identify and label the leaves in your drawing. (Picture A)

3 **Observe** the stem. Does it bend? Does it have branches? Identify and label the stem in your drawing.

4 Hold the pot upside down over the newspaper. Tap the pot gently until the plant and the soil come out. If the plant won't come out, run the plastic knife around between the soil and the inside of the pot. (Picture B)

Picture A

Picture B

5 Shake the soil from the roots until you can see them clearly. **Observe** the roots. Is there a single root, or are there many small roots? What shape are the roots? Use the ruler to **measure** the length of the roots. Are they thick or thin? Long or short? Use the hand lens to observe them more closely. What more can you say about them? Identify and label the roots in your drawing.

6 Put the soil and the plant back into the pot. Water the plant lightly to help it recover from being out of the pot.

Draw Conclusions

1. What are the parts of the plant you **observed**?

2. **Compare** the plant parts you identified with the parts of a large tree. How are they the same? How are they different?

3. **Scientists at Work** Scientists learn by making observations. What did you **observe** about each part of the plant?

Investigate Further What questions about plant parts could you answer if you had other measuring tools? Develop a testable question about plant parts. Then select the appropriate tools and make the observations you need to answer your question.

Process Skill Tip

When you **observe** something, you should use as many of your senses as you can. Don't just look at the plant. Touch it to see what it feels like and how thick or strong or dry it is. Smell its leaves and roots.

A63

What Vascular Plant Parts Do

Common Parts

FIND OUT

- **how vascular plants grow in different environments**
- **what roots, stems, and leaves do**

VOCABULARY

xylem
phloem
chlorophyll

There are more than half a million types of vascular plants on Earth. They range from tiny desert plants, smaller than a pencil eraser, to giant redwood trees, taller than a 25-story building. No matter how different they appear, vascular plants have three parts in common—roots, stems, and leaves.

These parts make it possible for vascular plants to live and grow almost everywhere. Vascular plants are found in dry deserts, wet jungles, and cold Arctic plains. Vascular plants are able to live in different environments because their roots, stems, and leaves are adapted to the environments in which they live.

✔ **What parts are common to most plants?**

◄ Some plants are able to grow through the cracks in a city sidewalk.

These crocuses bloom in low temperatures that would kill many other plants. ▼

Some tall trees have roots that spread out as far as their branches. They help keep the trees from falling over.

A thick mat of fibrous roots allows grasses to take in large amounts of water from the soil. ▶

Dandelions have long taproots. If you try to pull a dandelion out of the ground, part of the root may remain. The dandelion will grow back from the part that is left in the ground. ▶

Roots

The roots of many trees spread as far from the trunk as their branches do. Most plant roots act as anchors. They keep the plant from falling over or blowing away in the wind. Roots also take in water and minerals from the soil through tiny parts called *root hairs.* Some roots also store food for the plant.

Different types of roots are adapted to different environments. Some small desert plants have roots that spread far from the plant but grow close to the surface. These roots are able to take in large amounts of the little rain that falls in the desert.

Forest trees don't need the spreading roots of desert plants because there is more water in the forest soil. These trees need deep roots to anchor them. Some tree roots, called *prop roots,* begin above the ground.

These help keep trees that grow in loose, wet soil from being blown over by the wind.

Many plants have *fibrous* (FY•bruhs) *roots,* which look a little like tree branches. The fibrous roots of some grasses form a thick and tangled mat just under the surface of the soil. Fibrous roots help prevent soil erosion by wind and water because they anchor the soil as well as the plant.

Some plants have a single, thick root that grows straight down. These roots, called *taproots,* can reach water that is deep in the ground. Some taproots store food for the plant as well.

In tropical rain forests there are plants that grow on branches high in the trees. Their roots attach themselves to the trees and take water directly from the moist air.

✔ **What do plant roots do?**

A65

Storage Roots

Some plants store extra food and water to help them survive brief changes in their environments. Most plants cannot make food in the winter. In dry periods they may not be able to get all the water they need from the soil.

In good weather plants produce more food than they need and take in extra water. Some plants store extra food and water in their roots. Others store it in their stems.

Some plants store so much extra food in their roots that people grow them for their own food. You've probably eaten several kinds of storage roots. Beets, carrots, sweet potatoes, and turnips are called root vegetables. Because much of the food they store is in the form of sugar and starch, many root vegetables have a sweet taste.

✔ **What do some roots store?**

Stems

Stems do several things for plants. They hold the plant up, and they support the leaves so that they will be in sunlight. Stems also carry water and food to other parts of the plant.

Most plant stems grow upward. The leaves of long-stemmed plants can reach sunlight even in shady places. Some stems even turn during the day. This helps keep the leaves in sunlight, too.

Some plant stems grow sideways, instead of up. Wherever the stem touches the ground, it forms a root from which a new plant grows. Strawberry and spider plants are examples of this type of plant.

Many desert plants have stems that store food and water. The stem of the barrel cactus stores water for the plant. When rain is scarce, the cactus uses water from its stem.

Small plants, such as daisies and dandelions, usually have soft, green, flexible stems. The water inside the stem makes it firm enough to hold the plant up. You might have noticed that a cut flower begins to droop after a few days. Without a root, it can no longer get enough water to keep its stem firm. Most soft-stemmed plants live for just one growing season.

Large plants, such as bushes and trees, need extra support. For this reason, they usually have stiff, woody stems. Woody plants do not die at the end of one growing

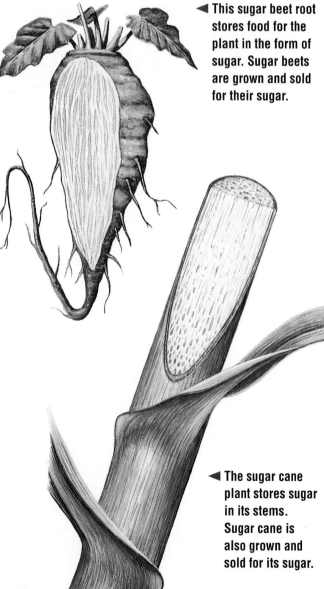

◀ This sugar beet root stores food for the plant in the form of sugar. Sugar beets are grown and sold for their sugar.

◀ The sugar cane plant stores sugar in its stems. Sugar cane is also grown and sold for its sugar.

season but continue to grow year after year. Some woody plants, such as the redwoods of California, may live for hundreds or even thousands of years.

Recall that plant stems contain narrow tubes that carry water, minerals, and food. The tubes that transport water and minerals are called **xylem** (ZY•luhm). They move water and minerals upward, from the roots to the leaves. The strings you find when you bite into a stalk of celery are xylem tubes.

The tubes that carry food are called **phloem** (FLOH•em). They move the food made in the leaves to other parts of the plant. The food that plants make and store is needed for growth by roots, stems, and leaves.

In plants with flexible stems, xylem and phloem are in bundles scattered all through the stem. In plants with woody stems, the xylem and phloem are arranged in rings. The xylem is toward the inside of the stem, while the phloem is toward the outside of the stem.

During each growing season, the stem of a woody plant gets thicker as new rings of xylem and phloem form. More xylem than phloem forms each year, so most of the thickness of a tree trunk is xylem. Older rings of xylem no longer transport water. They harden as they become filled with transported materials. This old xylem is the heartwood of a tree. People use the heart-wood of many kinds of trees as lumber to build houses and to make furniture.

✔ **Name the two types of tubes that transport materials in plant stems.**

Each year, trees produce a new layer of xylem, forming a *growth ring*. Counting the growth rings of a cut tree can tell you how many years old the tree was.

xylem

phloem

The trunk and branches of a tree are the plant's woody stems. The wood of a tree is old xylem. The bark is old phloem that is pushed outward as the trunk and branches grow thicker. ▶

A67

Leaves

Leaves have many shapes and sizes. Some are smaller than a postage stamp, while others are large enough to cover a school bus. But whether they are big or small, most leaves are thin and flat. This helps them make food.

Leaves are the "food factories" of plants. They use water and minerals from the soil, carbon dioxide from the air, and energy from sunlight to make food. The food-making process also produces oxygen, which the plants release into the air.

A *pigment*, or coloring matter, called **chlorophyll** (KLAWR•uh•fil) helps plants use light energy to produce sugars. Chlorophyll gives leaves their green color. In the fall, as the days get shorter, most leaves stop making chlorophyll. Then other pigments already in the leaves can be seen. So it's not frost but simply a lack of chlorophyll that makes the beautiful fall colors seen throughout most of the country.

A leaf is not as simple as it may appear. Inside are layers of cells containing microscopic *chloroplasts* (KLAWR•uh•plasts), which are full of chlorophyll. The food-making process takes place inside the chloroplasts. There are also veins, or bundles of xylem and phloem, running through a leaf. Veins bring water and minerals to the chloroplasts and take sugars from them.

Carbon dioxide enters a leaf, and oxygen and water leave it, through tiny holes called *stomata* (stoh•MAH•tuh). Stomata open wide during the day, when the plant is making food. They close at night, to conserve water. A waxy outer layer on

The leaves or stems of some plants are adapted as *tendrils*. Tendrils wrap themselves around poles or attach themselves to rough surfaces to help the leaves reach the sunlight they need to make food.

the top of most leaves helps conserve water during the heat of the day.

Some leaves "catch" food. The Venus' flytrap grows in places where the soil may not have all the nutrients the plant needs to make food. The plant's traplike leaves are adapted to snap shut when an insect lands on them. The leaves release chemicals that digest the insect and take from it the nutrients the plant needs.

Some leaves also store food. The fleshy layers of an onion bulb—the part we eat—are really leaves.

✔ **What is the main thing leaves do?**

The spines (leaves) of a cactus are an adaptation that protects the plant's food and water from desert animals. ▼

Summary

Each part of a vascular plant has a different function. Roots anchor a plant and take in minerals and water from the soil. A stem supports a plant and moves materials between the plant's parts. Leaves make the plant's food. All of these parts may be adapted to the environment and the needs of the plant.

Review

1. Why are the parts of some plants very different from those of other plants?

2. How are taproots and fibrous roots different?

3. Why do plants store food?

4. **Critical Thinking** What would happen to a green plant if you left it in a dark room for a long time?

5. **Test Prep** Some leaves change color in the fall. This is because —

   A they need to be replaced

   B they stop making chlorophyll

   C there is too much sunlight

   D the trees are dying

LINKS

MATH LINK

Ratio A ratio is a comparison that uses numbers. If a leaf is 6 cm long and 2 cm wide, the ratio of its length to its width is 3 to 1. Use a ruler to measure the length and width of a number of different leaves. Round each measurement to the nearest centimeter and record your measurements. What observations can you make about the ratio of length to width?

WRITING LINK

Informative Writing—Description
Suppose there were a world without trees. Write a story describing what such a world would be like. How would the world be different? What products would be missing from people's lives? Share your story with your classmates.

SOCIAL STUDIES LINK

Map Choose a type of plant and find out where in the United States it grows. Use a computer to make a map and identify the places where the plant grows. Then use the computer to make a chart showing the plant type, location, and climate.

TECHNOLOGY LINK

Learn more about plants by visiting the Harcourt Learning Site.

WELCOME TO
THE LEARNING SITE

www.harcourtschool.com/ca

LESSON 2

How Do Plants Recycle Materials?

In this lesson, you can . . .

INVESTIGATE how plants use carbon dioxide.

LEARN ABOUT how materials are reused in nature.

LINK to math, writing, social studies, and technology.

▼ Every cell in this bison's body uses oxygen and produces carbon dioxide.

How Plants Use Carbon Dioxide

Activity Purpose Remember that every time you inhale, or take a breath, your lungs take in oxygen. That oxygen then goes to your blood cells, which carry it to every other cell in your body. Body cells use oxygen for their life functions, or activities. Cell functions produce carbon dioxide, which the blood carries back to the lungs. When you exhale, or breathe out, carbon dioxide leaves your body. In this investigation you will **observe** how plants use carbon dioxide.

Materials

- safety goggles
- 2 beakers, 250 mL
- water
- dropper
- bromothymol blue (BTB), an indicator
- plastic straw
- elodea
- 2 test tubes with caps
- funnel
- clock

CAUTION

Activity Procedure

1 **CAUTION** Put on safety goggles, and leave them on until you complete Step 4. Fill one beaker about two-thirds full of water. Use the dropper to add BTB to the water until you have a blue solution. BTB is an indicator. It changes color when carbon dioxide is present.

2 **CAUTION** Don't suck on the straw. If you do accidentally, don't swallow the solution. Spit it out, and rinse your mouth with water. Put the plastic straw in the solution, and blow into it. What do you **observe**? **Record** your observations. (Picture A)

3 Put the elodea into one test tube, and use the funnel to fill the tube with BTB solution from the beaker. Fill the other test tube with the BTB solution only.

4 Seal the test tubes with the caps. Carefully turn the test tubes upside down, and place them in the empty beaker. (Picture B)

5 Put the beaker containing the two test tubes in a sunny window for 1 hour. **Predict** what changes will occur in the test tubes. After 1 hour, **observe** both test tubes, and **record** your observations.

Picture A

Draw Conclusions

1. What changes did you **observe** in the BTB solution when you blew into it through the straw? Explain.

2. What changes did you **observe** in the test tube of BTB solution after the elodea had been in it for 1 hour?

3. **Compare** the color of the BTB solution in the test tube that had the elodea with the color of the BTB in the test tube that did not have the elodea. Describe any differences.

4. **Scientists at Work** Scientists **observe** changes that happen during experiments. Then they **infer** what caused the changes. What can you infer about any changes that took place in the test tubes?

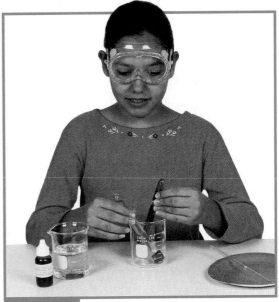
Picture B

Investigate Further In this investigation the color of the BTB solution is the dependent variable. What is the single, independent variable? What did you learn about plants' use of carbon dioxide from the data you collected on this variable? Find out what would happen to the BTB solution if you changed the independent variable.

Process Skill Tip

When you **infer** the cause of something, you try to explain why it happened. Your inference is based on what you **observe**.

How Natural Materials Are Reused

Natural Cycles

Many materials on Earth are used and then reused by living organisms. Earth also stores some materials for later use. The air, for example, stores large amounts of oxygen, nitrogen, and carbon dioxide. Materials such as iron, copper, magnesium, and calcium are stored in rocks.

Running water slowly wears away rocks, releasing stored materials. The materials dissolve in rivers and lakes or become part of the soil. When an animal drinks water, it gets some of the materials it needs. However, animals get most of the materials they need by eating. Animals, in turn, release materials into the environment in their wastes. These wastes are the products of cells making energy from food.

Plants get the materials they need to make food from the soil and from the air. Plants also release materials into the environment. When plants and animals die, their bodies decay. This releases more materials into the environment. The cycle continues as other plants and animals use these materials.

✔ **Where do animals and plants get the materials they need?**

FIND OUT

- how materials are reused in nature
- about the nitrogen and carbon dioxide–oxygen cycles
- how people can upset nature's recycling

VOCABULARY

nitrogen cycle
carbon dioxide–
   oxygen cycle

Animals get the materials they need by eating and by drinking water. ▼

Lightning "fixes" a small amount of nitrogen.

Most nitrogen gas is fixed by bacteria in the soil or in nodules on some plant roots.

Plants use nitrogen in the soil to make proteins.

Animals get nitrogen by eating plants and other animals.

Animal wastes and decaying plants and animals return nitrates and ammonia to the soil.

The Nitrogen Cycle

All living organisms need nitrogen (NY•truh•juhn). Plants make proteins from nitrogen in the soil. Animals get the nitrogen they need to make proteins when they eat plants or other animals that eat plants.

Earth's atmosphere is about 78 percent nitrogen. But most organisms can't use nitrogen in this form. In the **nitrogen cycle**, nitrogen gas is *fixed*, or changed, into forms of nitrogen that plants can use. These forms are nitrates and ammonia (uh•MOHN•yuh).

Bacteria in the soil and in nodules (NAHJ•ools), or small lumps, on the roots of certain plants fix most of the nitrogen gas.

A small amount of nitrogen gas is also fixed by lightning. Most fixed nitrogen remains fixed—only a small amount changes back into nitrogen gas.

Nitrates and ammonia are returned to the soil in two ways. First, they are returned through animal wastes. Solid waste from animals contains nitrates. The liquid waste, or urine, that animals produce contains ammonia. Second, when animals and plants die, bacteria release nitrates and ammonia from decaying protein.

✓ **What are two forms of fixed nitrogen?**

Farmers spread animal wastes on their fields to return nitrates to the soil.

The Carbon Dioxide–Oxygen Cycle

In the carbon dioxide–oxygen cycle, carbon and oxygen move among plants, animals, and the environment. All life on Earth is involved in this cycle.

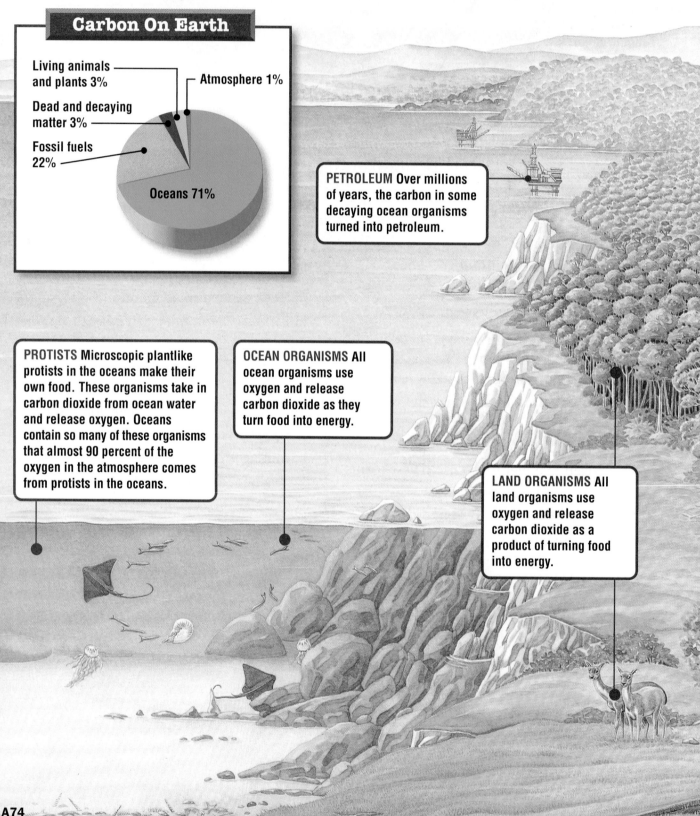

Carbon On Earth

Living animals and plants 3%

Atmosphere 1%

Dead and decaying matter 3%

Fossil fuels 22%

Oceans 71%

PETROLEUM Over millions of years, the carbon in some decaying ocean organisms turned into petroleum.

PROTISTS Microscopic plantlike protists in the oceans make their own food. These organisms take in carbon dioxide from ocean water and release oxygen. Oceans contain so many of these organisms that almost 90 percent of the oxygen in the atmosphere comes from protists in the oceans.

OCEAN ORGANISMS All ocean organisms use oxygen and release carbon dioxide as they turn food into energy.

LAND ORGANISMS All land organisms use oxygen and release carbon dioxide as a product of turning food into energy.

SOLAR ENERGY Sunlight provides the energy for all life on Earth.

COMBUSTION Oxygen is used in the burning, or combustion, of wood or coal. Carbon dioxide is a product of combustion.

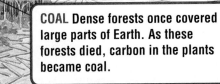

COAL Dense forests once covered large parts of Earth. As these forests died, carbon in the plants became coal.

DECAY Some carbon is stored for a while in the bodies of dead organisms. Bacteria and fungi break down the tissues of dead animals and plants and use some of the carbon as food. It is then released into the atmosphere as carbon dioxide.

PLANTS Plants use sunlight, water, and carbon dioxide to make food. Plants release oxygen into the atmosphere as a product of making food.

Changing the Balance

For hundreds of millions of years, the carbon dioxide–oxygen cycle stayed in balance, mostly by the processes of plants and animals. However, since the beginning of the Industrial Revolution, about 200 years ago, human activity has started to change the balance.

During the Industrial Revolution, humans began to use machines fueled by wood and coal. Factories needed huge amounts of these fuels. Large areas of forests were cut for timber, and deep mines were dug to remove coal from inside the Earth. The burning of wood and coal put tons of carbon dioxide into the air each year.

Slowly, new methods made it possible to replace wood and some coal with fossil fuels such as natural gas and petroleum. Factories, energy stations, heating systems, and cars, trucks, and airplanes all use fossil fuels. Burning these fuels adds even more carbon dioxide to the air.

Adding carbon dioxide to the air is a problem, because excess carbon dioxide is poisonous to animals. Although many people no longer use wood for fuel, large numbers of trees are still cut down for forest products, such as paper and lumber. Sometimes new trees are planted to replace the ones that are cut. But the total size of Earth's forests is less each year.

Forests are also cut to make room for other human needs, such as new farms and homes and growing cities. With forests becoming smaller, there are fewer trees to

Forests use large amounts of carbon dioxide. Smaller forests mean fewer trees to use the excess carbon dioxide in the air.

use the added carbon dioxide in the air. As a result, carbon dioxide continues to build up in the air. And too much carbon dioxide is poisonous to animals and humans.

✓ **How do trees and other plants help keep the carbon dioxide–oxygen cycle balanced?**

Summary

Most of the materials that organisms need are cycled through nature. Bacteria and lightning fix nitrogen gas into forms that plants can use to make proteins. Animal wastes and decaying organisms return nitrates and ammonia to the soil. Plants and animals cycle oxygen and carbon dioxide through the processes of making food and releasing energy from food. But human activities, such as burning fossil fuels and cutting down forests, upset the balance of the carbon dioxide–oxygen cycle.

Review

1. Name two places where carbon is stored.
2. Where do bacteria fix nitrogen gas?
3. How do plants and animals affect the carbon dioxide–oxygen cycle?
4. **Critical Thinking** How might building a shopping mall on land where there is now a park affect the amount of carbon dioxide in the air?
5. **Test Prep** Which human activity does **NOT** increase the amount of carbon dioxide in the air?
   A cutting down trees
   B heating buildings with coal
   C driving cars
   D planting corn

LINKS

MATH LINK

Calculate Each year human activity adds more than 7 billion tons of carbon dioxide to the air. This amount increases by 5 percent each year. If people add 7 billion tons of carbon dioxide to the air in the year 2000, how much will they add in 2001? In 2002?

WRITING LINK

Narrative Writing—Story Write a story for your family from the point of view of a material such as tin, copper, or iron. Begin your story inside a rock. Then describe what happens as you begin to dissolve in water and enter a natural cycle.

SOCIAL STUDIES LINK

Transportation Before the early 1900s, people didn't use cars to travel. Find out how people got around without cars. Write a report or make a poster showing methods of transportation people used before cars were invented.

TECHNOLOGY LINK

Learn more about cycles in nature by visiting this Internet site.
www.scilinks.org/harcourt

Nonvascular Plants

Activity Purpose Scientists classify plants by the way they transport water. You read in Lesson 1 that the stems of many plants have xylem that carries water from the roots to other parts of the plant. Now you will **observe** plants that have similar-looking parts. You will **infer** what these parts do by **comparing** them to the plant parts you observed in Lesson 1.

Materials
- moss
- liverwort
- hand lens

Activity Procedure

1. **Observe** the moss and the liverwort. **Record** what you see.

2. Now **observe** the plants with a hand lens. Can you see different parts? Do any of the parts you see look like the parts of the potted plant you observed in Lesson 1? (Picture A)

3. **Observe** the plants by touching them with your fingers. Are they soft or firm? Are they dry or moist? What else can you tell by feeling them? Describe what they feel like.

◄ Moss often grows in moist, shady forests. Many tiny plants grow close together to form a mat on tree trunks, rocks, or damp soil.

How Do Plants Reproduce?

In this lesson, you can . . .

INVESTIGATE nonvascular plants.

LEARN ABOUT plant reproduction.

LINK to math, writing, language arts, and technology.

Picture A

Picture B

4 Touch the plants with a pencil or other object while you **observe** them through the hand lens. Do the parts bend, or are they stiff? Do you see anything new if you push a part of the plant to one side? Describe what you see.

5 **Observe** the plants by smelling them. Do they have any kind of odor? Try to identify the odors. Describe what you smell. (Picture B)

6 Make drawings of the moss and liverwort, identify the parts you observed, and **infer** what each part does.

Draw Conclusions

1. What plant parts did you **observe** on the moss? What parts did you observe on the liverwort?

2. What do you **infer** each part of the plant does?

3. **Scientists at Work** Scientists use observations to **compare** things. Use the observations you made in this investigation to compare the moss and liverwort with a vascular plant.

Investigate Further **Observe** a fern. Based on your observations, would you **classify** a fern as a nonvascular plant, like the moss and the liverwort, or as a vascular plant, like the potted plant in Lesson 1?

> **Process Skill Tip**
>
> By knowing what observations help you **compare** things, you will be able to make better observations.

Different Methods of Reproduction

FIND OUT

• how nonvascular and vascular plants reproduce

VOCABULARY

spore
gymnosperm
pollen
angiosperm

Nonvascular Plants

Recall that mosses and liverworts are simple plants that usually grow in damp places. They need to stay moist because they do not have xylem tubes to transport water. They also lack phloem tubes.

Remember, plants that don't have xylem and phloem are nonvascular plants. Nonvascular plants can move water, minerals, and food only from one cell to the next. This is the reason why nonvascular plants are so small. Vascular plants, which have xylem and phloem, can grow much larger.

As you observed in the investigation, nonvascular plants have parts that look similar to those of vascular plants. Their leaflike parts, for example, have chloroplasts and use sunlight to manufacture food. Their thin, rootlike structures anchor the plants in the ground and take in some water and minerals. Their stemlike parts hold the leaflike parts up to the sunlight. However, these similar-looking parts are not true leaves, roots, or stems,

The spore capsules of moss plants contain hundreds of tiny spores. Each spore can grow into a new plant. ▼

Nonvascular Reproduction

Male and female cells join, and a spore stalk grows from the female plant.

The plants produce male and female cells.

The stalk releases spores.

Spores grow into new moss plants.

A80

because they do not have xylem and phloem.

Nonvascular plants do not have flowers, so they don't reproduce with seeds. Instead, they reproduce with spores (SPOHRZ). A **spore** is a single reproductive cell that grows into a new plant. During their life cycle, mosses produce male and female reproductive cells on separate plants. A male cell and a female cell unite and produce a stalk that grows out of the female plant. The stalk releases the spores that will grow into new moss plants.

✔ **What are the two major groups of plants, and how are they different?**

Simple Vascular Plants

Simple vascular plants include ferns and horsetails. Many people think of ferns as plants with lacy leaves. In fact, there are more than 11,000 kinds of ferns, with many different kinds of leaves.

About 325 million years ago, vast forests of tall tree ferns covered much of the Earth. Today most ferns are found in the tropics, though some grow in cool forests. A few kinds even grow in the Arctic.

Horsetails are much less common than ferns. There are only about 20 kinds of horsetails. Most are small, and all contain silica, a gritty material like sand. Years ago, people used dried horsetails to scrub pots and pans.

Like mosses and liverworts, simple vascular plants reproduce with spores. Also like nonvascular plants, ferns and horsetails have two different stages in their life cycles.

As is the case with mosses, ferns produce male and female reproductive cells. However, in ferns the united cell, or *zygote*, divides and grows into a separate spore-producing plant.

✔ **How do simple vascular plants reproduce?**

◄ The underside of a fern leaf contains spore cases.

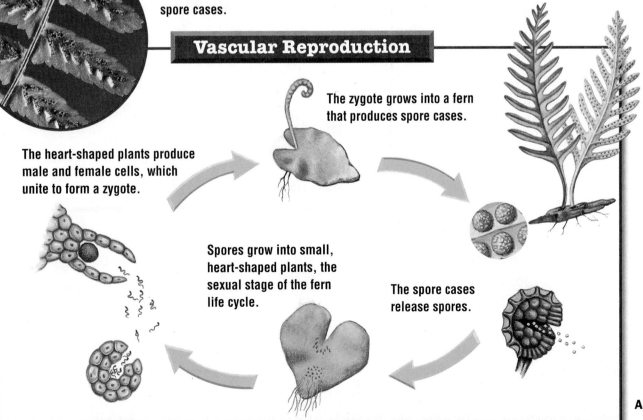

Vascular Reproduction

The zygote grows into a fern that produces spore cases.

The heart-shaped plants produce male and female cells, which unite to form a zygote.

Spores grow into small, heart-shaped plants, the sexual stage of the fern life cycle.

The spore cases release spores.

▲ The cones of
spruce trees hang
down. The cones
of pines grow up.

Conifer trees, such as this
Norway spruce, are common
in cold northern climates. ▶

Cone-Bearing Vascular Plants

Spore-producing plants make large numbers of spores. This adaptation makes sure that at least some of the spores will grow into new plants. Seed-producing plants make relatively fewer seeds, but a seed has a better chance of growing into a new plant than a spore does. This is because a seed contains a supply of food. This stored food helps the new plant grow until it can begin making its own food. Most vascular plants reproduce with seeds.

There are two kinds of seed-producing vascular plants. One type produces seeds with no protection. The other type produces seeds protected by some kind of fruit.

Plants with unprotected seeds are called **gymnosperms** (JIM•noh•spermz). The most common gymnosperms are the *conifers* (KAHN•uh•ferz), or cone-bearing plants, such as pine trees.

Most conifers produce both male and female cones on the same tree. Male cones produce **pollen**, structures that contain the male reproductive cells.

Female cones vary in size from 2 cm (about $\frac{3}{4}$ in.) to more than 75 cm (about 2 ft). Their shapes vary, too, but most have a kind of stem from which thin, woody plates grow. These plates are called *scales.*

Wind carries pollen from male cones to female cones. There the male and female reproductive cells unite. The resulting zygotes divide and grow into seeds. During dry weather the scales open and the seeds are released.

✔ **What is a gymnosperm?**

▲ Seeds develop
between the cone's scales.

Flowering Vascular Plants

Most of the plants you are familiar with are flowering plants, or **angiosperms** (AN•jee•oh•spermz). There are more than 235,000 kinds of angiosperms on Earth. These include grasses, herbs, shrubs, and many trees. Flowering plants are important sources of wood, fiber, and medicine. Nearly all the food that people eat comes directly or indirectly from flowering plants.

Flowers are an adaptation that is important to the success of angiosperms. They help make sure that pollen gets from the male part of a flower to the female part. Unlike gymnosperms, which are pollinated only by the wind, angiosperms are also pollinated by insects and other small animals. The colors, shapes, and odors of flowers attract these

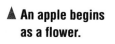

▲ An apple begins as a flower.

◄ There are more than 235,000 kinds of flowering plants. Flowers are important to the success of angiosperms.

▲ The seeds of the apple tree are protected by the fruit. As the fruit rots, it provides extra food for the growth of a new apple tree.

animals, which carry pollen from one flower to another as they move about.

Angiosperm seeds are also an adaptation for success. Unlike the gymnosperms, which produce unprotected seeds, angiosperms produce fruits that protect their seeds. These fruits include apples, oranges, tomatoes, peanuts, and acorns.

A fruit protects the seed or seeds inside it in several ways. It usually keeps birds and other animals from getting at them, even if they eat the outer part of the fruit. A fruit also serves as a covering that protects the seeds from cold weather. In addition, a rotting fruit provides extra food for a new plant when it begins to grow.

✔ **What is an angiosperm?**

Comparing Life Cycles

Both animals and plants go through stages in their lives. A flowering plant sprouts from a seed, grows and matures, flowers, and produces seeds of its own. An animal is born, grows into an adult, and reproduces its own kind. Each organism completes a cycle of life.

Some young animals look very much like their parents. Puppies and kittens are very small when they are born, but you can easily see what they will grow up to become.

Other young animals look very different from their parents. Who would guess that a caterpillar becomes a beautiful butterfly or that a fishlike tadpole becomes a frog?

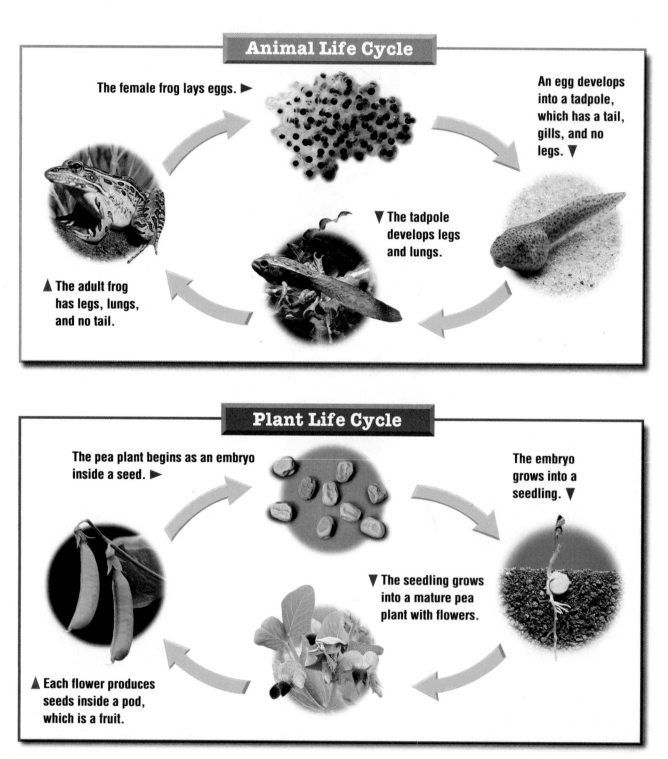

Animal Life Cycle

The female frog lays eggs. ▶

An egg develops into a tadpole, which has a tail, gills, and no legs. ▼

▼ The tadpole develops legs and lungs.

▲ The adult frog has legs, lungs, and no tail.

Plant Life Cycle

The pea plant begins as an embryo inside a seed. ▶

The embryo grows into a seedling. ▼

▼ The seedling grows into a mature pea plant with flowers.

▲ Each flower produces seeds inside a pod, which is a fruit.

In its earliest stages, a flowering plant is also very different from its parent plants. It starts as a tiny plant, called an *embryo,* inside a seed. When the seed sprouts, the embryo grows into a seedling that does not look much like the mature plant. As the plant grows and matures, it looks more and more like the plants it came from.

✔ **How does the life cycle of a flowering plant compare to that of an animal?**

Summary

Vascular plants have xylem and phloem. Nonvascular plants do not have these tubes. Nonvascular plants and simple vascular plants reproduce with spores. Gymnosperms and angiosperms are seed-producing vascular plants. Like animals, plants go through several stages in their life cycles.

Review

1. Why are nonvascular plants so small?
2. How do ferns reproduce?
3. How do conifers produce seeds?
4. **Critical Thinking** Why do you think night-blooming plants have less colorful flowers than day-blooming plants?
5. **Test Prep** The fruit produced by an angiosperm —

    A makes the seeds taste better

    B protects the seeds inside

    C attracts birds and insects

    D is more attractive than the cone of a gymnosperm

LINKS

MATH LINK

What Kind of Flower? Take a look at the plants around you—at home, at school, in parks. Are most of them vascular or nonvascular? Are they gymnosperms or angiosperms? Use a computer graphing program such as *Graph Links* to make a circle graph that compares the percentages of the types of plants you find.

WRITING LINK

Informative Writing—Explanation Write a paragraph explaining how you use plants each day. How many times do you use them? For what purposes? Would it be hard to get through a day without plants? Share your paragraph with your classmates.

LANGUAGE ARTS LINK

Prefixes In the word *nonvascular,* the prefix *non-* means "not." What do you think the words *nonsense, nonbreakable,* and *nonfat* mean? What other *non-* words can you think of? Make a list of words that begin with *non-* and write down what each one means.

TECHNOLOGY LINK

Learn more about flowering plants by visiting the Smithsonian Institution Internet site.
www.si.edu/harcourt/science

How Do People Use Plants?

In this lesson, you can . . .

INVESTIGATE how heat and moisture can change popcorn.

LEARN ABOUT the many uses of plants.

LINK to math, writing, music, and technology.

How many uses of plants or plant products do you see here? ▼

INVESTIGATE

Popcorn

Activity Purpose People eat many kinds of seeds as food, but popcorn is probably the most interesting, and the most fun. Popped popcorn is the exploded seeds of a type of corn plant. Popcorn seeds contain water, although you can't see it or feel it. Heating the seeds turns the water quickly to steam. As the steam expands, the popcorn seeds pop. In this investigation you will **predict** and **measure** how popping the seeds affects their volume and mass.

Materials

- large plastic measuring cup
- unpopped popcorn
- balance

Activity Procedure

1 Cover the bottom of the measuring cup with unpopped popcorn seeds.

2 **Estimate** the volume of the unpopped seeds. Put the cup on the balance, and **measure** the mass of the unpopped seeds. (Picture A)

3 **Predict** what will happen to the mass and the volume when the seeds are popped.

Picture A

Picture B

4 Your teacher will help you pop the popcorn. Return the popped seeds to the measuring cup.

5 **Measure** the volume and mass of the cup of popped popcorn. Were your **predictions** correct? (Picture B)

Draw Conclusions

1. How did the volume of the popcorn change?

2. How did the mass change? Explain.

3. **Scientists at Work** One reason why scientists **experiment** is to test predictions. If an experiment doesn't turn out the way they predicted, it may mean that their predictions were wrong. Or it may mean that they did not consider everything that could affect the experiment. Did you predict the volume and mass of the popped popcorn correctly? Explain.

Investigate Further What other questions do you have about popcorn? **Plan and conduct a simple investigation** to answer your questions. Write instructions that others can follow in carrying out the procedure.

> **Process Skill Tip**
>
> If you aren't careful when you **experiment**, something you may not have considered may affect your results.

The Uses of Plants

Plants as Food

FIND OUT

• how people use plants as food

• how people use plants as medicine

VOCABULARY

grain
fiber

People use plants more for food than for any other purpose. For example, breakfast cereal is made of **grain**, or the seeds of certain grasses. If you have a sandwich for lunch, you are eating grain again. The bread in the sandwich was made by grinding the seeds of wheat into flour. Does your sandwich have lettuce and tomato on it? Then you're also eating a plant leaf and a fruit. And if the sandwich is seasoned with mustard, you're eating something made from seeds.

People eat many different parts of many different plants. Beans, lentils, corn, and rice, for example, are seeds. Beets, radishes, turnips, and carrots are roots. Bamboo shoots and asparagus are stems. Spinach, lettuce, kale, and cabbage are leaves. Cherries, pears, oranges, and olives are fruits. Artichokes, cauliflower, and broccoli are flowers. And if you like cinnamon in your apple pie, you are eating the bark, the outer part of the stem, of a tree.

✔ **Name the plant parts that people eat.**

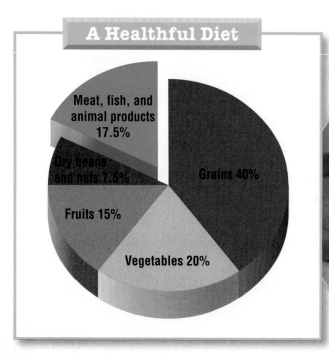

A Healthful Diet

Meat, fish, and animal products 17.5%

Dry beans and nuts 7.5%

Fruits 15%

Vegetables 20%

Grains 40%

In a healthful diet, most of the foods come from plants.

The Food Guide Pyramid

Grains form the largest part of this pyramid because they are the foundation of a healthful diet. The next level is shared by vegetables and fruits. Drinking fruit juice is more healthful than drinking soda, but you should also eat the fruits themselves.

Meats and dairy products are in a small part of the pyramid because they contain fats. Too much fat can harm your health. Fish and poultry have less fat than other meats. Milk, cheese, and yogurt are good for you, but they also are high in fat. Foods that are very high in fat, oil, or sugar are not healthful.

FATS, OILS, SWEETS
Foods in this group are generally not healthful, so don't eat a lot of them.

MILK, YOGURT, CHEESE GROUP
These foods contain fats, so limit yourself to 2–3 servings a day. A cup of milk is one serving.

MEAT, POULTRY, FISH, DRY BEANS, EGGS, NUTS GROUP
Eat 2–3 servings of foods from this group daily. A serving is one egg or about 3 oz of meat.

VEGETABLE GROUP
Eat 3–5 servings of vegetables a day. A half cup of chopped vegetables is one serving.

FRUIT GROUP
Eat 2–4 servings a day. A banana is one serving.

BREAD, CEREAL, RICE, PASTA GROUP
Eat 6–11 servings a day. A slice of bread, for example, is one serving.

◄ The leaves of the aloe plant store food. That food, a jellylike substance, is used in soaps, shampoos, makeup, skin cream, and sunscreens.

This fluffy cotton boll is made of tiny white fibers. The fibers are woven into cotton cloth, which is made into clothing. ▼

Plants as Medicines

Plants contain many substances that can be used to treat illnesses. Native Americans used the leaves and roots of hundreds of plants as medicines. They used them to reduce fevers, relieve pain, calm upset stomachs, and treat other problems.

About 40 percent of the medicines we use today are made from plants. For example, an important heart medicine called digitalis is made from the leaves of the foxglove plant. Foxglove grows in many parts of the United States. Quinine is made from the bark of a tree that grows in the Andes Mountains of South America. Quinine is used to treat malaria.

One of the best-known and most widely used pain medicines is also one of the oldest. Aspirin is a medicine invented in the 1800s. But thousands of years earlier, people took an almost identical medicine by chewing the bark of the willow tree.

✔ **What did some people do for pain before aspirin was invented?**

Other Uses for Plants

Clothing is another important product people get from plants. Blue jeans, for example, are made of fibers from the cotton plant. A **fiber** is any material that can be separated into thread. The dye that gives blue jeans their color was once made from the indigo plant.

Many kinds of trees provide wood for different purposes. Homes are often made of wood, and a lot of the furniture in most homes is wood. Musical instruments, such as guitars, violins, and pianos, are made with wood. And pulp, which is made from wood, is used to make paper.

Soaps and shampoos contain plant substances that can help make skin smooth and hair shiny. Many perfumes are made from flower petals. It takes about 100 kg (220 lb) of rose petals to make 30 mL (about 1 oz) of fragrance. This is one of the reasons why perfumes are expensive.

✔ **Name two products made from trees.**

This cancer medicine was once made from the bark of the yew. ▼

Summary

People eat the leaves, stems, roots, seeds, fruits, and flowers of various plants. When they are sick, people often use medicines made from plants. In fact, many things people use every day come from plants.

Review

1. Name three foods that are seeds or are made from seeds.

2. From which food group should you eat the most servings each day?

3. What percentage of the medicines people use comes from plants?

4. **Critical Thinking** Nutritionists say people shouldn't eat many French fries. In which food groups do French fries belong? What part of this food may not be healthful?

5. **Test Prep** Aloe is a plant that is used to make —
   A dye
   B skin cream
   C aspirin
   D fiber

LINKS

MATH LINK

How Much Fat? Most people should eat no more than 30 g of fat each day. Food labels list the fat in each serving. Add up the fat in the food you eat in one week. How close to 30 g per day is the amount of fat in your diet?

WRITING LINK

Persuasive Writing—Business Letter Some people think it's healthful to eat only plants. Others think it's important to eat both meat and plants. Write a letter to a health organization requesting information about the reasons for and against both of these diets.

MUSIC LINK

Wooden Instruments Today, some musical instruments are still made of wood. Report to the class on one of them. Explain why it is made of wood instead of some other material. Include a picture of the instrument, and play part of a recording of the instrument.

TECHNOLOGY LINK

Learn more about using plants for food by viewing *Genetic Tomatoes* on the **Harcourt Science Newsroom Video** in your classroom video library.

Potato Vaccines

Scientists are using biotechnology to turn common potatoes into vaccines against deadly diseases such as cholera.

Why Potato Vaccines?

Potatoes are an inexpensive, nutritious food that most children like to eat mashed, baked, or French fried. Biologists are using genetic engineering to insert a new gene into potatoes. This gene causes the plants to produce a chemical, called a B-protein, that is a harmless part of cholera toxin, or poison. When children eat a certain amount of these genetically altered potatoes, they become vaccinated against cholera.

What Is Cholera?

Cholera is an infectious disease that affects about 5 million people a year, particularly in poor areas of the world. It's highly contagious, so outbreaks of cholera can easily become epidemics. Cholera toxin causes pores in cells lining the intestines to remain open when they should be closed. Water diffuses from the blood into the intestines and

Potatoes are a good choice for edible vaccines because most people like them.

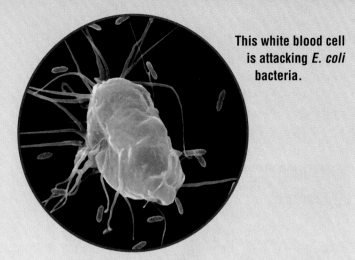

This white blood cell is attacking *E. coli* bacteria.

then out of the body as diarrhea. People with cholera can lose so much water so quickly that they become very sick and may even die.

How Does the Potato Vaccine Work?

Scientists at the Loma Linda University School of Medicine in California have added the gene that produces the cholera toxin's B-protein to the genes of potato plants. The B-protein attaches to cells in the intestines and triggers the production of antibodies against cholera.

Scientists tested the potato vaccines by feeding genetically altered potatoes to mice. Then they examined tissue from the mice's intestines to see what happened when it was exposed to cholera toxin. They found that only half as much water passed through this tissue compared with tissue from mice that had not eaten the altered potatoes.

People seldom eat potatoes raw, so scientists had to make sure that cooking wouldn't destroy the vaccine. They found that after cooking, the genetically altered potatoes had about half the vaccine they started with. But this is still enough vaccine to be effective. One cooked potato a week for one month provides enough cholera toxin B-protein to protect against the disease for years.

Other uses of the potato vaccine

Toxins produced by the cholera bacteria are nearly identical to toxins produced by another dangerous intestinal bacteria called *E. coli*. So the potato vaccine that works against cholera may also work against *E. coli* toxins. Scientists are also looking for ways to improve the potato vaccine so that it will help destroy the bacteria directly, not just the toxins the bacteria produce.

THINK ABOUT IT

1. Why do you think potato vaccines would be easier to distribute and give to people than injected vaccines?

2. What would be an advantage of inserting vaccine-producing genes into foods that are eaten raw, such as bananas?

WEB LINK:
For Science and Technology updates, visit The Learning Site.
www.harcourtschool.com/ca

Careers Geneticist

What They Do
Geneticists study the ways genes and chromosomes combine to produce variety in plants and animals.

Education and Training People wishing to become geneticists should earn an M.D. degree, specializing in genetics, or a Ph.D. degree in biology, specializing in cell biology.

Alice Eastwood

BOTANIST

"My own destroyed work I do not lament, for it was a joy to me while I did it, and I can still have the same joy in starting it again."

Alice Eastwood might never have become one of the world's greatest botanists if the great San Francisco earthquake and fire of 1906 had not taken place. One of the buildings destroyed in the disaster was the California Academy of Sciences, where Ms. Eastwood had spent more than 12 years building a huge collection of California plants. Although she managed to save nearly 1500 rare plant specimens just minutes before the academy was destroyed by fire, much of her work was lost. However, in the next six years, she produced a collection of more than 340,000 plants that was even better than the one she had lost in the fire.

Overcoming setbacks was nothing new for Ms. Eastwood. Her mother died when she was young, and because the family was poor, she couldn't finish high school with her classmates. After working for a few years, Ms. Eastwood finally graduated at the age of 20 as the top student in her class.

Although she never attended college, Ms. Eastwood continued to educate herself about plants, which had fascinated her from the time she was a young girl. She became known worldwide in the scientific community and at the age of 92 served as honorary president of the Seventh International Botanical Congress in Stockholm, Sweden. Ms. Eastwood died in 1953 at the age of 94.

THINK ABOUT IT

1. How did the San Francisco earthquake help Ms. Eastwood's career?
2. What can you infer about Ms. Eastwood's attitude toward the setbacks of life?

Ms. Eastwood working on her collection

Water in Plants

How does water move through plants?

Materials
- 5 toothpicks
- water
- dropper

Procedure

1. Break the toothpicks in half, but don't separate the parts. The two halves should remain connected.

2. Arrange the toothpicks like the spokes in a wagon wheel.

3. Put several drops of water in the center of the "wheel."

4. Observe any changes to the toothpicks.

Draw Conclusions

What happened to the water you put on the toothpicks? What happened to the toothpicks? Relate this to the way water moves through plants.

Yeast Beasts

What do simple organisms need to live?

Materials
- package of dry yeast
- 250-mL beaker
- 100 mL warm water
- sugar packet
- craft stick
- clock

Procedure

1. Empty the package of dry yeast into the beaker.

2. Add 100 mL of warm water and empty the packet of sugar into the water.

3. Stir the mixture with the craft stick for about 15 seconds. Put the beaker aside for 5 minutes.

4. After 5 minutes, measure the volume of the mixture in the beaker.

Draw Conclusions

What happened to the volume of the yeast, sugar, and warm water mixture? What do simple organisms need to live? Why is yeast used to make bread?

Chapter 3 Review and Test Preparation

Vocabulary Review

Use the terms below to complete the para-graph. The page numbers in ( ) tell you where to look in the chapter if you need help.

xylem (A67)   **spores** (A81)

phloem (A67)   **gymnosperms** (A82)

chlorophyll (A68)   **pollen** (A82)

nitrogen cycle (A73) **angiosperms** (A83)

carbon dioxide–oxygen cycle (A74)

A plant that contains tubes for the transport of water and food is called a vascular plant. The tubes that transport food are **1.** tubes; those that transport water are **2.** tubes. Plants that do not have these tubes are nonvascular plants. Whether or not they have transport tubes, all plants have a green pigment called **3.** , which enables them to make their own food. As plants make food, they use carbon dioxide and release oxygen. Plants and animals use oxygen and release carbon dioxide as they turn food into energy. These processes are part of the **4.** . Some plants fix nitrogen from the air. Most plants get nitrogen from nitrates and ammonia in the soil. These processes are part of the **5.** .

Plants have various means by which they reproduce. Plants will produce either seeds or **6.** , which will grow into a new plant when conditions are favorable. Conifers, or **7.** , produce unprotected seeds in cones. The flowers of **8.** produce protected seeds. In a flower, **9.** contains the male reproductive cells.

Connect Concepts

Write terms from the Word Bank to complete the chart.

angiosperms   **seeds**

gymnosperms   **spores**

nonvascular plants   **vascular plants**

The Two Main Groups of Plants Are
10. _____, which have no xylem or phloem.
11. _____, which have xylem and phloem tubes.

The Two Groups of Vascular Plants Are
12. plants that use _____ to reproduce.
13. plants that use _____ to reproduce.

The Two Groups of Seed-Producing Plants Are
14. _____, which include conifers, such as pines.
15. _____, which include flowering apple trees.

Check Understanding

Write the letter of the best choice.

16. Most leaves are thin and flat because —
    - **A** they look better that way
    - **B** this helps them make food
    - **C** they protect the plant from insects and birds
    - **D** they absorb water from the air

17. Nonvascular plants are limited in size because —
    - **F** they must pass water and minerals from one cell to the next
    - **G** they do not make their own food
    - **H** birds and other animals like to eat them
    - **J** they live in shady places

18. Animals get the nitrogen they need by —

A drinking liquid nitrogen

B eating nitrates

C fixing nitrogen gas

D decaying ammonia

19. Plants —

F use oxygen only and give off carbon dioxide only

G use carbon dioxide only and give off oxygen only

H use both oxygen and carbon dioxide and give off both

J use ammonia only and give off nitrates only

20. Large, colorful flowers are useful for a plant because —

A they look pretty

B they make food for plants

C they attract insects and birds that spread pollen

D they collect moisture

21. For a more healthful diet, eat more of foods that are —

F near the top of the Food Guide Pyramid

G mostly from the milk group

H high in sugar

J near the bottom of the Food Guide Pyramid

Critical Thinking

22. Could a plant live if all its leaves were cut off? Explain your answer.

23. In what way are fruits better than cones for carrying seeds?

Process Skills Review

24. What can you **observe** about a plant to help you identify the kind of plant it is?

25. **Infer** which products in your classroom are made from plants or plant parts.

26. **Predict** what would happen if trees did not have fruits or cones.

Performance Assessment

Design a Plant

Choose one condition from each set. Design a plant with roots, stems, and leaves that could live in a place with the conditions you choose.

a lot of rain
some rain
almost no rain

hot temperatures
moderate temperatures
cold temperatures

a lot of light
some light
almost no light

Chapter 4

Plant Processes

LESSON 1
How Do Plants Make Food? A100

LESSON 2
How Do Plants Respond to Light and Gravity? A108

LESSON 3
How Do Vascular Plants Reproduce Sexually? A114

LESSON 4
How Do Plants Grow? A120

SCIENCE AND TECHNOLOGY A128

PEOPLE IN SCIENCE A130

ACTIVITIES FOR HOME OR SCHOOL A131

CHAPTER REVIEW AND TEST PREPARATION A134

Plants depend on their environments. They need light, water, and carbon dioxide to make food. And they need wind or other organisms to help them flower and distribute their seeds.

Vocabulary Preview

epidermis
palisade layer
cellular
 respiration
tropism
gravitropism
fertilization
stamens
pistil
photosynthesis
phototropism
vegetative propagation

ovary
embryo
cotyledons
germinate
seedling
grafting
tissue
 culture

≡FAST FACT

There are about 248,000 different kinds of plants. About 9 out of every 10 of them are flowering plants.

Plant Species

Dicots (angiosperms)
170,000 species

Monocots (angiosperms)
50,000 species

Others
1300 species

Gymnosperms
529 species

Ferns
10,000 species

Bryophytes
16,600 species

The largest living thing in the world is not a giant sequoia tree or a whale. It is a fungus. The underground part of this fungus, growing in Washington state, covers 1500 acres.

FAST FACT

Plants have many ways of attracting animals to help with pollination. Sometimes a plant's shape and colors resemble an insect.

How Do Plants Make Food?

In this lesson, you can . . .

INVESTIGATE how plants use leaves.

LEARN ABOUT how plants make and use food.

LINK to math, writing, health, and technology.

Plants can be grown anywhere if they get what they need to survive. ▼

INVESTIGATE

How Plants Use Leaves

Activity Purpose What do leaves do for a plant? Why are they important? In this investigation you will **experiment** to determine the importance of leaves. Remember, experimenting involves carefully **controlling variables**.

Materials
- 3 potted plants
- labels
- scissors
- meterstick
- measuring cup

Activity Procedure

1. Label the plants *Normal, Half,* and *None.*

2. Using scissors, carefully cut off all the leaves of the plant labeled *None.* Cut off half the leaves of the plant labeled *Half.* The number of leaves is the variable. (Picture A)

3. Don't do anything to the plant labeled *Normal.* This plant is the control.

4. Use the meterstick to **measure** the height of each plant. **Record** the heights.

5. Put all three plants in a place where they will get plenty of sunlight. Water the plants as needed. Use the measuring cup to ensure they all get the same amount of water.
   What do you **hypothesize** about how the plants will grow?

Picture A

Picture B

6 **Measure** the heights of the plants every day, and **record** your data. Record anything else you **observe** about the plants. Cut off any new leaves that grow on the plants labeled *Half* and *None*. (Picture B)

7 At the end of two weeks, review your data.

Draw Conclusions

1. Which plant grew the most in height? Which plant grew the least? Does the data support your **hypothesis**? What can you conclude about the importance of leaves?

2. The number of leaves on each plant was the independent variable. What was the dependent variable in this investigation?

3. **Scientists at Work** Scientists always **control variables** when they **experiment**. What variables did you control in your investigation?

Investigate Further Does adding plant food really improve plant growth, as advertisements would have you believe? **Plan and conduct a simple investigation** to answer this question or another question you might have. Be sure you **control variables** in your investigation. Be sure you write instructions others can follow in carrying out the procedure.

Process Skill Tip

When you **control variables**, you are better able to draw valid conclusions about the data you collect as you **experiment**.

How Plants Make Food

Leaf Structure

You may remember that plants make their own food by using water, carbon dioxide, chlorophyll, and sunlight. The process by which plants make food is called **photosynthesis** (foh•toh•SIN•thuh•sis). You may already know the two parts of this word. *Photo* means "light" and *synthesis* means "putting together." In photosynthesis, plants put together materials to make food with the energy of sunlight.

Photosynthesis takes place mainly in a plant's leaves. Certain cells in a leaf have most of the leaf's chloroplasts. These structures contain chlorophyll, the pigment that gives plants their green color. During the day, chlorophyll takes in light energy from the sun and changes it into chemical energy needed for photosynthesis.

Most leaves also have a system of xylem and phloem tubes called veins. In addition to carrying water from the roots to the chloroplasts, veins carry food made in the chloroplasts back to the stem and roots. Veins also help keep leaves from wilting. As long as its veins are full of water and food, a leaf will keep its shape.

Photosynthesis takes place mainly near the upper surface of a leaf, where most of the sunlight is, so most leaves are thin and flat. This adaptation provides a large surface area for a leaf to get as much sunlight as possible. The leaves of most plants are not much thicker than the pages in this book.

The upper surface of a leaf has a single layer of cells that protects the inner cells in much the same way your skin protects your inner cells. This layer is called the upper **epidermis** (ep•uh•DER•mis). The epidermis is thin and flat, and sunlight easily passes through it.

FIND OUT

- about the structure of leaves
- how plants make and use food
- how energy from food supports different life forms

VOCABULARY

photosynthesis
epidermis
palisade layer
cellular respiration

A cornfield is like a factory, turning raw materials (water and carbon dioxide) into finished products (food and oxygen). ▼

Most photosynthesis takes place in the chloroplasts of the palisade cells. A single palisade cell may contain thousands of chloroplasts. Air spaces in the spongy layer connect to the stomata and allow gases to move back and forth between the outside air and the inside of the leaf. ▼

The upper epidermis helps reduce water loss from the surface of a leaf. Sometimes the epidermis has a waxy covering, called a *cuticle* (KYOO•ti•kuhl). The cuticle also protects against water loss.

Directly below the upper epidermis is the **palisade** (pal•uh•SAYD) **layer** of cells. The palisade layer is made up of long, thin, tightly packed cells. Each cell has many chloroplasts. Most photosynthesis takes place in the palisade layer.

The next layer of a leaf is made of loosely packed cells with many air spaces between them. For this reason, this layer is called the *spongy layer.* The air spaces allow carbon dioxide to pass among the cells and get to the chloroplasts. Cells in the spongy layer also have chloroplasts, but not nearly as many as the cells of the palisade layer do.

The bottom layer of a leaf is the lower epidermis. This layer protects the underside of the leaf. There are many openings, or *stomata,* in the lower epidermis. *Guard cells,* which form the edges of stomata, can change shape, depending on the amount of water in them. This causes the stomata to open and close. When the stomata are open, carbon dioxide can enter the leaf. At the same time, some of the oxygen produced during photosynthesis can leave the leaf. When the stomata are closed, at night or when there isn't much water, no photosynthesis takes place.

✔ **How do the materials needed for photosynthesis get to the chloroplasts?**

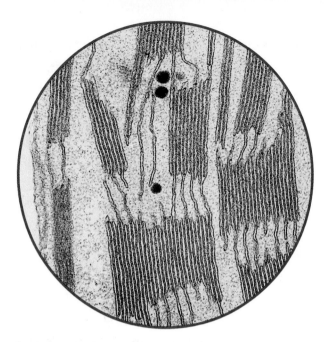

▲ This photograph of part of a chloroplast shows the layered *grana* where photosynthesis occurs.

How Photosynthesis Works

When sunlight falls on a leaf, the process of photosynthesis begins. Light energy is taken in by chlorophyll in the leaf's chloroplasts. Chlorophyll transforms, or changes, light energy into chemical energy.

This chemical energy starts a series of reactions in the chloroplast. In one reaction, water is split into the two materials that make it up—hydrogen and oxygen. Hydrogen combines with carbon dioxide to make a product called *glucose* (GLOO•kohs). Glucose is a type of sugar. Plants use some of the glucose as food. The rest is stored as starch, which is made up of many glucose particles joined together.

THE INSIDE STORY

Photosynthesis and Cellular Respiration Compared

Photosynthesis

Sunlight is taken in by chlorophyll. Light energy is turned into chemical energy, which is used to split water into hydrogen and oxygen. In a series of reactions, hydrogen combines with the carbon dioxide to form glucose and oxygen.

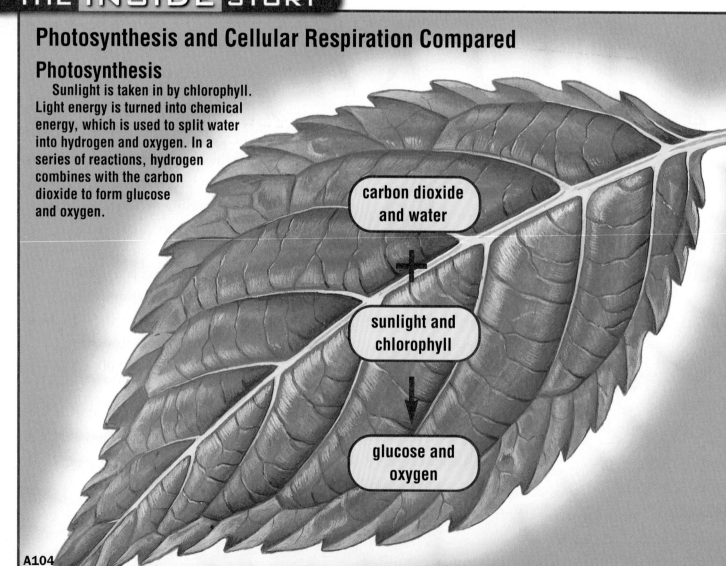

carbon dioxide and water

+

sunlight and chlorophyll

glucose and oxygen

Oxygen, which was once part of water, is another product of photosynthesis. The plant releases it into the air. Most living things could not survive without the oxygen plants produce. The following word formula summarizes photosynthesis. The formula reads: carbon dioxide and water, using sunlight and chlorophyll, make glucose and oxygen.

✔ **What are the products of photosynthesis?**

A plant that doesn't get enough light can't make food.

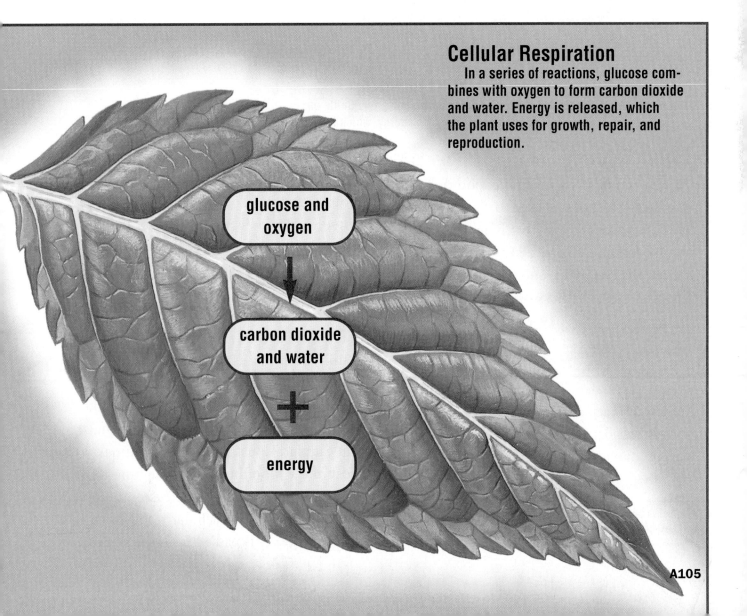

Cellular Respiration

In a series of reactions, glucose combines with oxygen to form carbon dioxide and water. Energy is released, which the plant uses for growth, repair, and reproduction.

glucose and oxygen

↓

carbon dioxide and water

+

energy

A105

The corn and hamburgers these people are eating started with energy from the sun.

▲ Grass uses the sun's energy to live and grow. Cattle eat grass to live and grow. In this way, the cattle are using the sun's energy, which is stored in the grass.

Food Energy

What do plants do with the food they produce? Most of it is used for the plant's life functions, such as growth, repair, and reproduction. The process by which plants release the energy in food to carry on these life processes is called **cellular respiration**. In the plant's cells, oxygen combines with glucose, forming carbon dioxide and water. During this process a large amount of energy is released. The following word formula summarizes cellular respiration. The formula reads: glucose and oxygen make carbon dioxide and water and energy.

Any extra food is stored in the plant. Different types of plants store food in their roots, their stems, or even their leaves. The stored food will be used whenever the plant is not able to make all the food it needs, such as on cloudy days or during dry periods.

A plant's extra food is usually stored in the form of starch. A potato, for example, is mainly stored starch. When the plant needs food, it turns the starch back into glucose.

Plants use about 90 percent of the food they make. The rest is available to animals that eat plants. Just as plants do, animals use most of the food they eat for life functions. And, as happens in plants, the energy stored in food is released by cellular respiration. In this way, energy is passed from the sun to the plant and then to the animal. Of all the food an animal eats, about 10 percent is stored in its body. An animal that eats another animal gets energy from the first animal. This energy can also be traced back to the sun.

✔ **In what form do plants store energy?**

Summary

Plants make food by a process called photosynthesis. In plant leaves, chlorophyll uses light energy to combine water and carbon dioxide, forming glucose and oxygen. Plants use most of the food they make. They store the rest. Any extra food is available to animals that eat plants. Plants and animals use food energy, which is released by cellular respiration.

Review

1. In what part of a plant do you find chlorophyll?
2. What three things do plants use to make food?
3. What gas that plants and animals use is a product of photosynthesis?
4. **Critical Thinking** Open stomata allow carbon dioxide, oxygen, and water to pass into and out of leaves. Using this information, explain why photosynthesis takes place early in the morning in many desert plants.
5. **Test Prep** Which cells would you expect to have the most chloroplasts?
   A guard cells
   B palisade cells
   C xylem cells
   D epidermis cells

LINKS

MATH LINK

Calculate If 10 percent of the food an animal eats is stored in its body, how many pounds of corn did a cow eat for every pound of hamburger made from its body?

WRITING LINK

Narrative Writing—Story What would life be like if people could make their own food, as plants do? Write a story for your class about some photosynthesizing friends who have lunch together.

HEALTH LINK

Be Prepared Plants store food for times when they cannot produce it. Humans store food in their bodies for times when they can't get it. Write a short report about how the human body stores food. As you write your report, include answers to the following questions: Why do people need the ability to store food? How can storing excess food be bad for a person's health?

TECHNOLOGY LINK

Learn more about the way plants make food by visiting the National Museum of Natural History Internet site.
www.si.edu/harcourt/science

How Do Plants Respond to Light and Gravity?

In this lesson, you can . . .

 INVESTIGATE how plants get the light they need.

 LEARN ABOUT how tropisms and other responses help plants.

LINK to math, writing, social studies, and technology.

▼ This plant is growing toward the light.

INVESTIGATE

How Plants Get the Light They Need

Activity Purpose You have learned that plants use light as energy for making their own food. You also know that plants can't move from place to place. How then do plants get the light they need for growth? In this investigation you will **compare** plants grown under different conditions to find out.

Materials

- 3 labels
- 2 potted plants
- measuring cup
- water

Activity Procedure

1 Write *Odd days* on one of the labels. Put the label on one side of a pot. Write *Even days* on a second label. Put this label on the other side of the same pot. Write *Don't move* on the third label, and put it on the other pot. (Picture A)

2 Place both potted plants in a sunny area. If you don't have a sunny area, put them under and to one side of a light source, such as a lamp. Make sure both plants are on the same side of and at the same distance from the lamp.

3 Use the measuring cup to give both plants the same amount of water at the same time each day. **Observe** the plants every day, and **record** your observations.

4 Turn the plant labeled *Odd days/Even days* one-half turn every day. If you start the **experiment** on an even-numbered day, place the pot so you

Picture A

Picture B

can see the *Even days* label. If you start on an odd-numbered day, place the pot so that you can see the *Odd days* label. Do not turn the plant labeled *Don't move*. (Picture B)

5 After ten days, write a summary of your **observations** about how the plants have grown. Draw pictures showing how the plants looked at the beginning and at the end of the **experiment**.

Draw Conclusions

1. What did you **observe** about the growth of the plants during the investigation?

2. **Compare** the two plants. What variable were the plants responding to?

3. **Scientists at Work** Scientists often **compare** organisms to help them understand how organisms respond to their environments. In this investigation, how did comparing the way the plants grew help you **draw conclusions** about the way plants respond to light? What other information is needed to support your conclusions?

Investigate Further **Hypothesize** about all plants needing the same amount of sunlight. Try putting two different plants in a very sunny window. **Observe**, and **record** your observations of the plants for two weeks.

Process Skill Tip

You can **compare** two organisms as a good way to **draw conclusions** about the results of an investigation.

A109

How Tropisms and Other Responses Help Plants

FIND OUT

- **how and why plants respond to their environments**
- **how light affects plants**
- **how gravity affects plants**

VOCABULARY

tropism
phototropism
gravitropism

Tropisms

All living things respond, or react, to their environments. For example, if the weather gets cold, you might respond by shivering. This response helps keep your body warm. No organism can survive if it can't respond to major changes in its environment.

A plant doesn't respond to everything in its environment, but many plants respond to certain stimuli (STIM•yoo•ly). A *stimulus* is anything that causes an organism to respond. A plant's response to a stimulus is called a **tropism** (TROH•piz•um).

In the investigation, you learned that plants grow toward light. This response to light is called **phototropism** (FOH•toh•troh•piz•uhm). Phototropism is caused by chemicals that direct the growth of a plant's stem. These chemicals cause cells in the stem on the side away from the light to get longer. Because the cells on the side of the plant toward the light are shorter, the plant bends toward the light.

Different amounts of light may cause different responses in some plants. In Bermuda grass, for example, the stems grow upright in shade. In full sun the stems grow along the ground.

✔ **What causes a plant to grow toward light?**

A plant's response to the stimulus of light can be easy to see. ▶

Plants also respond to the force of gravity. This tropism is known as **gravitropism** (GRAV•ih•troh•piz•uhm). Gravitropism is an adaptation that makes sure a plant's roots grow down into the soil and the stems grow up. This is important because roots must hold a plant in place and take in water and minerals from the soil. If plants did not respond to the stimulus of gravity, they would not be able to grow from seeds. Without gravitropism, if a seed landed upside down, its roots might never reach the soil or its leaves might never reach the light.

Gravitropism is caused by the pull of gravity on cells at the ends of roots. This causes growing roots to turn, if necessary, toward the center of the Earth and to grow in that direction. Scientists hypothesize that this may be caused by starch grains that move to the lower side of any root not growing down. In much the same way that cells on the shaded side of a stem are directed to grow longer, these starch grains cause cells on the lower side of a root to grow more slowly.

✔ **How does gravitropism help plants survive?**

▲ No matter which way this seedling was turned, its roots grew down into the soil and its stem grew up toward the light.

Although these trees are growing on a steep mountainside, their stems and roots are still affected by gravitropism. ▶

Other Responses

Remember the Venus' flytrap that catches insects for food? When the plant's traplike leaves snap shut on an insect that has landed on it, the plant is responding to the stimulus of touch.

The Venus' flytrap isn't the only plant that responds to touch. When an insect lands on a leaf of a sundew and touches one of its sticky hairs, other hairs bend in that direction. Soon the insect is trapped. The bending is caused by cells on one side of the hair growing very rapidly. They grow so fast that a hair pointing in one direction can bend in the opposite direction in less than a minute!

The mimosa, or "sensitive plant," also responds to touch. It has delicate, fernlike leaves. If you touch one leaf, even a little, all the leaves will curl up tightly. The touch response is an adaptation that protects the mimosa from animals that might eat its leaves.

All plants respond to light, but some respond to certain amounts of light. If they have either too much light or too little light, they won't bloom. These plants usually bloom only during the season that provides them with just the right amount of light.

For example, so-called short-day plants such as the poinsettia need only a few hours of sunlight for blooming. For this reason they bloom during the early spring or in the fall, when days are short. Long-day plants need many hours of sunlight each day to bloom. They usually bloom during the summer, when days are the longest. Plants that bloom no matter how many hours of sunlight they get are called day-neutral plants. The chart below shows how many hours of sunlight each plant needs to bloom.

Although plants need light to grow, the blooming of both long-day plants and short-day plants is actually controlled by the amount of darkness to which they are

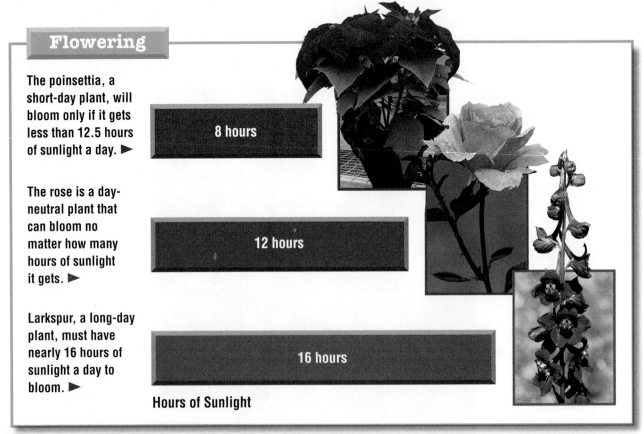

Flowering

The poinsettia, a short-day plant, will bloom only if it gets less than 12.5 hours of sunlight a day. ▶

8 hours

The rose is a day-neutral plant that can bloom no matter how many hours of sunlight it gets. ▶

12 hours

Larkspur, a long-day plant, must have nearly 16 hours of sunlight a day to bloom. ▶

16 hours

Hours of Sunlight

exposed. For example, the cocklebur, which needs short days, will not bloom if it gets as little as a minute of light during the night. The fact that plants "measure" darkness has an adaptive advantage. That way, cloudy or rainy days do not keep a plant from blooming.

✔ **What is the difference between long-day plants and short-day plants?**

Summary

Tropisms cause plants to respond to certain stimuli. Phototropism makes plants grow toward light. Gravitropism causes plant roots to grow down and stems to grow up. Some plants respond to touch. Other responses affect when plants will bloom. Responses to stimuli are adaptations that help plants survive.

Review

1. How does phototropism help plants survive?

2. What growing parts of a plant does gravitropism affect?

3. What happens if you touch a mimosa leaf? How does this help the plant?

4. **Critical Thinking** Suppose you put a poinsettia in a dark closet for 18 hours a day during the summer. How might this affect the plant's blooming?

5. **Test Prep** The parts of plants most affected by the number of hours of darkness are their —

   A leaves

   B stems

   C roots

   D flowers

LINKS

MATH LINK

Sunlight Hours The Biloxi soybean must have no more than 14 hours of sunlight each day to bloom. During the growing season, Chicago has an average of 10 percent more hours of sunlight than this, so the Biloxi soybean cannot grow there. How many hours of sunlight does Chicago average during the growing season?

WRITING LINK

Informative Writing—Report Choose a plant to research. Find out what growing conditions the plant needs, especially the number of hours of sunlight it needs to bloom. Write a report for your teacher that includes a picture of the plant and information about the environment in which it grows.

SOCIAL STUDIES LINK

Flowering Sometimes owners of plant nurseries want to make plants bloom for certain holidays, even when it is not their normal flowering season. Find out how nursery owners change conditions to make sure that certain plants bloom at the time they want.

TECHNOLOGY LINK

Learn more about plant responses by viewing *Pitcher Plants* on the **Harcourt Science Newsroom Video** in your classroom video library.

How Do Vascular Plants Reproduce Sexually?

In this lesson, you can . . .

INVESTIGATE
flower parts.

LEARN ABOUT
sexual reproduction in plants.

LINK to math, writing, literature, and technology.

INVESTIGATE

Flower Parts

Activity Purpose Have you ever looked closely at a flower's brightly colored petals? Have you ever wondered why some plants have such beautiful flowers? In this investigation you will find out more about flowers as you **observe** the structures of one.

Materials
- fresh flower
- paper towel
- hand lens
- ruler

Activity Procedure

1 Place a fresh flower on a paper towel.

2 **Observe** the outside of the flower. Notice the green, leaflike parts around the petals. These are called *sepals* (SEE•puhls). How many sepals does the flower have? What shape are the sepals? **Record** your observations. (Picture A)

3 Now **observe** the flower's petals. How many petals does the flower have? What shape are they? What color are they? Do the petals have any patterns, or are they one color? What do the petals feel like? **Record** your observations.

4 **Observe** the flower with your eyes closed. Does it have an odor? How would you describe the odor? What part of the flower do you think the odor is coming from? **Record** your observations about the flower's odor.

◀ As a butterfly drinks sweet nectar from deep inside several flowers, it spreads pollen from one flower to another.

Picture A

Picture B

5 Using the hand lens, **observe** the inside of the flower. What parts do you see? What are the shapes of these parts? **Measure** these parts. **Record** your observations about the inside of the flower. (Picture B)

6 Now make a drawing of the inside of the flower. As you draw each part, try to **infer** what it does.

Draw Conclusions

1. Colorful markings and strong odors often attract birds and insects to flowers. How might the location of the markings and odors attract birds and insects to the flower?

2. In the very center of a flower is the female reproductive part. Stalks surrounding the center contain male reproductive parts. **Infer** how it might help the plant to have the male parts around the female part.

3. **Scientists at Work** When scientists **infer** a part's function, they sometimes base their inferences on **observing** the part's location. Based on the sepals' location, what could you infer about the function of sepals?

Investigate Further **Observe** the parts of several other kinds of flowers. How do those flowers **compare** to the one you observed in this investigation? Do they have the same number of sepals? Are the petals arranged the same way? Do the flowers' inner parts look the same? **Classify** the flowers based on your observations.

> **Process Skill Tip**
>
> To **infer** the functions of all the parts of a flower, you might need to cut open some of the smaller parts and use a microscope to **observe** them.

Sexual Reproduction in Plants

FIND OUT

- how plants reproduce sexually
- about flower parts and their functions
- about pollination
- about the life cycle of a seed plant

VOCABULARY

fertilization
stamens
pistil
ovary

Fertilization and Pollination

Most plants reproduce sexually. In angiosperms and gymnosperms, **fertilization** (fuhr•tul•luh•ZAY•shuhn), the joining of a male reproductive cell with a female reproductive cell, produces seeds. Because of fertilization, a seed has characteristics of both the male parent and the female parent.

Gymnosperms have male and female parts in separate cones. Grains of pollen fall or are carried by the wind from a male cone to a female cone. After fertilization, seeds develop in the female cone.

In angiosperms, both male and female reproductive parts are usually in the same flower. The male parts, called **stamens** (STAY•muhnz), produce pollen. In the pollen grains are the male reproductive cells, or sperm. The female part, called a **pistil** (PIS•tuhl), contains the female reproductive cells, or eggs. Pollen is usually carried by the wind or by insects from the stamens of one flower to the pistil of another flower. Since some flowers can

▼ Male cones are small.

This spruce tree has male and female cones near the ends of its branches. ▼

The red maple tree is a flowering plant. ▼

The stamens of a maple's flower are longer than the petals. The pistil is in the center. ▼

Female cones are usually larger than male cones. ▼

pollinate themselves, fertilization can occur between reproductive cells of the same plant. However, most fertilizations occur between reproductive cells of different plants. After fertilization, seeds and their protective fruit develop in the pistil.

Before a flower blooms, or opens, it is called a *bud*. At that time the petals and reproductive parts are covered by the sepals. Petals can have thousands of shapes and colors, and they are usually pretty and easy to see.

Inside the petals are the reproductive parts. The stamens are long, thin stalks. A flower usually has several stamens. Anthers, small organs at the tops of the stamens, actually produce the pollen.

At the center of the flower is one pistil. Most of the pistil is a long, narrow tube called the *style*. The top of the pistil, the *stigma* (STIG•muh), is a little wider than the style. The stigma is often sticky, which helps it hold pollen grains tightly.

The transfer of pollen from an anther to the stigma is called *pollination*. After a pollen grain lands on the stigma, a tube begins to grow from a cell in the pollen. This pollen tube grows down through the style to an opening in the ovary (OH•vuh•ree), which is at the bottom of the pistil. The **ovary** has the eggs in one or more sections called *ovules* (AHV•yoolz).

Sperm cells move down the pollen tube and into the ovule. Fertilization occurs when a sperm cell joins with an egg to form a zygote.

✔ **What is the difference between pollination and fertilization?**

THE INSIDE STORY

Flower Details

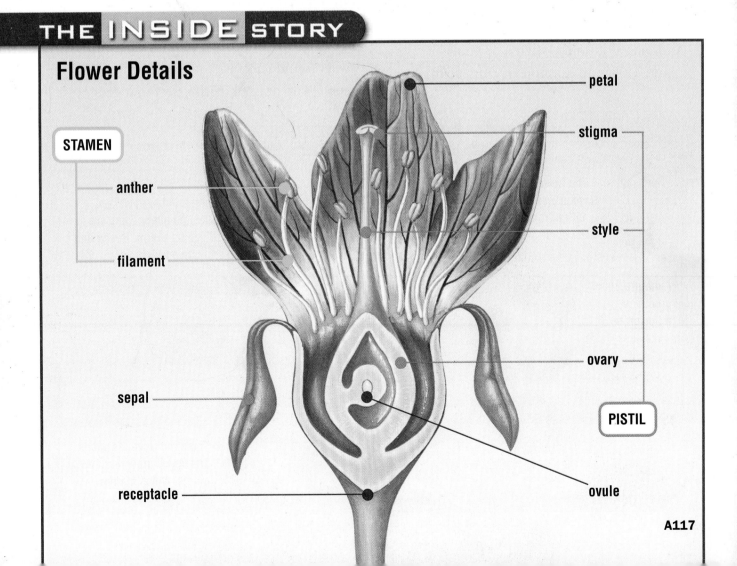

petal

STAMEN
— anther
— filament

stigma

style

ovary

PISTIL

sepal

ovule

receptacle

◀ Grasses have very small flowers. They depend on the wind for pollination.

◀ The color and the odor of some flowers attract insects. The insects carry pollen from flower to flower.

Methods of Pollination

Plants use many methods to ensure that pollen reaches the stigma. Pollination sometimes takes place inside a single flower. A pollen grain falls or is blown by a gentle breeze from an anther to the stigma. This type of pollination is called *self-pollination*.

Most pollination, however, takes place between different flowers. When Gregor Mendel experimented with pea plants, he took pollen from the anther of one plant and placed it on the stigma of another plant. This is an example of *cross-pollination*.

As the photographs above show, cross-pollination can occur in many ways.

Cross-pollination has adaptive benefits. It allows genetic traits to spread through a population of plants over time. Traits that help the plants survive will be passed to future generations.

Pollination itself is an example of a survival adaptation. Brightly colored petals or sweet odors attract insects and other animals to flowers. Many flowers have nectaries (NEK•ter•eez), which produce a sweet liquid (nectar) that some animals seek. As an animal drinks nectar, it gets

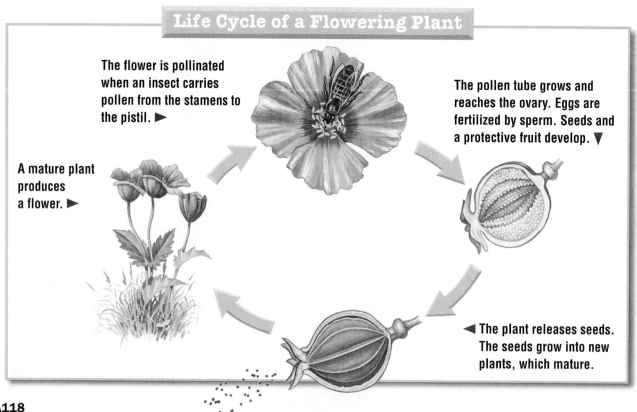

Life Cycle of a Flowering Plant

The flower is pollinated when an insect carries pollen from the stamens to the pistil. ▶

The pollen tube grows and reaches the ovary. Eggs are fertilized by sperm. Seeds and a protective fruit develop. ▼

A mature plant produces a flower. ▶

◀ The plant releases seeds. The seeds grow into new plants, which mature.

◀ Birds and other small animals seek the sweet nectar in some flowers. As this bat drinks, it gets pollen on its face.

pollen on its body. That pollen may be left on the next flower the animal visits.

✔ **Name two ways in which plants may be cross-pollinated.**

Summary

Most flowers have both male and female reproductive parts. Pollen, which has sperm cells, is produced by stamens. The pistil has the eggs. Pollen is transferred from the stamens to the pistil. After fertilization, eggs develop into seeds. Many flowers attract animals that carry pollen to the pistil. In some plants, pollination depends on the wind.

Review

1. What are the male and female reproductive cells of plants called?
2. Where is pollen produced?
3. What is cross-pollination?
4. **Critical Thinking** Why is wind pollination more useful for grasses than insect pollination?
5. **Test Prep** On what flower part must pollen land for fertilization to occur?
   A stigma
   B ovule
   C style
   D anther

LINKS

MATH LINK

Oldest Trees Some trees live a long time. This table shows the ages of some of the oldest trees in the United States.

Type of Tree	Age in Years
Bristlecone pine	4200
Redwood	3500
Giant sequoia	2500
Douglas fir	750
Bald cypress	500

How old was each of these trees the year the Declaration of Independence was signed?

WRITING LINK

Expressive Writing—Poem Write a poem for a friend about your favorite flower. Describe the way the flower looks or how it smells, and tell how you feel when you see it or smell it.

LITERATURE LINK

Fields of Daffodils Read William Wordsworth's poem "I Wandered Lonely as a Cloud." Make a list of the words and phrases the poet used to describe these flowers.

TECHNOLOGY LINK

Learn more about pollination by visiting the Smithsonian Institution Internet site. **www.si.edu/harcourt/science**

How Do Plants Grow?

In this lesson, you can . . .

INVESTIGATE the parts of a seed.

LEARN ABOUT how plants grow.

LINK to math, writing, health, and technology.

A coconut contains the seed of the coconut tree. This coconut floated onto the beach and began to grow into a new tree. ▼

INVESTIGATE

The Parts of a Seed

Activity Purpose The life cycle of a flowering plant begins with a seed. The seed sprouts and grows into a new plant. How does this happen? What parts do seeds have that allow them to grow? In this investigation you will find out by **observing** the parts of a bean seed.

Materials

- soaked lima beans
- paper towels
- hand lens
- dropper
- iodine solution

CAUTION

Activity Procedure

1. Put a soaked lima bean on a paper towel. **Observe** the seed with the hand lens. **Record** your observations by drawing a picture of what you see.

2. Carefully peel away the outer covering of the bean. This covering is called the *seed coat*. (Picture A)

3. Gently open the bean by splitting it in half. Use the hand lens to **observe** the parts inside the bean. **Record** your observations by drawing a picture of what you see.

4. Using the point of a pencil, carefully remove the part of the bean that looks like a tiny plant. This is called the *embryo*. Look through the hand lens to identify the parts of the embryo that look like leaves, a stem, and a root. (Picture B)

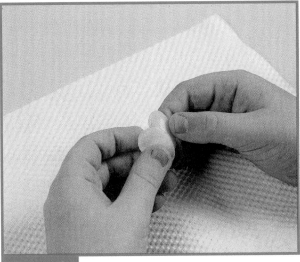

Picture A

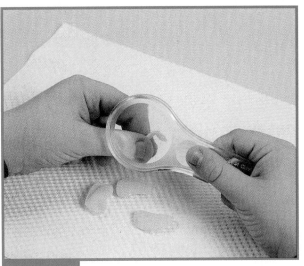

Picture B

5 **CAUTION** **Iodine can stain your hands and clothes.** Carefully put a drop or two of the iodine solution on the other parts of the bean. These parts are called the *cotyledons.* **Observe** what happens. **Record** your observations.

6 Label the seed coat, embryo, and cotyledons on your drawing from Step 3. On the embryo, label the parts that look like leaves, a stem, and a root.

Draw Conclusions

1. What words would you use to describe the seed coat of the bean? What do you **infer** is its function?

2. Iodine turns black in the presence of starch, a kind of food that plants store. Because of this, what do you **infer** is the function of the cotyledons?

3. **Scientists at Work** Scientists **observe** many plant parts. They often **communicate** to other scientists inferences they have made about the functions of certain parts. They use descriptions, data tables, graphs, and drawings. Write a report to communicate to a classmate your inferences and conclusions about the function of cotyledons. Be sure to include the results of the iodine test.

Investigate Further **Observe** other seeds that can be easily opened, such as green peas, squash seeds, or watermelon seeds. **Compare** them to the bean seed in this investigation.

Process Skill Tip

To help people understand what you **observe**, you need to **communicate** your ideas clearly. Choose the right words, make a graph, or draw a picture to help others learn what you know.

How Plants Grow

FIND OUT

- **about the parts of seeds**
- **how seeds germinate**
- **how some plants reproduce without seeds**

VOCABULARY

embryo
cotyledons
germinate
seedling
vegetative
    propagation
grafting
tissue culture

Seeds

A seed is like a package that has nearly everything a new plant needs in order to grow. The seed coat is a kind of "skin" that protects the seed. Inside the seed is an **embryo** (EM•bree•oh), a tiny plant that can grow into a mature plant. The seed also has stored food and some water that will keep the embryo alive until it can sprout and produce its own food.

A seed's food is stored in structures called **cotyledons** (kah•tuh•LEE•duhnz). The seeds of some angiosperms, such as corn, have one cotyledon. These plants are called *monocots*. Other angiosperms, such as beans, roses, and oak trees, have seeds with two cotyledons. They are called *dicots*.

✔ **What is the purpose of the cotyledons?**

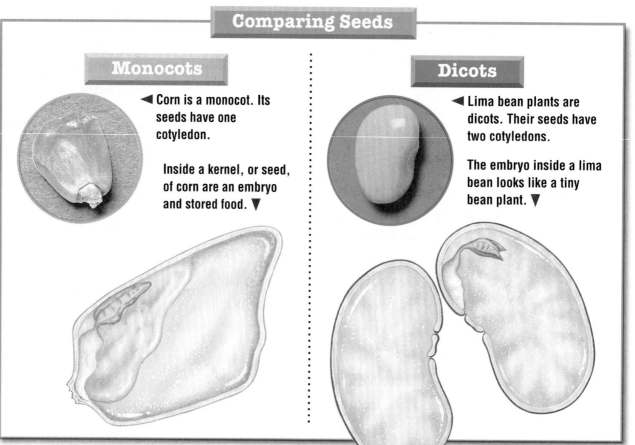

Comparing Seeds

Monocots

◄ Corn is a monocot. Its seeds have one cotyledon.

Inside a kernel, or seed, of corn are an embryo and stored food. ▼

Dicots

◄ Lima bean plants are dicots. Their seeds have two cotyledons.

The embryo inside a lima bean looks like a tiny bean plant. ▼

Seed Dispersal

Once the eggs of a plant have been fertilized and fruits have formed, the plant is ready to release the seeds. If the fruits fall next to the parent plant, the seeds do not have a good chance of growing. But plants are adapted in many ways to disperse, or scatter, fruits and seeds to places far away from the parent plant.

Maple trees, for example, produce wing-shaped fruits that spin as they fall. Spinning slows down their fall and makes it possible for wind to carry the fruit and its attached seed away from the parent tree.

In the Amazon rain forest, the fruits of some trees are dispersed by dropping into the Amazon River. The fruits are carried down the river, where they may wash up on a distant shore. There the seeds may sprout.

Many plants depend on animals to scatter their seeds. Oak trees, for example, produce fruits called acorns. Squirrels eat some acorns when they fall, and bury others to eat during the winter. The seeds inside buried acorns may sprout and grow into new oak trees.

Some seeds are covered by a fruit called a bur. The outside of a bur is usually rough, and it sticks to the fur of any passing animal. When it finally falls off, it may land on the ground and the seed inside may sprout.

✔ **Name two ways in which plants disperse seeds.**

The rough outside of a bur sticks to the fur of a passing animal or to a human's clothes.

Each dandelion seed is attached to a bit of fluff that can be blown by a light wind.

The seeds of this berry will be left in some other place with the bird's droppings.

When an animal eats a fruit, the seed may fall to the ground and sprout.

Seed Germination

A seed survives inside its protective seed coat until conditions are right for it to grow. These conditions usually include fertile soil, warm temperatures, and enough rainfall or moisture. Most seeds can survive for several years, and some seeds have survived for hundreds of years. When conditions are right, a seed will sprout, or **germinate** (JER•mih•nate).

First, the seed takes in water. This makes the seed larger. As the seed swells, the seed coat splits. The embryo then begins to grow and develop the parts it needs to live on its own. The first part to develop is the root, which begins to grow down, toward the center of the Earth.

Next, the stem emerges from the seed and begins to grow up, toward the light. The cotyledons are attached to the stem. At this stage, the growing plant, now called a **seedling**, uses food stored in the cotyledons to grow. Later the first leaves, which have also emerged from the seed, will begin to make food.

As it grows, the seedling produces longer and thicker roots. The stem gets taller and stronger. When the seedling is growing well and its leaves are making all the food the plant needs, the cotyledons drop off. The young, rapidly growing plant can now live on its own.

✔ **What is the first part to emerge from a germinating seed?**

▲ This seed has landed on rain-soaked, fertile soil. It will take in moisture, swell, and germinate.

▲ The first part to emerge from the seed is the root.

▲ As the root gets longer and thicker, a stem begins to emerge.

▲ The seedling now has a well-developed root system, and its first leaves are producing food.

▲ A strawberry plant's runners grow along the ground, putting out roots wherever they touch the soil.

▲ These offspring of the kalanchoe (kal•an•KOH•ee) plant develop on a leaf of the parent plant.

▲ Potato "eyes" are stem buds that can grow into a new potato plant.

◄ Irises grow from large underground buds, or *bulbs*. Several plants and many flowers may grow from a single bulb.

Vegetative Propagation

Some plants grow in places where there are few animals and little wind to help with pollination. Many of these plants are adapted to reproduce with or without seeds. This asexual reproduction—without seeds—is called **vegetative propagation** (VEJ•uh•tay•tiv prah•puh•GAY•shun).

Spider plants, for example, reproduce asexually by growing "babies" at the ends of long stalks. All these young plants are the same as the parent plant. Each develops roots while it is still joined to the stalk, and each will grow into a mature spider plant if it touches the soil.

Strawberry plants have flowers and seeds, but they also reproduce by sending out horizontal stems called *runners*. Like spider plant "babies," strawberry runners grow roots and become exact copies of the parent plant. Some types of grasses can completely take over lawns because new grass plants grow from a network of runners.

Potato plants have flowers and produce seeds. However, farmers rarely plant potato seeds because the seeds produce plants that have small *tubers*—the part we eat. Instead, farmers grow new plants from pieces of tubers that include a bud, or "eye." The buds are stem buds, not flower buds, that can grow into new plants.

The one disadvantage of vegetative propagation is that asexually produced plants have the same genes as the parent plants. As a result, there are fewer variations within a population of a particular plant. The population has fewer traits that may have adaptive benefits.

✔ **What is vegetative propagation?**

Artificial Reproduction

In the last lesson, you learned that cross-pollination leads to adaptive benefits for plants. It makes it possible for different characteristics to combine in the offspring. By controlling cross-pollination, scientists can artificially produce plants that have the characteristics people find useful. For example, one type of apple might be sweet but small, while another might be sour but large. Through cross-pollination, it's possible to produce a new kind of apple that is both sweet and large.

Grafting is a form of artificial reproduction that can produce desirable characteristics in woody plants. A stem or branch is slit open, and a stem or branch from a different plant is joined to it. When the "wound" heals, the two plants grow together. Grafting is often used to improve fruit trees. For example, black walnut trees have strong roots, but their nuts are not often eaten. English walnut trees have weak roots, but their nuts are prized as food. The branches of English walnut trees are often grafted onto the roots of black walnut trees.

It is also possible to grow a new plant from a piece of a plant. If the top of a pineapple is cut from the fruit and placed in

water or soil, the cutting will grow into a new pineapple plant. Some other plants can be grown from root cuttings or leaf cuttings.

Another method uses plant chemicals that speed up growth. If these chemicals are put on plant tissues, the cells may divide and become new plants. This process is known as **tissue culture**.

✔ **Why do scientists use artificial reproduction with plants?**

◄ The plants in this flask were grown from tissue cultures. Growth chemicals caused the cells to divide and specialize.

The small cactus was grafted onto the larger one. The plants grew together, and the two plants have become one plant. ►

◄ This "multi-fruit" tree is the result of grafting branches from several kinds of fruit trees. The close-up shows how the stems are grafted together.

Summary

Seeds contain embryo plants and stored food. Under the right conditions, seeds germinate. Seedlings are young plants that grow from the embryos. Some plants may reproduce asexually through vegetative propagation. Scientists and farmers use grafting and other types of artificial reproduction to grow useful plants.

Review

1. What does the seed coat do?
2. What is a seedling?
3. What are two characteristics of seeds dispersed by the wind?
4. **Critical Thinking** Some seeds have large cotyledons. Others have small ones. What does the size of cotyledons tell you about the time it takes for a seedling to begin making food?
5. **Test Prep** Which of these is **NOT** a type of vegetative propagation?

   A producing runners

   B growth from cuttings

   C grafting

   D cross-pollination

LINKS

MATH LINK

Counting Seeds Cut an apple into quarters, remove all the seeds, and count them. Your teacher will ask each student how many seeds he or she counted. Then use a calculator to find the average number of seeds in an apple.

WRITING LINK

Expressive Writing—Friendly Letter You have learned several ways in which plants and animals disperse seeds. Write a letter to a friend. Describe how and where some seeds are dispersed by plants and how animals help with seed dispersal.

HEALTH LINK

Seeds as Food The food that seeds store for growing embryos is good for people too. In fact, health experts say people should eat more seeds—especially grains—than any other kind of food. List all the seeds people eat. Find out what vitamins and other healthful things are in these seeds.

TECHNOLOGY LINK

Learn more about artificial reproduction in plants by visiting this Internet site. **www.scilinks.org/harcourt**

Corn Cards and Super Slurpers

Chemists and agricultural scientists are working together to find new ways to use plants. Their goal is to make useful products that won't cause pollution.

Why Use Plants to Make Plastic?

Products made from plastics make life simpler, but plastics can cause problems, too. Most plastics are made from petroleum, and when you throw them away, they aren't really gone. Petroleum-based plastics don't decompose (break down) in the environment. Each year people throw away almost 20 million tons of plastics. That's a lot of trash. Now scientists who work with plants have discovered how to use corn to produce plastics that do decompose. In a landfill or a backyard compost pile, these plastics break down into hydrogen, oxygen, and small bits of organic matter called humus. Humus helps enrich the soil.

Corn is one of America's most commonly grown crops.

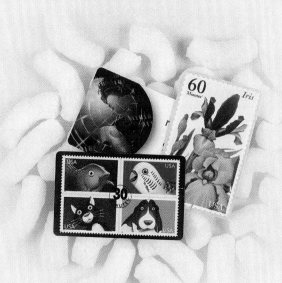

Packaging "peanuts" and phone cards can be made from corn.

Diapers? Not As Corny As It Sounds

What are corn-based plastics good for? Plenty! Companies use these environmentally friendly materials to make products ranging from disposable diapers to prepaid telephone calling cards.

Packaging "peanuts" made from cornstarch protect fragile products. After the peanuts have been exposed to moisture and sunlight for a few months, they fall apart.

Chemists at a U.S. Department of Agriculture laboratory discovered a way to use cornstarch to make a material they called hydrosorb. Its nickname is "Super Slurper." Why? Because it can soak up more than 300 times its own weight in water. Diapers containing hydrosorb help keep babies dry. Super Slurper filters remove water from fuels such as gasoline and heating oil. When mixed with soil, hydrosorb holds moisture near the roots of plants, helping them grow with less irrigation.

PLA Plastics

Other scientists have found ways to recombine the hydrogen, oxygen, and carbon in corn to make a material called polylactic acid resin, or PLA. Plastics made from PLA can be used just like petroleum-based plastics to make toys, TV sets, and other products.

Nebraska farmers grow nearly 30 million tons of corn each year. Scientists at the University of Nebraska say that they haven't found anything made with petroleum-based plastic that can't also be made from the PLA plastic that comes from corn.

THINK ABOUT IT

1. What other products could Super Slurpers be used for?
2. What are some advantages and disadvantages of corn-based plastics?

WEB LINK:
For science and technology updates, visit The Learning Site.
www.harcourtschool.com/ca

Careers Agronomist

What They Do
Agronomists study soils and plants to develop better ways to grow crops and to keep agricultural land productive.

Education and Training People wishing to become agronomists study plant biology and soil chemistry in college and graduate school.

Shirley Mah Kooyman

BOTANIST

"Our food, many of the things we wear, and even some parts of our homes come from plants. People also get enjoyment from looking at plants."

Because we depend on plants for so many things, the health of plants is important to our survival. Shirley Mah Kooyman feels that plants are sometimes taken for granted—that people forget they are living things. Ms. Kooyman is a botanist, or plant scientist, in Chanhassen, Minnesota. An important part of her work is discovering what makes plants grow. The knowledge that she gains is used by other scientists, who work to find ways to grow healthier plants that produce larger crops.

In her work, Ms. Kooyman seeks to better understand some of the growth processes of plants. She knows that in addition to light energy, water, proper temperature, and rich soil, plants need certain hormones. Hormones are chemical "messengers" that "tell" plants to grow. Plant hormones are produced in stems and roots. From there they travel to other parts of the plant.

Today scientists are able to make artificial plant hormones. Artificial hormones placed on a root tip make the root grow, just as natural hormones do. The advantage of artificial hormones is that they can be produced in greater amounts than natural hormones. Farmers can use artificial hormones to speed up plant growth and produce larger crops. This will make plant products more affordable. In addition to working with plant hormones in a laboratory and in the field, Ms. Kooyman teaches people about plants and the joys of gardening.

THINK ABOUT IT

1. Why is it important to understand what makes plants grow?
2. How might artificial hormones be used to produce a large crop of tomatoes?

Ms. Kooyman teaching a young gardener

Leaf Casts

How can you observe stomata?

Materials
- potted plant
- clear fingernail polish
- microscope slide
- microscope

Procedure

1 Paint a 2-cm square of fingernail polish on the underside of one leaf. Let the polish dry.

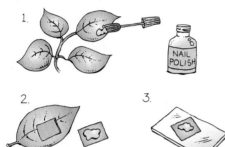

2 Add another layer of polish and let it dry. Repeat until you have 6 layers of polish.

3 Once the last layer of polish is dry, peel it off the leaf.

4 Put the polish, which contains a cast of the leaf epidermis, on a microscope slide.

5 Observe the slide by using the microscope.

Draw Conclusions

You should observe two types of cells. Compare the cells. Explain any differences between them. How do the guard cells form the stomata?

Seed Gravitropism

How do seeds respond to gravity?

Materials
- paper towel
- plastic sandwich bag
- water
- 4 lima beans

Procedure

1 Fold the paper towel to fit inside the plastic sandwich bag.

2 Add water to the bag until the paper towel is completely wet.

3 Put the lima beans facing in very different directions on the paper towel. Then lean the bag against something, as shown.

4 Observe the seeds as they germinate.

Draw Conclusions

What happens to the new roots as the seeds germinate? What force affects the growth of plant roots?

Making Food

Can a leaf make food without sunlight?

Materials

- geranium or other leafy plant
- ruler
- aluminum foil
- paper clip
- rubbing alcohol or fingernail-polish remover
- glass
- iodine
- shallow bowl
- tweezers
- paper towel
- dropper

Procedure

1. Use a paper clip to attach a 2-inch square of aluminum foil to one side of a geranium leaf. The aluminum foil should cover half of the front of the leaf and half of the back of the leaf.

2. Place the plant in direct sunlight for 4–6 days. Water the plant when the soil feels dry.

3. You will now test the leaf for the presence of starch. Much of the sugar a plant makes during photosynthesis is stored in the leaves and other parts of the plant as starch. Before testing for starch, however, you must remove most of the chlorophyll from the leaf. Remove the leaf from the plant and place it in the glass. To remove the chlorophyll from the leaf, pour enough alcohol or fingernail-polish remover into the glass to just cover the leaf. After 30 minutes, remove the leaf with the tweezers and let it dry on a paper towel.

4. Place the leaf in a shallow bowl and add several drops of iodine to it. The parts that turn black contain starch. The parts that do not turn black do not contain starch.

Draw Conclusions

What part of the leaf contained starch? How could you tell? Explain how the results show that plants need light to make food.

Growing Plants from Seeds

Which parts of seeds are essential for growth?

Materials

- 6 lima bean seeds, soaked overnight
- 6 corn seeds, soaked overnight
- knife and cutting board
- 6 plastic pots filled with potting soil
- saucers for the pots
- labels
- marker
- water

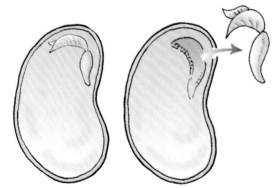

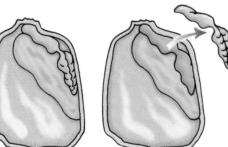

Procedure

1. Have an adult help you split all but two of the bean seeds in half. Keep the two best cotyledons with embryos.

2. Use your fingernail to remove the embryos from two cotyledons.

3. Label the pots *Complete seeds, No embryos,* and *No cotyledons.*

4. Plant the two complete seeds in one pot, the two cotyledons with no embryos in another pot, and the two embryos in a third pot. Water the pots and place them in a warm, sunny spot. Observe their growth for two weeks.

5. Since the corn seeds are monocots, you will not be able to split them. Have an adult remove the embryos from four of the corn seeds.

6. Plant two complete seeds in one pot, two cotyledons without embryos in another pot, and the two embryos in the last pot.

7. Label the pots as before, water the pots, and place them in a warm, sunny spot. Observe their growth for two weeks.

Draw Conclusions

Which pots of seeds grew best? Why did the cotyledons without embryos fail to grow? How did the embryos without cotyledons grow? Explain your results.

Vocabulary Review

Use the terms below to complete the sentences. The page numbers in ( ) tell you where to look in the chapter if you need help.

photosynthesis (A102)
epidermis (A102)
palisade layer (A103)
cellular respiration (A106)
tropism (A110)
phototropism (A110)
gravitropism (A111)
fertilization (A116)
stamens (A116)

pistil (A116)
ovary (A117)
embryo (A122)
cotyledons (A122)
germinate (A124)
seedling (A124)
vegetative propagation (A125)
grafting (A126)
tissue culture (A126)

1. ____ is the process plants use to make their own food.

2. Growing toward the light is an example of ____.

3. There may be many ovules in a flower's ____.

4. Planting a potato tuber with an "eye" is a form of ____.

5. The male reproductive parts of a flower are the ____.

6. A seed will not ____ unless it has enough water.

7. An embryo plant whose root and stem have started growing is called a ____.

8. A plant's response to a stimulus is called a ____.

9. The joining of an egg and a sperm cell is called ____.

10. The ____ is the part of the seed that will become the plant.

11. Most photosynthesis takes place in the ____ of cells.

12. Making stems from two different plants grow together is called ____.

13. The ____ is the female reproductive part of a flower.

14. ____ contain stored food that helps an embryo plant grow.

15. ____ causes roots to grow down.

16. The process by which organisms release energy stored in food is ____.

17. Growing new plants from plant tissues is called ____.

18. The upper layer of cells in a leaf is the ____.

Connect Concepts

Write the letter of the plant part that best fits each description.

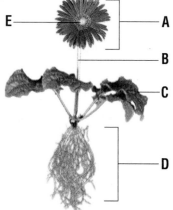

____ 19. Produce pollen

____ 20. Bends toward light

____ 21. Exchange of gases

____ 22. Usually brightly colored

____ 23. Most photosynthesis occurs here

____ 24. Grows toward center of Earth

____ 25. Produces nectar

Check Understanding

Write the letter of the best choice.

26. Phototropism changes the growth of cells in the plant's —

A roots

B leaves

C stem

D flowers

27. The ovary is part of a flower's —

F stamens

G pistil

H style

J sepals

28. Nectaries and colorful petals attract insects and other animals that help in —

A pollination

B germination

C grafting

D dispersal

29. Embryo plants grow by using the food stored in —

F tubers

G stems

H cotyledons

J seed coats

30. In order to germinate, seeds have to absorb —

A carbon dioxide

B water

C nectar

D starch

Critical Thinking

31. The leaves of some plants have edges that are sharp enough to cut your finger. How would this be an adaptive benefit to the plant?

32. A weed is sometimes defined as "any plant growing where it is not wanted." Why do farmers and gardeners try to get rid of weeds?

Process Skills Review

33. Do bean seeds need warm temperatures to germinate? **Plan and carry out an experiment** to find out.

34. **Compare** cross-pollination and self-pollination. Which do you think has more adaptive benefits?

Performance Assessment

Design a Flower

Work with a partner to design a flower. Your flower may be as unusual as you wish, but it must contain all the flower parts you learned about in this chapter. Draw a picture or make a model of your flower. Label its parts. Describe how the flower is pollinated.

Unit Project Wrap Up

Here are some ideas for ways to wrap up your unit project.

Display at a Science Fair

Display the fold-outs in a school science fair. You may want to include photographs of the living things you showed in your project.

Write a Disclaimer

Think of an ad for a service that claims to improve your health, such as for a fitness center. Write a paragraph, called a disclaimer, that explains why some people might not get the results described in the ad.

Draw a Cartoon

Use a computer and drawing software to make a cartoon showing a person moving in some way. Explain how the bones, muscles, and nerves work together to enable him or her to move.

Investigate Further

How could you make your project better? What other questions do you have about animals and plants? Plan ways to find answers to your questions. Use the Science Handbook on pages R2-R9 for help.

Weather and Space

UNIT B

EARTH SCIENCE

Weather and Space

Chapter 1   Earth's Air and Water   **B2**

Chapter 2   Earth's Weather   **B36**

Chapter 3   Weather Prediction and Climate   **B64**

Chapter 4   Earth and the Moon   **B88**

Chapter 5   The Solar System   **B112**

Unit Project

Weather Station

Make a weather station for your classroom. Make instruments to help you measure the weather. Use charts and tables to record changes in the weather. Prepare a weather report each day, and predict the weather for the following day. Be sure to support your prediction with data you've collected. Then compare your prediction with the actual weather.

Chapter 1

LESSON **1**
What Makes Up Earth's Atmosphere? B4

LESSON **2**
How Are Atmospheric Conditions Measured? B10

LESSON **3**
What Role Do Oceans Play in the Water Cycle? B18

LESSON **4**
Why Is the Water Cycle Important? B24

SCIENCE AND TECHNOLOGY B30

PEOPLE IN SCIENCE B32

ACTIVITIES FOR HOME OR SCHOOL B33

CHAPTER REVIEW AND TEST PREPARATION B34

Earth's Air and Water

The water you washed with this morning has been around for millions of years. It has been rain, snow, sleet, and hail. It has flowed over thousands of waterfalls and been frozen in hundreds of glaciers. Dinosaurs might have drunk it. But it has always returned to the ground, the ocean, or the air again and again.

Vocabulary Preview

atmosphere
air pressure
troposphere
stratosphere
weather
humidity
precipitation
evaporation
condensation
water cycle
transpiration

≡FAST FACT

Waterfalls move. Niagara Falls is moving toward Lake Erie as it slowly wears away the rock at its top. It will reach the lake in about 23,000 years.

About 75 percent of Earth's surface is covered by salt water. Most of it is in Earth's four oceans.

Earth's Oceans

Ocean	Surface Area (millions of km²)	Volume (millions of km³)
Pacific	166.0	723.7
Atlantic	82.0	321.9
Indian	73.6	292.1
Arctic	12.2	13.5

FAST FACT

If all of Earth's glaciers and ice caps were to melt, the oceans would rise about 60 meters (200 feet), covering thousands of large coastal cities, such as Venice, Italy.

LESSON 1

What Makes Up Earth's Atmosphere?

In this lesson, you can . . .

INVESTIGATE a property of air.

LEARN ABOUT Earth's atmosphere.

LINK to math, writing, art, and technology.

A Property of Air

Activity Purpose Everything around you is matter. Matter is anything that takes up space and has weight. In this investigation you will **observe** a property of air. Then you will **infer** whether air is matter.

Materials

- metric ruler
- piece of string about 80 cm long
- scissors
- 2 round balloons (same size)
- safety goggles
- straight pin

◆ CAUTION

Activity Procedure

1 Work with a partner. Use the scissors to carefully cut the string into three equal pieces. **CAUTION** Be careful when using scissors.

2 Tie one piece of the string to the middle of the ruler.

◄ Oxygen is part of the air you breathe. High on a mountain the particles of air are far apart. The climber can't get enough oxygen from the air. He needs extra oxygen from a tank to keep his body working properly.

B4

3 Blow up the balloons so they are about the same size. Seal the balloons. Then tie a piece of string around the neck of each balloon.

4 Tie a balloon to each end of the ruler. Hold the middle string up so that the ruler hangs from it. Move the strings so that the ruler is balanced. (Picture A)

5 **CAUTION** **Put on your safety goggles.** Use the straight pin to pop one of the balloons. **Observe** what happens to the ruler.

Picture A

Draw Conclusions

1. Explain how this investigation shows that air takes up space.

2. Describe what happened when one balloon was popped. What property of air caused what you **observed?**

3. **Scientists at Work** Scientists often **infer** conclusions when the answer to a question is not clear or can't be **observed** directly. Your breath is invisible, but you observed how it made the balloons and the ruler behave. Even though you can't see air, what can you infer about whether or not air is matter? Explain.

Investigate Further What other questions do you have about air? **Plan and conduct a simple investigation** to answer one of your questions. Write instructions that others can follow to carry out the procedure.

Earth's Atmosphere

The Air You Breathe

FIND OUT

- **some properties of air**

- **the layers of the atmosphere**

VOCABULARY

atmosphere
air pressure
troposphere
stratosphere

You can live for a few days without water and for many days without food. But you can live only a few minutes without air. Nearly all living things need air to carry out their life processes. The layer of air that surrounds our planet is called the **atmosphere** (AT•muhs•feer). When compared to the size of Earth, the atmosphere looks like a very thin blanket surrounding the entire planet.

The atmosphere wasn't always as it is today. It formed millions of years ago as gases from erupting volcanoes collected around the planet. This mixture of gases would have poisoned you if you had breathed it. But bacteria and other living things used the gases of this early atmosphere. They released new gases as they carried out their life processes. Over time, the gas mixture changed slowly to become the atmosphere Earth has now.

The atmosphere now is made up of billions and billions of gas particles. Almost four-fifths of these gas particles are nitrogen. Oxygen, a gas that organisms use in cellular respiration, makes up about one-fifth of the atmosphere. Other gases, including carbon dioxide and water vapor, make up the rest of the atmosphere.

Although you can't see all of it, a thin blanket of air called the atmosphere surrounds Earth. ▼

Plants and some protists use carbon dioxide during the process of photosynthesis. They give off oxygen as photosynthesis occurs. Carbon dioxide also absorbs heat energy from the sun and from Earth's surface. This helps keep the planet warm.

Air has certain properties. As you saw in the investigation, air takes up space and has weight. All the particles of air pressing down on the Earth's surface cause **air pressure** (PRESH•er). Air pressure changes as you go higher in the atmosphere. The picture shows what a column of air might look like. At the surface of Earth, air particles are close together. The higher you go in the atmosphere, the farther apart the air particles are. So the air pressure is less as you go higher in the atmosphere.

✔ **What is the atmosphere?**

1 Air particles in the upper atmosphere have the least weight of other particles pressing on them. The particles are far apart. Air in this part of the atmosphere is much less dense than air lower in Earth's atmosphere.

2 Air near the middle of the atmosphere has more weight of other particles pressing down on it. So it is denser than air higher above Earth.

3 The weight of the entire column of air presses down on the air particles closest to Earth, forcing them close together. This makes air densest at Earth's surface. Air pressure is greatest where air is densest.

1 meter

1 meter

1

2

3

10000KG

The mass of a 1-m × 1-m column of Earth's atmosphere is about 10,000 kg. ▶

Atmosphere Layers

Scientists divide Earth's atmosphere into four layers. The layer closest to Earth is called the **troposphere** (TROH•poh•sfeer). We live in the troposphere and breathe its air. Almost all weather happens in this layer. In the troposphere, air temperature decreases as you go higher.

Some airplanes fly in the **stratosphere** (STRAT•uh•sfeer). The stratosphere contains most of the atmosphere's ozone, a kind of oxygen. Ozone protects living things from the sun's harmful rays. Temperatures in the stratosphere increase with height.

In the *mesosphere* (MES•oh•sfeer), air temperature decreases with height. In fact, the mesosphere is the coldest layer of the atmosphere. The *thermosphere* (THER•moh•sfeer) is the hot, outermost layer of atmosphere. In the thermosphere, temperature increases quickly with height. Temperatures high in the thermosphere can reach thousands of degrees Celsius.

✔ **What are the four layers of the atmosphere?**

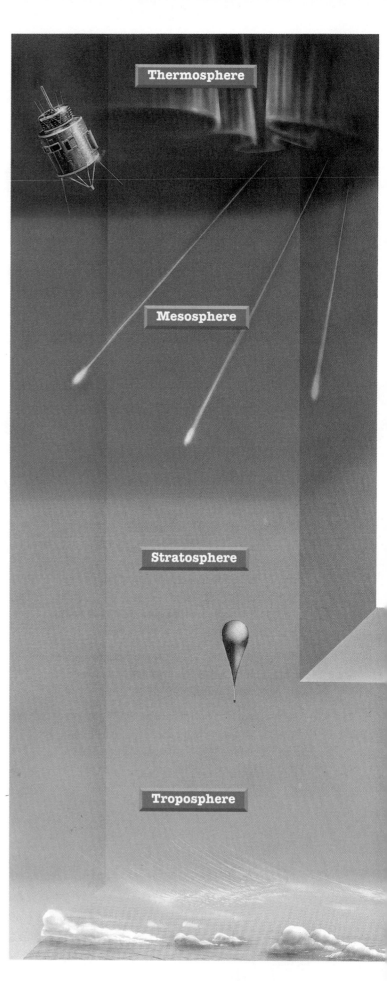

Earth's atmosphere is divided into four layers based on changes in air temperature. Each layer actually blends into the next. The thermosphere fades into outer space, where there is no air at all. ▶

Summary

The thin blanket of air that surrounds Earth is called the atmosphere. Earth's atmosphere is divided into four layers based on changes in temperature. The layers, starting with the one closest to Earth, are the troposphere, stratosphere, mesosphere, and thermosphere.

Review

1. What is the atmosphere?
2. How does air pressure change with height?
3. How is the atmosphere divided?
4. **Critical Thinking** Compare and contrast the stratosphere and the mesosphere.
5. **Test Prep** In which layer of the atmosphere does most weather occur?

   A troposphere
   B stratosphere
   C mesosphere
   D thermosphere

LINKS

MATH LINK

Atmospheric Temperatures In the troposphere the air temperature drops about 6.5°C for every kilometer increase in height. If the troposphere is about 10 kilometers thick and the air temperature at the ground is 30°C, what is the air temperature at a height of 2 kilometers?

WRITING LINK

Informative Writing—Description Pretend that you are falling from space toward Earth. For your teacher, write a story describing what you see and feel as you go through each layer of the atmosphere.

ART LINK

Atmosphere Layers Paint a picture showing the atmosphere as you would see it from space. Label the layers.

TECHNOLOGY LINK

Learn more about Earth's atmosphere and weather by visiting this Internet site. **www.scilinks.org/harcourt**

How Are Atmospheric Conditions Measured?

In this lesson, you can . . .

INVESTIGATE and measure atmospheric conditions.

LEARN ABOUT air pressure and weather.

LINK to math, writing, art, and technology.

◀ A Midwest tornado

Measuring Atmospheric Conditions

Activity Purpose People have always been affected by the weather. Today's weather scientists use many instruments to **measure** and **collect data** about conditions in the atmosphere. Then they use the data to help **predict** what the weather will be like today, tomorrow, or next weekend. In this investigation you will measure and collect data about atmospheric conditions in your area.

Materials

- weather station

Activity Procedure

1 Make a copy of the Weather Station Daily Record table. You will use it to **record** the date, the time, the temperature, the amount of rain or snow, the wind direction and speed, and the cloud conditions each day for five days. Try to **record** the weather conditions at the same time each day.

2 Place the weather station in a shady spot, 1 m above the ground. **Record** the temperature. (Picture A)

3 Be sure the rain gauge will not collect runoff from any buildings or trees. **Record** the amount of rain or snow (if any).

Weather Station Daily Record

Date					
Time					
Temperature					
Rainfall or snowfall					
Wind direction and speed					
Cloud conditions					

Picture A

4 Be sure the wind vane is located where wind from any direction will reach it. **Record** the wind direction and speed. Winds are labeled with the direction from which they blow. (Picture B)

5 Describe and **record** the cloud conditions by noting how much of the sky is covered by clouds. Draw a circle and shade in the part of the circle that equals the amount of sky covered with clouds.

6 Use the temperature data to make a line graph showing how the temperature changes from day to day.

Draw Conclusions

1. Use your Weather Station Daily Record to **compare** the atmospheric conditions on two different days.

2. From the **data** you **gathered** in this activity, how might scientists use this data to **predict** the weather?

3. **Scientists at Work** Scientists learn about the weather by **measuring** atmospheric conditions and **gathering data** from other sources. What could you **infer** by measuring the amount of rain your area received during the week?

Investigate Further Newspaper and television weather reports usually describe the sky or cloud conditions as sunny, mostly sunny, partly sunny, partly cloudy, mostly cloudy, or cloudy. Using the data from your table, **classify** each day's cloud conditions as if you were writing a newspaper report.

Picture B

Process Skill Tip

Measurements are a kind of observation. You **measure** when you use a tool, such as a thermometer or rain gauge, to **gather data** about something.

B11

Weather

FIND OUT

- where most weather occurs
- how conditions in the atmosphere are measured
- how clouds form

VOCABULARY

weather
humidity
precipitation
evaporation
condensation
water cycle

Where Weather Occurs

Almost all weather occurs in the lowest layer of atmosphere that surrounds Earth. **Weather** is the condition of the atmosphere at any moment. The atmosphere stretches about 1000 km (620 mi) from Earth's surface to outer space. The lowest layer of the atmosphere, the troposphere, is where most water is found and where most clouds form. The troposphere is about 15 km (9 mi) thick at the equator.

Very little weather occurs above the troposphere. There is a little water in the stratosphere, so a few clouds form there. From the stratosphere to the edge of space, there is no water and too little air for any weather to occur.

✔ **In what layer of the atmosphere does most of Earth's weather occur?**

Blizzards, at the left, and hurricanes, at the right, are among the largest and most powerful weather systems of Earth's troposphere.

A *thermometer* measures air temperature. ▼

Air pressure is the weight of the atmosphere. A *barometer* measures air pressure. ▼

A *rain gauge* measures the amount of precipitation. ▼

◀ Water in the air is called humidity. A *hygrometer* (hy•GRAHM•uht•er) measures humidity.

A *wind vane* measures the direction from which the wind is blowing. An *anemometer* (an•uh•MAHM•uht•er) measures wind speed. ▶

Measuring the Condition of the Atmosphere

Weather changes because the atmosphere is constantly changing. Sometimes the air is cold and sometimes it's warm. As air warms, air pressure lessens. Warm air holds more water, or has more **humidity**, than cold air. These and other conditions of the atmosphere can be observed and measured.

The weather instruments shown on this page are used to measure certain atmospheric conditions—air temperature, air pressure, **precipitation** (rain, snow, sleet, or hail), humidity, wind direction, and wind speed. Other atmospheric conditions, such as cloud type, can be observed directly.

Why do people measure atmospheric conditions? One reason is to predict what the weather will be. For example, a change in air pressure or cloud type often means there will be a change in the weather.

✔ **What are some atmospheric conditions that can be measured?**

Air Pressure and Weather

You probably don't feel the atmosphere weighing you down. But you know from Lesson 1 that air does have weight. The atmosphere pushes on you all the time, and in all directions.

There are several types of barometers for measuring air pressure. A mercury barometer, like the ones shown at the right, consists of a glass tube about 1 m (3 ft) long. Air is removed from the tube, and the glass is sealed at the top. Then the tube is turned upside down, and the open end is placed in a dish of mercury. The weight of the air pushing down on the mercury in the dish pushes mercury up into the glass tube. The mercury rises in the tube until its weight exactly balances the weight of the air pushing down on the mercury in the dish. The height of the mercury in the tube is a measure of air pressure. This measure is compared to a standard, or average, air pressure of about 76 cm (30 in.) of mercury.

Warm air weighs less than cold air. A mass of cold air is called a *high-pressure area,* because it will measure more than 76 cm of mercury. A mass of warm air is called a *low-pressure area,* because it will measure less than 76 cm of mercury.

Weather changes because high- and low-pressure areas move. In the winter, areas of high pressure often move from northwestern Canada toward the southeastern United States, bringing cool, dry weather. In the summer, areas of low pressure often move from the Gulf of Mexico to the northeastern United States, bringing warm, wet weather.

As high-pressure and low-pressure areas move, barometer readings in their paths change. Therefore, changing barometer

HIGH AIR PRESSURE

The mercury in this barometer is high. Areas of high pressure usually have fair weather.

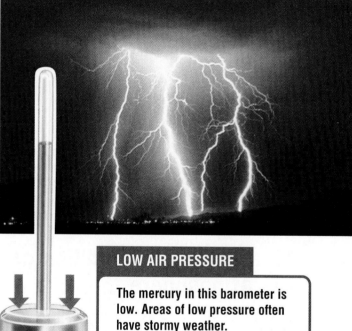

LOW AIR PRESSURE

The mercury in this barometer is low. Areas of low pressure often have stormy weather.

readings can be used to predict changes in weather. If the barometer is rising, the weather will probably become fair. If the barometer is falling, stormy weather is probably coming.

✔ **How can changing air pressure be used to predict changing weather?**

Water in the Air

In addition to temperature and air pressure, humidity, or the amount of water in the air, is an important factor in describing weather. But how does water get into the air?

Earth's oceans are the biggest source of water. As the sun heats the oceans, liquid water changes into an invisible gas called *water vapor,* which rises into the air. The process of liquid water changing to water vapor is called **evaporation**. High up in the atmosphere, where the air is cooler, water vapor turns back into liquid drops of water, forming clouds. This process is called **condensation**.

When cloud drops come together, gravity returns the water to the Earth's surface as precipitation—usually rain. If the temperature in the clouds is below freezing, the precipitation is sleet, hail, or snow. This transferring of water from the Earth's surface to the atmosphere and back is called the **water cycle**.

THE INSIDE STORY

The Water Cycle

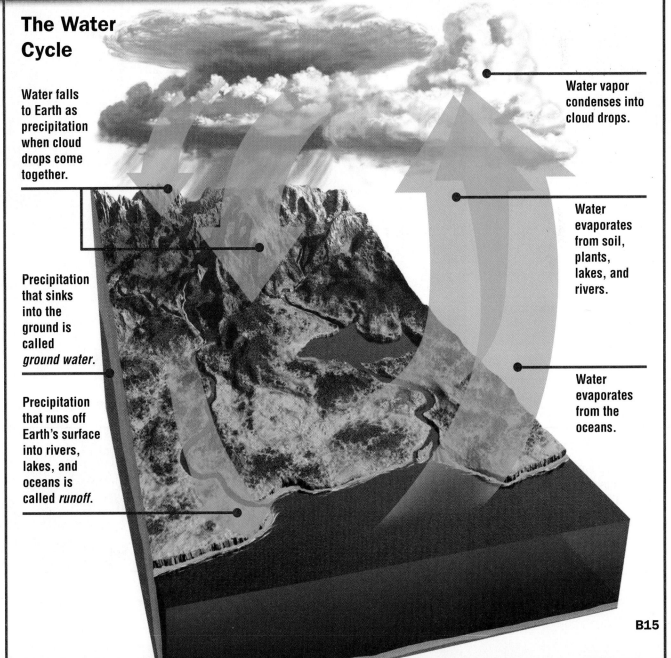

Water falls to Earth as precipitation when cloud drops come together.

Precipitation that sinks into the ground is called *ground water*.

Precipitation that runs off Earth's surface into rivers, lakes, and oceans is called *runoff*.

Water vapor condenses into cloud drops.

Water evaporates from soil, plants, lakes, and rivers.

Water evaporates from the oceans.

On clear nights, when the surface of the Earth cools quickly, water vapor may condense to form a cloud near the ground. This low cloud is called *fog*. If you have ever walked through fog, you know what the inside of a cloud is like.

Whether a cloud forms near the ground or high in the atmosphere, it forms in the same way. Water vapor condenses onto dust and other tiny particles in the air when it rises and cools. Another way in which air cools enough for water vapor to condense is by moving from a warm place to a colder place. For example, moist air that moves from over a warm body of water to over cooler land forms clouds or fog.

Even though all clouds form by condensation, different atmospheric conditions produce different types of clouds. Weather scientists, or *meteorologists* (meet•ee•uhr•AHL•uh•juhsts),

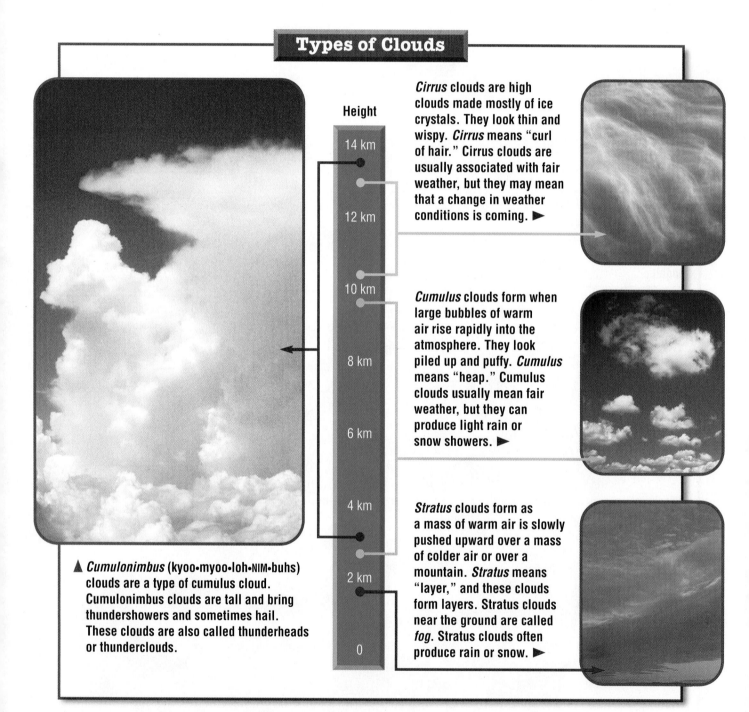

Types of Clouds

Height

14 km

12 km

10 km

8 km

6 km

4 km

2 km

0

Cirrus clouds are high clouds made mostly of ice crystals. They look thin and wispy. *Cirrus* means "curl of hair." Cirrus clouds are usually associated with fair weather, but they may mean that a change in weather conditions is coming. ▶

Cumulus clouds form when large bubbles of warm air rise rapidly into the atmosphere. They look piled up and puffy. *Cumulus* means "heap." Cumulus clouds usually mean fair weather, but they can produce light rain or snow showers. ▶

Stratus clouds form as a mass of warm air is slowly pushed upward over a mass of colder air or over a mountain. *Stratus* means "layer," and these clouds form layers. Stratus clouds near the ground are called *fog*. Stratus clouds often produce rain or snow. ▶

▲ *Cumulonimbus* (kyoo•myoo•loh•NIM•buhs) clouds are a type of cumulus cloud. Cumulonimbus clouds are tall and bring thundershowers and sometimes hail. These clouds are also called thunderheads or thunderclouds.

give clouds three basic names—cirrus (SEER•uhs), cumulus (KYOO•myoo•luhs), and stratus. Along with other information, the types of clouds in the atmosphere can be used to help predict weather changes. Some basic types of clouds and their descriptions are shown on page B16.

✔ **How do clouds form?**

Summary

Most of Earth's weather takes place in the troposphere, the lowest layer of the atmosphere. Weather conditions such as temperature, air pressure, humidity, wind speed and direction, and the amount of precipitation can be observed and measured. Certain weather conditions, such as changing air pressure and types of clouds, can be used to predict changes in the weather.

Review

1. How do weather scientists **observe** and **measure** weather conditions?

2. How is water recycled in the water cycle?

3. What causes clouds to form?

4. **Critical Thinking** It is a gray, cloudy day, and a light rain is falling. What type of clouds would you expect to see? Explain your answer.

5. **Test Prep** The process by which water vapor turns into liquid water drops is known as —

   A condensation
   B evaporation
   C precipitation
   D the water cycle

LINKS

MATH LINK

Measurement Many meteorologists in the United States measure air pressure in units called *millibars*. At sea level, standard air pressure is 1013.2 millibars. If 1013.2 millibars equals 76 cm of mercury, what would a barometer reading of 75 cm of mercury equal in millibars?

WRITING LINK

Informative Writing—Report Suppose that you are a meteorologist who has just spotted a large cumulonimbus cloud moving toward a city. Write a weather report for the city's residents.

ART LINK

Stormy Weather Make a drawing that includes one or more of the cloud types shown on page B16. Show the weather conditions that are associated with those cloud types.

TECHNOLOGY LINK

Learn more about Earth's atmosphere by visiting the Harcourt Learning Site.
www.harcourtschool.com/ca

WELCOME TO
THE
LEARNING
SITE

What Role Do Oceans Play in the Water Cycle?

In this lesson, you can . . .

INVESTIGATE how to get fresh water from salt water.

LEARN ABOUT Earth's ocean water.

LINK to math, writing, social studies, and technology.

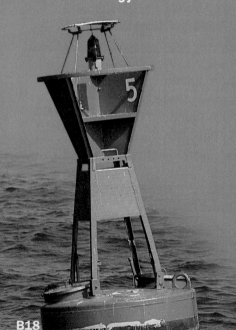

◄ Buoys float but are held in place by anchors. They mark paths where the water is deep enough for ships.

INVESTIGATE

Getting Fresh Water from Salt Water

Activity Purpose If you've ever been splashed in the face by an ocean wave, you know that sea water is salty. The salt in ocean water stings your eyes, leaves a crusty white coating on your skin when it dries, and tastes like the salt you put on food. In this investigation you'll evaporate artificial ocean water to find out what is left behind. From your **observations** you will **infer** how you can get fresh water from salt water.

Materials

- container of very warm water
- salt
- spoon
- cotton swabs
- large clear bowl
- small glass jar
- plastic wrap
- large rubber band
- piece of modeling clay
- masking tape

Activity Procedure

CAUTION

1 Stir two spoonfuls of salt into the container of very warm water. Put one end of a clean cotton swab into this mixture. Taste the mixture by touching the swab to your tongue. **Record** your observations. **CAUTION** Don't share swabs. Don't put a swab that has touched your mouth back into any substance. Never taste anything in an investigation or experiment unless you are told to do so.

Picture A

Picture B

2 Pour the salt water into the large bowl. Put the jar in the center of the bowl of salt water. (Picture A)

3 Put the plastic wrap over the top of the bowl. The wrap should not touch the top of the jar inside the bowl. Put a large rubber band around the bowl to hold the wrap in place.

4 Form the clay into a small ball. Put the ball on top of the plastic wrap right over the jar. Make sure the plastic wrap doesn't touch the jar. (Picture B)

5 On the outside of the bowl, use tape to mark the level of the salt water. Place the bowl in a sunny spot for one day.

6 After one day, remove the plastic wrap and the clay ball. Use clean swabs to taste the water in the jar and in the bowl. **Record** your **observations.**

Draw Conclusions

1. What did you **observe** by using your sense of taste?

2. What do you **infer** happened to the salt water?

3. **Scientists at Work** The movement of water from the Earth's surface, through the atmosphere, and back to Earth's surface is called the water cycle. From what you **observed,** what can you **infer** about the ocean's role in the water cycle?

Investigate Further Put the plastic wrap and the clay back on the large bowl. Leave the bowl in the sun until the water in the large bowl is gone. **Observe** the bowl and the jar. What can you **conclude** about the water that evaporates from ocean water? What other information do you need to support your conclusion?

Process Skill Tip

Observing and inferring are different things. You **observe** with your senses. You **infer**, or form an opinion, based on what you have observed and what you know about a situation.

Ocean Water

Salt Water to Fresh Water

FIND OUT

- about processes that turn salt water into fresh water
- why ocean water is salty

Much of the Earth is covered by water. Almost all of that water is ocean water. Even though ocean water is salty, it provides most of Earth's fresh water. Earth's water is always being recycled. As the model in the investigation showed, heat from the sun causes fresh water to evaporate from the oceans, leaving the salt behind. This water vapor condenses to form clouds. Fresh water falls from clouds to Earth's surface as rain. During the water cycle, water changes from a liquid to a gas and back to a liquid. The diagram shows the role of the oceans in the water cycle. It includes the parts played by the sun, the water, the air, and the land.

✔ **What is the role of the oceans in the water cycle?**

The sun warms the ocean, causing the water particles to move faster and faster. After a while, they have enough energy to leave the water and enter the air as water vapor. This is evaporation. When water evaporates from the oceans, salt is left behind. Clouds form when water vapor condenses high in the atmosphere. Cloud drops are fresh water.

Near places where rivers empty into the ocean, the ocean water is less salty than it is farther from the shore. This is because the fresh water mixes with the salt water. Ocean water is a little saltier near the equator, where it is hot and water evaporates faster. And ocean water is a little less salty near the North and South Poles, where it is colder and water evaporates more slowly.

✓ **What is in ocean water?**

Summary

The waters of the ocean provide fresh water for Earth through the water cycle. As water moves through this cycle, it changes from a liquid to a gas and back to a liquid through the processes of evaporation and condensation. The water returns to Earth as precipitation. Sodium chloride is the most common salt in the ocean. The salts and other substances dissolved in ocean water make it denser than fresh water.

Review

1. What is the source of energy for evaporation in the water cycle?
2. Explain how the oceans play a major role in the water cycle.
3. What factors affect the saltiness or density of ocean water?
4. **Critical Thinking** How could you make salt water denser?
5. **Test Prep** Which of these processes occurs when a gas changes to a liquid?
   A evaporation
   B condensation
   C precipitation
   D salinity

LINKS

MATH LINK

Compare Fresh Water and Salt Water Use library reference materials to find out more about the amounts of fresh water and salt water on Earth. Draw a large square on a sheet of paper, and divide it into fourths. Color the squares to show the amounts of land and ocean. Stack pennies or checkers on the squares to stand for the amounts of fresh water and salt water.

WRITING LINK

Narrative Writing—Story Suppose you are sailing alone around the world. For your teacher, write down some of your thoughts that describe the ocean and what it is like to have nothing but water all around you.

SOCIAL STUDIES LINK

Currents Find out what ocean currents are. Locate major currents on a world map. Write a report that explains what causes ocean currents and how they affect weather.

TECHNOLOGY LINK

Learn more about Earth's water systems by visiting the National Air and Space Museum Internet site. **www.si.edu/harcourt/science**

Why Is the Water Cycle Important?

In this lesson, you can . . .

INVESTIGATE how water moves through air.

LEARN ABOUT human activity and the water cycle.

LINK to math, writing, literature, and technology.

INVESTIGATE

Water, Water Everywhere

Activity Purpose Every day, you have some contact with water. You drink it, you bathe in it, and maybe you watch it fall from the sky. But have you ever wondered where your water comes from, where it goes, or why we never run out of it? In this activity you will **measure** water as it cycles.

Materials

- graduate
- water
- small plastic cup
- zip-top plastic bag

Activity Procedure

1 Using the graduate, **measure** and pour 100 mL of water into the cup. (Picture A)

2 Open the plastic bag, and carefully put the cup inside. Then seal the bag. Be careful not to spill any water from the cup.

3 Place the sealed bag near a sunny window. **Predict** what will happen to the water in the cup. (Picture B)

◄ The warmth of the sun will change the snow into liquid water.

Picture A

Picture B

4 Leave the bag near a window for 3 to 4 days. **Observe** the cup and the bag each day. **Record** what you see.

5 Remove the cup from the bag. **Measure** the amount of water in the cup by pouring it back into the graduate. **Calculate** any difference in the amount of water you poured into the cup and the amount of water you removed from the cup.

Draw Conclusions

1. What did you **observe** during the time the cup was inside the bag?

2. Where do you infer the water in the bag came from? Explain.

3. **Scientists at Work** Scientists often **infer** the cause of something they **observe**. What can you infer about the amount of water in the bag?

Investigate Further Develop a testable question about where the missing water went. Decide what equipment you will need, and then **plan and conduct a simple investigation** that will help you answer your question. Be sure to write instructions so that others can follow your procedure.

Why the Water Cycle Is Important

Fresh Water

As seen from space, Earth looks like a big blue marble. Seas, oceans, lakes, and rivers cover about 75 percent of Earth's surface. Earth's water moves through the environment in the water cycle. In the investigation, you inferred that liquid water in the cup became water vapor in the air of the plastic bag. The water vapor then became liquid water on the surface of the bag.

As you saw in the last lesson, most of the water on Earth is salt water. Suppose that all of Earth's water just fills a 1-liter bottle. Of that liter, 972 mL would be salt water. Only 28 mL would be fresh water. And most of the fresh water isn't available either.

If all of Earth's water could be held in a 1-liter bottle, the contents would be divided up like this:

Salt water: 972 mL

Fresh water: 28 mL

B26

Most fresh water is frozen in the polar ice caps and in glaciers. So only 15 percent of Earth's fresh water is available for living organisms.

All living organisms need water to survive. In fact, living organisms are made up mostly of water. About 70 percent of the human body is water. Living organisms get the water they need in different ways. Plants use their roots to take in water that seeps into the soil. Most animals get the water they need by drinking from lakes or streams. Some animals get all the water they need from the food they eat.

Plants and animals also put water back into the environment. Plants give off water through their stomata. This process is called **transpiration** (tran•spuh•RAY•shuhn). Animals give off water vapor from their lungs when they exhale. And most of the urine animals produce is water.

✔ **Where is most of Earth's fresh water stored?**

All the water you use keeps recycling. The heat of the sun evaporates water from the ocean's surface. High in the air, water condenses into tiny droplets to form clouds. Winds sweep clouds over the land. When clouds rise over a mountain, water falls as precipitation. Some rainwater runs off the land and returns to the ocean or to lakes. Some rainwater seeps into the Earth and becomes ground water.

Some communities get the water they need from surface supplies, such as rivers or lakes. Others get water from underground sources. A few places even get the water they need by removing the salt from ocean water. What is the source of water for your community?

The 28 mL of fresh water is divided up like this:

Ice caps: 22 mL
Glaciers: 1.5 mL

Groundwater: 4 mL

Lakes and rivers: 2 drops

Water in soil and air: 1 drop

Average Daily Water Use

Laundry	60 gal
Bath	36 gal
Dishwashing	12 gal
Lawn watering	10 gal/min
Cooking	8 gal
Toilet per flush	5–6 gal
Shower	5 gal/min
Leaky faucet	5 gal/hr
Leaky toilet	3 gal/hr
Drinking water	0.26 gal

Humans and the Water Cycle

All the water on Earth today is the same water that was here billions of years ago. Yet every year the need for water grows. In addition to drinking, bathing, cooking, and waste removal, people use water to grow crops, feed livestock, and make materials, such as plastic, aluminum, and paper.

Less than 1 percent of the Earth's fresh water can be used because most of it is frozen in ice caps and glaciers. Yet the limited sources of fresh water are sometimes affected by human activity. Rainwater running off the land washes harmful chemicals such as oil

Although trash is more visible, this stream also carries harmful chemicals, such as pesticides, motor oil, and gasoline. ▶

and road salt into lakes and rivers. Expensive forms of water treatment must be used to make lakes and rivers safe for human use.

Rainwater seeping into the soil carries harmful chemicals such as fertilizers and pesticides into groundwater supplies. It stays there for thousands of years. Groundwater supplies provide many people with water for use in their homes. Farmers also use underground supplies to water their crops.

There are ways to conserve water and to improve water quality. For example, in

Some landscaping in west Texas uses native desert plants instead of grass and trees. ▼

many states, factories must remove harmful chemicals from their waste water. In some places, used motor oil is recycled into new products. And people everywhere can conserve water by using washers and toilets that don't need much water. People in arid places can also landscape with native plants instead of grasses and trees that need a lot of water.

✓ **How do harmful chemicals on the land get into ground water?**

Summary

In the water cycle, water on Earth's surface evaporates into the atmosphere. There it condenses into cloud droplets and then falls back to Earth as precipitation. Plants and animals return water to the environment through transpiration and respiration. Fresh water is a limited resource that people need to conserve and keep clean.

Review

1. What is the process by which liquid water becomes water vapor?
2. What is the process by which water vapor becomes cloud droplets?
3. Where is most of Earth's fresh water?
4. **Critical Thinking** What do you think causes dew to form on plant leaves during a cool night?
5. **Test Prep** About how much of all the fresh water on Earth can be used by people and other land organisms?
   A less than 1 percent
   B more than 10 percent
   C more than 97 percent
   D 100 percent

LINKS

MATH LINK

Water Use An average person uses about 60 gallons of water a day. Calculate how much water a person uses in a month (30 days) and in a year (365 days). How much would a family of four people use in a year?

WRITING LINK

Informative Writing—Business Letter As you read, the amount of water available for human use is very limited. Write a letter to your community's water department. Ask them to send you information on the source of the water they provide. Also ask for information on water treatment and ways to conserve water.

LITERATURE LINK

A Drop of Water Check out either of these two books about water: *A Drop of Water* by Walter Wick (Scholastic, 1998) or *Squishy, Misty, Damp and Muddy: The In-Between World of Wetlands* by Molly Cone (Sierra, 1997). Learn about the importance of water and wetlands.

TECHNOLOGY LINK

Learn more about the water cycle and water treatment by viewing *Natural Water Treatment* on the **Harcourt Science Newsroom Video** in your classroom video library.

WETLANDS WITH A PURPOSE

Wetlands are among the most productive ecosystems on Earth. Many kinds of organisms—fish, birds, reptiles, amphibians, insects, and mammals—find food and shelter in wetlands.

What Wetlands Do

In addition to providing habitats for wildlife, wetlands improve water quality. Aquatic plants and microorganisms that live on the plants filter waste materials and pollutants from the water.

Scientists are combining technology with ecology to build artificial wetlands to treat wastewater. An artificial wetland is a wetland with a purpose. Over 500 communities in the United States have already built artificial wetlands to treat sewage effluent (wastewater) and storm runoff.

Technology Imitates Nature

Artificial wetlands are designed to do what natural wetland ecosystems do. The processes are carried out by water, plants, animals, microorganisms, sun, soil, and air working together. What happens is that microorganisms, such as the bacteria and fungi in the soil and on the plants, change organic wastes into nutrients that plants can use. The plants take in materials such as nitrogen and phosphorus from the wastewater.

The Show Low wetland in northeastern Arizona was one of the first artificial wetlands in the country. In 1979 the U.S. Forest Service, the Arizona Fish and Game Commission, and Show Low city officials teamed up to build the wetland. Wastewater was

An artificial wetland

Great blue herons

pumped into a natural low area, making Pintail Lake. Then 14 small islands were built in the lake to attract water birds. The islands and the shoreline were seeded with wetland plants, such as cattails, water grass, duckweed, and bulrushes. In the following years, several more marshes and lakes were made. Now the wetlands complex covers about 81 hectares (200 acres) and receives 5.37 million liters (about 1.42 million gallons) of wastewater daily. Instead of being released into a nearby river, the water stays in the treatment area until it evaporates.

Why Build Wetlands?

Artificial wetlands are very efficient at removing pollutants from municipal,

agricultural, and industrial wastewater at little or no cost. It takes less energy, fewer supplies, and far fewer people to run an artificial wetland than it does to run a conventional water treatment plant.

Artificial wetlands are an example of human technology working with natural processes. In addition to treating wastewater, artificial wetlands provide habitats for wildlife and an environment in which people can enjoy and explore nature.

THINK ABOUT IT

1. For what purposes are artificial wetlands built?
2. How do artificial wetlands combine technology with natural processes?

WEB LINK:
For science and technology updates, visit The Learning Site.
www.harcourtschool.com/ca

Careers — Heavy-Machine Operator

What They Do Heavy-machine operators drive earth-moving and construction machines, such as road scrapers, cranes, forklifts, bulldozers, and front-end loaders.

Education and Training People wishing to become heavy-machine operators may attend special trade schools to learn the basics of how to drive and operate the machinery. They also need on-the-job training and experience.

Denise Stephenson-Hawk

ATMOSPHERIC SCIENTIST

Denise Stephenson-Hawk always loved school and was especially good in math. She skipped her senior year in high school and entered Spelman College. While there, she received a scholarship to a summer program at the National Aeronautics and Space Administration (NASA). She worked on a project to test panels for the space shuttle to make sure the panels would withstand the high temperatures they experience upon reentry into Earth's atmosphere. Dr. Stephenson-Hawk was so excited by what she learned about the atmosphere that she decided to apply her math skills to the study of atmospheric science.

Dr. Stephenson-Hawk's first job was at AT&T Bell Laboratories. There she made computer models to learn how sound travels in the ocean. After teaching mathematical modeling at Spelman College, Dr. Stephenson-Hawk moved to Clark Atlanta University in Georgia. There she works as a senior research scientist and associate professor of physics.

Dr. Stephenson-Hawk is also a member of the Climate Analysis Center (CAC) at the National Oceanic and Atmospheric Administration (NOAA). The CAC uses computer models to

analyze and predict climate changes that happen in a short time. Dr. Stephenson-Hawk's special project has been building computer models of the effects of El Niño, a series of events set off by warmer-than-normal surface-water temperatures in the Pacific Ocean. Dr. Stephenson-Hawk and the other scientists working on this project are trying to more accurately predict the impact of El Niño so that people can better prepare for unusual weather.

THINK ABOUT IT

1. Why else might scientists be interested in studying El Niño?
2. Why do you think atmospheric scientists use computer models?

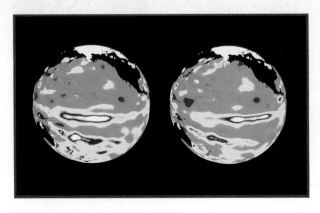

El Niño water temperature maps

Air Pressure

How strong is air pressure?

Materials

- plastic sandwich bag
- drinking straw
- tape
- heavy book

Procedure

1 Put one end of the straw in the plastic bag. Then seal the bag shut with tape.

2 Put the plastic bag on a table and lay the book on part of the bag as shown.

3 Blow through the straw into the bag, and observe what happens.

Draw Conclusions

Describe what happened to the bag and the book. Explain what happened. Try to think of a situation where air pressure could be used like this.

Sidewalk Graph

How does sunlight speed up evaporation?

Materials

- sunny sidewalk
- 500 mL water
- chalk
- clock

Procedure

1 Pour about 500 mL of water onto a sidewalk that is in full sunlight.

2 Draw a line around the outside of the puddle with the chalk.

3 Draw a new line around the puddle every 5 min for 20 min.

4 Repeat the experiment on a sidewalk in the shade.

Draw Conclusions

Compare the sizes of the puddles at each 5-min interval. Based on your observations, predict how long it would take for each puddle to evaporate.

Chapter 1 Review and Test Preparation

Vocabulary Review

Use the terms below to complete the sentences. The page numbers in ( ) tell you where to look in the chapter if you need help.

atmosphere (B6)
air pressure (B7)
troposphere (B8)
stratosphere (B8)
humidity (B13)
precipitation (B13)
evaporation (B15)
condensation (B15)
water cycle (B15)
transpiration (B27)

1. The _____ is the thin blanket of air that surrounds Earth.

2. In the atmosphere the layer that contains the most ozone is the _____.

3. In the atmosphere the layer that contains the air we breathe is the _____.

4. Liquid water changes to water vapor through the process of _____.

5. Water vapor turns back to liquid water through a process called _____.

6. Rain, sleet, and snow are called _____.

7. The amount of water vapor in the air is called _____.

8. The weight of air is known as _____.

9. Plants give off water from their stomata in a process called _____.

10. Water vapor, clouds, rain, and the ocean are part of the _____.

Connect Concepts

Complete the diagram by using terms from the Word Bank.

atmosphere   stratosphere
troposphere   thermosphere

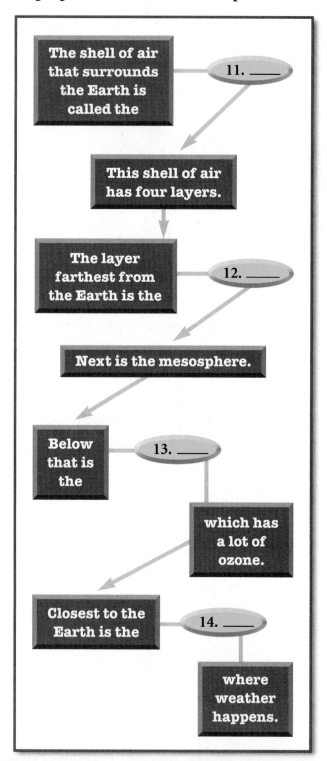

The shell of air that surrounds the Earth is called the

11. _____

This shell of air has four layers.

The layer farthest from the Earth is the

12. _____

Next is the mesosphere.

Below that is the

13. _____

which has a lot of ozone.

Closest to the Earth is the

14. _____

where weather happens.

Check Understanding

Write the letter of the best choice.

15. As you go higher in the atmosphere, the space between air particles —
  A decreases   **C** increases
  B doesn't change   **D** masses

16. As air warms, —
  F air pressure increases
  G air pressure decreases
  H temperature decreases
  J humidity changes

17. A wind vane indicates the —
  A air pressure
  B humidity
  C amount of precipitation
  D direction in which air is moving

18. Where is the most fresh water on Earth?
  F lakes   **H** rivers
  G glaciers   **J** oceans

19. During transpiration, plants give off —
  A water
  B carbon dioxide
  C salt
  D nitrogen

20. The ___ provides energy for Earth's water cycle.
  F atmosphere   **H** moon
  G land   **J** sun

21. Oceans are a mixture of water and —
  A other liquids   **C** grains of sand
  B dissolved salts **D** different gases

Critical Thinking

22. Why do mountain climbers use oxygen tanks?

23. Would it be easier to float in the great Salt Lake or Lake Michigan? Explain your answer.

24. There are just a few white, fluffy clouds in the sky. What kind of day is it? What is likely to happen if the clouds multiply, grow very tall, and darken?

Process Skills Review

25. **Infer** which property of air keeps a beach ball inflated.

26. Which would you **predict** would be saltier, the Gulf of California or the Gulf of Mexico? Explain.

27. Suppose you will **measure** weather conditions over the next five days, using different weather instruments. Make a table for recording the data you will collect.

Performance Assessment

Water Cycle Art

Make a mural or poster that traces a drop of water through the water cycle. Include how long the drop of water stays in each stage of the cycle. For example, it might stay 10 years in a lake, 12 days in a cloud, and so on. Label each part of the cycle.

Chapter 2

LESSON 1
What Causes Wind? B38

LESSON 2
How Do Air Masses Affect Weather? B44

LESSON 3
What Causes Severe Storms? B50

SCIENCE THROUGH TIME B58

PEOPLE IN SCIENCE B60

ACTIVITIES FOR HOME OR SCHOOL B61

CHAPTER REVIEW AND TEST PREPARATION B62

Earth's Weather

Everyone talks about the weather, but weather forecasters get paid to talk about it. Many people depend on weather forecasts to plan their day. Sometimes forecasts of severe weather can even save lives.

Vocabulary Preview

local winds
prevailing winds
air mass
front
thunderstorm
hurricane
tropical storm
tornado

Right now, 2000 thunderstorms are happening around the Earth. While you are reading this sentence, lightning will strike the Earth about 500 times!

Never underestimate the power of a flood! Just fifteen centimeters (about 6 in.) of fast-moving water can knock you off your feet. Sixty centimeters (about 2 ft) of water can carry away an automobile!

≡FAST FACT

If you're a famous baseball player, your number will be retired. If you're a really destructive hurricane, your name will be retired! Instead of a batting average or ERA, a hurricane has a scale rating. Here's how it works:

Saffir-Simpson Hurricane Scale

Category	Wind Speed (kilometers per hour)	Wind Speed (miles per hour)
1	119–153	74–95
2	154–177	96–110
3	178–209	111–130
4	210–249	131–155
5	over 249	over 155

What Causes Wind?

In this lesson, you can . . .

INVESTIGATE the rates at which water and soil absorb and release heat.

LEARN ABOUT uneven heating of the Earth's surface as the cause of wind.

LINK to math, writing, music, and technology.

The Sun's Energy Heats Unevenly

Activity Purpose If you've ever walked barefoot from pavement to grass on a sunny day, you know that different materials absorb heat differently. On a larger scale, uneven heating like this is what produces wind. In this investigation you will **predict** which material heats up and cools off faster—water or soil. Then you will test your predictions.

Materials

- 2 tin cans (lids removed)
- water
- dry soil
- spoon
- 2 thermometers

Activity Procedure

1. Fill one can about $\frac{3}{4}$ full of water and the other can about $\frac{3}{4}$ full of soil. (Pictures A and B)

2. Place one thermometer in the can of water and the other in the can of soil. Put the cans in a shady place outside. Wait for 10 minutes, and then **record** the temperatures of the water and the soil.

3. Put both cans in sunlight. **Predict** which of the cans will show the faster rise in temperature. **Record** the temperature of each can every 10 minutes for 30 minutes. In which can does the temperature rise faster? Which material—soil or water—heats up faster?

◀ Energy to fly this kite starts with the sun.

Picture A

Picture B

4 Now put the cans back in the shade. **Predict** in which of the cans the temperature will drop faster. Again **record** the temperature of each can every 10 minutes for 30 minutes. In which can does the temperature drop faster? Which material—soil or water—cools off faster?

5 Make line graphs to show how the temperatures of both materials changed as they heated up and cooled off.

Draw Conclusions

1. What was the dependent variable in this investigation? What independent variables did you test?

2. From the results you graphed in this investigation, which would you **predict** heats up faster—oceans or land? Which would you predict cools off faster? Explain.

3. **Scientists at Work** Scientists learn by **predicting** and then testing their predictions. How did you test your predictions about water and soil? What variables did you control?

Investigate Further **Predict** how fast other materials, such as moist soil, sand, and salt water, heat up and cool off. **Plan and conduct a simple investigation** to test your predictions. Then write a report of your investigation that includes tests conducted, data collected, and conclusions drawn.

Process Skill Tip

A prediction is based on previous observations. Before you **predict**, think about what you have already observed.

B39

The Causes of Wind

FIND OUT

- what causes the wind
- about Earth's wind patterns

VOCABULARY

local winds
prevailing winds

Uneven Heating

The illustration below shows how the sun's rays strike the Earth's surface and the atmosphere. The atmosphere absorbs some of the sun's energy and reflects some of it back into space. Some of the energy that reaches the Earth's surface is reflected back into the atmosphere. However, much of the sun's energy is absorbed by the Earth's surface.

In the investigation you discovered that soil heats up faster and cools off faster than water. In the same way, when the sun's rays strike the Earth's surface, land absorbs the sun's energy more quickly and heats up faster than bodies of water, such as lakes, rivers, and oceans. And land releases heat and cools off faster when the sun goes down than bodies of water do.

✔ **What happens to the energy from the sun's rays that reach Earth?**

The atmosphere absorbs energy directly from the sun and from energy reflected from the Earth's surface. ▼

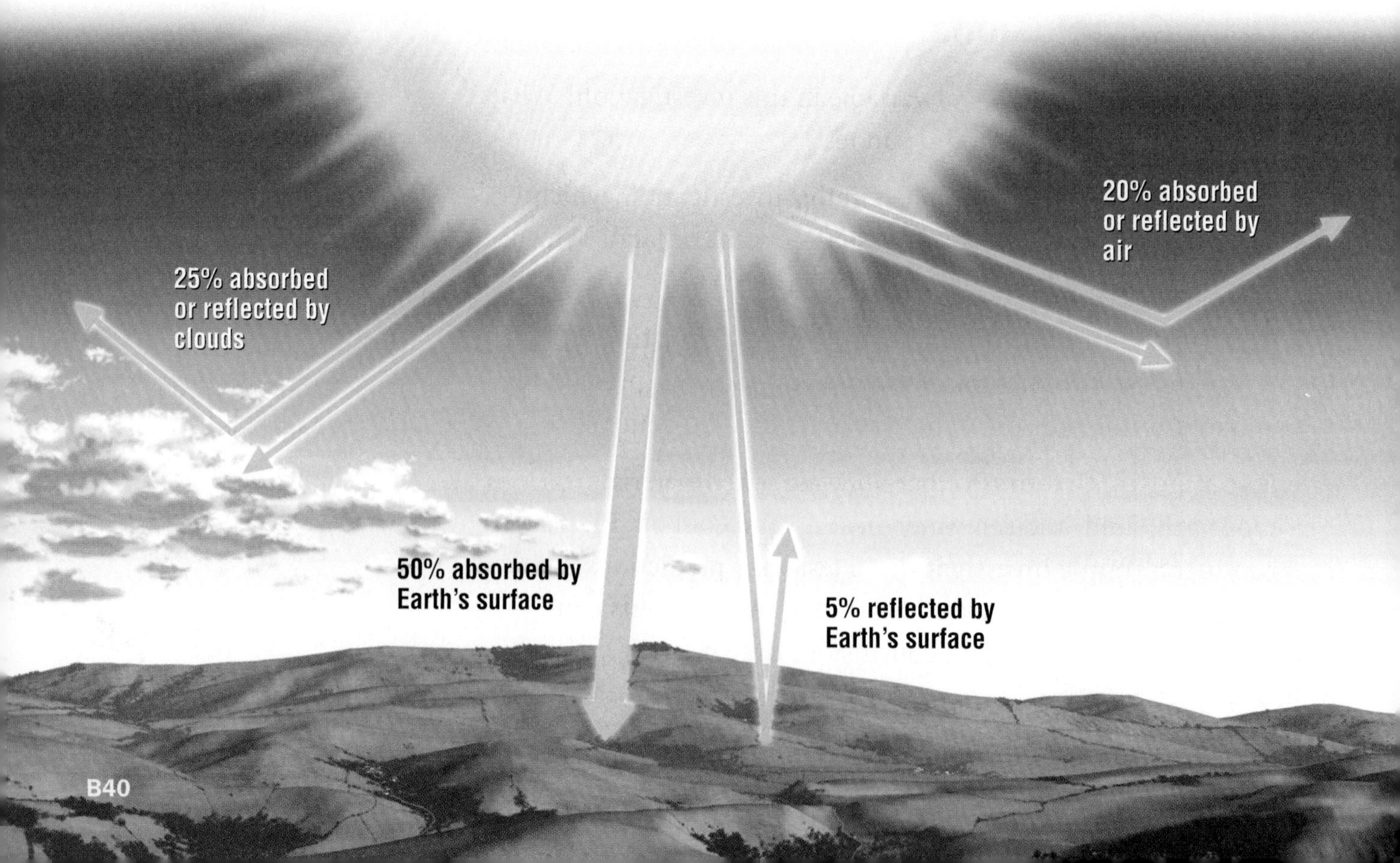

25% absorbed or reflected by clouds

20% absorbed or reflected by air

50% absorbed by Earth's surface

5% reflected by Earth's surface

Local Winds

Because the Earth's surface is heated unevenly, the air above it is in constant motion. Cold air is heavier than warm air, so it sinks, forcing lighter, warm air to rise. The upward movement of warm air in the atmosphere produces *updrafts*. You may have seen birds soaring on updrafts.

At the surface, two places can often have differences in temperature and, therefore, differences in air pressure. These differences cause air to move from the area of higher pressure to the area of lower pressure. This horizontal movement of air is called *wind*. Winds can be local, affecting small areas, or global, affecting large parts of the Earth.

Local winds depend on local changes in temperature. The illustrations below show an example of local winds at the seashore. During the day, the land heats up more quickly than the water does, so the breezes blow from the sea to the land. But at night, air over the water is warmer than air over the land, so the breezes blow from the land to the sea.

✔ What causes local winds?

▲ Uneven heating of the Earth's surface produces air masses of different temperatures. Cold air sinks, forcing warm air to rise.

Prevailing Winds

In the age of sailing ships, sailors relied on prevailing winds to carry them across the oceans. **Prevailing winds** are global winds that blow constantly from the same direction. Prevailing winds are caused by the uneven heating of large parts of Earth's atmosphere.

To understand prevailing winds, first suppose an Earth that doesn't rotate. The sun would warm the air over the equator, while air over the North and South Poles would be very cold. The cold, heavy polar air would flow toward the equator, forcing an upward movement of the warmed air at the equator. This air then would flow north and south toward the poles. Far from the equator, the warm air would cool and sink at the poles, where it would once again flow toward the equator. This flow from the equator to the poles and then back again would be continuous. On the real Earth, rotation influences the direction of the air flow, so the prevailing winds do not flow exactly north and south.

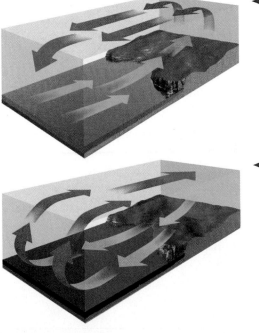

◄ During the day, the land heats up faster than the sea. Cooler sea air moves toward the land. This is called a sea breeze.

◄ At night, the land loses heat faster than the sea. Cooler air over the land moves toward the sea. This is called a land breeze.

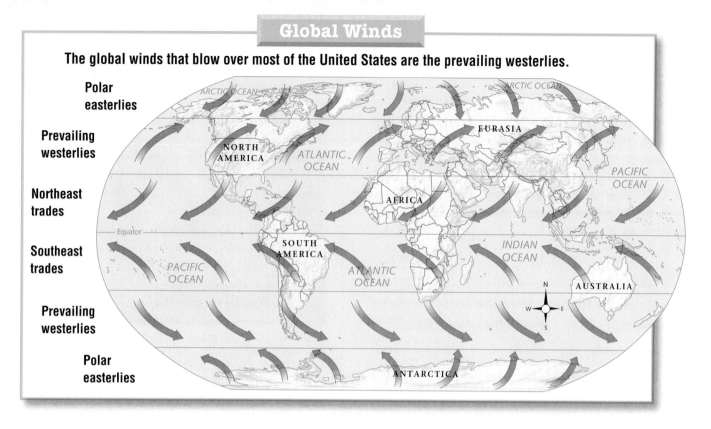

Global Winds

The global winds that blow over most of the United States are the prevailing westerlies.

Polar easterlies

Prevailing westerlies

Northeast trades

Southeast trades

Prevailing westerlies

Polar easterlies

ARCTIC OCEAN ARCTIC OCEAN NORTH AMERICA ATLANTIC OCEAN EURASIA PACIFIC OCEAN AFRICA Equator SOUTH AMERICA PACIFIC OCEAN ATLANTIC OCEAN INDIAN OCEAN AUSTRALIA ANTARCTICA

Now suppose Earth rotates from west to east. This rotation makes north and south winds curve. You can see this by placing a sheet of paper on a turntable. As the paper spins, try drawing a straight line from the center of the turntable to its edge.

Winds that blow toward the poles curve east. Winds that blow toward the equator curve west. In most of the United States, the prevailing winds curve to the east, producing west winds, or *westerlies*.

The prevailing westerlies cause most weather systems in the United States to move from west to east. Weather conditions on the West Coast today often move to the middle of the country tomorrow and from there to the East Coast the next day.

✔ **What causes weather systems to move from west to east?**

◀ The arrow of a weather vane points to the direction from which the wind is blowing.

Summary

Changes in air pressure, from uneven heating of Earth's surface and the air above it, cause the wind to blow. Local winds depend on local changes in temperature. Prevailing, or global, winds are caused by the sun's uneven heating of large parts of the atmosphere and by Earth's rotation on its axis. Prevailing winds in the United States are from the west, so weather systems tend to move from west to east.

Review

1. How does uneven heating of Earth's surface produce wind?

2. Suppose you're at the seashore on a sunny summer day. In which direction is the wind blowing? Why?

3. How do the prevailing winds affect weather systems in the United States?

4. **Critical Thinking** Shortly after daybreak at the seashore, the air temperature over sea and land is about the same. What sort of wind, if any, is blowing? Explain.

5. **Test Prep** The Global Winds map shows —
   A precipitation
   B how and where weather systems move
   C local winds
   D prevailing winds

LINKS

MATH LINK

Calculate Suppose 35 percent of the sun's rays that reach the Earth are reflected back into space. Another 15 percent are absorbed or reflected by the atmosphere. What percentage of the sun's rays would reach the Earth's surface?

WRITING LINK

Expressive Writing—Friendly Letter Suppose you are on vacation. Write a postcard describing the weather to a friend. Include temperature, wind speed, and wind direction.

MUSIC LINK

Weather Songs Many songs are about the weather or compare something to the weather. Some examples are "You Are My Sunshine," "The Itsy Bitsy Spider," and "Sunny Day." Work with a partner to see how many weather songs you can list.

TECHNOLOGY LINK

Learn more about wind by visiting the Harcourt Learning Site.
www.harcourtschool.com/ca

WELCOME TO **THE LEARNING SITE**

LESSON 2

How Do Air Masses Affect Weather?

In this lesson, you can . . .

INVESTIGATE wind speed.

LEARN ABOUT what causes weather.

LINK to math, writing, health, and technology.

Wind, which is air in motion, keeps these kites fluttering in the sky. ▼

INVESTIGATE

Wind Speed

Activity Purpose Have you ever flown a kite? A strong wind makes the kite flutter and soar through the air. A gentle breeze is usually not enough to keep the kite flying. In this investigation you will make an instrument to **measure** wind speed.

Materials

- sheet of construction paper
- tape
- hole punch
- 4 gummed reinforcements
- glue
- piece of yarn about 20 cm long
- strips of tissue paper, about 1 cm wide and 20 cm long

Activity Procedure

1. Form a cylinder with the sheet of construction paper. Tape the edge of the paper to keep the cylinder from opening.

2. Use the hole punch to make two holes at one end of the cylinder. Punch them on opposite sides of the cylinder and about 3 cm from the end. Put two gummed reinforcements on each hole, one on the inside and one on the outside. (Picture A)

3. Thread the yarn through the holes, and tie it tightly to form a handle loop.

Wind Scale			
Speed (km/h)	Description	Objects Affected	Windsock Position
0	no breeze	no movement of wind	
6–19	light breeze	leaves rustle, wind vanes move, wind felt on face	
20–38	moderate breeze	dust and paper blow, small branches sway	
39–49	strong breeze	umbrellas hard to open, large branches sway	

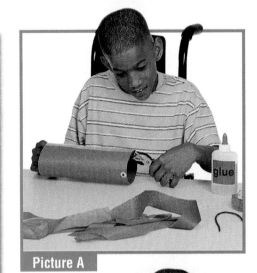

Picture A

4. Glue strips of tissue paper to the other end of the cylinder. Put tape over the glued strips to hold them better. Your completed windsock should look like the one shown in Picture B.

5. Hang your windsock outside. Use the chart above to **measure** wind speed each day for several days. **Record** your measurements in a chart. Include the date, time of day, observations of objects affected by the wind, and the approximate wind speed.

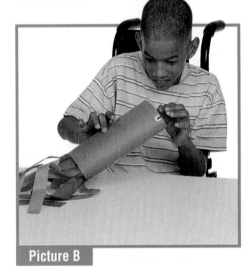

Picture B

Draw Conclusions

1. How fast was the weakest wind you **measured**? How fast was the strongest wind?

2. How did you determine the speed of the wind?

3. **Scientists at Work** *Light*, *moderate*, and *strong* are adjectives describing wind speed. Scientists often use **measurements** to describe things because, in science, numbers are more exact than words. What do you **infer** the wind speed to be if the wind is making large tree branches sway?

Investigate Further Determine which direction is north. **Measure** both wind speed and direction each day for a week. **Record** your data in a chart.

> **Process Skill Tip**
>
> The use of standard **measurements** allows people to communicate precisely. Telling someone there is a gentle breeze is not as exact as saying the wind is blowing at 8 km/h.

Air Masses and Weather

Air Masses

FIND OUT

- what makes an air mass
- what happens when air masses meet

VOCABULARY

air mass
front

If you could see the air around Earth from outer space, you would see large clumps of it forming, moving over Earth's surface, and slowly changing. These huge bodies of air, which can cover thousands of kilometers, are called air masses.

Like air heated by a hot road, an **air mass** has the same general properties as the land or water over which it forms. Two properties—moisture content and temperature—are used to describe air masses. Moist air masses form over water. Air masses that form over land are generally dry. Air masses that form near Earth's poles are cold. Air masses that form in the tropics, or areas near the equator, are warm.

✔ **What is an air mass?**

THE INSIDE STORY

Storm Front

When two air masses meet, they form a front. Thunderstorms and high winds often happen as a cold front moves through an area. After the front has passed, wind speed is lower, the sky is clear of clouds, and the temperature is lower.

1 When a cold air mass meets a warm air mass, a cold front forms. Because cold air is denser than warm air, the cold air mass pushes the warm air up.

Air Masses Meet

What do you think happens when different air masses meet? When two air masses meet, they usually don't mix. Instead they form a border called a **front**. Most of what you think of as weather happens along fronts.

A cold front is shown below. It forms when a cold air mass moves in to replace a warm air mass. The colder air mass forces the warmer air up into the atmosphere. As the warm air is pushed upward, it cools and forms clouds. Rain develops. Thunderstorms often occur along a cold front.

A warm front forms when a warm air mass moves over a cold air mass. The warm air slides up over the colder, denser air. Clouds form, sometimes many miles ahead of where the front is moving along the ground. Steady rain or snow may fall as the front approaches and passes. Then the sky becomes clear of clouds and the temperature rises.

Sometimes a front stops moving. Such a front is called a stationary front. A stationary front can stay in one place for several days. The constant fall of snow or rain along a stationary front can produce many inches of snow or flooding rains.

✔ **What is a front?**

Air Masses Move

You can see air masses moving from place to place by watching how weather forms and changes. In the investigation you built a

2 As the warm air is forced up, it cools. It can no longer have as much water vapor. The extra water vapor begins to form clouds.

3 Dense, puffy clouds with flat bottoms form along cold fronts. Sometimes these clouds are called thunderheads. They often produce lightning, thunder, and lots of rain in a short time.

device to measure wind speed. Wind speed often increases as a front approaches. Wind direction changes as a front passes.

Air pressure also changes as air masses move over an area. As a warm front moves closer, air pressure usually drops. Air pressure rises as a cold front passes.

Temperature, too, changes as a front moves over an area. Warmer air is brought into a region by a warm front. Likewise, the temperature goes down when a cold front moves through an area. The maps at the right show the movement of warm and cold fronts.

✔ **How does air pressure change as a front moves through an area?**

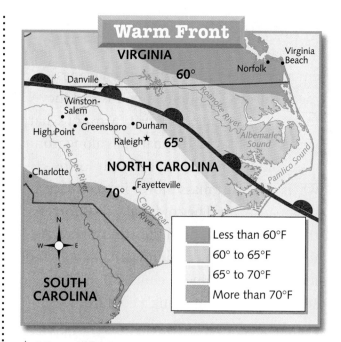

▲ A line with half-circles is the symbol for a warm front. The half-circles point in the direction the front is moving. The air is warmer behind this front than ahead of it.

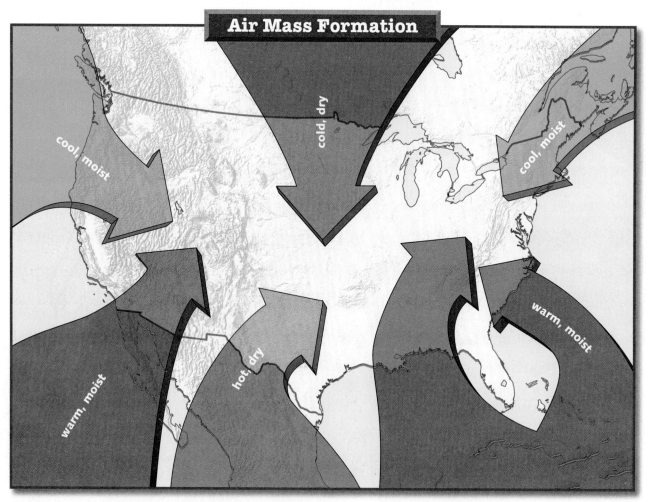

▲ This map shows where air masses form. Cool air masses are in blue colors. Warm air masses are in red colors.

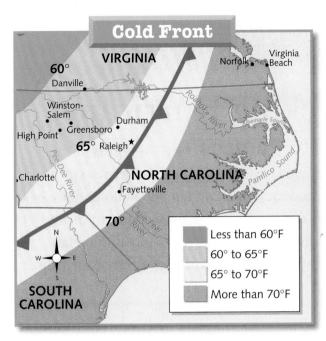

A line with triangles is the symbol for a cold front. The air is colder behind a cold front than ahead of it. The triangles point in the direction of movement. In which direction is this front moving?

Summary

Air masses form over continents and oceans. They have the same general properties as the land or water over which they form. When two air masses meet, they form a front. Fronts are the areas where most weather happens.

Review

1. What is an air mass?
2. What is a weather front?
3. How does a cold front form?
4. **Critical Thinking** Why are weather forecasts based on the movements of fronts?
5. **Test Prep** What kind of front forms when a warm air mass moves over a cold air mass?

   A a warm front   C a rain front
   B a cold front   D a hot front

LINKS

MATH LINK

Make a Rain Gauge Rain is usually measured in inches. Find out what a rain gauge is. Make one, and use it to measure daily rainfall for two weeks. Make a table to organize your data. Check your measurements against those shown in a newspaper or on TV.

WRITING LINK

Expressive Writing—Poem Use what you've learned in this chapter so far. For a third-grade student, write a short poem about weather. Use these words in your poem: *air mass, cold front, warm front, rain,* and *clouds.*

HEALTH LINK

Storm-Front Safety Find out what types of frontal weather most often affect your area. Find out how to prepare for bad weather associated with fronts. Also find out what to do to stay safe during flooding rains or heavy snows.

TECHNOLOGY LINK

Learn more about air masses by visiting this Internet site.
www.scilinks.org/harcourt

What Causes Severe Storms?

In this lesson, you can . . .

INVESTIGATE how meteorologists track the paths of hurricanes.

LEARN ABOUT how storms develop and what you can do to protect yourself from them.

LINK to math, writing, social studies, and technology.

Satellite images like this one help meteorologists track hurricanes, Earth's largest storms.

INVESTIGATE

Tracking Hurricanes

Activity Purpose Meteorologists at the National Weather Service track dangerous storms so that, if necessary, they can tell people to prepare or to move. In this investigation you will get an inside view of one of a meteorologist's most important jobs—tracking the movement of a hurricane. You will track the progress of a fictional storm—Hurricane Zelda.

Materials
- hurricane tracking chart
- 3 different-colored pencils or markers
- history table for Hurricane Zelda
- current advisory for Hurricane Zelda

Activity Procedure

1 On the hurricane tracking chart, plot the path taken by Hurricane Zelda. Use the data from the history table and the current advisory. On the tracking chart, draw a small circle for each location listed on the history table. Use an ordinary pencil for this step.

2 Your first circles show Zelda as a tropical depression. When winds exceed 39 mi/hr, a tropical depression is classified as a tropical storm and is given a name. Fill in the tropical depression circles with one color. Write *Tropical Storm Zelda* under the location where the tropical depression first becomes a tropical storm. Choose a different color for the tropical storm circles.

3 When winds exceed 74 mi/hr, a tropical storm becomes a hurricane. Write *Hurricane Zelda* under the location where Zelda first reaches hurricane strength. Use the color for the tropical storm to fill in all the circles from the one labeled in Step 2 to the one labeled here. Choose a different color for the hurricane circles, and fill in all of those.

History of Hurricane Zelda

Date and Time	Latitude	Longitude	Maximum Wind Speed
07/27 3:00 UT*	23.0°N	66.0°W	35 mi/hr
07/27 9:00 UT	23.5°N	67.0°W	35 mi/hr
07/27 15:00 UT	24.0°N	67.5°W	40 mi/hr
07/27 21:00 UT	24.5°N	67.5°W	45 mi/hr
07/28 3:00 UT	25.5°N	69.0°W	55 mi/hr
07/28 9:00 UT	27.0°N	72.0°W	60 mi/hr
07/28 15:00 UT	29.0°N	72.5°W	70 mi/hr
07/28 21:00 UT	31.0°N	73.0°W	75 mi/hr
07/29 3:00 UT	31.0°N	76.0°W	85 mi/hr

*UT means Universal Time and is the same as Greenwich Mean Time. In this 24-hour system, the time one hour after 12:00 noon is 13:00.

Current Advisory

BULLETIN

HURRICANE ZELDA FORECAST/ADVISORY NUMBER 10

NATIONAL WEATHER SERVICE MIAMI FL

15:00 UT JUL 29

HURRICANE CENTER LOCATED NEAR 32°N,
78°W AT 15:00 UT 7/29

PRESENT MOVEMENT TOWARD THE
NORTHWEST AT 20 MI PER HR

MAX. SUSTAINED WINDS 90 MI PER HR WITH
GUSTS TO 100 MI PER HR

Draw Conclusions

1. Look at the track of the storm on the map. What general patterns can you **infer** from the storm's direction and wind speed?

2. Use the tracking chart and the latest data on Zelda's speed and direction to **predict** where and when the storm will strike the coast.

3. **Scientists at Work** Scientists who track hurricanes often **predict** using probabilities. They list the probability of a storm's striking a spot on the coast as low, medium, or high. To which parts of the coastline would you give low, medium, and high probabilities of being hit by Hurricane Zelda?

Process Skill Tip

When you use data to **predict**, you need to decide whether you should use only the most recent patterns shown by the data or the pattern shown overall, by the whole set of data.

Severe Storms

Thunderstorms

About 2000 thunderstorms are taking place on Earth at any given moment. A **thunderstorm** can be a very strong storm with a lot of rain, thunder, and lightning.

A thunderstorm begins to form when warm, humid air is pushed high into the atmosphere. As the warm air is pushed upward, it begins to cool, and a cloud forms. Soon, the weight of the condensed water vapor becomes too much for the air to support. The water falls to the ground, pulling cool air with it.

Electric charges build up in the cloud. The charges increase until they are so strong that electricity travels through the air as lightning. It may travel between parts of the cloud or between the cloud and the Earth's surface.

The air along the path of a lightning bolt is heated to temperatures that can be greater than 28,000°C (about 50,000°F). This intense heat makes the air expand so fast that the shock waves make the sound of thunder.

Most thunderstorms are over within an hour. The precipitation and cool

FIND OUT

- how thunderstorms, hurricanes, and tornadoes form
- what to do to stay safe in severe storms

VOCABULARY

thunderstorm
hurricane
tropical storm
tornado

About 45,000 thunderstorms occur on Earth every day. They result in lightning, thunder, heavy precipitation, and sometimes hail. ▶

The large volumes of warm air being pushed upward add height to the cloud that forms. These upward movements of air, called updrafts, can reach speeds of 100 km/hr (62 mi/hr).

air moving downward through a thunder-cloud stop more warm air from moving up into the cloud. Sometimes, however, the cool air rushing down to the Earth's surface pushes more warm air upward to form another thundercloud.

✔ **Why do most thunderstorms stop?**

Precipitation forms a cool downdraft, a downward movement of air, near the original warm updraft. This cool air eventually shuts off the thunderstorm's fuel supply, the warm air below. When it does, the storm weakens and breaks up.

Thunderstorm Safety

Lightning that travels between a cloud and the Earth's surface can be deadly. It is usually attracted to the highest point in the area and to materials that easily conduct electricity, such as water, wiring, and metals. Here are some rules that can protect you in a thunderstorm:

1. If you are outside, try to get indoors. Avoid small buildings that are far from other buildings.
2. Don't touch faucets, plumbing pipes, electric outlets, or telephones with cords, except in an emergency.
3. If you can't get indoors, you will be safe in a car, as long as you are not touching any of the car's metal parts.
4. If you are out in the open, lie down flat.
5. Don't take shelter under a tree.
6. Stay out of water. If you are in a boat, get to shore as soon as a storm threatens, even if it seems far away.

Thunderstorm updrafts can carry moisture all the way to the edge of the stratosphere, where it forms a flat-topped, anvil-shaped cloud.

Falling ice crystals gather water droplets that freeze to form a coating around them. The lumps—called hailstones—are carried upward by updrafts and fall again. Each time this happens, the hailstones get bigger.

Hurricanes

Hurricanes are large, spiraling storm systems that can be as much as 600 km (about 372 mi) across. They can travel for thousands of kilometers and last for more than a week. Their winds can reach speeds of 300 km/hr (about 186 mi/hr).

A hurricane starts as a low-pressure area over an ocean. This area is called a tropical depression, because the air pressure is low, or "depressed." Winds blow into the low-pressure area, and the rotation of the Earth causes them to spiral around the low. If the winds reach a constant speed of 63 km/hr (about 39 mi/hr), the tropical depression is a **tropical storm**. About half of the tropical storms that form each year develop winds that exceed 119 km/hr (about 74 mi/hr). When the winds reach this speed, the storms are hurricanes.

THE INSIDE STORY

Anatomy of a Hurricane

The center of a hurricane, called the eye, is about 20 km (13 mi) wide. Within the eye the winds drop and there is no rain. The eye is caused by dry, cool air that is pulled down from above.

Around the eye is the eye wall. This area is the most intense part of the storm. The warm, wet air that rushes to the center of a hurricane is pulled upward in the eye wall. As the air travels upward, it causes low pressure at the surface, pulling in more air.

Heat and moisture from below feed both the upward-moving and the downward-moving air. As long as the storm stays over warm water, it can continue to strengthen.

The spiral is made up of cumulus clouds that can stretch 12 km (about 8 mi) into the atmosphere.

The hurricane's fastest winds spiral around the eye in the eye wall.

Warm, wet air is pulled into the base and the sides of the hurricane.

When a hurricane reaches land, extremely strong rains can cause flooding, and violent winds can destroy buildings. Waves of up to 12 m (about 40 ft) high hit the shoreline, and a storm surge of water up to 3 m (about 10 ft) high is also pushed ahead of the storm. These can cause serious damage to beaches and barrier islands.

✔ **What causes the winds to rush toward hurricanes?**

Hurricane Safety

Meteorologists carefully track hurricanes by satellite so that people can be warned well before a hurricane affects their area. If you live in the area where a hurricane is approaching, you should follow these safety rules:

1. If your home is sturdy and on high ground, stay there. If not, go to a shelter.
2. Bring inside or tie down any loose outdoor objects that might be damaged or cause damage if the storm blows them around.
3. Board up windows, or crisscross them with tape to prevent the glass from shattering.
4. Make sure you have medical supplies, canned food, fresh water, flashlights, candles, a portable radio, and extra batteries. You should have enough supplies for about two weeks.
5. If the eye of the hurricane passes over your area, it may seem safe to go outside. But dangerous weather will return very soon. Listen to your radio to learn when it is safe to go outside.

Cool, dry air is pulled down into the eye of the hurricane. As a result the eye is a place of calm and quiet. However, it is quiet only for a short time. As the storm moves, the eye wall with its extreme weather once again moves over an area.

The hurricane is pushed by the prevailing winds at 15–40 km/hr (about 9–25 mi/hr).

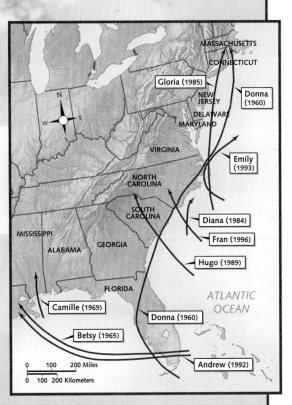

This map shows the tracks of some of the strongest hurricanes to reach the United States since 1960. Which states seem most at risk from these storms? ▶

MASSACHUSETTS
CONNECTICUT
Gloria (1985)
NEW JERSEY
Donna (1960)
DELAWARE
MARYLAND
VIRGINIA
Emily (1993)
NORTH CAROLINA
SOUTH CAROLINA
Diana (1984)
Fran (1996)
MISSISSIPPI
Hugo (1989)
ALABAMA
GEORGIA
FLORIDA
ATLANTIC OCEAN
Camille (1969)
Donna (1960)
Betsy (1965)
Andrew (1992)

0   100   200 Miles
0 100 200 Kilometers

Tornadoes

Far from the ocean, an area of the Great Plains from northern Texas through North and South Dakota has hundreds of Earth's most violent storms each year. This area is known as Tornado Alley.

A **tornado** is an intense windstorm that often forms within a severe thunderstorm. The winds of a tornado spin in a column of air that extends from the bottom of a thundercloud. The swirling updrafts can reach speeds of 480 km/hr (about 300 mi/hr). When a tornado touches the ground, its winds can destroy almost everything in their path.

✔ **What kind of storm can cause a tornado?**

Tornado Safety

When you hear a tornado warning or see a tornado, act quickly.

1. Stay inside, if possible. However, some homes, such as mobile homes, are not sturdy enough to withstand the force of a tornado.
2. Go to an inside room on the lowest floor of the building. A basement is best, but an inside hallway or bathroom is good. Stay away from windows and doors.
3. Stay underneath a staircase, a bed, or a strong table or desk.
4. If you can't get inside a building, lie in a ditch with your hands over your head. Don't stay in a car or other vehicle.

A small funnel begins to form at the bottom of a wall cloud, a circular bulge on the bottom of a thundercloud. Strong updrafts are already present in this bulge. With Doppler radar, meteorologists can detect tornadoes as they form in clouds.

◄ The swirling funnel starts to descend. By the time the funnel is visible, the winds may already be swirling debris around on the ground below.

Summary

Lightning, thunder, high winds, hail, and tornadoes can accompany thunderstorms. Hurricanes are large, spiraling storms with high winds and heavy rain. Tornadoes are violently rotating columns of air that can form in severe thunderstorms. The winds of a tornado can be exceptionally destructive.

Review

1. Why do hurricanes form over oceans?
2. Why is a mobile home an unsafe place to be during a tornado?
3. **Critical Thinking** Why do most thunderstorms form in the afternoon?
4. **Test Prep** The most violent weather in a hurricane is in the —

   A eye   **C** downdraft

   B eye wall   **D** spiral

◄ The funnel touches the ground. If this tornado is like many others, it will travel for about 15 minutes in a north-easterly direction at about 55 km/hr (34 mi/hr). It may cause a path of destruction about 140 m (459 ft) wide and about 15 km (9 mi) long.

LINKS

MATH LINK

Rates During a thunderstorm, you hear thunder after you see the lightning that causes it. You can figure out how far away a thunderstorm is, based on the difference between the speed of light and the speed of sound. If there is a lapse of 5 seconds between seeing the lightning and hearing the thunder, the storm is about 1.6 km (1 mi) away. How far away is the storm if the lapse is 12 seconds?

WRITING LINK

Informative Writing—Explanation Find out about waterspouts. Write and illustrate a short magazine article for your classmates that explains what waterspouts are, how and where they form, and what effects they have.

SOCIAL STUDIES LINK

Geography Rotating tropical storms can form over the Indian and western Pacific Oceans. Learn more about these storms and the damage they can do. What are these storms called?

TECHNOLOGY LINK

Learn more about tornadoes and the people who study them by viewing *Tornado Tracking* on the **Harcourt Science Newsroom Video** in your classroom video library.

Major Events in Weather Forecasting

In ancient times, weather predictions were based on superstitions. It seemed to make sense that good weather depended on the happiness of the gods. Yet as early as the year 100, Egyptian scientists showed that air expanded when it was heated. This early discovery led to other advances in meteorology, the study of weather.

Observing Weather Systems

In 1735 scientists observed that the sun heated areas near the equator more strongly than areas north or south of the equator. They also discovered that as air above the equator expands, it moves toward the cooler latitudes. This movement results in a global wind pattern, which causes a global weather pattern.

This discovery was followed by the discovery of the "trade winds" north and south of the equator and other wind zones in the Northern Hemisphere. In 1835 French physicist Gustave Coriolis described the movement of air masses north and south of the equator. He showed how winds north or south of the equator curve in different directions. Coriolis realized that these curved air routes were caused by the rotation of Earth.

Modern Forecasting

Wind vanes had long been used to determine wind direction, but it wasn't until the 1600s that instruments were invented that could accurately measure other weather conditions. In 1644 the first barometer was

The History of Weather Forecasting

300 B.C.
Aristotle writes *Meteorologica,* a book about weather observations.

1902
Scientists discover that the atmosphere has layers. The troposphere and stratosphere are identified.

400 B.C.   A.D. 1600   A.D. 1700   A.D. 1800

1600
Early weather instruments are invented.

1835
Coriolis discovers what is later called the "Coriolis Effect."

1890
Congress forms an agency called the Weather Bureau, later renamed the National Weather Service.

made. In 1754 G. D. Fahrenheit made the first mercury thermometer.

At least 100 years ago, scientists knew that they could improve their forecasts if they had measurements from enough weather stations around the world. Today there are tens of thousands of weather stations. Each station takes many measurements—temperature, humidity, cloud cover, wind speed and direction, and barometric pressure. Modern communication systems allow scientists to share this information almost instantly. This allows warnings to be issued to people who might be affected by severe weather events.

Weather satellites, first launched in the 1960s, provide the most important data for modern weather forecasting. Satellite data helps scientists understand the global forces that cause local weather conditions. Today countries around the world share satellite weather data.

THINK ABOUT IT

1. What causes winds to curve?

2. What is the most important instrument for weather forecasters today? Explain.

Jacob Bjerknes discovered the warm current, called El Niño, that sometimes produces severe weather along the Pacific coast.

1950s
Bjerknes makes the connection between the El Niño current and certain reversed weather patterns.

1980s
Doppler radar is first used.

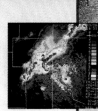

A.D. 1900   A.D. 2000

1960s
The first weather satellites are launched.

NIMBUS SPACECRAFT

1990s
International cooperation and the use of satellites increases understanding of worldwide weather patterns.

Carolyn Kloth

METEOROLOGIST

"A lot of people tend to think that you need to be able to look out of a window to assess the weather. With the use of radar, weather satellites, and all of the other weather data available, you can do the job almost anywhere."

From the time she was in elementary school, Carolyn Kloth knew what she wanted to do—fly airplanes and chase storms. Today Ms. Kloth is doing both of these things as a pilot and a meteorologist at the National Severe Storms Forecast Center in Kansas City, Missouri. She specializes in tracking severe thunderstorms and giving information about them to airplane pilots.

At the severe storms center, Ms. Kloth receives weather data every hour from across North America. The data includes images of cloud patterns, locations of fronts, and the number of lightning strikes. She also studies measurements of air pressure, humidity, precipitation, and temperature, both at the ground and at various levels in the atmosphere. Once all the data has come in, Ms. Kloth uses computers to analyze it. Then she predicts where severe thunderstorms are likely to form across the continent and over nearby coastal waters.

Ms. Kloth issues severe storm warnings to pilots for any storm that has winds of more than 26 m/s, hail larger than 19 mm in diameter, or clouds that may form tornadoes. She finds that about 1 percent of all thunderstorms fit into one or more of those categories. The warnings that Ms. Kloth issues help pilots avoid thunderstorms and result in safer and more comfortable flights.

THINK ABOUT IT

1. How can Ms. Kloth gather weather data without looking out a window?
2. How do you think Ms. Kloth's experience as a pilot helps her in her job at the National Severe Storms Forecast Center?

A large storm system

Relative Wind Speed

What is a way to measure relative wind speed?

Materials

- pattern (TR p.107)
- cardboard
- scissors
- permanent marker
- plastic straw
- long pencil
- masking tape
- paper fastener
- small paper cup

Procedure

1 **CAUTION** Be careful when using scissors. Trace the pattern pieces onto the cardboard and cut them out. Add the scale markings.

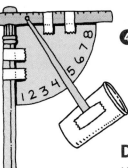

2 Cut a hole for the pencil in the middle of the straw. Push the pencil eraser into the hole. Tape the straw and pencil to the corner of the cardboard wedge.

3 Use the fastener to attach the cardboard strip. Tape the cup to the strip.

4 Push the pencil point into the ground in an open, windy area. Observe and record relative wind speed twice a day for one week. Use the table on page B45 to help you match gauge readings to actual wind speeds.

Draw Conclusions

How did the gauge help you measure wind speed?

Weather Fronts

How can water model a weather front?

Materials

- tall, clear jar
- hot and cold tap water
- pitcher
- food coloring
- thermometer

Procedure

1 Fill the jar halfway with cold water.

2 Fill the pitcher with hot water. Add 10 drops of food coloring.

3 Tilt the jar of cold water. Then slowly trickle the hot water down the inside of the jar. Slowly put the jar upright. Observe what happens in the jar.

4 Use the thermometer to measure the temperature of the hot water in the jar. Carefully move the thermometer down to measure the cold water in the jar. Can you find the front by using the thermometer?

Draw Conclusions

How did the hot water and cold water interact? How were they like air masses?

Chapter 2 Review and Test Preparation

Vocabulary Review

Use the terms below to complete the sentences. The page numbers in ( ) tell you where to look in the chapter if you need help.

local winds (B41) **thunderstorm** (B52)
prevailing winds (B41) **hurricane** (B54)
air mass (B46) **tropical storm** (B54)
front (B47) **tornado** (B56)

1. Global winds that blow constantly from the same direction are known as ____.

2. Winds that are caused by temperature changes in an area are called ____.

3. A large body of air that has the same characteristics throughout is an ____.

4. A ____ forms when two air masses meet.

5. A storm that produces rain, thunder, and lightning is called a ____.

6. A ____ is a spinning column of air that dangles from the bottom of a thunder-cloud.

7. When winds exceed 39 mi/hr, a tropical depression becomes a ____.

8. A strong storm that forms over the ocean and has a central eye is a ____.

Connect Concepts

Complete the concept map by filling in the blanks below.

> **Severe storms include:**
> 9. _____
> 10. _____
> 11. _____
> **Which are related to:**
> 12. _____
> **Air masses collide at:**
> 13. _____
> **Air masses are pushed by:**
> 14. _____

Check Understanding

Write the letter of the best choice.

15. The winds that move air masses across land and water are caused by —
    - **A** the thinning of the atmosphere at high elevations
    - **B** uneven heating of Earth by the sun
    - **C** Earth's ozone layer absorbing ultraviolet energy
    - **D** the aurora borealis

16. A passing front usually brings ____.
    - **F** a change of weather
    - **G** a hurricane or tornado
    - **H** warmer weather
    - **J** cooler weather

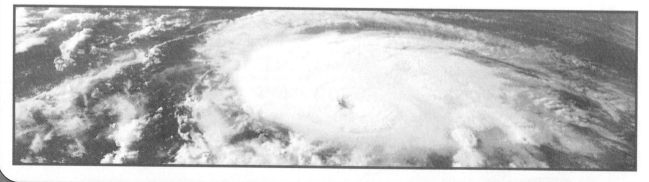

17. A continental air mass from Canada is about to move into your area. What can you expect the weather to become?

A warmer and drier

B warmer and wetter

C cooler and wetter

D cooler and drier

18. Local winds are caused by —

F air moving from the land to the sea

G air moving from the sea to the land

H air moving from an area of high pressure to an area of low pressure

J uneven heating of the oceans

19. What happens to air pressure as a warm front moves toward and then over an area?

A First it drops, then it rises.

B First it rises, then it drops.

C It depends on where you live.

D It depends on local winds.

20. The most violent weather in a hurricane is in the —

F central eye   H downdraft

G eye wall   J outer edge

21. If you see a tornado while you are outside, you should —

A hold onto a tree

B lie down in a ditch

C stay in a car

D stand by a building

22. Which storms are usually the shortest?

F thunderstorms   H hurricanes

G blizzards   J tornadoes

Critical Thinking

23. You hear a weather report that a cold front is coming. What weather changes can you expect?

24. Suppose you watch the weather report each day for five days. Each day the average temperature is the same and the air pressure doesn't change. What could be happening?

25. Which do you predict would heat up faster on a sunny day—a pond or a meadow? Explain.

Process Skills Review

26. How is a **measurement** of wind speed different from a word description of air speed?

27. You hear a clap of thunder and then you see a flash of lightning. What can you **infer**?

28. **Predict** whether breezes at the seashore during the day will blow from the land to the sea or from the sea to the land.

Performance Assessment

Fronts

Use a smooth, waterproof globe and colored water to demonstrate the effect of Earth's rotation on wind direction in the Northern Hemisphere. First, demonstrate how winds would blow if Earth didn't rotate. Then, show the effect of rotation. Summarize your results with a diagram.

Chapter 3

LESSON **1**
How Can Weather Be
Predicted?   **B66**

LESSON **2**
What Is Climate and
How Does It Change?   **B74**

SCIENCE AND TECHNOLOGY   **B82**

PEOPLE IN SCIENCE   **B84**

ACTIVITIES FOR HOME
OR SCHOOL   **B85**

CHAPTER REVIEW AND
TEST PREPARATION   **B86**

Weather Prediction and Climate

Does weather begin or end?
Or does it just keep moving from
place to place? Many things
contribute to making weather
and to changing it.

Vocabulary Preview

forecast
station model
surface map
weather balloon
weather map
climate
microclimate
El Niño
greenhouse effect
global warming

≡ FAST FACT

The United States is a country of many weather extremes.
Below are some record-breaking weather measurements.

Heavy Weather		
What	**Where**	**How Much**
Highest Temperature	Death Valley, CA	134°F
Lowest Temperature	Prospect Creek, AK	⁻79.8°F
Heaviest Snowfall	Mount Shasta, CA	189 in.
Most Snow in a Year	Mount Rainier, WA	1224.5 in.
Strongest Wind	Mount Washington, NH	231 mi/hr
Most Rain in a Year	Kukui, HI	739 in.

Each summer an average of 6–12 tropical storms form in the Atlantic Ocean, the Caribbean Sea, or the Gulf of Mexico and move toward the United States. If a storm's winds reach 74 miles an hour or more, the storm is called a hurricane.

FAST FACT

In 1816 a volcano in Asia blew huge amounts of dust into the atmosphere, blocking some of the sun's rays. That year average temperatures around the world dropped several degrees. In June there were even a few days of snow in the northeastern United States.

How Can Weather Be Predicted?

In this lesson, you can . . .

INVESTIGATE how to make a station model.

LEARN ABOUT methods and tools for predicting weather.

LINK to math, writing, social studies, and technology.

One way to collect data from a storm is to fly into it. This plane carries meteorologists and their equipment into the eye of a hurricane.

Making a Station Model

Activity Purpose Throughout the United States hundreds of weather stations **collect data** on local weather conditions. In this investigation you will learn how to make a station model that records weather conditions in your area.

Materials
- weather station

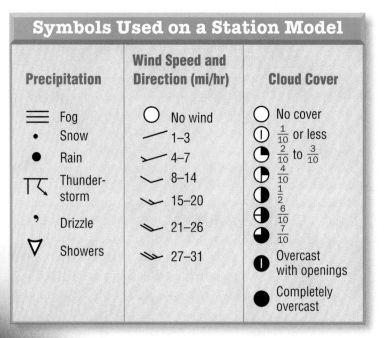

Symbols Used on a Station Model		
Precipitation	**Wind Speed and Direction (mi/hr)**	**Cloud Cover**
≡ Fog	◯ No wind	◯ No cover
• Snow	╱ 1–3	◐ $\frac{1}{10}$ or less
● Rain	⤙ 4–7	◗ $\frac{2}{10}$ to $\frac{3}{10}$
⊤⌐ Thunderstorm	⤛ 8–14	◑ $\frac{4}{10}$
' Drizzle	⤜ 15–20	◑ $\frac{1}{2}$
▽ Showers	⤝ 21–26	⊕ $\frac{6}{10}$
	⤞ 27–31	◗ $\frac{7}{10}$
		◉ Overcast with openings
		● Completely overcast

Activity Procedure

1 Using the weather station or other appropriate tools, **measure** and **record** the current weather conditions. Include temperature, air pressure, wind speed and direction, amount of precipitation, and cloud cover.

2 Use symbols from the table on page B66 to **record** your station model for four days in a chart.

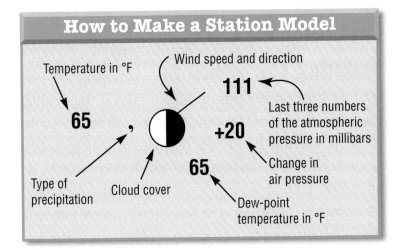

How to Make a Station Model

Temperature in °F

Wind speed and direction

111

Last three numbers of the atmospheric pressure in millibars

65

+20

65

Change in air pressure

Type of precipitation

Cloud cover

Dew-point temperature in °F

3 Use your observations to **predict** what the weather for Day 5 will be like. **Record** your prediction for Day 5. Then **record** the actual weather for Day 5.

Draw Conclusions

1. How did the station-model symbols help you summarize and **record data**?

2. How did making station models for four days give you information to **predict** the weather? What other information do you **infer** might be useful in predicting the weather?

3. **Scientists at Work** Meteorologists must carefully **measure** conditions to **gather** and **record data** to put together maps that will help them **predict** the weather. How would the measurements from a weather satellite differ from those that you took? How would this be helpful to meteorologists?

Investigate Further Try making a long-range weather forecast. After **recording data** on weather conditions from several station models, **predict** the weather for the next three days. Then write a summary report that includes data collected and conclusions drawn from that data.

Process Skill Tip

As you **gather data**, you often need to **measure**. Measurements should be carefully checked before they are recorded. The recorded information should be checked again to make certain that it is accurate.

Weather Prediction

Forecasting the Weather

FIND OUT

- **how meteorologists make station models and surface maps**

- **what tools and technology meteorologists use to forecast weather**

VOCABULARY

forecast

station model

surface map

weather balloon

weather map

One of the greatest benefits of meteorology is the weather **forecast**, a prediction of what the weather will be like in the future. Before making their forecasts, meteorologists make a station model for each location from which they have data. A **station model** is an arrangement of symbols and numbers that show the weather conditions recorded at a weather station. Station models are shown on daily maps from the National Weather Service. From the station models meteorologists construct a surface map. A **surface map** includes station models and information about fronts and about centers of high pressure and low pressure.

Although large weather systems are complex, most of the tools for collecting data at each station are simple. Many of these

Some instruments can measure several conditions at once. This device measures both the temperature and the relative humidity. ▶

▲ The National Weather Service launches more than 1000 weather balloons every day to gather information from the troposphere.

▲ Weather satellites view the Earth from heights greater than 35,000 km (about 22,000 mi) above the surface. In a single view, they give a clear picture of atmospheric conditions across the country.

tools are placed inside an instrument shelter. The shelter protects the instruments inside from sun, rain, and wind, but it allows air from outside to reach them. It is usually placed in a grassy area that does not collect or reflect heat as concrete does.

Instruments inside the shelter include a thermometer and a barometer. They may also include thermometers that record the highest and lowest temperatures of the day, and instruments that keep a continual record of changes in temperature and air pressure. Outside the shelter is a rain gauge. Also outside is an anemometer.

Meteorologists read the shelter's instruments at regular intervals. They also take measurements to find the *dew point*, the temperature at which water vapor in the air will condense. The closer the temperature of the air is to the dew point, the higher is the air's relative humidity.

Weather forecasters also use information about conditions high above the ground. They record data on how cloudy it is, the types of clouds, their movement, and their height. Forecasters may also release balloons into the atmosphere. A **weather balloon** carries a package of instruments that record data about temperature, air pressure, and humidity. This data is transmitted back to the ground by radio. The instruments work at heights up to about 30,000 m (100,000 ft).

✔ **Name three instruments used in weather forecasting.**

Weather forecasters are often more interested in how the pressure has changed than in its current measurement. Some barometers are connected to instruments that keep a record of every change. ▶

▲ As the cups of an anemometer catch the wind, they spin. A dial shows the wind speed. The wind vane swings with the wind and shows wind direction.

◀ Doppler radar is one of meteorology's newest tools. Not only can it identify storms, but it can also detect the motion and speed of the winds inside a storm. This is especially useful in forecasting severe weather conditions such as tornadoes.

Weather Maps

The weather in any one place is part of a larger pattern. Local weather is produced by a combination of atmospheric conditions that are both nearby and far away. Because of this, the best way to communicate information about the weather is with a map. A **weather map** shows data about recent weather conditions across a large area. It shows precise data for separate locations, and it shows how this data relates to each other. Weather maps are useful tools for making forecasts.

The National Weather Service (NWS) is the main source of weather maps in the United States. Several times each day, forecasters at about 350 major weather stations (and many smaller ones) around the country send data to the NWS. The NWS plots this information on surface maps. New surface maps are prepared every three or six hours.

By comparing the information from the station models on a surface map, NWS meteorologists can identify larger patterns in the weather. They mark maps to show storms, regions of high or low pressure, and fronts. They add information sent by radio from weather satellites, weather balloons, and ocean buoys. The final maps show recent weather conditions across the nation.

The maps on the next page show a low-pressure system passing through New England. On the top map, the area ahead

A weather map helps to show what is happening nearby. Fronts, pressure systems, precipitation, and temperature are often shown on weather maps. The symbols used on weather maps are the same all over the world. Using standard symbols allows everyone to share data about the weather, wherever the data has been collected.

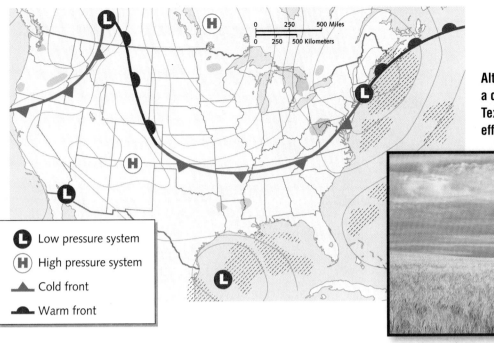

Legend:
- **L** Low pressure system
- **H** High pressure system
- ▲ Cold front
- ● Warm front

Although the map shows a cold front approaching Texas, it hasn't had any effect on the weather yet. ▼

of the system has rainy weather, because of the air mass that hangs over the ocean. Station models from Cape Cod would show warm temperatures, southwest winds, and heavy cloud coverage.

The map at the bottom of the page shows the United States 24 hours later. A cold front has moved through the area, bringing the changes that you might expect. The warm, humid air has been pushed far off the coast, and the weather has become sunny and cooler. These are common changes as weather systems move across the country, pushed by the prevailing westerlies.

Meteorologists use weather maps like these to help predict how the weather will change. By also reading the station models on both sides of a front, meteorologists can predict what the air masses will do next.

✔ **What will the weather just behind a cold front be like?**

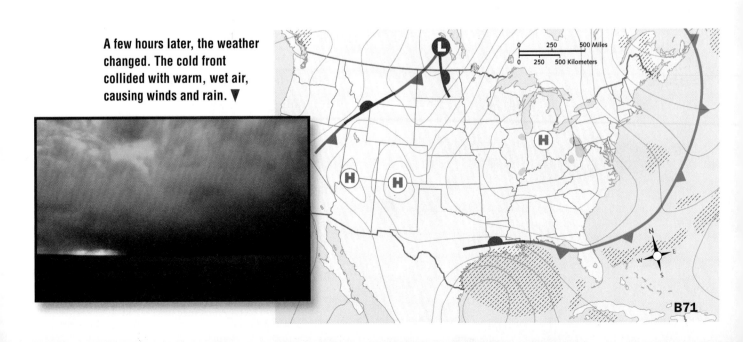

A few hours later, the weather changed. The cold front collided with warm, wet air, causing winds and rain. ▼

▲ A satellite image shows the intensity of thunderstorms, but it cannot pinpoint where tornadoes are likely to form.

▲ Winds blowing toward a Doppler radar tower show up as blue-green. Winds blowing away show up as yellow-red. When these colors appear next to each other, a tornado is likely to form.

Satellite and Doppler Technology

Advances in technology have helped make weather forecasts more and more accurate. Two developments, weather satellites and Doppler radar, have actually helped save many lives. Because of these devices, forecasters have been able to warn people of dangerous weather.

Weather satellites have been orbiting Earth since the 1960s. They are especially useful for tracking the paths of hurricanes and large winter storms. The earliest satellites gave meteorologists their first look at clouds over the Earth and allowed them to track storms far out at sea. Today, weather satellites can measure humidity and temperature and even detect fog forming at night.

Additional weather data is collected by a network of Doppler radar stations across the country. Doppler radar uses the reflection of radio waves to accurately measure wind speeds and precipitation. It can also determine the direction of winds. Information about wind direction is extremely important in forecasting

◄ Tornadoes form from funnel-shaped thunderclouds. Although these storms last a short time and cover a small area, they cause extreme damage. The winds in a tornado can approach speeds of 480 km/hr (about 300 mi/hr).

tornadoes. Doppler radar detects the opposing directions of rotating winds. When meteorologists see these conditions, they can issue tornado watches and warnings to communities that are likely to be affected.

✔ **How do weather satellites and Doppler radar help meteorologists forecast severe weather?**

Summary

Meteorologists use data collected at weather stations to make surface maps. These maps include station models and symbols for systems such as fronts and for centers of high and low pressure. The information in station models is gathered using a variety of tools. Weather maps also use data collected by weather satellites, Doppler radar, and weather balloons.

Review

1. What is a station model?
2. What does Doppler radar show?
3. Why aren't instrument shelters built on concrete surfaces?
4. **Critical Thinking** If the National Weather Service doubled the number of its employees and the amount of its equipment, would its forecasts become twice as accurate as they are now? Explain your answer.
5. **Test Prep** Which weather prediction tool is most useful for identifying conditions under which a tornado might form?

   A weather maps   **C** Doppler radar

   B surface maps   **D** weather satellites

LINKS

MATH LINK

Forecasting Suppose a cold front has traveled 800 km from the Great Plains to the Great Lakes over the past 24 hours. Buffalo, New York, is 400 km from the cold front now. Assuming the front continues to travel at the same speed, in how many hours will the front reach Buffalo?

WRITING LINK

Narrative Writing—Story The writer Mark Twain once said, "Everyone talks about the weather, but no one does anything about it." Write a story that includes a weather saying and an explanation of what it means.

SOCIAL STUDIES LINK

How Weather Shaped the Modern World In 1588 the English navy won an important sea battle against the Spanish Armada. This event helped shape the history of the modern world. Find out how weather played an important role in this historic event.

TECHNOLOGY LINK

Learn more about weather forecasting by investigating *Umbrella or Not?* on the **Harcourt Science Explorations CD-ROM.**

What Is Climate and How Does It Change?

In this lesson, you can . . .

INVESTIGATE local weather conditions.

LEARN ABOUT climates and how they change.

LINK to math, writing, literature, and technology.

INVESTIGATE

Local Weather Conditions

Activity Purpose Why does the temperature change as you go from the city to the country? Why is a city park cooler than nearby streets and sidewalks? You know that different parts of the country often have different weather conditions. In this investigation you'll find out if places very close to each other can have different weather conditions, too.

Materials

- 4 metersticks
- 4 weather stations

Activity Procedure

1. Make a table like the one shown on page B75.

2. Choose four locations near your school to study. Select different kinds of locations, such as a shady parkway, a sunny playground, a parking lot on the south side of your school, and a ball field on the north side. For the same time on any given day, **predict** whether the temperature, wind direction, and wind speed will be the same or different at the different locations.

3. At the chosen time, four people should each take a meterstick and a weather station to a different one of the selected locations. Use the meterstick to locate a point 1 m above the ground. **Measure** and **record** the temperature at that point. Use the weather station to determine the wind direction and speed, too. Record the data in your table. (Picture A)

Picture A

Local Weather Conditions	1	2	3	4
Location				
Temperature				
Wind Direction				
Wind Speed				

4. Make a double-bar graph to show the temperatures and wind speeds recorded at all the locations. Write the wind direction at each location on the appropriate wind-speed bar.

Draw Conclusions

1. Use your table to **compare** the temperature, wind direction, and wind speed at the different locations. What differences, if any, did you find?

2. Local weather conditions affect the organisms that live in a location. Do you think wind speed or temperature is more likely to affect living organisms? Explain.

3. Based on your investigation, how would you define the phrase *local weather conditions*?

4. **Scientists at Work** Scientists learn about local weather conditions by **comparing** weather data from different locations. **Draw conclusions** about local weather conditions, based on the locations you studied. What other information is needed to support your conclusions?

Investigate Further What other factors, in addition to temperature, wind direction, and wind speed, might affect local weather conditions? **Hypothesize** about a factor that might affect local weather conditions. Then **plan and conduct a simple investigation** to test your hypothesis. Write instructions that others could follow in carrying out the procedure.

Process Skill Tip

You **compare** before you **draw conclusions** about what is the same and what is different about weather conditions in different locations.

Climates and How They Change

Climate

FIND OUT

• what determines a climate

• how human activity can affect climate

VOCABULARY

climate
microclimate
El Niño
greenhouse effect
global warming

The weather in your area probably changes from day to day and from season to season. Yet year after year many of the same weather conditions are repeated. These repeating conditions, or patterns, make up your area's climate. **Climate** is the average of all weather conditions through all seasons over a period of time. Temperature and precipitation are the major factors that determine climate. Wind speed and direction are also factors.

Temperature is also a major factor of microclimates. A **microclimate** is the climate of a very small area. You probably pass several microclimates on your way to school each day. If you live in a city, you may know that a wooded park has a cooler, wetter climate than a parking lot has. Observing microclimates, as you did in the investigation, is a good way to learn about climates.

These photos of Mount Wheeler, in New Mexico, show different climates on the slope of a high mountain. In addition to certain weather conditions, each climate has its own typical plants and animals adapted to living in that climate.

✔ **What is climate?**

At the top of the mountain, you will find a cold, dry climate with few trees or animals. ▼

▲ On the sides of the mountain, the climate is cool and moist, and there are tall trees and forest animals.

▲ At the base of the mountain, the climate is warm and dry. Desert animals and plants such as sagebrush live there.

The coast of northern Maine is covered with snow in the winter. The average daily temperature is in the 20s.

On the Outer Banks of North Carolina, winter temperatures may reach the 40s or 50s.

In Florida the average daily temperature in winter is in the 60s or 70s.

MAINE
NEW HAMPSHIRE
MASSACHUSETTS
RHODE ISLAND
CONNECTICUT
NEW JERSEY
DELAWARE
MARYLAND
VIRGINIA
NORTH CAROLINA
SOUTH CAROLINA
GEORGIA
FLORIDA

Lake Superior
Lake Michigan
Lake Huron
Lake Ontario
Lake Erie

ATLANTIC OCEAN

Gulf of Mexico

Climate and Location

The United States has many different climates. There is the cold, *polar* climate of northern Alaska and the hot, *tropical* climate of Hawai'i and Puerto Rico. Most of the country has more moderate, or *temperate*, climates. But among temperate climates, there are big differences in average temperature and precipitation. Along the East Coast of the United States, for example, average temperatures vary quite a bit—from Florida, in the south, to Maine, in the north. These temperature differences are determined by *latitude*, or the distance a place is from the equator.

Most areas near the equator have tropical climates. There the sun is directly overhead nearly all year, which causes intense heating of the Earth's surface. Farther from the equator, in temperate climates, the sun is directly overhead only part of the year, causing less heating of the Earth's surface. These temperate climates have warm summers but cold winters. Near the poles the sun is never directly overhead. The decreased heating of the Earth's surface at latitudes far from the equator results in cold, polar climates.

In addition to latitude, nearness to large bodies of water, especially the ocean, affects weather and climate. Recall that water and land heat and cool at different rates. So the ocean has a moderating effect on the air temperature of nearby land areas. Air temperatures in these areas are usually cooler in summer and warmer in winter than are places farther from the water.

✔ **Why does Florida have a warmer average temperature than Maine?**

B77

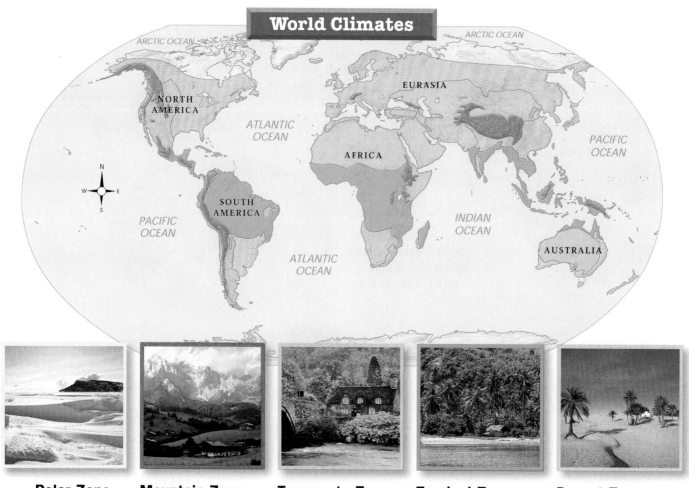

Polar Zone
Cold all year; light precipitation

Mountain Zone
Cold winters, cool summers; moderate to heavy precipitation

Temperate Zone
Cold winters, warm summers; moderate precipitation

Tropical Zone
Hot all year; moderate to heavy precipitation

Desert Zone
Hot summers, cool winters; light precipitation

World Climates

So many factors affect an area's climate that no two places on Earth have exactly the same climate. Anything that affects temperature or precipitation affects climate.

Climate is also affected by prevailing winds. In the United States, the prevailing westerlies help to moderate the hot summer climate by pushing cooling air masses across the country.

Ocean currents can affect climate, too. On the West Coast, the cold California Current flows south from the North Pacific. It keeps the summers cool along the coastal areas of Washington, Oregon, and northern California.

Yet another factor that affects climate is the shape of the land itself. A mountain can have a wet climate on the side facing the prevailing winds and a dry climate on the other side.

Although no two places on Earth have exactly the same climate, Earth's climates can be grouped into five major zones—polar, mountain, temperate, tropical, and desert. Each zone has its own weather patterns and its own typical kinds of life. For example, a polar climate supports small plants and animals like the polar bear. A tropical climate supports lush forests and animals such as monkeys.

✔ **What are the five climate zones?**

Climate Changes

Have you ever heard an older relative say, "When I was young, the winters were much colder than they are now. Why, some days the snow was piled up to the windows."

Your relative may be right. Climate does change over time. Scientists have been measuring the Earth's winds, temperatures, and precipitation for many years. Based on this data and other evidence, they know that Earth's climate is slowly warming. As recently as 50 or 60 years ago, average temperatures in parts of the United States were a degree or two cooler than they are now.

Earth's climate hasn't always been warming up. About 20,000 years ago, Earth was in the middle of an Ice Age. When the climate cools enough, large areas of Earth are covered by sheets of ice, or *glaciers*. Earth has gone through many Ice Ages. During the most recent one, glaciers covered 30 percent of Earth's surface. Evidence of this period can still be seen in the glaciers of Greenland and the Canadian Rockies.

At other times, Earth has had a warmer climate than it does today. Look at the graph to see how Earth's temperature has increased and decreased over time.

▲ One effect of El Niño's heavy rains is mudslides.

▲ During most winters, the weather in California is mild and cool, with only moderate precipitation.

Sometimes Earth's climate changes for just a year or so. The **El Niño** (EL NEEN•yoh) effect is a short-term climate change. Every two to ten years, weather conditions around the Pacific Ocean change dramatically because of changing ocean currents. The normally wet countries of Southeast Asia become dry, while heavy rains fall on the normally dry western coasts of Mexico and California. The photographs above show California during a normal winter and during a winter of heavy El Niño rains.

✔ **What evidence is there that Earth's climate is constantly changing?**

Changes in Earth's temperature might be caused by a change in the size or shape of Earth's orbit or a change in the tilt of Earth's axis.

To determine which areas of North America were once covered by ice, scientists look for evidence of glacial erosion and deposition.

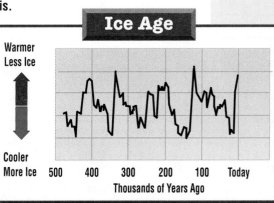

Ice Age

Warmer
Less Ice

Cooler
More Ice

500   400   300   200   100   Today

Thousands of Years Ago

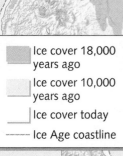

- Ice cover 18,000 years ago
- Ice cover 10,000 years ago
- Ice cover today
- Ice Age coastline

Humans Affect Climate

You know that a city is warmer than the surrounding countryside. In fact, city temperatures may be as much as 8°C (15°F) warmer than surrounding areas. Cities are warmer for several reasons. Buildings, roads, and sidewalks hold heat longer than trees and grass. Cars, buses, and trucks increase city temperatures. Large buildings block winds that might otherwise blow warm air away. All of these factors combine to make a city an area of warm air surrounded by cooler air, or a *heat island*.

Warm air also results from an effect of the burning of fossil fuels such as gasoline. Fossil fuels give off carbon dioxide when burned. Carbon dioxide in the atmosphere absorbs some of the heat given off by Earth. This process, commonly called the **greenhouse effect**, is necessary for life. Without carbon dioxide and other gases in the atmosphere, all of Earth's heat would go off into space, leaving the planet too cold for life. However, too much carbon dioxide in the air may cause climate changes.

Many scientists hypothesize that excess carbon dioxide will lead to **global warming**,

an abnormally rapid rise in Earth's average temperature. If Earth's average temperature rises just a few more degrees, the polar icecaps will begin to melt. The melting ice will raise the sea level around the world, flooding many coastal cities.

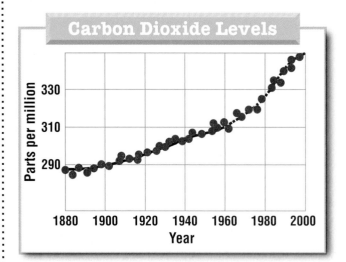

▲ The level of carbon dioxide (CO_2) in the atmosphere has increased over the past century.

▼ Earth's average temperature over the past century has increased at about the same rate.

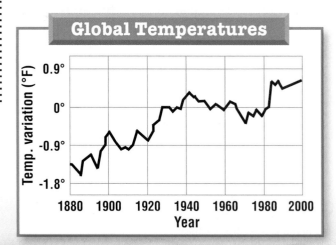

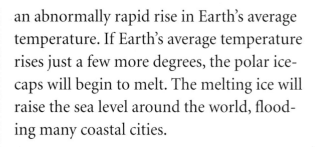

Cities have microclimates that are affected by humans. One reason is that a city has buildings, roads, and vehicles that hold or produce heat.

To reduce this possibility, many countries have agreed to try to reduce the amount of carbon dioxide released into the atmosphere. One way to do this is to burn less fossil fuel.

✓ **What are some ways in which humans affect climate?**

Summary

Climate is the average of all weather conditions through all seasons over a period of time. Temperature and precipitation are the major factors that determine climate. Earth's climate has changed over time as average temperatures have risen and fallen. Human activities, such as burning fossil fuels, can affect climate.

Review

1. What is the difference between climate and microclimate?
2. List four factors that affect climate.
3. What causes an Ice Age?
4. **Critical Thinking** During an Ice Age, what is likely to happen to the levels of oceans around the world?
5. **Test Prep** Burning fossil fuels affects climate by —
   A reducing the number of trees
   B decreasing the amount of sunlight that reaches Earth's surface
   C raising Earth's average temperature
   D changing the prevailing winds

LINKS

MATH LINK

Estimation Look at the graph on page B80 showing global temperature variations. Find the highest and lowest values. Estimate how much Earth's average temperature has varied over the last 100 years.

WRITING LINK

Persuasive Writing—Request Do you think the recent measurements of Earth's temperatures are really evidence of global warming? Write a persuasive letter to the editor of a newspaper, requesting that your point of view be printed. Be sure to include facts to support your point of view.

LITERATURE LINK

Earthmaker's Tales Read *Earthmaker's Tales: North American Indian Stories About Earth Happenings* by Gretchen Will Mayo. Earth and its atmosphere are the subjects of this collection of Native American legends about the origins of thunder, tornadoes, and other weather features.

TECHNOLOGY LINK

Learn more about changes in climate by viewing *El Niño Erosion* and *Global Warming* on the **Harcourt Science Newsroom Video** in your classroom video library.

TRACKING EL NIÑO

Scientists use satellites and other technology to scan the ocean for changes that can cause severe weather.

Why look at the ocean for weather changes?

The temperature of the ocean affects the air above it. Warm water evaporates faster than cold water and can cause more storms to form. Depending on wind patterns, the storms can affect nearby land.

Winds normally push a current of warm water westward across the Pacific Ocean, toward Australia. El Niño begins when winds pushing warm water west weaken and allow it to return to the east, toward South America. As a result, a band of unusually warm water—an El Niño current—forms across the Pacific. The warmer ocean increases the formation of clouds and storms in the Pacific. This changes weather patterns in Australia, East Africa, and

Southeast Asia, as well as in North and South America.

How do satellites and other hardware help forecast El Niño?

Meteorologists use satellites, weather balloons, ground weather stations, and radar to gather data on the atmosphere and the ocean each day.

To forecast El Niño, meteorologists add a couple of extra tools. The TOPEX/Poseidon satellite measures the surface level of the Pacific Ocean every 10 days. Although the satellite orbits 1336 km (about 830 mi) above Earth's surface, its measurements are accurate to 13 cm (about 6 in.). Because the winds that form an El Niño current raise ocean water levels in the eastern Pacific, a rise in ocean levels is a clue that El Niño is beginning.

Meteorologists also get data from a group of ocean buoys. The buoys send data on air temperature, water temperature, wind, and humidity to data centers in the United States. The information allows forecasters to quickly spot weather changes caused by El Niño.

▲ A TOPEX/ Poseidon view of the Pacific Ocean

Why is it important to know when El Niño will occur?

An El Niño pattern in the Pacific causes severe weather that can harm millions of people. An El Niño pattern occurred between late 1997 and mid-1998. As a result, storms from the Pacific pounded the west coast of North and South America. Drought struck Australia, while floods destroyed crops in Africa. Predicting El Niño events can help people prepare for these storms' damaging effects.

THINK ABOUT IT

1. Why is it important to track El Niño systems?
2. How do meteorologists use satellites to track El Niño?

WEB LINK:
For Science and Technology updates, visit The Learning Site.
www.harcourtschool.com/ca

Careers | Tornado Chaser

What They Do
Tornado chasers work in areas where tornadoes are common. They place instruments in the paths of tornadoes to collect information.

Education and Training A tornado chaser must have a background in geography, physics, meteorology, and computer science. Those who work in the field need at least a bachelor's degree.

Edward Lorenz

METEOROLOGIST

Edward Lorenz teaches meteorology at the Massachusetts Institute of Technology (MIT). Dr. Lorenz used the ideas of chaos theory to show why accurate long-range weather prediction is not possible. In his studies he observed that even the smallest change in one variable that contributes to a weather system can have a big effect on how the system develops. That means that all atmospheric conditions measured to the smallest fraction of a degree would have to be known completely to make predictions more than four or five days into the future.

After serving as a weather forecaster in the U. S. Army, Dr. Lorenz began to wonder if weather forecasting could be improved. He decided to write a computer program that would make long-range predictions. The computer model showed how much weather conditions change over time.

For the computer model, Dr. Lorenz used the numbers from an earlier run that had produced a particular weather pattern. He put the numbers back into the computer, expecting the computer to produce the same pattern. But instead of using the exact numbers carried out to six decimal places, he rounded them to three. The change was so small that he thought it wouldn't matter. But it did. The resulting weather pattern varied from the original—first a little and then more and more. He called this "the butterfly effect," because a tiny difference in weather conditions, such as the breeze caused by the flapping of the wings of a butterfly in China, could alter the weather over the United States weeks later.

THINK ABOUT IT

- Why did Dr. Lorenz hypothesize that accurate long-range weather forecasting would be impossible?

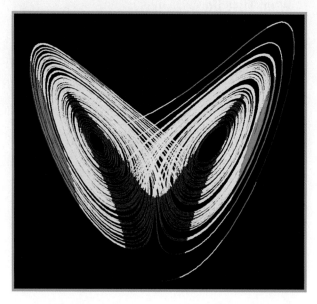

The shape produced by a computer graphing Dr. Lorenz's equations

Figuring Out Fronts

How do air masses behave when they meet?

Materials
- 22.5-cm (9-in.) glass pie plate
- 240 mL (1 cup) water, colored blue
- 240 mL (1 cup) cooking oil
- clay

Procedure
1. Use the clay to build a barrier across the middle of the pie plate.

2. Gently pour the colored water into one side of the plate and the oil into the other side.

3. Remove the barrier, disturbing the liquids as little as possible.

4. Quickly bend down and observe how the liquids move in the plate.

Draw Conclusions
Which liquid is heavier or more dense? How can you tell? What kind of air mass do you think the water represents? What does the oil represent? Where is the front?

Low Pressure

How does low pressure affect weather?

Materials
- 2 medium-sized balloons
- 2 lengths of string, each 30 cm (1 ft)

Procedure
1. Inflate the balloons to equal sizes and knot them shut.

2. Tie one end of one string to a balloon. Tie one end of the other string to the second balloon.

3. Hold the other ends of the strings and position the balloons about 7.5 cm (3 in.) apart in front of your face.

4. Blow a steady stream of air between the balloons and observe how they respond.

Draw Conclusions
The "wind" blowing between the balloons lowered the air pressure between them. How did the balloons respond? How do you think that blowing between the balloons is similar to what happens when a tornado forms?

Vocabulary Review

Use the terms below to complete the sentences. The page numbers in ( ) tell you where to look in the chapter if you need help.

forecast (B68)

station model (B68)

surface map (B68)

weather balloon (B69)

weather map (B70)

climate (B76)

microclimate (B76)

El Niño (B79)

greenhouse effect (B80)

global warming (B80)

1. Many people use a _____ to predict the weather.

2. One example of a short-term climate change is _____.

3. The current weather at a particular weather station can be shown by the numbers and symbols of a _____.

4. Scientists at the National Weather Service make a _____ to show the data collected at weather stations.

5. The process by which carbon dioxide in the atmosphere absorbs some of the heat given off by the sun is called the _____.

6. The average of an area's weather conditions through all seasons over a period of time is called _____.

7. A prediction of upcoming weather can be made with the help of data from a _____, which is released into the atmosphere.

8. Excess carbon dioxide in the atmosphere may lead to _____.

9. The climate of a small area is called a _____.

10. A prediction of upcoming weather is called a _____.

Connect Concepts

Copy and complete the idea clusters below, which describe climate.

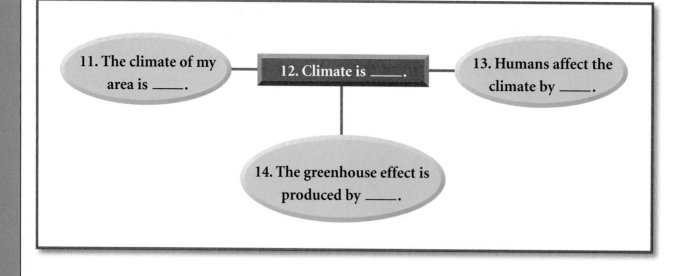

11. The climate of my area is _____.

12. Climate is _____.

13. Humans affect the climate by _____.

14. The greenhouse effect is produced by _____.

Check Understanding

Write the letter of the best choice.

15. Florida has a warmer climate than Maine because Florida —

   A is closer to the South Pole

   B is closer to the Equator

   C is nearer to the Atlantic Ocean

   D receives more precipitation

16. Most of the eastern United States and West Coast have a climate that is —

   F mountain   **H** desert

   G polar   **J** temperate

17. Scientists hypothesize that an abnormally rapid rise in Earth's average temperature would lead to —

   A the greenhouse effect

   B global warming

   C a microclimate

   D El Niño

18. Wind speed is measured with —

   F an anemometer

   G a barometer

   H a thermometer

   J a speedometer

19. Which weather prediction tool is most useful for identifying conditions under which a tornado might form?

   A weather balloon

   B Doppler radar

   C weather satellites

   D surface map

Critical Thinking

20. What would help the National Weather Service make faster, more accurate forecasts of severe weather?

21. How does the location of Hawaiʻi, in the Pacific Ocean near the equator, affect its climate?

22. What two factors in addition to temperature, wind direction, and wind speed might affect weather conditions?

Process Skills Review

23. Suppose you want to record the average weather conditions in your town on a monthly basis. What instruments would be most useful for **measuring** the conditions? How would you **gather the data**? What format would you use for the record?

24. Using the data gathered in the activity described in question 23 above, what factors might you be able to **compare**? What **conclusions** could you **draw** from the data?

Performance Assessment

Your Weather

Look at the three weather maps of the United States your teacher gives you. Arrange the maps in chronological order. Explain where the weather in your area comes from. Describe any conditions, such as mountains or large lakes, that affect your local weather.

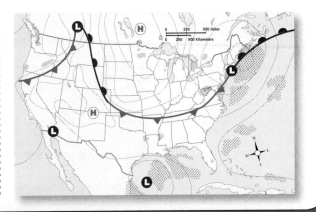

Chapter

LESSON **1**
**How Do Earth and
the Moon Compare?** B90

LESSON **2**
**How Have People
Explored Space?** B98

SCIENCE THROUGH TIME   B106

PEOPLE IN SCIENCE   B108

ACTIVITIES FOR HOME
OR SCHOOL   B109

CHAPTER REVIEW AND
TEST PREPARATION   B110

Earth and the Moon

Although Earth moves through space very rapidly, it doesn't *seem* to move at all. That's why the sun and the moon both seem to move around Earth. It took astronomers a long time to realize that Earth actually moves around the sun.

Vocabulary Preview

revolve
orbit
rotate
axis
eclipse
telescope
satellite
space probe

FAST FACT

Observatories located near growing cities are no longer very useful. The city lights and the pollution in the air make it impossible to see the stars clearly. But on the summit of Mauna Kea in Hawai'i, many miles from city lights and pollution, scientists can see the stars quite clearly.

Once Around the Sun

Planet	Earth Days
Mercury	88
Venus	224.7
Earth	365.26
Mars	687
Jupiter	4,332.6
Saturn	10,759.2
Uranus	30,685.4
Neptune	60,189
Pluto	90,777.6

The next total solar eclipse in the United States will not take place until August 21, 2017. It will move across the country from Oregon to South Carolina. You can safely view a solar eclipse the way the photograph shows.

How Do Earth and the Moon Compare?

In this lesson, you can . . .

INVESTIGATE how Earth, the moon, and the sun move through space.

LEARN ABOUT Earth and its moon.

LINK to math, writing, music, and technology.

Earth, from the surface of the moon ▽

How Earth, the Moon, and the Sun Move Through Space

Activity Purpose You may not feel as if you're moving right now, but you're actually speeding through space. Earth makes a complete spin once every 24 hours. So if you stand on the equator, you're moving at about 1730 km/hr (1075 mi/hr)! Earth also moves around the sun at about 107,000 km/hr (66,489 mi/hr). At the same time, the moon, which also spins, moves around Earth at about 3700 km/hr (2300 mi/hr). In the investigation you will **make a model** of Earth, the moon, and the sun to **compare** how they move through space.

Materials

- beach ball
- baseball
- Ping Pong ball

Activity Procedure

1 You will work in a group of four to **make a model** of the sun, Earth, and the moon in space. One person should stand in the center of a large open area and hold the beach ball over his or her head. The beach ball stands for the sun. A second person should stand far from the "sun" and hold the baseball overhead. The baseball stands for Earth. The third person should hold the Ping Pong ball near "Earth." The Ping Pong ball stands for the moon. The fourth person should **observe** and **record** what happens.

2 The real Earth moves around the sun in a path like a circle that has been pulled a little at both

ends. This shape, called an *ellipse* (ee•LIPS), is shown here. For the model, Earth should move around the sun in an ellipse-shaped path. Earth should also spin slowly as it moves around the sun. The observer should **record** this motion. (Picture A)

ellipse

Picture A

3 While Earth spins and moves around the sun, the moon should move around Earth in another ellipse-shaped path. The moon should spin once as it moves around Earth. The same side of the moon should always face Earth. That is, the moon should spin once for each complete path it takes around Earth. The observer should **record** these motions. (Picture B)

Picture B

Draw Conclusions

1. Your model shows three periods of time—a year, a month, and a day. Think about the time it takes Earth to spin once, the moon to move around Earth once, and Earth to move around the sun once. Which period of time does each movement stand for?

2. **Compare** the movements of the moon to those of Earth.

3. **Scientists at Work** Scientists often **make models** to show **time and space relationships** in the natural world. However, models can't always show these relationships exactly. How was your model of Earth, the moon, and the sun limited in what it showed?

Investigate Further Develop a testable question about the amount of sunlight that reaches Earth. Then **plan and conduct a simple investigation** to show how the amount of sunlight reaching Earth changes as Earth moves around the sun. Write instructions others can follow to carry out the procedure.

Process Skill Tip

Making a model of the sun-Earth-moon system allowed you to **use time and space relationships** to learn how objects in space move and interact.

How Earth and the Moon Compare

Earth and the Moon in Space

The moon is the brightest object in the night sky and Earth's nearest neighbor in space. Together, Earth and the moon are part of the sun's planetary system. Pulled by the sun's gravity, the Earth-moon system **revolves**, or travels in a closed path, around

FIND OUT

- about the Earth-moon system
- what causes lunar and solar eclipses
- how Earth and the moon are alike and different

VOCABULARY

revolve
orbit
rotate
axis
eclipse

❸ FIRST QUARTER
About one week after a new moon, the moon looks like a half-circle. This phase is called the first quarter because the moon is a quarter of the way around Earth.

❹ WAXING GIBBOUS
The word *gibbous* (GIB•uhs) comes from a word meaning "hump."

❺ FULL MOON
About two weeks after a new moon, we see the entire sunlit half.

❻ WANING GIBBOUS
A waning moon appears to get smaller.

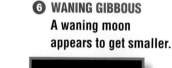

❼ LAST QUARTER
About three weeks after a new moon, the moon is three-fourths of the way around Earth.

the sun. The path Earth takes as it revolves is called its **orbit**. Earth's orbit is an ellipse, a shape that is not quite circular.

As Earth orbits the sun, it **rotates**, or spins on its axis. The **axis** is an imaginary line that passes through Earth's center and its North and South Poles. Earth's rotation results in day and night. When a location on Earth faces the sun, it is day in that place. When that location faces away from the sun, it is night.

Pulled by Earth's gravity, the moon revolves around Earth in an ellipse-shaped orbit. When the moon is closest to Earth, it is about 356,400 km (221,463 mi) away.

Like Earth, the moon rotates on its axis. However, the moon takes 27.3 Earth days to complete one rotation. This makes a cycle on the moon of one day and one night that is 27.3 Earth days long.

Even though the moon rotates, the same side of the moon always faces Earth. This is because the moon orbits Earth in 27.3 days—exactly the same amount of time it takes to rotate once on its axis.

Although the moon shines brightly at night, it does not give off its own light. We see the moon from Earth because sunlight is reflected off its surface. As the moon orbits Earth, its position in the sky changes. This produces the different shapes, or phases, of the moon we see each month. The phases of the moon, as seen from Earth, are shown in the photographs below and on page B92.

✔ **How do Earth and the moon move through space?**

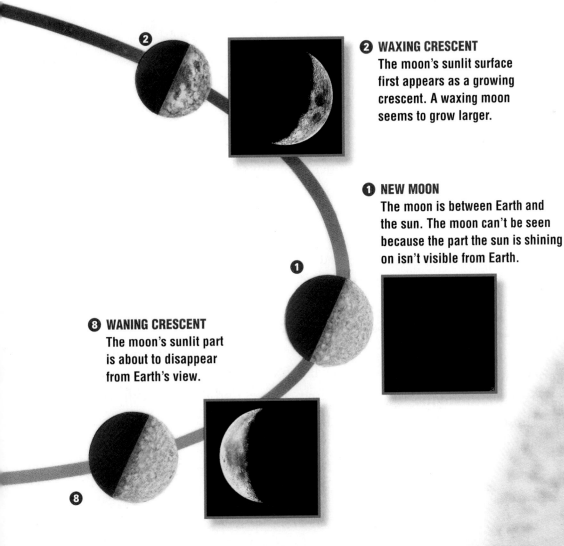

❷ **WAXING CRESCENT**
The moon's sunlit surface first appears as a growing crescent. A waxing moon seems to grow larger.

❶ **NEW MOON**
The moon is between Earth and the sun. The moon can't be seen because the part the sun is shining on isn't visible from Earth.

❽ **WANING CRESCENT**
The moon's sunlit part is about to disappear from Earth's view.

Solar Eclipse

▲ **Solar eclipse** A total solar eclipse lasts no more than 7.5 minutes. That's how long it takes for a point on Earth to rotate through the shadow of the moon.

Lunar Eclipse

▲ **Lunar eclipse** A total lunar eclipse lasts more than two hours. It may be seen from any place on Earth that is facing the moon.

Solar and Lunar Eclipses

All bodies in the solar system produce shadows in space. An **eclipse** (ee•KLIPS) occurs when one object passes through the shadow of another. A solar eclipse or a lunar eclipse may occur during a new moon or full moon, when Earth, the sun, and the moon line up.

A solar eclipse occurs when Earth passes through a new moon's shadow. During a total solar eclipse, the moon completely covers the sun. The sky darkens, and only the sun's outer atmosphere is visible. It can be seen glowing as a bright circle around the moon. A partial solar eclipse occurs when Earth passes through part of the moon's shadow.

A lunar eclipse occurs when the full moon passes through Earth's shadow. When Earth passes between the sun and the moon, it blocks the sun's light. However, Earth's atmosphere bends certain colors of light, especially red. This makes the eclipsed moon look like a dim red circle.

You may wonder why eclipses do not occur twice each month—at every new moon and full moon. This is because the moon's shadow usually passes above or below Earth, or the moon passes above or below Earth's shadow. Only seven eclipses—two lunar eclipses and five solar eclipses—occur in a single year. And most of those are partial eclipses.

✔ **How does a solar eclipse differ from a lunar eclipse?**

The Moon's Surface

When the moon first formed, its surface was hot, molten rock. As the surface cooled, it formed a rocky crust. If you look at the moon through a telescope, you can see three types of landforms—craters, highlands, and dark, flat areas.

Some moon craters are very large. Tycho (TY•koh) crater, for example, is 87 km (about 54 mi) across. Other craters are so small that a hundred of them could fit on your fingernail.

The moon also has dark, flat areas known as *maria* (MAH•ree•uh). The word *maria* is Latin for "seas." For many years people thought these flat, dark areas on the moon were seas filled with water. But maria are really areas of hardened lava.

Maria formed when hot, molten rock flowed from the interior through cracks in the moon's surface. This molten rock overflowed some craters and spread across the moon's surface. It then cooled to form a dark rock called *basalt*. The largest mare (MAH•ray) is 1248 km (about 775 mi) across. The illustration below shows craters and other landforms found on the moon's surface.

✔ **What are some landforms found on the moon's surface?**

Lunar landforms include craters, maria, ray craters, rilles, highlands, and volcanic domes. Ray craters are thought to be new craters. The "rays" formed from molten rock that splashed out. Rilles are lunar valleys. Some lunar highlands are as high as Earth's mountains. Volcanic domes may be like some volcanoes on Earth. ▶

Comparing Earth's and the Moon's Features

Earth and its moon are alike in several ways. Both are rocky and fairly dense. The same materials that make up Earth—calcium, aluminum, oxygen, silicon, and iron—are found on the moon. Craters occur on both, although there are many more craters on the moon than on Earth.

There are also important differences between Earth and the moon. Unlike Earth, the moon has no atmosphere and no liquid water. Because of this, the moon's landscape has not been eroded by wind and water. The moon's surface weathers very slowly, staying the same for millions of years.

Comparing Earth and the Moon

Earth

Moon

Craters

Both Earth and the moon have craters. However, the surface of the moon has many more craters than the surface of Earth. Many meteorites burn up in Earth's atmosphere before they reach the surface.

Weathering

Since the moon has no wind or rain, footprints left by astronauts will remain on its surface for millions of years. Most footprints left on Earth's surface are worn away within a few days.

Water

Life on Earth depends on water. Since the moon has no liquid water, it has no life. However, frozen water has recently been discovered in craters at the moon's poles.

Look at the photographs on page B96 to compare features of the moon and Earth. The photographs on the right were taken on the moon. Those on the left were taken on Earth.

✔ **Compare and contrast features of Earth and the moon.**

Summary

The moon revolves around Earth, while the Earth-moon system orbits the sun. Both Earth and the moon rotate on axes and have day-night cycles. As Earth, the moon, and the sun travel through space, they sometimes line up to produce eclipses. Many of the features on Earth and the moon are different, although some landforms occur on both.

Review

1. Why does the same side of the moon always face Earth?
2. Describe a lunar eclipse.
3. How does a mare differ from a crater?
4. **Critical Thinking** Lunar rocks are very old and do not look as if they were eroded by water. Also, no rocks have been found that contain water combined with minerals, as are found on Earth. What can you **infer** about how long the moon has been without water?
5. **Test Prep** The path that Earth takes around the sun is called its —

   A axis
   B orbit
   C cycle
   D rotation

LINKS

MATH LINK

Moon Fractions During a full moon, we see half of the moon's surface. During a first or third quarter, what fraction of the moon's surface do we see?

WRITING LINK

Narrative Writing—Story Some early people were afraid of solar eclipses. They believed that the sun might not return. They made up stories and myths to explain eclipses. For example, a myth might say that a dragon or wolf ate the sun and then spit it out again. Write a story or myth for your class explaining what happens during a solar eclipse.

MUSIC LINK

Moon Music The moon has given people many ideas for songs. Work with a group to list ideas for as many new titles of songs about the moon as you can think of. Then write a song about the moon. You may find it easier to write words to a tune you already know.

TECHNOLOGY LINK

Learn more about the discovery of ice near the moon's poles by viewing *Ice on the Moon* on the **Harcourt Science Newsroom Video** in your classroom video library.

How Have People Explored Space?

In this lesson, you can . . .

INVESTIGATE how the moon's craters were formed.

LEARN ABOUT how people explore the solar system.

LINK to math, writing, art, and technology.

Astronaut working in space ▽

INVESTIGATE

The Moon's Craters

Activity Purpose As Earth's nearest neighbor in space, the moon was the first object in the solar system that people studied. People **observed** that the moon's surface was very different from the Earth's surface. One difference was the large number of craters on the moon. In the investigation you will **make a model** of the moon's surface to **infer** how the craters formed.

Materials

- newspaper
- aluminum pan
- large spoon
- water
- flour
- safety goggles
- apron
- marble
- meterstick

CAUTION

Activity Procedure

1 Copy the table below.

Trial	Height	Width of Craters
1	20 cm	
2	40 cm	
3	80 cm	
4	100 cm	

2 Put the newspaper on the floor. Place the pan in the center of the newspaper.

3 Use a large spoon to mix the water and flour in the aluminum pan. The look and feel of the mixture should be like thick cake batter. Now lightly cover the surface of the mixture with dry flour. (Picture A)

4 **CAUTION** Put on the safety goggles and **apron** to protect your eyes and clothes from flour dust. Drop the marble into the pan from a height of 20 cm. (Picture B)

5 Carefully remove the marble and **measure** the width of the crater. **Record** the measurement in the table. Repeat Steps 4 and 5 two more times.

6 Now drop the marble three times each from heights of 40 cm, 80 cm, and 100 cm. **Measure** the craters and **record** the measurements after each drop.

Picture A

Picture B

Draw Conclusions

1. **Compare** the height from which each marble was dropped to the size of the crater it made. How does height affect crater size?

2. The Copernicus (koh•PER•nih•kuhs) crater on the moon is 91 km across. Based on your model, what can you **infer** about the object that formed this crater?

3. **Scientists at Work** Most of the moon's craters were formed millions of years ago. Scientists **use models** to **infer** events that occurred too long ago to **observe** directly. What did you infer from the model about how the moon's craters formed? What other information do you need to **draw conclusions** about the formation of the moon's craters?

Process Skill Tip

You can **use a model** to **infer** how something happened a long time ago, such as how the moon's craters formed.

Space Exploration

FIND OUT

- about the history of space exploration
- how spacesuits work

VOCABULARY

telescope
satellite
space probe

Exploring the Solar System

Thousands of years ago, people observed the night sky and recorded their observations in cave paintings and rock art. These early observations were made without telescopes or other devices. About the only things early people could see were the phases of the moon and some of the moon's larger features. They could also see some of the planets and many stars. Then, about 400 years ago, the telescope was invented. It allowed people to observe objects in space in much greater detail.

In 1609 Galileo used this telescope to observe the sun, moon, and planets. His telescope had two curved pieces of glass, or lenses, one at each end of a long tube.

900–1200	1200–1500	1500–1800

The Mayas, in Central America, built many *observatories*, or places for viewing the stars and planets. This one at Chichén Itzá, in Mexico, was built about 900.

This telescope was designed by English scientist Sir Isaac Newton in 1668. It used two mirrors and one lens to produce sharper images than Galileo's telescope could.

In 1609 the Italian scientist Galileo (gal•uh•LEE•oh) was possibly the first person to use a new invention—the telescope—to observe the sky. A **telescope** is an instrument that magnifies, or makes larger, distant objects. With this telescope Galileo observed the moon and saw mountains, valleys, and craters that had never been seen before. He also observed the phases of Venus and four moons orbiting Jupiter. About fifty years later, English scientist Sir Isaac Newton used an even better telescope to observe other objects in space.

The modern age of space exploration began in 1957, when the Soviet Union launched *Sputnik I*, an artificial satellite. A **satellite** is any natural body, like the moon, or artificial object that orbits another object. *Sputnik*, which was about twice the size of a soccer ball, carried instruments to measure the density and temperature of Earth's upper atmosphere. The United States launched its own satellite the next year. Soon both countries were launching humans into space.

✔ **How did the telescope help people learn more about objects in space?**

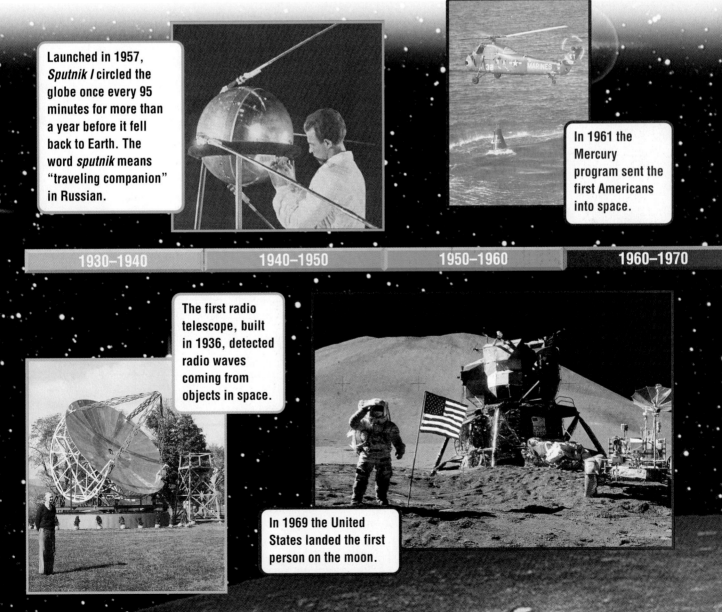

Launched in 1957, *Sputnik I* circled the globe once every 95 minutes for more than a year before it fell back to Earth. The word *sputnik* means "traveling companion" in Russian.

In 1961 the Mercury program sent the first Americans into space.

1930–1940   1940–1950   1950–1960   1960–1970

The first radio telescope, built in 1936, detected radio waves coming from objects in space.

In 1969 the United States landed the first person on the moon.

To the Moon and Beyond

One of the best-known American space programs was Project Apollo. The Apollo missions landed 12 humans on the moon between 1969 and 1972. These astronauts set up experiments and brought back samples of rock. Their work helped scientists learn more about the moon.

In 1977 the *Voyager 1* and *Voyager 2* space probes were launched. A **space probe** is a robot vehicle used to explore deep space. The Voyager space probes have sent back pictures of Jupiter, Saturn, Uranus, and Neptune. Both Voyagers are still traveling through space beyond the solar system.

Other early space probes included *Viking I* and *Viking II*, which landed on Mars in 1976, and the Pioneer probes, which used instruments to "see" through thick clouds that cover Venus. Today's scientists use the Hubble Space Telescope, satellites, and space probes to better understand Earth, the solar system, and what lies beyond.

✔ **What was Project Apollo?**

Space shuttles, which have been in use since 1981, have many uses. They lift heavy cargoes into orbit and provide labs for carrying out scientific research in space. They also provide a place to launch, bring back, and repair satellites.

1970–1980

1980–1990

Two Viking spacecraft landed on Mars in 1976. They photographed their landing sites and sent back data about Mars' soil and atmosphere.

The Hubble Space Telescope, launched in 1990, produces images five times as sharp as those from any telescope on Earth.

Spacesuits

The Apollo spacesuit below, once worn by Neil Armstrong, is a $10 million outfit made to protect an astronaut from the moon's hostile environment. The spacesuit must keep an astronaut from "cooking" in direct sunlight or freezing in cold shadows. It must provide the person who wears it with air, water, and waste removal for a moonwalk that may last up to eight hours. The spacesuit must also be flexible enough for an astronaut to walk, twist, turn, bend over, and pick up objects in the reduced gravity on the moon. Flightsuits, such as the one at the right, are much less bulky.

The visor reflects the sun's intense light.

▲ A shuttle flightsuit

Communications gear allows astronauts to talk with each other, with other astronauts in orbit, and with scientists at Mission Control.

A drinking bag is located inside the helmet.

Medical monitors check heartbeat rate and body temperature.

The spacesuit protects against extreme heat and cold and against tiny objects speeding through space.

Stretchy mesh, liquid-cooled underwear is worn under the spacesuit.

Gloves allow as much flexibility as possible.

Boots are made for walking on the moon's surface.

Space Exploration in the Future

The launch of the first modules of the International Space Station in 1998 marked the beginning of a new era in space exploration. As many as seven scientists at a time will be able to live and work in space. When completed, the station will be nearly 80 m (about 260 ft) long and have a mass of more than 455,000 kg. In the future, larger stations could have room for a thousand people or more.

Settlements may one day be built on the moon, or even on Mars. Although there are as yet no plans to build bases on the moon, they could be possible by 2020.

A moon base could be used as a research station, like those in Antarctica. To save money, some materials needed to build and run the base could come from the moon itself. For example, some of the moon's rocks contain oxygen. This oxygen could be taken from the rocks and used by people living on the moon. Recently a probe discovered enough ice at the poles to supply a moon base with water. For electricity the base could use solar energy. And some minerals could be mined from the moon and sent back to Earth for processing.

✔ **How could people live on the moon?**

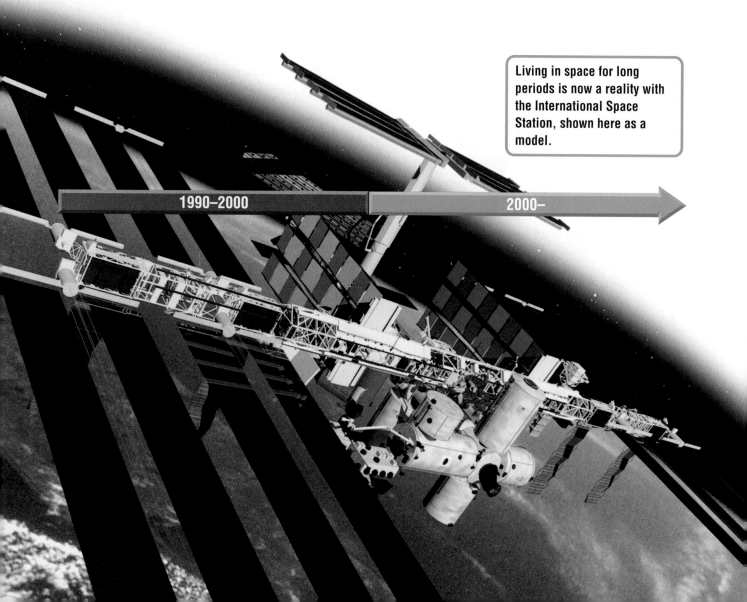

Living in space for long periods is now a reality with the International Space Station, shown here as a model.

1990–2000

2000–

Summary

People have observed and studied the moon and other objects in space since ancient times. The invention of the telescope allowed people to see features and objects that had never been seen before. Today scientists use telescopes, satellites, and space probes to study objects in the solar system and beyond. In the future, people may live and work on space stations and moon bases.

Review

1. What event marked the start of the space age?
2. What are space shuttles used for?
3. What problems have to be solved to build a permanent research station on the moon?
4. **Critical Thinking** A spacesuit weighs more than most astronauts. How can astronauts wear an outfit that is heavier than they are?
5. **Test Prep** The Apollo missions landed humans on —
   A Mercury
   B Venus
   C Mars
   D the moon

LINKS

MATH LINK

Calculation Earth spins once every 24 hours. A person standing still on the equator is moving with Earth's rotation at more than 1730 km/hr. How far does he or she move in a 24-hour day?

WRITING LINK

Persuasive Writing—Request Suppose that you have been invited to enter an essay contest. The winner will be the first student astronaut in space. Write a one-page essay to the judges requesting that they choose you. Explain why you are the best candidate.

ART LINK

Space Art Design a permanent space station or moon base. Draw a picture to show what it will look like. Label all the major parts, explaining how they will help people live and work in space or on the moon.

TECHNOLOGY LINK

Learn more about the solar system by visiting this Internet site.
www.scilinks.org/harcourt

The History of Rockets and Spaceflight

As with many inventions, it is likely that the first rockets were produced partly by accident. Trying to scare off evil forces, the ancient Chinese lit bamboo tubes filled with a combination of charcoal, saltpeter, and sulfur. Perfectly sealed tubes produced loud explosions.

But once in a while an imperfectly sealed tube would shoot off into the air. At some point the Chinese began to produce these tubes, which they called "fire arrows," as weapons.

Rockets of War

Through the centuries, knowledge of how to make rockets spread through Asia, the Middle East, Europe, and the Americas. The "rockets' red glare" that Francis Scott Key wrote about in "The Star-Spangled Banner" were fired by British troops on Fort McHenry near Baltimore, Maryland, during the War of 1812.

The first liquid-fuel rockets were developed during the 1920s by American scientist Robert H. Goddard. These powerful rockets were a great advance in rocket technology. During World War II, a team of German scientists started the Space Age with the launch of the A4 rocket. It traveled 193 km (about 120 mi). Although it was designed to be a weapon of war, the A4 was the first modern rocket, a guided missile. After the war many German rockets were redesigned to collect data from Earth's upper atmosphere.

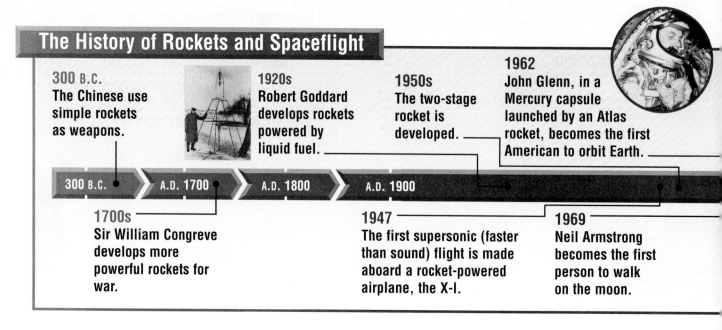

The History of Rockets and Spaceflight

300 B.C.
The Chinese use simple rockets as weapons.

1920s
Robert Goddard develops rockets powered by liquid fuel.

1950s
The two-stage rocket is developed.

1962
John Glenn, in a Mercury capsule launched by an Atlas rocket, becomes the first American to orbit Earth.

300 B.C.   A.D. 1700   A.D. 1800   A.D. 1900

1700s
Sir William Congreve develops more powerful rockets for war.

1947
The first supersonic (faster than sound) flight is made aboard a rocket-powered airplane, the X-I.

1969
Neil Armstrong becomes the first person to walk on the moon.

The Race to Space

In 1957 the Soviet Union used a German-designed rocket to launch *Sputnik,* the first Earth-orbiting satellite. The next year NASA (National Aeronautics and Space Administration) launched the first American satellite, *Explorer I,* and the space race was on. In 1961 a Soviet cosmonaut became the first person in space. Then President Kennedy promised that an American astronaut would be the first person to land on the moon. Competition between the Soviet Union and the United States was fierce. National pride was at stake. In 1964 the United States sent a space probe to Mars. In 1965 a Soviet cosmonaut became the first person to "walk" in space. In 1968 three American astronauts orbited the moon. Finally, in July 1969, the *Eagle* lander of *Apollo 11* touched down on the moon. Neil Armstrong became the first person to walk on another body in space.

Cooperation in Space

The space race ended with the flight of *Apollo 11.* Soon cooperation, not competition, became the key to space exploration. In 1988 Japan, Canada, the United States, Russia, and nine members of the European Space Agency agreed to construct the International Space Station. Many parts have already been built, and the process of launching them on American space shuttles and Russian rockets is underway. Once in orbit, the parts are joined by astronauts from several countries.

Rockets began as weapons of war and were improved as sources of national pride. But they have become cargo carriers and transports for scientific research in space.

THINK ABOUT IT

1. Why do you think rockets were first used as weapons?
2. Why do you think the space race ended with *Apollo 11*?

The Mir space station

1981
The first space shuttle, *Columbia,* is launched.

A.D. 2000

1986
The Soviet Union launches the Mir space station.

1998
Russia and the United States launch the first parts of the International Space Station.

Harrison Schmitt

GEOLOGIST, ASTRONAUT

Harrison (Jack) Schmitt is a geologist. He was also the first scientist to fly in space and the only scientist to do research on the moon. In 1971 he was the lunar module pilot for *Apollo 17*. The spacecraft landed in the Taurus-Littrow region of the moon. This area is noted for volcanic cinder cones and steep-walled valleys. At this location Dr. Schmitt collected samples of both young volcanic rock and older mountain rock.

Dr. Schmitt's involvement with the space program began at the United States Geological Survey's Astrogeology Center in Flagstaff, Arizona. There he developed geologic field techniques that were used by all Apollo crews. In 1965 Dr. Schmitt became an astronaut. As the only geologist-astronaut, he trained Apollo astronauts in geology observations. He also studied lunar rock samples and documented the geologic findings of each Apollo flight.

Following his resignation from NASA in 1975, Dr. Schmitt was elected to the United States Senate and served six years as senator from New Mexico. Today Dr. Schmitt is a consultant on issues concerning business, geology, space, and public safety.

THINK ABOUT IT

1. Why was it important for Apollo crew members to have a knowledge of geology?
2. What kinds of information do you think might be gained from samples of lunar rock?

Taking a ride on the moon

Paper Moon

How can the moon be used to make a calendar?

Materials

- clock
- 28 white paper plates
- scissors

Procedure

1. Observe the moon at the same time each night for 4 weeks.

2. Cut one paper plate each night to represent the shape of the moon as you observed it.

3. Hang the paper-plate moons on a wall to make a record of your observations.

Draw Conclusions

How did the shape of the moon change over the length of your observations? What pattern do you notice about the changing shape of the moon? An Earth calendar has 12 months. How many months (moon cycles) would there be in a moon calendar?

Solar-System Distances

How far is it to Pluto?

Materials

- table of planets' distances from the sun
- roll of toilet paper
- wood dowel
- marker

Procedure

1. Round off all distances on the table to the nearest million kilometers.

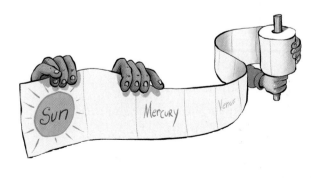

2. Use one square of toilet paper to represent the distance from the sun to Mercury.

3. Divide the distance from the sun to Mercury into all the other distances. The quotient for each problem will be how many toilet-paper squares each planet is from the sun.

4. Put the dowel into the toilet-paper roll. Unroll the paper, count the squares of paper, and label the position for each planet.

Draw Conclusions

How many squares of toilet paper does it take to show the location of Pluto? How much farther from the sun is Pluto than Mercury? Distances in the solar system are huge. The toilet-paper model helps you visualize those distances. What kind of model could you make to show the sizes of the planets?

Chapter 4 Review and Test Preparation

Vocabulary Review

Use the terms below to complete the sentences. The page numbers in ( ) tell you where to look in the chapter if you need help.

revolves (B92)   eclipse (B94)

orbit (B93)   telescope (B101)

rotate (B93)   satellite (B101)

axis (B93)   space probe (B102)

1. Any natural or artificial object that orbits another object is called a ____.

2. Both Earth and the moon have day-night cycles because they each ____, or spin on an ____.

3. The path the moon takes around Earth is its ____.

4. Galileo used a ____ to observe four of Jupiter's moons.

5. A ____ is a vehicle that is used to explore deep space.

6. As a planet travels around the sun, the planet ____.

7. During an ____, one object in space passes through the shadow of another object.

Connect Concepts

Write terms and phrases from the Word Bank below where they belong in the Venn diagram.

revolve   weathering

rotate   almost no weathering

life   craters

no known life   rocky

liquid water   atmosphere

no liquid water   no atmosphere

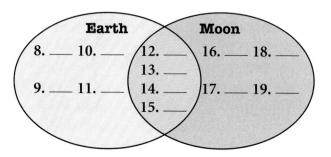

Earth   **Moon**

8. ____ 10. ____ 12. ____ 16. ____ 18. ____
                    13. ____
9. ____ 11. ____ 14. ____ 17. ____ 19. ____
                    15. ____

Check Understanding

Write the letter of the best choice.

20. The diagram below shows Earth's —

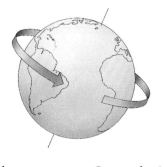

A orbit   C revolution

B rotation   D moon

21. During the new-moon phase, a person on Earth cannot see the moon because the sun is shining —

F on the far side of the moon

G on the Earth

H on the moon's axis

J from behind and below the moon

22. The diagram below shows a —

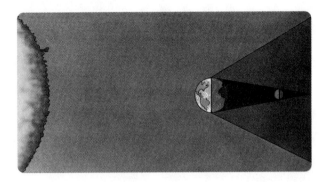

  A solar eclipse   **C** full moon

  B lunar eclipse   **D** new moon

23. The Apollo flights gave scientists first-hand knowledge of —

  F the moon

  G Earth's atmosphere

  H Mars

  J the sun

24. Which of the following must a spacesuit provide for an astronaut?

  A life support, including air

  B protection from intense heat and cold

  C a means to orbit the Earth

  D both A and B

Critical Thinking

25. Why does the moon appear to wax, or grow larger, and then wane, or get smaller?

26. The moon has many craters that are millions of years old. Although Earth was hit by large objects from space, just as the moon was, it has few such craters today. Explain why.

27. On Earth the moon appears to rise and set. If you could look at Earth from the moon, would Earth appear to rise and set? Explain why or why not.

Process Skills Review

28. How can you **use a model** to learn more about the moon?

29. You want to **compare** the moon's landforms with landforms on Earth. What processes will you consider? What tools can you use to **observe** the moon's landforms?

30. On the moon, the sun might rise on July 1 and not set until July 14. **Infer** the effects of such a long day on people living on a moon base.

Performance Assessment

On the Moon

Work with a partner to write a dialogue between an astronaut on the moon and Mission Control on Earth. From the astronaut's point of view, describe the moon's landforms and environment. Include a few details about your spacesuit, too.

Chapter 5

LESSON 1
What Are the
Features of the
Sun?   B114

LESSON 2
What Are the
Planets Like?   B122

LESSON 3
Why Do the Planets
Stay in Orbit?   B130

SCIENCE AND TECHNOLOGY   B136

PEOPLE IN SCIENCE   B138

ACTIVITIES FOR HOME
OR SCHOOL   B139

CHAPTER REVIEW AND
TEST PREPARATION   B142

The Solar System

Have you ever looked up at night and seen the Milky Way Galaxy? It's hard to miss because it's the *only* thing you can see. All of the stars and planets visible to your eyes—including Earth— are part of it. Beyond the Milky Way Galaxy are hundreds of billions of other galaxies. How many planets like Earth do you think there might be?

Vocabulary Preview

photosphere
corona
sunspot
solar flare
solar wind
solar system
planet
asteroids
comet
orbit
law of universal gravitation

FAST FACT

On a clear night you can see more than 2000 stars without using a telescope. However, there are 50,000,000 times as many stars in the Milky Way Galaxy alone.

≣FAST FACT

In 1989 the *Magellan* spacecraft was launched to Venus from a space shuttle. If you ever get to spend a day on Venus, take plenty of clean clothes. It takes just over 243 Earth days for Venus to rotate once on its axis.

Long Days, Short Days	
Planet	**Day**
Jupiter	9 hr 50 min
Saturn	10 hr 39 min
Neptune	16 hr 3 min
Uranus	17 hr 14 min
Earth	23 hr 56 min
Mars	24 hr 37 min
Pluto	153 hr 18 min
Mercury	1392 hr 30 min
Venus	5832 hr 32 min

≣FAST FACT

Saturn's rings are made up of chunks of ice, some of which are bigger than most houses. The Voyager space probes showed that Jupiter, Uranus, and Neptune also have rings.

LESSON 1

What Are the Features of the Sun?

In this lesson, you can . . .

INVESTIGATE sunspots.

LEARN ABOUT the sun's structure and features.

LINK to math, writing, and technology.

▼ The surface of the sun

Sunspots

Activity Purpose The sun always seems the same from Earth. But is it always the same? What changes take place on the sun? You can find out about some of them as you **observe** sunspots in this investigation.

Materials

- white paper
- clipboard
- tape
- small telescope
- large piece of cardboard
- scissors

Activity Procedure

CAUTION

1. **CAUTION** **Never look directly at the sun. You can cause permanent damage to your eyes.** Fasten the white paper to the clipboard. Tape the edges down to keep the wind from blowing them.

2. Center the eyepiece of the telescope on the cardboard, and trace around the eyepiece.

3. Cut out the circle, and fit the eyepiece into the hole. The cardboard will help block some of the light and make a shadow on the paper.

4. Point the telescope at the sun, and focus the sun's image on the white paper. **Observe** the image of the sun on the paper. (Picture A)

5. On the paper, outline the image of the sun. Shade in any dark spots you see. The dark spots are called *sunspots*. **Record** the date and time on the paper. **Predict** what will happen to the sunspots in the next

Picture A

Picture B

day or two. *Note:* Since the image of the sun on the paper is reversed, any movement you **observe** will also be reversed. For example, movement from right to left on the image represents movement from west to east on the sun.

6 Repeat Step 5 each sunny day for several days. **Record** the date, the time, and the positions of the sunspots each day. (Picture B)

Draw Conclusions

1. How did the positions of the sunspots change?

2. What can you **infer** from the movement of sunspots?

3. **Scientists at Work** Scientists **draw conclusions** from what they **observe**. Galileo was the first scientist to observe that it takes a sunspot about two weeks to cross from the left side of the sun's surface to the right side. Two weeks later, the sunspot appears on the left side of the sun's surface again. From this information, what conclusions can you draw about the time it takes the sun to make one complete rotation? What other information do you need to support your conclusions?

Investigate Further Does the sun always have the same number of spots? Do sunspots change in size? **Plan and conduct a simple investigation** to find answers to these and any other questions you might have about sunspots. Write instructions others can follow to carry out the procedure.

> **Process Skill Tip**
>
> You need to use logical reasoning to **draw conclusions** based on what you **observe**.

The Sun

Energy from the Sun

FIND OUT

• how the sun's energy affects life on Earth

• about the sun's layers

• about the sun's visible features

VOCABULARY

photosphere
corona
sunspot
solar flare
solar wind

◄ The sun is the source of most energy on Earth.

The sun is Earth's "local star"—the star at the center of the solar system. It has no permanent features, like Earth's mountains and oceans, because the sun is a huge ball of very hot gases.

The sun is the source of almost all energy on Earth. Plants are the link between the sun's energy and people. Plants take the sun's energy and change it to food energy. When an animal eats plants—or eats animals that have eaten plants—it gets food energy that comes from the sun.

When organisms die, they decay. Some organisms that died long ago became fossil fuels. So the energy that lights homes and runs cars comes from the sun.

The sun's energy is also the source of wind and other weather on Earth. Recall that when the sun's rays strike Earth's surface, land heats up faster than water. This uneven heating causes weather by producing differences in air pressure.

The sun is the source of most energy on Earth, but where does the sun's energy come from? On Earth, energy often comes from fuel. For example, burning gas or coal produces energy. But the sun's energy doesn't come from burning fuels. It comes from the fusing, or combining, of small particles to form larger ones.

Like all stars, the sun is a huge ball of gases, mostly hydrogen and helium. The temperature at the center of the sun is about

Solar energy from the sun travels as waves. Some of these waves can be seen as light, while others can be felt as heat. ▼

15 million °C (27 million °F). At that temperature, and under enormous pressure, particles of hydrogen smash into each other and produce helium. Every time this happens, the sun releases energy as light and heat.

This process is called *fusion* because hydrogen particles fuse, or join together, to produce helium. The fusion of an amount of hydrogen the size of a pinhead releases more energy than the burning of 1000 metric tons of coal. And the sun fuses about 600 million metric tons of hydrogen every second.

Energy from the sun travels in waves, as shown in the illustration below. There are several kinds of waves. Each kind carries a different amount of energy. We see some of the waves as visible light. We feel infrared waves as heat, and ultraviolet waves tan or burn the skin. The sun even produces radio waves, which we hear as radio or TV static. Some of the sun's energy, such as X rays, is harmful to life on Earth. But the atmosphere keeps most of the harmful energy from reaching Earth's surface.

✔ **How does the sun affect life on Earth?**

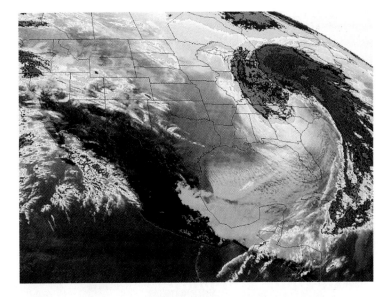

▲ Solar energy produces differences in air pressure, causing storms, such as hurricanes and blizzards. This photograph is a satellite image of a large winter storm.

Sometimes particles from the sun stream into space. When these particles reach Earth's atmosphere, they can produce colorful bands of light such as the *aurora borealis,* or northern lights. ▶

Through the process of photosynthesis, plants convert solar energy into food energy. ▼

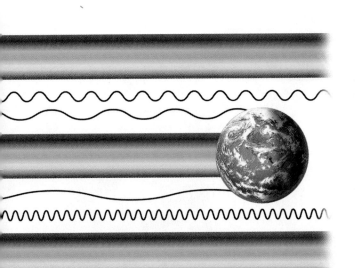

B117

Exploring the Sun

The sun's diameter is 1.4 million km (about 870,000 mi)—more than 100 times that of Earth. The sun is large enough to hold 1 million Earths. Since the sun is so much closer to Earth than other stars are, astronomers study it to understand stars. They have discovered that the sun has several layers of gases. The layers don't have definite boundaries. Instead, each layer blends into the next.

The layer at the center of the sun is the *core*. As you can see in the illustration, the core is small in comparison with the entire sun. However, most of the sun's mass is in its core.

THE INSIDE STORY

The Sun's Structure

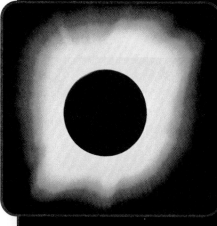

The sun's *corona*, or atmosphere, is visible only during an eclipse. Streams of tiny particles, called the *solar wind*, travel outward from the corona through the solar system.

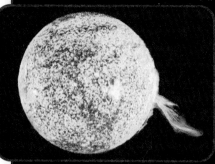

The photosphere has a grainy look. Its surface is made up of hot, bright areas, called *granules*, surrounded by cooler, darker areas. A *solar flare*, at the far right, is a brief burst of energy from the sun's photosphere.

A *sunspot* is a dark area on the photosphere. Sunspots appear dark because they are cooler than the rest of the sun. Many sunspots are larger than Earth. ▼

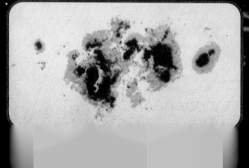

As energy from the sun's core moves outward, it passes through the *radiation zone*. Energy from the core heats this layer as a radiator heats the air in a room. From there it moves to the sun's outer layer, the *convection zone*. In the convection zone, energy moves to the surface by a process called convection. In convection, cooler particles are pulled down by gravity, pushing warmer particles up. This is the same way bubbles move energy to the surface of boiling water.

The surface of the sun is known as the **photosphere**, or "sphere of light." This is the part of the sun we see. Above the photosphere is the sun's atmosphere, the **corona**. This area of hot gases extends 1 million km (about 600,000 mi) from the photosphere.

✔ **What are the layers of the sun?**

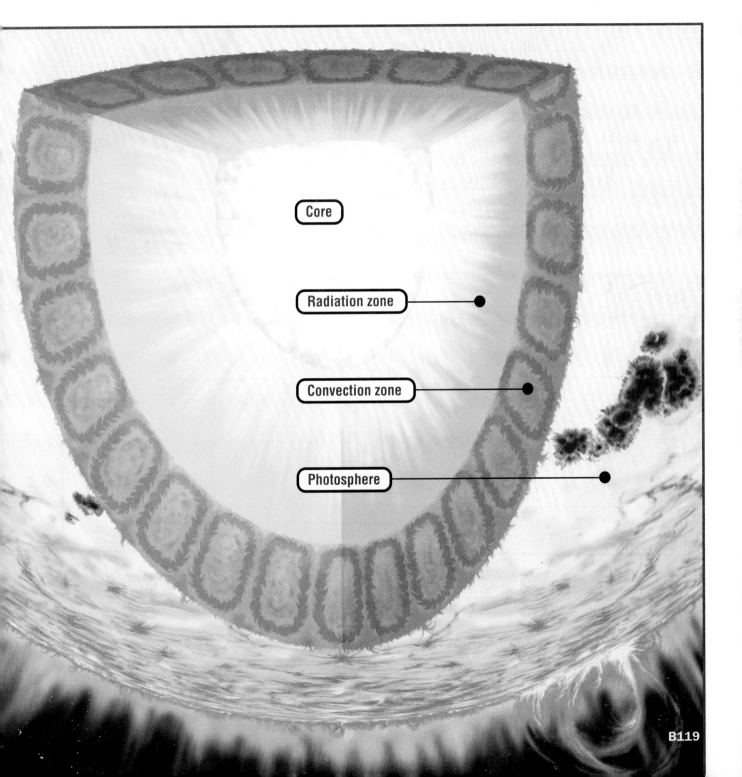

Core

Radiation zone

Convection zone

Photosphere

Solar Features

The sun has several features visible at different times at or near its surface. Bright spots on the photosphere are called *granules*. Granules are the tops of columns of rising gases in the convection layer. Darker areas between granules contain cooler gases.

Dark spots, called **sunspots**, are the most obvious features. Sunspots look dark because they are cooler than the rest of the photosphere. If you could see them by themselves, they would actually look very bright.

Scientists have observed sunspots for thousands of years. In the past few hundred years, they have recorded the number of sunspots observed each year. Scientists noticed that the number of sunspots increases and decreases over a period of about 11 years. This is called a sunspot cycle. The graph below shows sunspot cycles over a period of 300 years.

Sunspots can produce **solar flares**. These are brief bursts of energy from the photosphere. Much of a solar flare's energy is ultraviolet waves, radio waves, and X rays. As the energy is released, a fast-moving stream of particles is thrown into space. These particles are called the **solar wind**. When the solar wind reaches Earth, the particles can cause magnetic storms. These storms disturb compasses and energy and communication systems. They also produce auroras in the northern skies.

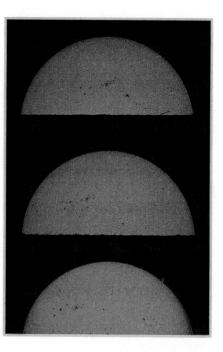

As the sun rotates, groups of sunspots seem to move across its surface. After a few days, the same spots are seen in a different location on the sun's surface, as you saw in the investigation. ▶

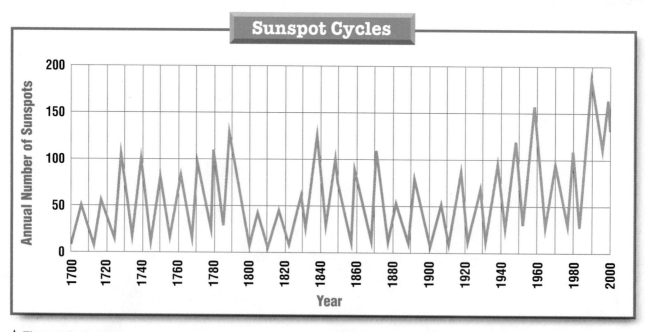

▲ The graph shows how the average number of sunspots varies in cycles. Years with a large number of sunspots are called *sunspot maximums*. Years with a low number of sunspots are called *sunspot minimums*.

A sun feature similar to a solar flare is called a *solar prominence*. A solar prominence is a bright loop or sheet of gas in the corona. It may hover there for days. Or it may explode and disappear in minutes. The photo on page B114 shows a spectacular solar prominence.

✓ **Compare sunspots, solar flares, and solar wind.**

Summary

The sun is a huge mass of hot gases that produces huge amounts of energy. It is the source of most of the energy on Earth. The sun has several layers: the core, the radiation zone, the convection zone, the photosphere, and the corona. Some of the visible features of the sun are solar prominences, solar flares, granules, and sunspots.

Review

1. How does life on Earth depend on the sun?

2. How is energy produced by the sun?

3. Draw a diagram of the sun, showing each layer.

4. **Critical Thinking** Suppose an astronomer observes a huge solar flare. Predict its effect on Earth in the next day or so.

5. **Test Prep** Solar prominences are loops of gas in the sun's —

    A corona
    B radiation zone
    C core
    D photosphere

LINKS

MATH LINK

Far Out Because distances in the solar system are so large, astronomers use a unit of measure called an astronomical unit, or AU. An AU is the distance between Earth and the sun, about 150 million km. At this distance, energy from the sun reaches Earth in about 8 minutes. Copy the table below, and complete it to show how long it takes the sun's energy to reach each planet.

Planet	Distance (AU)	Time (min)
Mercury	0.4	
Venus	0.7	
Earth	1.0	8
Mars	1.5	
Jupiter	5.2	
Saturn	9.5	
Uranus	19.2	
Neptune	30.0	
Pluto	39.5	

WRITING LINK

Informative Writing—Description Suppose scientists built a space probe that could withstand the sun's high temperatures. Write a description for your teacher of the information the probe might send back as it descends through the sun's layers to its core.

TECHNOLOGY LINK

Learn more about suns and solar systems by viewing *Extra-Solar Planets* on the **Harcourt Science Newsroom Video** in your classroom video library.

What Are the Planets Like?

In this lesson, you can . . .

INVESTIGATE distances between planets.

LEARN ABOUT the planets in our solar system.

LINK to math, writing, technology, and other areas.

INVESTIGATE

Distances Between Planets

Activity Purpose If you've ever used a map, you know what a scale model is. A scale model is a way to compare large distances in a smaller space. In this investigation you will **use measurements** to **make a scale model** that shows the distances between planets in our solar system.

Materials

- piece of string about 4 m long
- meterstick
- 9 different-colored markers

Activity Procedure

1 Copy the chart shown on the next page.

2 At one end of the string, tie three or four knots at the same point to make one large knot. This large knot will stand for the sun in your model.

3 In the solar system, distances are often measured in astronomical units (AU). One AU equals the average distance from Earth to the sun. In your model, 1 AU will equal 10 cm. Use your meterstick to accurately measure 1 AU from the sun on your model. This point stands for Earth's distance from the sun. Use one of the markers to mark this point on the string. Note in your chart which color you used. (Picture A)

◄ Europa (you•ROH•puh) is one of Jupiter's many moons. This natural satellite has a diameter of 3100 kilometers (about 1925 mi) and takes about $3\frac{1}{2}$ Earth days to orbit Jupiter.

Planet	Average Distance from the Sun (km)	Average Distance from the Sun (AU)	Scale Distance (cm)	Marker Color	Planet's Diameter (km)
Mercury	58 million	$\frac{4}{10}$	4		4876
Venus	108 million	$\frac{7}{10}$	7		12,104
Earth	150 million	1			12,756
Mars	228 million	2			6794
Jupiter	778 million	5			142,984
Saturn	1429 million	10			120,536
Uranus	2871 million	19			51,118
Neptune	4500 million	30			49,532
Pluto	5900 million	39			2274

4 Complete the Scale Distance column of the chart. Then measure and mark the position of each planet on the string. Use a different color for each planet, and **record** in your table the colors you used.

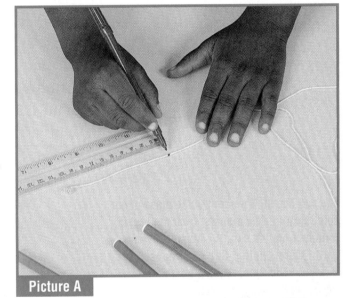

Picture A

Draw Conclusions

1. In your **model**, how far from the sun is Mercury? How far away is Pluto?

2. What advantages can you think of for using AU to measure distances inside the solar system?

3. **Scientists at Work** Explain how it helped to **make a model** instead of trying to show actual distances between planets.

Investigate Further You can use a calculator to help make other scale models. The chart gives the actual diameters of the planets. Use this scale: Earth's diameter = 1 cm. Find the scale diameters of the other planets by dividing their actual diameters by Earth's diameter. Make a scale drawing showing the diameter of each planet.

Process Skill Tip

You can **make a model** to study objects or events that are too small or too large to observe directly. A scale model shows large objects or areas in smaller sizes so that they can be more easily studied.

The Planets

The Inner Planets

FIND OUT

- **about the planets in our solar system**
- **how moons and rings may have formed**

VOCABULARY

solar system
planet
asteroids
comet

Our solar system is made up of the sun and nine planets. A **solar system** is a group of objects in space that move around a central star. A **planet** is a large object that moves around a star. The planets can be divided into two groups—the inner planets, near the sun, and the outer planets.

Mercury, the planet closest to the sun, is about the size of Earth's moon. Mercury, which is covered with craters, even looks like the moon. Very small amounts of some gases are present on Mercury, but there aren't enough of them to form an atmosphere.

Venus, the second planet from the sun, is about the same size as Earth. But Venus is very different from Earth. Venus is dry and has a thick atmosphere that traps heat. The temperature at the surface is about 475°C (887°F). The thick atmosphere presses down on Venus with a weight 100 times that of Earth's atmosphere. Also, Venus spins on its axis in a direction opposite from that of Earth's rotation.

The sun has 99.8 percent of the mass of our solar system. The planets, from nearest to farthest from the sun, are Mercury, Venus, Earth, Mars, Jupiter, Saturn, Uranus, Neptune, and Pluto. Each planet travels in its own path around the sun. ▶

Mercury has a diameter of 4876 kilometers (about 3031 mi) and is 58 million kilometers (about 36 million mi) from the sun. This inner planet has no moons and takes about 59 Earth days to make one rotation, or turn once on its axis. Mercury orbits the sun in about 88 Earth days.

Venus has a diameter of 12,104 kilometers (about 7517 mi) and is 108 million kilometers (about 67 million mi) from the sun. This inner planet has no natural satellites. It takes Venus about 243 Earth days to make one rotation and 225 Earth days to orbit the sun.

Earth, the third planet from the sun, is the largest of the inner planets. It has one natural satellite, the moon. Earth is the only planet that has liquid water. It is also the only known planet that supports life. Earth's atmosphere absorbs and reflects the right amount of solar energy to keep the planet at the correct temperature for living things such as humans to survive.

Mars, the fourth planet from the sun, is sometimes called the Red Planet because its soil is a dark reddish brown. Mars has two moons and the largest volcano in the solar system—Olympus Mons (oh•LIHM•puhs MAHNS). Space probes have shown us that nothing lives on Mars. Dust storms can last for months and affect the whole planet. Although no liquid water has been found on Mars, it is believed that liquid water once existed there. This is because probes and satellites have found deep valleys and sedimentary rocks. These features probably were formed by flowing water.

✔ **List the inner planets in order from the sun.**

Earth has a diameter of 12,756 kilometers (about 7922 mi). Our planet is 150 million kilometers (about 93 million mi) from the sun. Earth has one moon and takes almost 24 hours to complete one rotation on its axis. It takes about 365 days to orbit the sun.

Not to scale

Mars has a diameter of 6794 kilometers (about 4230 mi) and is 228 million kilometers (about 142 million mi) from the sun. This inner planet has two moons. Mars completes a rotation in about 24.5 hours. Mars takes about 687 Earth days to complete one orbit around the sun.

The Outer Planets

Jupiter is the largest planet in our solar system. A thin ring that is hard to see surrounds it. At least 16 moons orbit around it. Jupiter's atmosphere is very active. Its energy causes a circular storm known as the Great Red Spot. This weather, which is a lot like a hurricane, has lasted more than 300 years. It is so big around that three Earths would fit inside it.

Saturn is a planet known for its rings. Space probes have found that other planets also have rings. But Saturn's are so wide and so bright that they can be seen from Earth through a small telescope. Saturn has at least 18 named moons.

Uranus (YOOR•uh•nuhs), the seventh planet from the sun, is the most distant planet you can see without using a telescope. Uranus, a giant blue-green ball of gas and liquid, has at least 15 moons as well as faint rings around it.

Not to scale

Neptune, the farthest away of the giant gas balls, has at least eight moons and a faint ring. It also has circular storms, but none have lasted as long as the Great Red Spot on Jupiter.

In the investigation you saw that *Pluto* is the planet farthest from the sun. You also learned that Pluto is the smallest planet. From Pluto's surface the sun looks like a very bright star. Little heat or light reaches Pluto or its one moon. Unlike the other outer planets, Pluto is not a ball of gas. Instead, Pluto has a rocky surface that is probably covered by frozen gases.

Asteroids and comets are other objects that move around the sun. **Asteroids** are small and rocky. Most of them are scattered in a large area between the orbit paths of Mars and Jupiter. Some scientists hypothesize that these asteroids are pieces of a planet that never formed. All the asteroids put together would make an object less than half the size of Earth's moon.

A **comet** is a small mass of dust and ice that orbits the sun in a long, oval-shaped path. When a comet's orbit takes it close to the sun, some of the ice on the comet's surface changes to water vapor and streams out to form a long, glowing tail.

✔ **Which planets are outer planets?**

Uranus has a diameter of 51,118 kilometers (about 31,700 mi). This planet is 2870 million kilometers (1782 million mi) from the sun. Uranus makes one rotation in 17 hours and one orbit around the sun in about 84 Earth years.

Pluto has a diameter of 2274 kilometers (about 1366 mi) and is 5900 million kilometers (about 3664 million mi) from the sun. It takes Pluto about 7 days to complete one rotation and 249 Earth years to complete one revolution.

Neptune has a diameter of 49,532 kilometers (about 30,740 mi) and is 4500 million kilometers (about 2795 million mi) from the sun. Neptune completes one rotation in a little more than 16 hours and one revolution in about 165 Earth years.

▲ Titan, Saturn's largest moon, has a diameter of 5150 kilometers (about 3200 mi). Titan has no clouds in its atmosphere and is very cold.

▲ The rings around Saturn are made up of dust, ice crystals, and small bits of rock coated with frozen water. The rings are about 270,000 kilometers (about 167,700 mi) across but only about 10 kilometers (about 6 mi) thick.

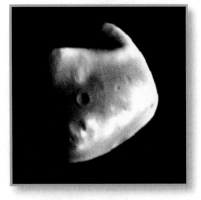

Io (EYE•oh) is a moon of Jupiter. Io has a diameter of 3630 kilometers (about 2254 mi) and has several active volcanoes on its surface. The volcanoes are the big orange patches. ▶

▲ Deimos (DY•muhs) is one of the two Martian moons. It has many craters and an uneven shape. It is about 14 kilometers (9 mi) in diameter.

Moons and Rings

Every planet except Mercury and Venus has at least one natural satellite, or *moon.* Earth's moon is round and rocky, and it has many craters. Others, like the two moons of Mars or the outer moons of Jupiter, are small and rocky and have uneven shapes. Jupiter and Mars orbit near the asteroid belt. So, their moons may be asteroids pulled in by the planets' gravity. The large moons of Jupiter and Saturn are almost like small planets. Io, one of Jupiter's larger moons, has active volcanoes. Titan (TYT•uhn), one of Saturn's moons, has a dense atmosphere that glows red-orange.

Besides having moons, each of the gas giants has a system of rings. These rings are made of tiny bits of dust, ice crystals, and small pieces of rock. Saturn's rings may have formed as a moon was pulled apart by gravity because it got too close to the planet.

✔ **What are planet rings made of?**

▲ Phobos (FOH•buhs) is the other moon that orbits Mars. Like Deimos, it is a small, rocky object. Its diameter is about 22 kilometers (14 mi). Phobos makes three trips around its planet each Martian day.

Summary

The inner planets—Mercury, Venus, Earth, and Mars—are small and rocky. Four of the five outer planets are giant balls of gas. They are Jupiter, Saturn, Uranus, and Neptune. The outer planet that is farthest from the sun is Pluto, another rocky planet. Most of the planets have at least one moon. The gas giants also have rings.

Review

1. Name the inner planets, starting with the planet closest to the sun.
2. What can be thought of as the dividing line between the inner planets and the outer planets?
3. Which planets have no moons?
4. **Critical Thinking** Compare and contrast Venus and Earth.
5. **Test Prep** The outer planet that is **NOT** a giant ball of gas is —
   A Jupiter
   B Saturn
   C Neptune
   D Pluto

LINKS

 MATH LINK

Graphing Planet Data Make a bar graph showing the diameter of each planet. Use data from the table on page B123 and a computer program such as *Graph Links*.

WRITING LINK

Persuasive Writing—Opinion Suppose you are a real-estate agent trying to get adults to move to the planet of your choice. Write a newspaper ad pointing out all the benefits of living on your chosen planet.

ART LINK

View of a Planet Paint or draw a realistic landscape of the surface of another planet. Or paint the view of the planet as it would be seen from one of its moons.

LITERATURE LINK

The Wonderful Flight to the Mushroom Planet Read this book by Eleanor Cameron to find out what happens when two boys go on an adventure in space. Compare the planet with Earth.

 TECHNOLOGY LINK

Learn more about planets by investigating *Planet Hopping* on the **Harcourt Science Explorations CD-ROM.**

Why Do the Planets Stay in Orbit?

In this lesson, you can . . .

INVESTIGATE orbits.

LEARN ABOUT the orbits of planets and moons.

LINK to math, writing, social studies, and technology.

This mechanical model, known as an *orrery* (OHR•er•ee), shows the solar system as it was known in the 1800s. ▼

INVESTIGATE

Orbits

Activity Purpose At the age of 23, Isaac Newton developed three laws of motion. The first law states that an object in motion will continue moving in a straight line at a constant speed until an outside force acts on it. In this investigation you will **make a model** to see how this law helps explain why moons and planets stay in orbit.

Materials
- 2 m string
- metal washers
- safety goggles

CAUTION

Activity Procedure

1 Tie three or four metal washers securely to one end of the string.

2 **CAUTION** **Take the string with the washers outside to an open area. Be sure that you are far from any buildings or objects and that no one is standing close to you. Put on the safety goggles.** Hold the loose end of the string. Slowly swing the string and washers in a circle above your head. **Observe** the motion of the washers. (Picture A)

3 **Predict** what will happen if you let go of the string while swinging it in a circle.

4 **CAUTION** Again, make sure that there are no people, buildings, or other objects near you. Swing the string and washers in a circle again. Let the string slip through your fingers. **Observe** the motion of the washers. How does it **compare** with your prediction? (Picture B)

5 Using a drawing, **record** the motion of the washers in Steps 2 and 4. Be sure to show the forces acting in each situation. Now make a drawing of the moon orbiting Earth. **Compare** the two drawings.

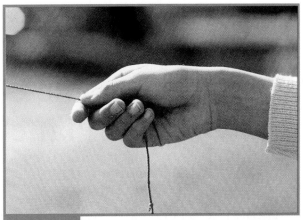

Picture A

Draw Conclusions

1. **Compare** the path of the washers while you were swinging them with their path once you let go of the string.

2. The string and washers can be used to **model** the moon orbiting Earth. **Compare** the motion of the washers circling your head with the motion of the moon orbiting Earth.

Picture B

3. **Scientists at Work** When scientists **experiment,** they must **communicate** their results to others. One way of doing this is with diagrams. Look at the drawing you made of the washers. What motions and forces does it show?

Investigate Further **Hypothesize** about the effect the length of the string has on the time the washers take to complete one revolution. Test your hypothesis. Then write a report that includes tests conducted, data collected or evidence examined, and conclusions drawn.

Process Skill Tip

After you **experiment,** you need to **communicate** your results by using a graph, a chart, a table, a written summary, or a drawing.

The Orbits of Planets and Moons

Orbits

In the investigation you made a model of an orbit. An **orbit** is the path one body in space takes as it revolves around another body. All of the planets in our solar system are in orbit around the sun. The moon orbits Earth. The orbit you modeled in the investigation was like the moon's orbit in two ways. First, the moon moves around Earth in much the same way as the washers moved around your head. Second, forces acted on the washers to keep them circling in the same way that forces act on the moon to keep it in orbit.

Think about what happened to the washers when you let go of the string. They flew away from you instead of continuing in a circle. This is an example of the first law of motion. A moving object will continue to move in a straight line until an outside force acts on it. This property of an object is called *inertia*. The inertia of the washers made them fly away when you let go. In the

FIND OUT

- how inertia and gravity interact to make an orbit
- what the law of universal gravitation is

VOCABULARY

orbit

law of universal gravitation

The shuttle's inertia tries to keep it moving in a straight line while gravity tries to pull it toward Earth. The result is that the shuttle orbits Earth.

same way, inertia would make the moon fly off in a straight line unless another force was acting on it.

What is the other force? In your model it was the force exerted by the string, which pulled the washers toward your hand. In the moon's orbit, the other force is gravitation between Earth and the moon. The moon's orbit is the path that results when inertia and gravitation act together.

✔ **What keeps the moon in orbit around Earth?**

Universal Gravitation

In addition to three laws of motion, Isaac Newton stated a law of gravitation. The **law of universal gravitation** is that all objects in the universe are attracted to all other objects. This attraction is observable only when the masses of the objects are huge. The masses of Earth and the moon produce a strong gravitational pull between them. The gravitational pull between two paperclips on a table isn't enough to pull them together because their masses are small.

The law of universal gravitation, when combined with the property of inertia, also explains why planets orbit the sun. The size of a planet's orbit is related to the planet's speed and its mass. Earth moves around the sun at an average speed of about 30 km/sec. The outer planets move in much longer, slower orbits.

✔ **Why is gravitation between small objects not observed?**

> After launch, the shuttle separates from its booster rockets and then from its fuel tank. Inertia tries to keep the objects moving forward, but gravity pulls them back to Earth.

In *Principia Mathematica*, Isaac Newton presented three laws of motion and the law of universal gravitation. ▼

Earth and the Moon

A moon is a body that orbits a planet. Earth has one moon. Some planets have no moons, while Jupiter has 17.

As a planet orbits the sun, the planet's moons orbit with it. In the same way, the planets move with the sun as it orbits the center of the Milky Way Galaxy.

Earth and the moon move together around the sun. Because the moon is always orbiting Earth while the Earth-moon system orbits the sun, the moon's path around the sun is a series of loops.

Inertia and the pull of gravity keep the moon in a nearly circular orbit around Earth.

Newton saw the universe as a giant machine. This model of the solar system, built in 1712, reflects that view. Turning the crank, like winding a clock, sets the planets in motion. ▶

Summary

The moon circles Earth in a path called an orbit. Gravitation between Earth and the moon keeps the moon from flying off into space because of its inertia. The balance between inertia and gravitation keeps Earth in orbit around the sun. It also keeps other planets and moons in their orbits.

Review

1. What is an orbit?
2. What keeps Earth in orbit around the sun?
3. What is the law of universal gravitation?
4. **Critical Thinking** Suppose the gravitation between Earth and the sun suddenly stopped. What path would Earth follow?
5. **Test Prep** Gravitation between Earth and the moon pulls on the moon as the moon orbits. What property of the moon keeps it from crashing into the Earth?

   A gravitation

   B inertia

   C mass

   D momentum

LINKS

MATH LINK

Calculate For a certain satellite to remain in orbit around Earth, it must move forward at about 8 km/sec. This satellite takes about 90 minutes to make one orbit. About how far does it travel in one orbit?

WRITING LINK

Informative Writing—Explanation Some people say that to learn something really well, you should teach it. Write a short lesson for a younger student. Explain why Earth stays in orbit around the sun. Make diagrams to go with your lesson.

SOCIAL STUDIES LINK

History of Astronomy Two important astronomers before Newton were Tycho Brahe and Johannes Kepler. Find out more about them and their contributions to the study of the solar system. Report to your class on your research.

TECHNOLOGY LINK

Learn more about orbits by visiting the National Air and Space Museum Internet site.
www.si.edu/harcourt/science

MAGNETARS

Some people say "there's nothing new under the sun." Astronomers might laugh at this! They are always finding new things in the universe. One exciting discovery is a different kind of star. Stars of this kind spin rapidly and send out gigantic bursts of energy. They might also be the most powerful magnets in the universe. Astronomers call them magnetars.

Surprise in the Sky

The first data about magnetars came from spy satellites. The U.S. government wanted to know when certain countries were testing nuclear weapons. So it launched a series of satellites to detect radiation from nuclear explosions. To government scientists' amazement, the satellites picked up radiation coming from outer space! Bursts of gamma rays seemed to be coming from everywhere in the universe. Government scientists communicated with civilian astronomers about this mysterious energy from space. Using satellites and radio telescopes, astronomers began measuring the energy bursts. Some of the larger bursts released as much energy in one second as the sun does in 1000 years!

Radio telescopes are also used to identify unknown energy sources from space.

This drawing of a magnetar shows its magnetic force field.

A few astronomers hypothesized that these stars have solid crusts and magnetic fields so strong that they cause the crusts to crack, releasing radiation. So magnetars may have starquakes, just as Earth has earthquakes.

A Giant Magnet

What's so different about this new kind of star? For one thing, if you were close enough, a magnetar's huge magnetic field would rearrange the atoms in your body. You wouldn't be you anymore! Think of this star as a giant magnet. Even if it were as far away as the sun, it could pull metal objects, such as paper clips, out of your pockets. The pull of gravity on its surface would flatten you like a pancake. And a magnetar spins very, very fast! While Earth takes 24 hours to complete one rotation, some magnetars take less than 6 seconds.

Luckily for us, the closest magnetars are thousands of light-years away. Astronomers have identified several of them and hypothe-

size that there are millions of others. From studying magnetars, scientists can learn more about magnetism, gravity, and other forces. And, since magnetars seem to have formed after massive stars exploded, they might help scientists learn more about how stars develop and change.

THINK ABOUT IT

1. How are magnetars different from other stars?
2. Why would it be dangerous for a spacecraft to fly near a magnetar?

WEB LINK:
For Science and Technology updates, visit The Learning Site.
www.harcourtschool.com/ca

Careers   Astrophysicist

What They Do

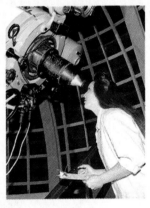

Astrophysicists work in space agencies, universities, or observatories. They study the stars and galaxies to find out more about radiation, magnetism, and other processes in the universe.

Education and Training A person wishing to become an astrophysicist needs to study math, physics, and chemistry. He or she also needs training in using equipment such as radar and telescopes. Some astrophysicists learn how to use satellites to get data from distant stars.

Julio Navarro
ASTRONOMER

"If you look at a galaxy far away, you're seeing the galaxy as it was many years ago. You're looking at the universe as it was when it was young."

Julio Navarro is a theoretical astronomer who studies galaxies. Instead of looking through telescopes, Dr. Navarro works with numerical data from the Hubble Space Telescope and from ground-based telescopes. He uses this data in computer models that help him study the formation of galaxies and other bodies in the universe.

Dr. Navarro explains that the light from distant galaxies can take billions of years to reach our telescopes. So we're not seeing those galaxies as they appear now, but as they appeared billions of years ago.

When he was growing up in Argentina, no one would have guessed that Dr. Navarro would become an astronomer. He was more interested in music. However, an essay assignment in high school changed everything. "I was looking through a lot of books, and I became interested in astronomy," says Dr. Navarro. He kept reading, and his interest grew.

Dr. Navarro earned a bachelor's degree and a Ph.D. in astronomy before leaving Argentina to work and study in North America and Europe. Today Dr. Navarro is at the University of Victoria, in British Columbia, Canada, where he teaches astronomy and does research on the formation of galaxies.

THINK ABOUT IT

1. Why does Dr. Navarro study distant galaxies?
2. How does Dr. Navarro gather data for his studies?

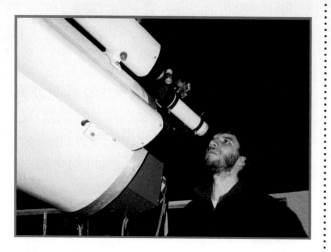

Looking into the past

A Model Sun

What are some sun features?

Materials
- yellow construction paper
- ruler
- scissors
- markers
- black construction paper
- glue
- white legal-sized paper

Procedure

1 Cut a 20-cm circle from the yellow paper to represent the photosphere. Using markers, make sunspots on the photosphere.

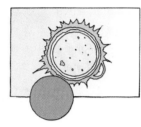

2 Cut a 20-cm circle from the black paper to represent the moon during a solar eclipse.

3 Glue the yellow circle to the white paper.

4 Using the markers, color jagged shapes around the sun to represent the sun's corona.

5 Use your black "moon" to eclipse the sun's photosphere to study its corona.

Draw Conclusions

Why did you cut out the moon for the total eclipse the same size as the sun? Scientists learn a great deal about the sun during total eclipses. Why is this an important time to study the sun? What benefits are there to blocking out the sun's photosphere?

Astrolabe

How do people navigate by the stars?

Materials
- 15-cm cardboard square
- protractor
- pencil
- drinking straw
- tape
- 20-cm piece of string
- metal washer

Procedure

1 Using the protractor, and starting in one corner of the cardboard square, draw a line at an angle of 5°. Draw additional lines at 10°, 15°, and so on.

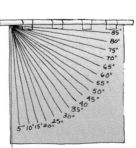

2 Tape the straw to the cardboard as shown.

3 At the point where all the lines meet, make a hole in the cardboard. Push the string through the hole and tie a knot to keep it from pulling through the hole. Tie the washer to the other end of the string.

4 Look at the North Star through the straw. Measure the angle of the North star by noting the angle of the string.

Draw Conclusions

The angle of the North Star tells you your latitude on the Earth. What is the angle of the North Star where you live? What is the latitude where you live?

Spinning Planets

How does rotation help a planet maintain its position in orbit?

Materials

- 25-cm (10-in.) cardboard circle with a small hole in the exact center
- 0.9 m (1 yd) of heavy string
- 4 large, metal paper clips

Procedure

❶ Push one end of the string through the hole in the cardboard disk. Knot the other end so that it will not pull through. The disk represents an orbiting planet.

❷ Attach the paper clips evenly around the outside of the planet.

❸ Holding the end of the string, swing the planet back and forth. Observe how it moves.

❹ With your hand, quickly spin the planet toward you. Then swing it again as it spins and observe how it moves.

Draw Conclusions

What happened when you swung the planet in Step 3? What happened when you swung the planet in Step 4? What does the spinning represent?

Plants on Other Planets

Why does Earth support life?

Materials

- 6–9 seeds, such as dried beans or sunflower seeds
- 3 small, plastic cups nearly filled with soil
- 1 shoe box lined with aluminum foil
- refrigerator freezer
- water

Procedure

❶ Plant two or three seeds in each cup, water lightly, and put them in a sunny spot until they sprout. Label the pots "Earth," "Jupiter," and "Mercury."

❷ Leave "Earth" where it is, and water its soil when it feels dry. Put "Jupiter" in the freezer. Do not water it. Put "Mercury" in the box, put the box in the sun, and do not water.

❸ Observe the growth in all three cups after a week.

Draw Conclusions

How does this experiment model growth on other planets?

Analyzing Starlight

How do scientists learn about the distant stars?

Materials

- window facing the sun
- pan of water
- small mirror

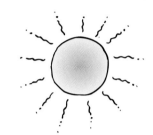

Procedure

❶ Place the pan so sunlight shines into it.

❷ Put the mirror inside the pan, facing the window. Lean it against the side of the pan, with its bottom partly under water.

❸ Adjust the position of the mirror until a pattern, a spectrum of colors, appears on the wall.

Draw Conclusions

How did the mirror and water work together to change the white light from the sun? What can scientists learn by studying the colors of the sun and other stars?

Building a Telescope

How does a reflecting telescope magnify objects?

Materials

- window facing the moon on a clear night
- curved shaving or makeup mirror
- small, flat mirror
- hand lens

Procedure

❶ Place the curved mirror so the magnifying side faces the moon.

❷ Position the flat mirror facing the curved mirror.

❸ Adjust both mirrors so the moon is reflected from the curved mirror into the flat mirror.

❹ Use the lens to examine the image of the moon in the flat mirror.

Draw Conclusions

What does the curved mirror do? What does the hand lens do? What would you see if you simply looked out the window and examined the moon with the hand lens?

Vocabulary Review

Use the terms below to complete the sentences. The page numbers in ( ) tell you where to look in the chapter if you need help.

photosphere (B119)

corona (B119)

sunspot (B120)

solar flare (B120)

solar wind (B120)

solar system (B124)

planet (B124)

asteroid (B127)

comet (B127)

orbit (B132)

law of universal gravitation (B133)

1. The sun's atmosphere is the ____.

2. A dark area on the sun that is caused by twists and loops in the sun's magnetic field is a ____.

3. A ____ is a brief burst of energy that occurs above a sunspot.

4. The ____ is a fast-moving stream of particles ejected into space.

5. The sun's ____ is the layer we see.

6. A statement of the ____ might be this: Everything is attracted to everything else.

7. An ____ is the path a body in space takes.

8. A ____ is a group of planets and their moons that orbit a central star.

9. Venus is a ____ that revolves around the sun.

10. An ____ is a rocky object that orbits the sun in a path between Mars and Jupiter.

11. A ____ is a space object made of ice, dust, and gases.

Connect Concepts

Write the names of the objects in the diagram.

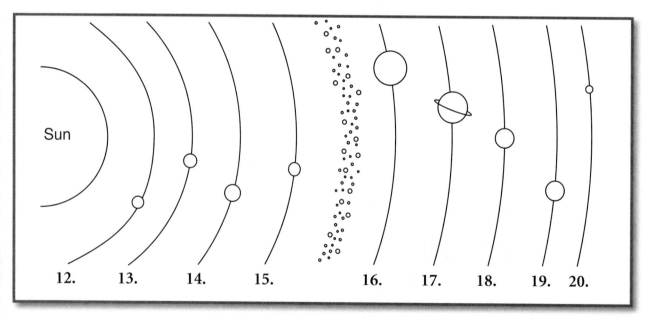

Sun

12.   13.   14.   15.   16.   17.   18.   19.   20.

Check Understanding

Write the letter of the best choice.

21. The sun is a huge mass of —
    A metals   C gases
    B light   D liquids

22. The sun provides ____ of the energy to the solar system.
    F most   H none
    G little   J some

23. Which of these is a giant ball of gas?
    A Earth   C Jupiter
    B moon   D Pluto

24. Planetary rings are made up of —
    F ice, dust, and rock
    G satellites
    H soil and lava
    J asteroids

25. Particles thrown off by the sun that can cause magnetic storms and disturb communications systems are —
    A coronal storms
    B solar flares
    C solar wind
    D granules

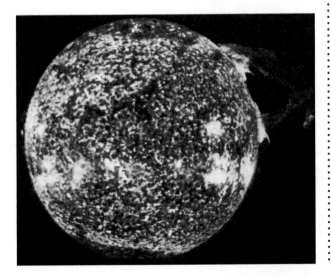

Critical Thinking

26. Gravitation attracts all objects in the universe toward each other, so why don't all of the clothes hanging in a closet cling together?

27. Would there be life on Earth without the sun? Explain.

28. How are asteroids like planets? How are they different?

Process Skills Review

29. From the graph on page B120, you can **observe** that sunspots appear and disappear in cycles that average about 11 years. As a cycle starts, the number of sunspots increases for 5 to 6 years. Then it decreases for 5 to 6 years. Using what you know about the relationship between solar flares and sunspots, **draw a conclusion** about when solar flares might be most frequent.

30. Describe an experiment you could conduct to demonstrate the law of universal gravitation. How would you **communicate** your results?

Performance Assessment

Solar-System Model

Make a model of the solar system. Try to get it as close to scale as possible. What measurements will you need to make for your model? What should you include in addition to the nine planets? You might want to use the data from the investigation on pages B122–B123.

Unit Project Wrap Up

Here are some ideas for ways to wrap up your unit project.

Produce a Weather Program

Videotape your daily weather reports and forecasts, and play the tapes for the school.

Write Guidelines

Write directions that tell how to use your weather instruments. Include information about why and how each instrument works.

Make a Chart

For a week, evaluate how accurately the weather was forecast by professional meteorologists. Make a chart to organize your data.

Investigate Further

How could you make your project better? What other questions do you have? Plan ways to find answers to your questions. Use the Science Handbook on pages R2-R9 for help.

Matter and Energy

UNIT C

PHYSICAL SCIENCE

Matter and Energy

Chapter 1	Matter and Its Properties	C2
Chapter 2	Atoms and Elements	C36
Chapter 3	Energy	C60

Unit Project

Let's Cook!

Suppose you are a cook in a restaurant. Develop a menu of foods that could demonstrate ways matter can change. Prepare the items, keeping records of the changes that take place. Identify physical and chemical changes. Invite others to predict whether the changes are reversible, and let them test their predictions. Then, look for advertisements for foods. Find an ad that makes a claim you can test. For example, one cereal manufacturer says its cereal stays crisp longer in milk. Plan and conduct a simple investigation to test the claim.

LESSON 1
How Can Physical Properties Be Used to Identify Matter? **C4**

LESSON 2
How Does Matter Change from One State to Another? **C12**

LESSON 3
How Does Matter React Chemically? **C20**

SCIENCE AND TECHNOLOGY **C28**

PEOPLE IN SCIENCE **C30**

ACTIVITIES FOR HOME OR SCHOOL **C31**

CHAPTER REVIEW AND TEST PREPARATION **C34**

Matter and Its Properties

Do you know why water, a liquid, can also be a solid (ice) and a gas (water vapor)? Actually, *every* substance can be a solid, a liquid, and a gas. The form a substance takes depends on its temperature and how fast particles of the substance move.

Vocabulary Preview

matter
physical properties
mass
weight
volume
density
solubility
solid
liquid
gas
evaporation
condensation
reactivity
combustibility

⁝⁝⁝FAST FACT

Water expands as it freezes. Water freezing in tiny cracks in rocks makes the cracks bigger. Over millions of years, this process can turn a mountain into a pile of sand.

People used to think that glass was a liquid, not a solid, because old glass windows are thicker at the bottom than at the top. However, at normal temperatures, glass is still more like a solid than it is like a liquid.

How cold can it get? There is a lowest possible temperature, called absolute zero. At this temperature the particles that make up a substance stop moving.

Hot and Cold Temperatures

Temperature	Celsius	Fahrenheit
Absolute zero	−273.15°	−459.67°
Water freezes	0.0°	32.0°
Human body	37.0°	98.6°
Water boils	100.0°	212.0°

LESSON 1

How Can Physical Properties Be Used to Identify Matter?

In this lesson, you can . . .

INVESTIGATE physical properties.

LEARN ABOUT how to measure and use physical properties.

LINK to math, writing, physical education, and technology.

Even apples have different physical properties. ▶

Using Physical Properties to Identify Objects

Activity Purpose Some objects, such as a tree and a rock, are so easy to identify that you almost don't have to think about it. But how do you identify two different trees? You have to **observe** their properties, or characteristics, more closely. In this investigation you will use properties to identify objects that are very similar.

Materials

- apples
- balance
- ruler
- string

Activity Procedure

1 Carefully **observe** the apple your teacher gave you. What properties of your apple can you discover just by observing it? **Record** all the properties you observe.

2 Use the balance, ruler, and string to **measure** some properties of your apple. **Record** the properties you measure. (Picture A)

3 Put your apple in the pile of apples on your teacher's desk. Don't watch while your teacher mixes up the apples.

Picture A

Picture B

④ Using the properties that you recorded, try to identify your apple in the pile. (Picture B)

⑤ Using the balance, ruler, and string, **measure** this apple. **Compare** the measurements to those you recorded earlier. Then decide whether the apple you chose from the pile is yours. If someone else chose the same apple, comparing measurements should help you decide whose apple it really is.

Draw Conclusions

1. **Compare** your apple with a classmate's apple. How are the two apples alike? How are they different?

2. Why was it helpful to **measure** some properties of your apple in addition to **observing** it?

3. How did you use the string to **measure** the apple?

4. **Scientists at Work** Scientists use both observations and measurements to identify substances. Which is faster, **observing** or **measuring**? Which provides more exact information?

Investigate Further **Compare** the list of your apple's properties with a classmate's list. Then, using both lists, come up with a way to **classify** apples based on their physical properties.

Process Skill Tip

Some properties can only be observed. When you **observe**, you use only your senses. Some properties can be measured with instruments. Being able to **measure** something you are studying will help you identify it.

The Importance of Physical Properties

Matter and Physical Properties

FIND OUT

- what physical properties are
- how to measure some physical properties
- examples of physical properties that can be used to identify substances

VOCABULARY

matter
physical properties
mass
weight
volume
density
solubility

The objects you used in the investigation were all alike—they were all apples. But would you believe that apples, parrots, candy, computers, humans, and even the air around you are all alike in one way? They are all made of matter. **Matter** is anything that has mass and takes up space.

Objects made of matter can be very different from each other. Each object has its own set of characteristics, or *properties*. For example, one property of a piece of candy is its color. Another is its taste.

Color, hardness, and taste are examples of physical properties. An object's ability to conduct heat, sound, or electricity or to become a magnet are also physical properties. **Physical properties** are characteristics of a substance that can be observed or measured without changing the substance into something else.

Some physical properties, such as color, can be observed directly. Other physical properties, such as length, must be measured. Measurements are especially useful in science because they provide more exact descriptions of matter than direct observations do.

✔ **What are some examples of physical properties?**

◀ You can tell these balls apart by examining the physical properties of size, mass, and color.

Mass and Weight

One physical property that can be measured is mass. **Mass** is the amount of matter in an object. The mass of an 18-wheel truck is greater than the mass of a small car, because the truck has more matter. In this example you can easily see the difference in the amount of matter. Sometimes the difference in the amount of matter between two objects is very small. In fact, some matter may have so little mass that it is difficult to measure. But all matter has some mass.

It's easy to confuse mass with another physical property—weight. Weight depends on the amount of matter in an object. However, weight also depends on the force of gravity. So **weight** is a measure of the pull of gravity on an object. While the mass of an object is always the same, the weight of an object is not. For example, a car that weighs 12,000 newtons (about 2698 lb) on Earth would weigh only 2000 newtons (about 450 lb) on the moon! This is because the force of gravity is 6 times greater on Earth than it is on the moon. Because weight can vary,

▲ The mass of the foam, on the balance, will be the same no matter what shape it is given. The mass of the gel, in the container at the left, will also stay the same, even though it takes the shape of its container.

mass is a better measurement of the amount of matter in an object.

Different equipment is used to measure weight and mass. Weight is measured on a spring scale. How much the spring in the scale is squeezed or stretched depends on the pull of gravity and the mass of the object being weighed. Mass is measured on a balance to avoid also measuring the pull of gravity. On a balance the mass of an object is compared to a known mass.

✔ **How are mass and weight alike? How are they different?**

An astronaut weighs less on the moon than on Earth. However, the astronaut has the same mass on the moon as on Earth. ▶

Volume

Matter not only has mass but also takes up space. **Volume** is the amount of space that an object takes up. Volume can be measured in several ways.

The volume of a liquid can be measured using a graduated cylinder. A *graduated cylinder* is a clear tube that is marked in milliliters. When liquids are poured into a graduated cylinder, they stick slightly to the tube, forming a curved surface. To measure the volume of a liquid accurately, you need to read the volume at the bottom of this curve.

The volume of some solids can be calculated. First, measure the length, width, and height of the object. Then multiply as shown in this formula:

Volume = length × width × height

For example, the volume of a box 38 cm long, 21 cm wide, and 13 cm high is calculated as follows:

Volume = 38 cm × 21 cm × 13 cm = 10,374 cm³

The volume of the rock is equal to the difference in the volume of the water before and after the rock is placed in it.

Although most solids do not have regular shapes, their volumes can still be measured. One way to do this is to measure the amount of liquid, such as water, that the solid *displaces*, or takes the place of. To do this, partially fill a measuring container with water and place the solid in the liquid. You will observe that the level of the liquid rises. The volume of the water and solid together is greater than the volume of the water alone. The volume of the solid is the difference between these two volumes.

✔ **What are two ways to measure the volume of a solid?**

◀ The 250 mL (about 8 oz) of juice in the box can be measured in a graduated cylinder. Notice that the volume of a liquid does not depend on the shape of the container.

Density

Mass and volume are physical properties that can be measured. By themselves, neither can be used to identify unknown objects or substances. However, if you have measured the mass and the volume of an object, you can calculate its density. You can then use this property to identify some objects.

Density is the concentration of matter in an object. It is the amount of matter in a certain volume. Density is calculated by using the following formula:

Density = mass ÷ volume

For example, the density of a substance with a mass of 10 g and a volume of 2 cm³ is calculated as follows:

Density = 10 g ÷ 2 cm³
= 5 g/cm³

Pure substances always have the same density when measured under the same conditions. The density of diamond, for example, is always 3.51 g/cm³ (2.03 oz/in.³).

▲ The copper cube, made with the densest matter, has the greatest mass. The aluminum cube is less dense than the copper cube. The wooden cube is the same size but is made with the least-dense matter. It has the smallest mass.

Because density is always the same for a pure substance, this property can be used for identification. Suppose you were given a gemstone and didn't know whether it was a diamond or a zircon—a mineral that looks like a diamond but is much less valuable. If you had instruments that were exact enough, you could measure the gemstone's mass on a balance and find out its volume by the amount of water it displaced. Then you could calculate its density. If the density is 4.7 g/cm³ (2.72 oz/in.³), you have a zircon. If the density is 3.51 g/cm³ (2.03 oz/in.³), you have a diamond!

The Density of Copper

Mass	8.96 g	89.6 g	134.4 g
Volume	1 cm³	10 cm³	15 cm³
Density	8.96 g/cm³	8.96 g/cm³	8.96 g/cm³

▲ No matter how large or how small a copper ball is, its density is always the same.

✔ **Will different volumes of the same substance have the same density or different densities?**

Mixtures and Solutions

Most of the objects around us are not pure substances. Instead, they are mixtures. A *mixture* is a combination of two or more different kinds of matter, each of which keeps its own physical properties.

In some mixtures it's easy to tell that each type of matter keeps its physical properties, because you can still see the parts of the mixture. If sugar and iron filings are mixed together, for example, you can still see the individual sugar grains and the iron filings.

Mixtures can be separated into the substances that make them up. The method used to separate a mixture depends on the physical properties of the substances in the mixture. In a mixture of iron filings and sugar, the iron filings keep their physical property of magnetism. Since sugar doesn't have this property, you can separate the mixture with a magnet.

If sugar is mixed with water, it's not easy to tell what is in the mixture. The sugar seems to disappear. But if you taste the mixture, you will find that the water is sweet. The sugar has kept its physical property of taste. In a mixture of sugar and water, the sugar dissolves in the water. When one substance dissolves in another, the two form a solution. A *solution* is a type of mixture in which particles of the two substances are evenly mixed. Solutions cannot be easily separated.

The **solubility** (sahl•yoo•BIL•uh•tee) of substances, or their ability to be dissolved, can be used to help identify them. Sugar, for example, is soluble in water, but ground black pepper is not.

The air in the diver's tank is a mixture of mostly nitrogen and oxygen. ▶

Sea water is a mixture of salts and water. The salts in sea water can be separated from the water by evaporation.

Gases in Air

Other gases 1%

Oxygen 21%

Nitrogen 78%

Sand is a mixture of solids. You can still see the different types of solids after they are mixed together.

In the sugar and water solution, a solid is mixed with a liquid. Rubbing alcohol is a solution of two liquids: water and alcohol. But solutions don't have to include a liquid. Mixtures of metals are solutions of solids. Brass is a solution of zinc and copper. It is made by melting the two metals together. Gases can form solutions, too. Air is a solution of several gases, as the circle graph on page C10 shows.

✔ **What is an example of a mixture?**

Summary

Matter is anything that has mass and takes up space. Physical properties can be used to identify different types of objects and substances. Some physical properties (such as mass, volume, and density) can be measured. Physical properties such as density and solubility help scientists identify different substances.

Review

1. How can physical properties be used to identify objects and substances?

2. Does an object on Earth have the same mass as it does on the moon? Explain.

3. What physical properties are used to calculate the density of an object?

4. **Critical Thinking** Are all solutions mixtures? Are all mixtures solutions? Explain with examples.

5. **Test Prep** All of these are physical properties except —

   A mass

   B volume

   C density

   D time

LINKS

MATH LINK

The International System of Units (SI) SI uses prefixes to tell you how many times to multiply or divide by 10. Put these measurements in order from shortest to longest: 2 dam, 4 m, 60 dm, 500 cm, 10,000 mm.

Prefix	Abbreviation	Multiply By
kilo	k	1000
hecto	h	100
deca	da	10
deci	d	$\frac{1}{10}$
centi	c	$\frac{1}{100}$
milli	m	$\frac{1}{1000}$

WRITING LINK

Informative Writing—Description Suppose you find an unknown substance growing out of the sidewalk in front of your home. Decide on its physical properties, and write a paragraph for your science teacher describing them.

PHYSICAL EDUCATION LINK

Swimming Research to find the dimensions of an Olympic-sized pool. Then figure out the volume of water it can hold.

TECHNOLOGY LINK

Learn more about the physical properties of matter by visiting this Internet site.
www.scilinks.org/harcourt

How Does Matter Change from One State to Another?

In this lesson, you can . . .

INVESTIGATE changes in states of matter.

LEARN ABOUT three states of matter.

LINK to math, writing, physical education, and technology.

Ice (water) changes state from a solid to a liquid when it is warmed by the heat of a human hand. ▼

INVESTIGATE

Changing States of Matter

Activity Purpose   Liquid water, ice, and water vapor are all the same substance, but they have different physical properties. That's because they are all different states, or forms, of the same substance. In this investigation you will **observe** and **infer** changing states of matter.

Materials

- 5 ice cubes
- zip-top plastic bag
- balance
- thermometer
- glass beaker
- safety goggles
- hot plate

CAUTION

Activity Procedure

1 Place five ice cubes in a zip-top plastic bag. Be sure to seal the bag. Use the balance to **measure** the mass of the ice cubes and the bag. **Observe** the shape of the ice cubes. **Record** your observations and measurements. (Picture A)

2 Set the bag of ice cubes in a warm place. **Observe** what happens to the shape of the ice cubes. **Measure** the mass of the melted ice cubes and the bag. Unzip the bag slightly and insert the thermometer. Measure the temperature of the water. **Record** your observations and measurements. Use your observations to **infer** that a change of state is occurring.

Picture A

Picture B

3 After the ice has completely melted, pour the water into a glass beaker. **Observe** what happens to the water's shape, and **record** the water's temperature. (Picture B)

4 **CAUTION** **Put on the safety goggles.** Your teacher will use a hot plate to heat the water in the beaker until it boils. **Observe** what happens to the water when it boils. **Record** the temperature of the boiling water. Use your observations to **infer** that another change of state has occurred.

Draw Conclusions

1. Identify the different states of water at different points in this investigation.

2. **Compare** the mass of the ice to the mass of water after it melted. What does this show about changes in state?

3. What temperatures did you **record** as the water changed states? Make a table or a graph of your data.

4. **Scientists at Work** After scientists use their senses to **observe** the properties of substances, they can **infer** whether a change in state has taken place. What did you observe in this investigation? What did you infer about a change of state from each observation?

Investigate Further The physical change that happens to water when it is boiled produces water vapor—an invisible gas. Develop a testable question or a hypothesis about the relationship between the mass of the water vapor and the mass of the liquid water.

Changes in State

Three States of Matter

FIND OUT

- what three states of matter are
- how substances change state

VOCABULARY

solid
liquid
gas
evaporation
condensation

In the investigation you learned that water exists in three states—solid, liquid, and gas. Most matter exists in one or more of these states. Which state it is in depends on the conditions at the time, such as temperature and pressure. A **solid** has a definite shape and a definite volume. A **liquid** has a definite volume but no definite shape. For example, when you pour orange juice, a liquid, from a jug into a glass, the shape of the juice changes to fit the container. The volume of juice, however, doesn't change. A **gas** does not have a definite shape or volume. If you put air into a tire, for example, it takes the same shape as the tire. But even when the tire seems full, you can put more air into it.

✔ **What are three states of matter?**

Two states of water are shown in this picture. A third can be inferred. The snow is solid water. Melted snow and ice are liquid water. Water vapor released into the air by the geysers (GY•zerz) is a gas. However, the steam that can be seen near the geysers is liquid water, not water vapor.

Particles of Matter

Why does a solid keep its shape? Why does a liquid flow? Why can the volume of a gas change? You can better understand the differences between states of matter if you think of matter as particles in motion.

In a solid the particles are very close together. Because there is very little space between particles, they can't be squeezed any closer together. This gives a solid a definite volume and shape. It also keeps particles in a solid from moving very much. In fact, they are packed together so tightly that each particle stays in the same place and just vibrates.

Particles are not packed together as tightly in a liquid, so they move more freely than they do in a solid. This allows a liquid to flow and take the shape of its container. You can see the motion of particles in a liquid by placing a drop of dye in a glass of water. As the particles bump into one another, the dye slowly spreads through the water.

The particles in a gas are packed together the least. Because the particles are freer to move around in gases than in solids or liquids, gas particles move the fastest. Like a liquid, a gas flows and takes the shape of its container. But the density of particles in a gas is so low that an increase in pressure can move the particles closer together. If the pressure is high enough, a gas becomes a liquid.

✔ **In which state of matter are the particles closest together? Farthest apart?**

A solid feels firm when you touch it because the particles that make it up are packed tightly together. A solid can be used to make gear that protects you, like this bicycle helmet.

The particles in a liquid move freely enough to slide past one another. This allows liquids to change shape, as the milk has done in this splash.

The particles in a gas are the farthest apart and move the fastest. Bubbles of carbon dioxide gas are lighter than the liquid in this glass, so they float to the top and escape into the air.

C15

Changes Between States

You may be used to seeing many substances in only one state. Nitrogen is usually a gas, for example, and aluminum is usually a solid. But all substances can change states. Liquid nitrogen is used to cool other materials to very low temperatures. Liquid aluminum can be poured into molds to make objects.

You may have seen puddles freeze and turn to ice when it gets cold. *Freezing* changes a substance from a liquid to a solid.

When the sun comes out and warms the ice, it melts. *Melting* is a change in state from a solid to a liquid.

In the investigation you saw water boiling on a hot plate. *Boiling* changes a substance from a liquid to a gas. Even when the temperature of a liquid has not yet reached its boiling point, some of the particles near the surface may be moving fast enough to evaporate. **Evaporation** occurs when particles escape from a nonboiling liquid and become a gas.

THE INSIDE STORY

Changing States

When enough heat is removed from a liquid, it freezes. The particles slow down and move closer together. They become tightly packed and a solid is formed. ▼

When a solid melts, the addition of heat makes the particles move faster. ▼

Melting

Freezing

◀ This is the solid state of sulfur.

Condensation (kahn•den•SAY•shuhn) changes a substance from a gas to a liquid. This is what happens when drops of water appear on the outside of a glass of cold water on a hot day. Water vapor in the air is cooled on the surface of the glass. It condenses, forming water drops.

Particles can also escape from the surface of a solid and become a gas. *Sublimation* (sub•luh•MAY•shuhn) is a change in state from a solid to a gas. Dry ice, which is solid carbon dioxide, sublimes. Without ever melting, in warm air it forms a cold gas that looks like smoke.

Changes in state do not change a substance. Water is still water whether it is a solid, a liquid, or a gas. Changes in state are also reversible.

Changes in state occur when heat is added or removed. When heat is added to a substance, the particles gain energy. They move faster, and farther apart. When heat is removed from a substance, the particles slow down. When enough heat has been removed, the particles move closer together.

✔ **What process is the opposite of evaporation?**

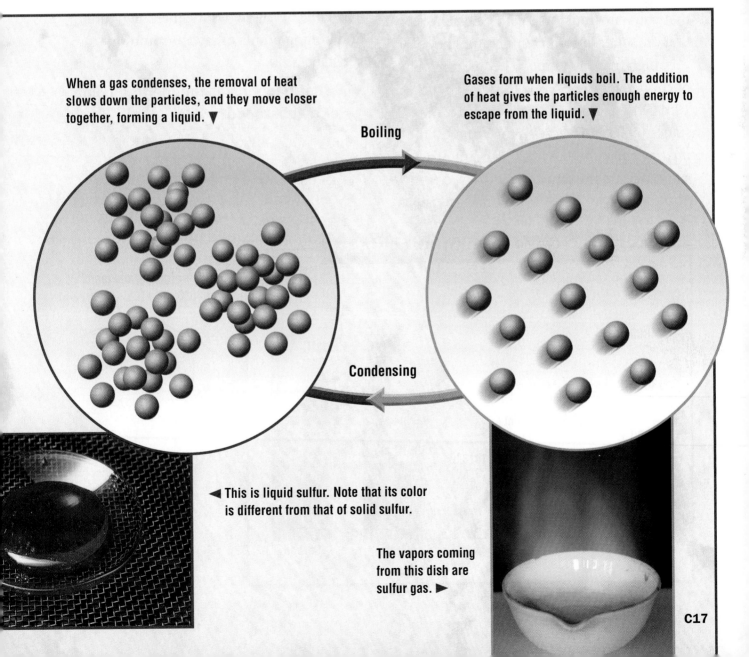

When a gas condenses, the removal of heat slows down the particles, and they move closer together, forming a liquid. ▼

Gases form when liquids boil. The addition of heat gives the particles enough energy to escape from the liquid. ▼

Boiling

Condensing

◄ This is liquid sulfur. Note that its color is different from that of solid sulfur.

The vapors coming from this dish are sulfur gas. ►

C17

Melting and Boiling Points

Farmers who grow oranges and grapefruit worry when the outdoor temperature drops below 0°C (32°F). That's because all water, including the water inside the fruit, freezes at 0°C. Freezing and thawing can damage fruit, making it worthless.

When a weather forecaster says there will be freezing temperatures, the word *freezing* refers to the temperature at which water freezes. But every substance has its own temperature at which it changes from a liquid to a solid. This temperature is the substance's *freezing point*.

Not all freezing points are temperatures that you may think of as cold. Substances that are solids at room temperature have very high freezing points. The freezing point of copper, for example, is 1083°C (about 1981°F)! The temperature at which a substance melts and freezes is the same. So the *melting point* and the freezing point of a substance are the same.

The temperature at which a substance changes from a liquid to a gas is called its *boiling point*. The boiling point of water is 100°C (212°F). Boiling points are not always temperatures you would consider to be hot. Substances that are gases at room temperature have very low boiling points. The boiling point of oxygen, for example, is -183°C (about -297°F).

At normal air pressure, the temperatures at which a substance melts and boils are always the same. However, different substances melt and boil at different temperatures. So most substances can be identified by their melting points and boiling points. The table below shows the melting points and boiling points of several common substances.

✔ **What happens at the melting point of a substance?**

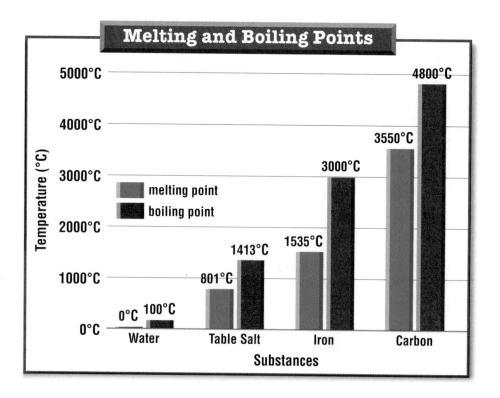

Melting and Boiling Points

- melting point
- boiling point

Water: 0°C, 100°C
Table Salt: 801°C, 1413°C
Iron: 1535°C, 3000°C
Carbon: 3550°C, 4800°C

Temperature (°C) / Substances

Water freezes and melts at 0°C (32°F). ▼

Summary

Three states of matter are solid, liquid, and gas. Changes in state are physical changes. Particles of matter move faster as heat is added and slow down as heat is removed. Every substance has a melting point, the temperature at which it changes from a solid to a liquid. It also has a boiling point, the temperature at which it changes from a liquid to a gas.

Review

1. What are the three states in which most matter occurs?

2. List two substances that are solids, two that are liquids, and two that are gases at room temperature.

3. What happens to the particles of matter when a liquid changes to a gas?

4. **Critical Thinking** Why can boiling points and freezing points be used to identify substances?

5. **Test Prep** The process by which a liquid becomes a gas without boiling is called —

   A sublimation   **C** melting

   B precipitation   **D** evaporation

◀ **Water boils and condenses at 100°C (212°F).**

LINKS

MATH LINK

Estimate The volume of a gas varies with pressure. The higher the pressure, the smaller the volume. If a sample of gas has a volume of 150 mL, will its volume be larger or smaller if the pressure doubles?

WRITING LINK

Narrative Writing—Personal Story Suppose you are a particle in a substance. Write a story about what happens to you as the substance changes its state from a solid to a liquid and then to a gas. Read your story to your class.

PHYSICAL EDUCATION LINK

Sports and Water Many sports use water in different states. For example, hockey is played on solid water—ice. With a partner, make a list of as many sports as you can that use water in some state.

TECHNOLOGY LINK

Learn more about freezing points by viewing *Absolute Zero* on the **Harcourt Science Newsroom Video** in your classroom video library.

LESSON 3

How Does Matter React Chemically?

In this lesson, you can . . .

INVESTIGATE chemical properties of matter.

LEARN ABOUT changes in matter.

LINK to math, writing, social studies, and technology.

Heat and smoke are signs of chemical reactions that occur when the space shuttle lifts off. ▶

Chemical Properties

Activity Purpose If you were in the kitchen at home and had to decide whether a cup of solid, white grains was sugar or salt, you could taste them. While tasting might be fairly safe in your own kitchen, you should never taste an unknown substance in a science laboratory. Tasting in the laboratory is very dangerous! Instead, you can use chemical properties to identify substances. *Chemical properties* are characteristics of a substance related to changing the substance into something else. In this investigation you will **experiment** to discover some chemical properties of matter.

Materials

- masking tape
- marking pen
- 3 test tubes
- apron
- safety goggles
- measuring spoon
- baking soda
- 3 droppers
- water
- vinegar
- iodine solution
- cornstarch
- talcum powder
- baking powder

CAUTION

Activity Procedure

1. Use the masking tape and marking pen to label your test tubes *water*, *vinegar*, and *iodine*.

2. **CAUTION** Put on the apron and safety goggles. Leave them on for the entire activity.

3. Put about $\frac{1}{3}$ spoonful of baking soda in each test tube. Add a dropper of water to the test tube labeled *water*. **Observe** and **record** what happens.

4. Add a dropper of vinegar to the test tube labeled *vinegar*. **Observe** and **record** what happens this time. (Picture A)

5. Add a dropper of iodine solution to the test tube labeled *iodine*. **CAUTION** **Iodine is poisonous if swallowed and can cause stains. Be careful not to spill or touch the iodine solution. Wash your hands if you get iodine on them.** **Observe** and **record** what happens.

6. Wash the test tubes with soap and water. Repeat Steps 3–5 three more times using cornstarch, talcum powder, and baking powder in the test tubes instead of baking soda. Be sure to wash the test tubes between tests. **Observe** and **record** what happens each time. (Picture B)

7. Get an "unknown" sample from your teacher. It will be one of the substances you have already tested. Test it with water, vinegar, and iodine solution, just as you did before. **Observe** and **record** what happens when you add each of the liquids. What is your unknown substance?

Picture A

Picture B

Draw Conclusions

1. Vinegar is one of a group of substances called *acids*. Acids react with substances called *bases*. Of the substances you tested, which are bases? How can you tell?

2. Baking powder is not a pure substance. It is a mixture of two of the other substances you tested. Based on your results, what do you **infer** are the two substances in baking powder?

3. **Scientists at Work** Scientists **experiment** to find out if substances react. What signs of reactions (dependent variables) did you identify? What **variables** did you **control**? What was the independent variable (the one you changed) in each experiment? What did you learn as you changed this variable?

Investigate Further Suppose you wanted to discover some of the chemical properties of chalk. First develop a testable question. Then **experiment** to answer your question.

Process Skill Tip

When you **experiment**, it is important to vary only one factor at a time. This helps make clear which factor is the cause of the results you observe. Varying one factor at a time is called **controlling variables**.

Changes in Matter

Physical and Chemical Changes

FIND OUT

- about physical and chemical changes
- how physical and chemical changes can be used to identify substances and to separate mixtures
- about the law of conservation of matter

VOCABULARY

reactivity
combustibility

When ice melts, it changes into liquid water. When liquid water boils, it changes into water vapor. But through all the changes, it is still water. Changes in which no new substances are formed are physical changes. All changes in state are physical changes.

When you shape clay on a potter's wheel, you change its form. This is a physical change. Cutting up a piece of paper is also a physical change. Gases such as hydrogen and oxygen can be cooled and squeezed until they become liquids. When this happens, the gases go through changes in state, volume, and density. These are all physical changes!

But if an electric current is sent through water, a different kind of change takes place. Gases are produced, but the gases are not water. They are oxygen and hydrogen, the substances that make up water. In the space shuttle's main engines, liquid oxygen and liquid hydrogen are mixed and burned as a fuel. Water—a new substance—is produced. Changes in which one or more new substances are formed are called chemical changes, or *chemical reactions*.

A marshmallow melting is an example of a physical change. A marshmallow burning is an example of a chemical change. ▼

Burning is one kind of chemical reaction. When charcoal burns, for example, carbon reacts with oxygen to produce carbon dioxide. Carbon and oxygen are *reactants*, the starting substances in a chemical reaction. Carbon dioxide is a *product* of the reaction. It is a new substance.

Some substances are more likely than others to react. Chlorine gas reacts chemically with many different substances. But neon gas does not. The ability of a substance to react chemically is called **reactivity**.

There are some clues that can help you identify chemical reactions. They include a change in color or the production of light, heat, or a gas. Paper turns black as it burns, for example. When baking soda is mixed with vinegar, it bubbles. This shows that carbon dioxide has been produced. A candle produces heat and light as it burns.

However, it's sometimes hard to tell the difference between a physical change and a chemical reaction. Cherry-flavored drink powder is pale pink. When you mix it with water, it turns bright red. But the powder has only dissolved. It has gone through a physical change, not a chemical reaction. When you open a cold soft drink, bubbles are produced. But a chemical reaction has not taken place. The carbon dioxide has simply come out of solution. And if you rub your hands quickly back and forth across a surface, they become hot. But the heat is due to friction, not a chemical reaction.

✔ **What is the difference between a physical change and a chemical reaction?**

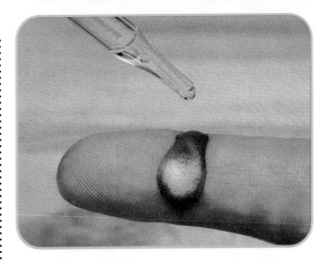

▲ Production of a different kind of gas shows that a chemical reaction has taken place. When hydrogen peroxide is used to clean a wound, it reacts with a substance in blood, forming oxygen and water.

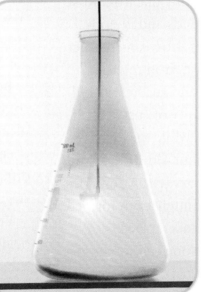

◄ When sodium combines with chlorine to make sodium chloride (salt), light is produced. This new product shows that a chemical reaction has occurred.

Steel wool burns, but only in pure oxygen, not in air. Steel wool is not as reactive as charcoal, which does burn in air. ▼

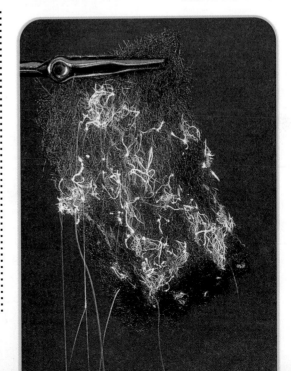

Using Physical and Chemical Properties

Chemical reactions often form products with properties that are different from those of the reactants. So observing the chemical and physical properties of a substance can help you decide whether a chemical change or a physical change has taken place.

For example, when iron rusts, it turns red or brown. But is this a chemical reaction or a physical change? Is rust a new substance, or is it still iron?

If you examine rust carefully, you will find that it is no longer shiny like iron. Rust is powdery, while iron bends and is easily formed into other shapes. Iron can conduct electricity, but rust cannot. Iron melts at 1535°C (about 2795°F), and rust at 1594°C (about 2901°F). The density of rust is 5.18 g/cm³ (about 323 lb/ft³), while the density of iron is 7.86 g/cm³ (about 491 lb/ft³). And rust does not react with oxygen as iron does. A new substance has definitely been formed. A chemical reaction has taken place.

Chemical properties alone can sometimes be used to identify substances. Since charcoal burns, it has the chemical property of **combustibility** (kuhm•buhs•tuh•BIL•uh•tee). Some substances can be identified by certain characteristics of their combustibility. Flame tests can be used to identify substances based on the color of the flame they produce when burned. Barium, for example, produces a green flame. Sodium produces a yellow flame, and potassium produces a violet flame.

Chemical properties are also important in deciding how certain substances can be used. For example, many solutions are either acids or bases. Acids are sour, and weak acids can be used to flavor foods. Weak bases can be used in cleaning products. However, strong acids and strong bases are dangerous. Therefore, it's important to be able to measure their strengths. The strengths of acids and bases are measured using dyes called *indicators*. Indicators react chemically with acids and bases and turn different colors depending on their strengths.

Physical and chemical properties can also be used to separate mixtures or to identify substances in mixtures. Remember that the

Gold can be separated from sand by panning, because gold is more dense than sand.

Acids can be used to identify limestone because they react easily with it, producing bubbles of carbon dioxide. Acid rain can damage limestone statues for the same reason; it reacts chemically with them.

substances that make up mixtures keep their physical properties. They also keep their chemical properties.

One industry that uses physical and chemical properties to separate mixtures is the mining industry. Metals must be separated from their ores before they can be made into useful products. An *ore* is a combination of a metal and other substances, such as oxygen, sulfur, carbon, or silicon. Several methods can be used to separate metals from their ores. Some impurities, or unwanted substances, are less dense than water, so they float in water and can be washed away. Others, like sulfur, can be burned away.

If a mixture contains a substance that is magnetic, a magnet can be used to separate the mixture. For example, a magnet can be used to separate steel from a mixture of car parts containing steel, aluminum, and plastics. The steel can then be recycled into new car parts.

Some liquid mixtures can be separated by spinning at very high speeds—up to 80,000 turns per minute. The force of the spinning pushes solids and other dense substances to the bottom of the container. This process can be used to separate heavy blood cells from the liquid, called plasma. It can also be used to separate the lighter cream from the heavier milk. This produces skim milk.

A solution of a solid and a liquid can be separated by boiling away the liquid, leaving the solid behind. When salt water is boiled, the water boils away and the salt is left as crystals in the container. The water can be recovered by collecting the water vapor and condensing it. This process is called *distillation*. Distillation is used to separate petroleum into products such as gasoline, motor oil, and asphalt.

Sometimes both a physical change and a chemical reaction are used to recover a substance from a mixture. For example, suppose you wanted to recover some copper from a mixture of copper, sugar, and charcoal. Since sugar is the only substance of the three that is soluble in water, water can be added to dissolve the sugar. The sugar water can be removed from the mixture by pouring it through filter paper. Sugar water will pass through the filter paper, but the large particles of copper and charcoal won't. After the charcoal-and-copper mixture dries, the charcoal can be burned away, leaving only copper.

✔ **What physical and chemical properties are used to separate metals from their ores?**

Conservation of Matter

Physical changes and chemical reactions cause matter to look different. But neither can change the amount of matter present. Matter is neither created nor destroyed during a physical change or a chemical change. Scientists call this the *law of conservation of matter*.

This law is easier to prove for some changes than it is for others. If you cut a piece of paper into tiny pieces, you have more pieces of paper, but you have not made more paper. However, when water changes from a liquid to a gas, there may appear to be more matter because the volume of water vapor is greater. But no new matter has been produced. The density of the water is less, so the same mass of water takes up more space. If you measured carefully, you would discover that the mass of the water before the change of state is equal to the mass of water vapor produced.

It may be harder to believe that matter is not produced or destroyed during a chemical change. The reactants seem to disappear and the products seem to appear. However, in the 1700s, Antoine Lavoisier (lah•vwah•ZYAY), a French chemist, was among the first scientists to carefully measure chemical reactions. He found that during a chemical change, the mass of the products equals the mass of the reactants. Because there is no change in mass after a chemical reaction, there is no more and no less matter than there was before the reaction.

Sometimes the masses involved in a chemical change may be harder to measure than those in a physical change. For example, one of the reactants of combustion reactions is oxygen from the air. If the oxygen is not included in the mass of the reactants, then the mass of the products appears to be greater than the mass of the reactants. It looks as if matter has been produced!

✔ **Give an example of a physical change, and explain how matter was neither created nor destroyed.**

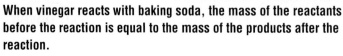

When vinegar reacts with baking soda, the mass of the reactants before the reaction is equal to the mass of the products after the reaction.

Summary

Physical changes do not result in the formation of new substances. However, new substances are formed during chemical changes. Physical and chemical properties can be used to identify substances and to separate mixtures. Matter is neither produced nor destroyed during physical and chemical reactions.

Review

1. Give an example of a physical change and a chemical change for iron.
2. Give an example of a chemical change that produces light and heat.
3. Does distillation produce a chemical change or a physical change in petroleum? Explain your answer.
4. **Critical Thinking** Describe how to use physical properties to separate a mixture of ice cubes and nails.
5. **Test Prep** The law which says that matter is neither produced nor destroyed in a physical or chemical reaction is the law of —
   - **A** conservation of matter
   - **B** metallurgy
   - **C** chemical properties
   - **D** physical changes

LINKS

MATH LINK

Conservation of Mass Sometimes it is easier to calculate the mass of a gas involved in a chemical reaction than it is to measure it. If 56 g of iron react with oxygen gas to produce 80 g of rust, calculate the mass of the oxygen that reacted.

WRITING LINK

Persuasive Writing—Opinion Scientists sometimes don't agree whether a certain change is physical or chemical. They use data from experiments to support their positions. Choose an example that you think is a physical or chemical change, and then write a persuasive paragraph for your teacher using experimental data to support your opinion.

SOCIAL STUDIES LINK

History The progress of science is often affected by politics. Research the life of Antoine Lavoisier to find out how the politics in France during the late 1700s may have affected the progress of science.

TECHNOLOGY LINK

Learn more about physical and chemical changes by investigating *Matter Mania* on the **Harcourt Science Explorations CD-ROM.**

Self-Healing Asphalt

T he tissue of many living organisms heals itself. Trim away branches of a tree, for example, and it quickly produces new shoots. Can nonliving things also repair themselves? Some asphalt seems to.

Tired Pavement

Asphalt is the sticky, black stuff used to pave roads and parking lots. It is made from petroleum and crushed rock. After it dries, fresh asphalt feels smooth under the wheels of a car. As it gets old, however, asphalt cracks and crumbles from the weight of many vehicles rolling over it.

It's hard to repair roads that are busy all day.

Highway repair takes a lot of time, money, and machinery.

This cracking and crumbling is called fatigue. If the cracks widen and deepen, potholes appear. Eventually the road falls apart. In some places, however, asphalt cracks just seem to disappear. Researchers have conducted tests to find out why some asphalt repairs itself.

In one test a heavy machine imitates traffic on test pavement. Then engineers measure how much cracking has occurred. A day later they measure the pavement again. Remarkably, the cracks in some of the test pavement "heal" overnight. Somehow, resting gives some kinds of asphalt a chance to recover.

Cracking the Mystery

Why does some asphalt heal itself? Molecules in any material—asphalt, glass, or anything else—bond with molecules around them. When a material cracks, the bonds between molecules break. Why do molecules in some kinds of asphalt reconnect after the asphalt rests, but the bonds in other kinds do not? Scientists are studying the ingredients in different asphalts. They hope to find out which ones produce healing.

Some researchers hypothesize that they can speed up asphalt healing with microwaves. Heating the asphalt causes more molecules to reconnect. But it would be impractical to do this on a large scale. Engineers suggest building wider roads. During the day, driving lanes could be alternated, giving each lane a rest period. Whichever process is used, self-healing roads could save taxpayers millions of dollars in repairs each year.

THINK ABOUT IT

1. What are some ways the healing process in roads could be speeded up?

2. Why do you think asphalt gets more "rest" in some locations than others?

 WEB LINK:
For science and technology updates, visit The Learning Site.
www.harcourtschool.com/ca

Careers   Highway Engineer

What They Do
Highway engineers plan, design, construct, and inspect highways, tunnels, and other structures. They analyze speed limits, study the soil, and work with asphalt mixtures.

Education and Training   To become a highway engineer, a person needs to study civil and environmental engineering. Math, chemistry, physics, and computer skills are also important.

Theophilus Leapheart
CHEMIST

"No one can put the whole puzzle together alone. Chemists, engineers, mathematicians, and physicists all need to work together to solve problems and to develop new products. To be successful, you have to know how to work with others."

Theophilus Leapheart is the leader of a group of chemists who make new chemical compounds. An important part of this job is finding out the structures of the compounds being made. To do this, Mr. Leapheart's team uses the technology of NMR spectroscopy. The letters *NMR* stand for *n*uclear *m*agnetic *r*esonance.

When the team is ready to test a new compound, they take a sample and dissolve it in a solvent. Then they place the sample in the NMR machine, which produces a strong magnetic field. The magnetic field causes molecules of the sample compound to line up in a certain way, just as Earth's magnetic field causes a compass needle to point north.

The NMR spectrum of a compound is like its fingerprint—no two compounds produce exactly the same spectrum. By looking at an NMR spectrum, Mr. Leapheart can tell which atoms are present and how many are present. In this way he can determine the structure of even the most complicated molecules.

THINK ABOUT IT

1. How does an NMR spectrum help identify a compound?
2. Why is it important for chemists to communicate the processes they use and the results of their work?

An NMR spectrum

Density Column

Why do some liquids separate?

Materials
- 250-mL graduate
- 50 mL cooking oil
- 50 mL water
- blue food coloring
- 50 mL corn syrup
- 50 mL alcohol
- small cork
- glass marble
- small rock
- wood cube
- metal nut

Procedure

1. Add the food coloring to the water.

2. Pour the liquids into the graduate in order: corn syrup, colored water, oil, and alcohol.

3. Predict in which layers the cork, marble, rock, wood, and metal will end up.

4. Gently drop in the cork, marble, rock, wood, and metal and observe.

Draw Conclusions

Why do the liquids separate into four layers? In which liquid does each of the objects end up? How does this match your predictions? Why do some of the objects sink, while others float?

Mix It Up

How can some mixtures be separated?

Materials
- coffee filter
- scissors
- 3 different-colored water-soluble markers
- small paper cups
- water

Procedure

1. Cut the coffee filter into three strips, each 3 cm X 10 cm.

2. Touch a different-colored marker near one end of each of the pieces of filter paper.

3. Put the bottom edge of each piece of filter paper in a paper cup containing a small amount of water.

4. Observe what happens.

Draw Conclusions

Most inks are mixtures of different-colored pigments. As water traveled up the filter papers, the pigments separated. Which pigments made up the colors you tested? Why do you think some of the pigments traveled farther up the paper than others?

Cabbage Juice Indicator

How can you use cabbage juice as an indicator?

Materials

- head of red cabbage
- large pot
- boiling water
- folded paper towel
- glass jar
- funnel
- tablespoon
- several small glasses
- marker
- substances to test, such as bleach, soft drinks, baking powder, vinegar, soap, fruit juices, milk, antacids, tea, and oven cleaner

Procedure

❶ To make the cabbage juice, cut up about half of the cabbage. Place it in a pot and cover it with boiling water. After 15 minutes, the juice should be cool enough to handle.

❷ Place the folded paper towel in the funnel. Put the funnel in the mouth of the glass jar. Hold it steady while a partner pours the mixture through the filter. Now you have a jar of cabbage juice indicator.

❸ Put several tablespoons of cabbage juice into each glass. Label each glass with the name of the substance you will test. Then add the test substances to the glasses. Make sure you crush any solids before putting them into the glasses. Add only small amounts of dark substances, because they make the cabbage juice hard to see.

❹ Cabbage juice is an indicator. When you add it to another substance, it changes color to indicate the presence of an acid or a base. After a few minutes, compare each glass to the jar of cabbage juice. If the cabbage juice in the glass is pink, the substance being tested is an acid. If the cabbage juice is blue or green, the substance is a base.

Draw Conclusions

Make a chart showing which of the substances you tested were acids and which were bases.

Hot or Cold?

How do Epsom salts make water colder?

Materials

- 1/2 cup water at room temperature
- outdoor thermometer
- stopwatch (or watch with a second hand)
- 1/2 cup Epsom salts at room temperature
- spoon

Procedure

❶ Put the thermometer in the water for 20 seconds. Record the temperature, and remove the thermometer.

❷ Add the Epsom salts to the water and stir for about 20 seconds.

❸ Measure and record the water temperature again.

Draw Conclusions

What happened to the temperature of the water after you added the Epsom salts? Is this an example of a physical change or a chemical change? How do you know?

Pennies and Paper Clips

How does acid affect copper?

Materials

- plain steel paper clip
- about 30 copper pennies (Pennies made before 1983 contain more copper.)
- plastic cup of vinegar

Procedure

❶ Put the pennies in the vinegar. Drop in the paper clip so it rests on top of them. Make sure the pennies and clip are covered by the vinegar.

❷ Allow the jar to sit undisturbed for 24 hours.

❸ Observe the color of the pennies and the paper clip. If the color of the paper clip has not changed, rub it with steel wool or sandpaper, and start over.

Draw Conclusions

How did the color of the paper clip change? The color of the pennies? What do you think happened to change the color of the pennies and the paper clip?

Chapter 1 Review and Test Preparation

Vocabulary Review

Use the terms below to complete the sentences. The page numbers in ( ) tell you where to look in the chapter if you need help.

matter (C6)
physical properties (C6)
mass (C7)
weight (C7)
volume (C8)
density (C9)
solubility (C10)
solid (C14)
liquid (C14)
gas (C14)
evaporation (C16)
condensation (C17)
reactivity (C23)
combustibility (C24)

1. _____ is a measure of the amount of matter in an object.

2. _____ is the amount of space that an object takes up.

3. A substance's ability to be dissolved is its _____.

4. A measure of the pull of gravity on an object is _____.

5. _____ are properties that can be observed or measured without changing a substance into a new substance.

6. The concentration of matter in an object is its _____.

7. Particles escape from a nonboiling liquid and become a gas during _____. _____ is a change in state from a gas to a liquid.

8. _____ is anything that has mass and takes up space.

9. Three states of matter are _____, _____, and _____.

10. _____ is a kind of _____ that refers to a substance's ability to burn.

Connect Concepts

Diagrams that stand for three states of matter are shown below. Fill in the blanks (11–13) to identify each state shown. Describe how changes in state take place by labeling the arrows between the diagrams (14–19). The mass of a substance in one state is given. Give the mass of the substance in the other two states by filling in the blanks (20, 21). Add arrowheads to the lines labeled *volume* and *density* to show the direction in which they increase (22, 23).

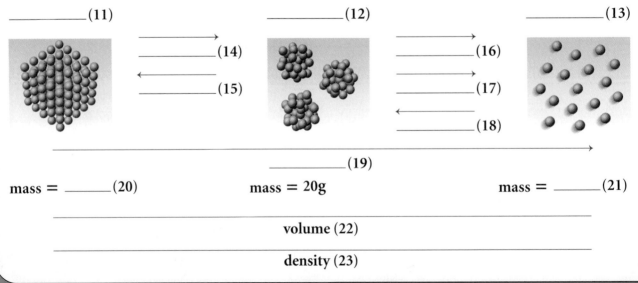

_____(11)   _____(12)   _____(13)

_____(14)   _____(16)

_____(15)   _____(17)

_____(18)

_____(19)

mass = _____ (20)   mass = 20g   mass = _____ (21)

volume (22)

density (23)

Check Understanding

Write the letter of the best choice.

24. Which of the following is **NOT** a physical property of an iron nail?

  A It rusts.   **C** It bends.

  B It's shiny.   **D** It's a solid.

25. Bill weighs 135 lb and Rodney weighs 175 lb. Bill's mass is ____ Rodney's mass.

  F more than   **H** the same as

  G less than   **J** unknown

26. If solid copper sulfate is mixed with water, ____ is formed.

  A a mixture   **C** a solvent

  B a solution   **D** both **A** and **B**

27. A substance seems to completely fill a container, but more can be forced in. The substance is a —

  F solid   **H** liquid

  G gas   **J** none of these

28. A liquid is usually ____ a gas.

  A denser than

  B less dense than

  C the same density as

  D lighter than

29. Nitrogen can be compressed and cooled into a liquid at a very low temperature. So, nitrogen normally exists as a —

  F solid   **H** gas

  G liquid   **J** none of these

30. The melting point of gold is 1064°C. The freezing point of gold —

  A is 1064°C

  B is greater than 1064°C

  C is less than 1064°C

  D cannot be determined from the information given

31. Because paper will burn, it has the property of —

  F combustibility   **H** evaporation

  G condensation   **J** sublimation

Critical Thinking

32. Choose an object in the room, and describe some of its physical and chemical properties.

33. Explain a possible way to separate a mixture of water, ethanol, and sand.

Process Skills Review

34. What properties of your apple were you able to **observe**? What properties of your apple were you able to **measure**?

35. What change of state can you **infer** when you **observe** that the water level in a pan is lower after the water has boiled for ten minutes?

36. In your **experiment** with baking powder, which substance did you vary?

Performance Assessment

Matter Models

Work with two other students. Use marbles and boxes of different sizes to make models that show the density and behavior of particles in solids, liquids, and gases.

Chapter  **2**

Atoms and Elements

LESSON **1**
What Are Atoms and Elements?   C38

LESSON **2**
What Are Compounds?   C46

SCIENCE THROUGH TIME   C52

PEOPLE IN SCIENCE   C54

ACTIVITIES FOR HOME OR SCHOOL   C55

CHAPTER REVIEW AND TEST PREPARATION   C58

The Statue of Liberty has stood in New York Harbor for more than one hundred years—but it has never been completely still. Every particle of the statue is constantly in motion. These particles are so small that they can barely be seen with the most powerful microscopes.

Vocabulary Preview

nucleus
proton
neutron
electron
element
atom
molecule
periodic table
compound

FAST FACT

The copper skin of the Statue of Liberty was once shiny, like a new penny. A chemical change produced a *patina*, or covering, that protects the copper from the salt air of New York Harbor.

FAST FACT

Oxygen makes up about half of the mass of Earth's water, soil, and rocky crust. However, it's not the most common substance in Earth's atmosphere.

The Composition of Air

Gas	Percent of Air
Nitrogen	78.00
Oxygen	20.90
Argon	0.93
Carbon dioxide	0.03
All other gases	0.14

FAST FACT

Diamonds, graphite, and coal are all made of carbon. They have different properties because the particles of each material are arranged in different ways.

What Are Atoms and Elements?

In this lesson, you can . . .

 INVESTIGATE objects you cannot see or touch.

 LEARN ABOUT atoms and elements.

LINK to math, writing, health, and technology.

Many of the treasures in this chest are metals and other natural materials. ▼

INVESTIGATE

Mystery Boxes

Activity Purpose It's easy to study the characteristics of an object you can see and touch. You can **observe** them directly. You can pick up the object to see patterns and feel textures. You can also **measure** its mass, volume, and dimensions. In this investigation you will study characteristics of an object you can't see or touch. You will have to **infer** information from indirect observations.

Materials

- sealed box provided by your teacher
- ruler
- balance
- magnet

Activity Procedure

1 With a partner, **observe** the sealed box your teacher gave you. **Record** any observations you think might help you learn about what's inside the box.

2 Use the ruler to **measure** the outside of the box. Use the balance to find the mass of the box. **Record** your results. (Picture A)

3 Carefully tilt and shake the box. How many objects do you **infer** are in the box? How big do you infer the objects are? **Record** your inferences and the reasons for them.

4 Hold the magnet to the surface of the box. Then tilt the box. Are any of the objects in the box attracted to the magnet? Repeat this at several places on the surface of the box. (Picture B)

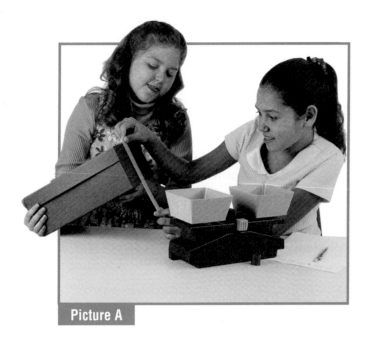

Picture A

Picture B

5 What objects do you **infer** are inside the box? Base your inferences on your measurements and observations.

6 What do you **infer** about the inside of the box? Draw a picture of what you think the inside of the box looks like.

7 Now open the box. **Compare** your inferences about the objects in the box with the objects the box really contains. Also compare your inferences about what the box looks like inside with what it really looks like.

Draw Conclusions

1. How did what you **inferred** about the objects inside the box **compare** with what was really inside?

2. How did what you **inferred** about the inside of the box **compare** with the way it really looked inside?

3. **Scientists at Work** Different scientists may **infer** different things about objects they can't **observe** directly. Compare your inferences about the contents and the inside of the box with the inferences of others.

Investigate Further Construct your own mystery box, and place various objects inside it. Exchange boxes with a classmate. **Observe** the box and **draw conclusions** about its contents based on your observations. Indicate whether additional information is needed to support your conclusions.

> **Process Skill Tip**
>
> When you can't **observe** something directly, you may be able to **infer** some of its characteristics. To do this, you might observe how the object reacts under certain conditions.

Atoms and Elements

The Atomic Theory

FIND OUT

- what matter is made of
- what atoms are made of
- about elements and metals

VOCABULARY

nucleus
proton
neutron
electron
element
atom
molecule

In the investigation you probably found it difficult to identify an object you couldn't see. Early scientists had the same difficulty in trying to understand what matter was made of.

The theory that matter is made of tiny particles that can't be divided was first proposed by a Greek philosopher, Democritus (di•MAHK•ruh•tuhs), in 400 B.C. The particles Democritus proposed were too small to be seen. Aristotle (AIR•is•taht•uhl), a Greek philosopher who lived after Democritus, believed that matter was not made of particles. This theory was widely accepted for 2000 years. However, neither of these theories was based on experimental evidence.

By the early 1800s, scientists had begun to measure chemical reactions. The measurements made it possible for John Dalton, an English chemist, to propose an atomic theory of matter that was based on experimental evidence. Dalton's atomic theory is that all matter is made up of tiny particles called *atoms*.

✔ **What is the atomic theory?**

The helium in these balloons is made up of one of more than a hundred different kinds of atoms. ▼

The Structure of an Atom

How small is an atom? About 5 million atoms could be lined up across the period at the end of this sentence. When Dalton proposed his theory, it was thought that atoms were the smallest particles of matter. There was no evidence of smaller particles.

Scientists now know that atoms are made up of even smaller particles called *subatomic particles*. The **nucleus** (NOO•klee•uhs) is the very tiny center of an atom. The nucleus is made up of protons and neutrons. A **proton** (PROH•tahn) is a subatomic particle with a positive charge. A **neutron** (NOO•trahn) is a subatomic particle with no charge. The rest of an atom is made up of electrons, which surround the nucleus. An **electron** (ee•LEK•trahn) is a subatomic particle with a negative charge.

In 1913, Niels Bohr proposed a model of the structure of an atom. In his model, electrons circle the nucleus at fixed distances from it. The paths in which the electrons move are called *orbits*. They are also referred to as *energy levels,* because their distance from the nucleus depends on the energy of the electrons in them. Low-energy electrons orbit close to the nucleus. High-energy electrons orbit farther away.

Although the nucleus is very tiny, almost all of an atom's mass is in its nucleus. The mass of a proton is nearly 2000 times the mass of an electron. Protons and neutrons have about the same mass.

Although their masses are very different, electrons and protons have charges that are equally strong. Part of what holds atoms together is the attraction between the positive protons and the negative electrons. If an atom has more protons than electrons, it has a positive charge. If it has more electrons than protons, it has a negative charge. An atom with the same number of protons and electrons is called a *neutral atom,* because the positive and negative charges cancel each other.

✔ **What subatomic particles make up an atom?**

The Bohr model of a helium atom shows electrons orbiting the nucleus, much as planets orbit the sun.

The modern atomic model shows spherical orbitals (blue haze) instead of circular orbits. Orbitals are areas where electrons are likely to be found.

Elements

An **element** (EL•uh•muhnt) is a substance made up of only one kind of atom. For example, gold is an element. If a single atom is taken from a nugget of gold, that single atom is still gold. An **atom** is the smallest unit of an element that has all the properties of that element.

Each element has an *atomic number,* which is the number of protons in one atom of that element. There are more than 100 elements. An atom of each element has a specific number of protons in its nucleus. The nucleus of a hydrogen atom, for example, has only one proton. So the atomic number of hydrogen is 1. The atomic

number of plutonium is 94. All atoms that have 94 protons are plutonium atoms.

Most matter, including the matter that makes up living organisms, contains only a few kinds of elements. For example, a hamburger, gasoline, and paper are all made of carbon, hydrogen, and oxygen.

The atoms of most elements do not occur alone. Instead, they are linked together. Two or more atoms linked together form a **molecule**. When atoms are linked only to atoms of the same kind, they are in a pure state. Oxygen gas, for example, is made up of oxygen molecules. Oxygen molecules are made up of two oxygen atoms linked together.

✔ What is an element?

Graphite

Anthracite

◄ Diamond, graphite, and anthracite are all made up of carbon atoms, which have six protons. These materials have different properties because their carbon atoms are arranged differently.

This diagram of a carbon atom shows six protons and six neutrons in the nucleus. The six, fast-moving electrons are somewhere in the "cloud" surrounding the nucleus.▼

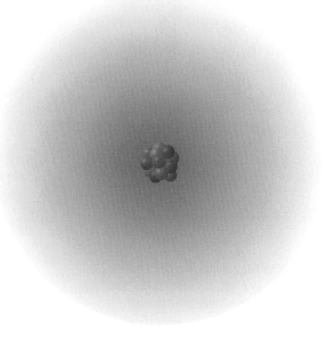

Diamond

Some Common Elements

NAME	NUCLEUS MODEL	USES
Oxygen Oxygen is a colorless gas. It makes up about 20 percent of Earth's atmosphere. Oxygen is the most common element in Earth's crust. It is combined with other elements in many metal ores and minerals.	**Atomic number 8**	The mask supplies oxygen for the pilot.
Sodium Sodium is a soft, silver-colored metal. It is a waxlike solid at room temperature, but it becomes brittle as the temperature falls. Sodium combines easily with nonmetals to form salts such as sodium chloride—table salt.	**Atomic number 11**	The sodium vapor in this light glows when electricity passes through it.
Aluminum Aluminum is a silver-colored metal solid. Because it combines easily with oxygen, it is never pure in nature. Aluminum is the third most common element in Earth's crust.	**Atomic number 13**	Most baseball bats are now made of aluminum, instead of wood.
Silicon Silicon is a dark nonmetal solid. It is the second most common element in Earth's crust. Silicon combines mainly with oxygen to form a mineral that is found in many beach sands.	**Atomic number 14**	Electric circuits are printed on thin pieces of silicon.
Chlorine Chlorine is a greenish yellow gas with a sharp odor. It is 2.5 times as dense as air, and it forms a pale yellow solution in water. Chlorine combines easily with metals to form salts, such as sodium chloride—table salt.	**Atomic number 17**	Chlorine bleach is a solution of chlorine gas in water.
Iron Iron is a silver-white metal solid. There are large amounts of minerals containing iron in Earth's crust. Many useful materials, such as steel, are made from iron. Iron is also found in blood. It carries oxygen to cells.	**Atomic number 26**	Iron can be shaped more easily if it is red hot.

Metals

Elements are classified by their properties. About one-fourth of all elements are classified as nonmetals. The rest are metals. All metals except mercury are solid at room temperature.

Metals have many familiar properties. Gold is used in jewelry because of its high *luster,* or shininess. Most metals, like silver and nickel, have a gray or silver luster.

Most metals are said to be *malleable* (MAL•ee•uh•buhl). They can be hammered or rolled into thin sheets. The foil used to cover and store food is a thin sheet of aluminum. Metals are also *ductile* (DUHK•til). They can be formed into wires. Copper and aluminum are used in electric wiring.

Copper and aluminum are used in electric wiring because of another property. Metals *conduct,* or transfer, electricity. The electrons farthest from the nucleus of a metal atom are not held by just that atom. They are free to move to other metal atoms. This freedom of electrons allows metals to conduct electricity.

Electrons in materials such as glass, plastic, and rubber are bound tightly to their atoms. These materials conduct hardly any electricity. They are *insulators.*

Metals also conduct heat. Have you ever noticed that when a car has been sitting in the sun, its metal parts are much hotter than its plastic parts? Metal conducts heat better than plastic does. For this reason the

▼ Metal can be rolled into very thin sheets, called foil, that can be used to decorate buildings.

▼ Copper is often used on the bottom of pans because it conducts heat easily.

Metals such as aluminum and copper are good conductors of electricity. Most electric wiring is made of these metals.

handles of pots and pans are often made of plastic.

Some metals are not pure elements. They are actually *alloys,* or mixtures of metals or metals and other elements. Bronze is an alloy of copper and tin. Steel is an alloy of iron and carbon. Brass is an alloy of copper and zinc. Other metals, such as iron, aluminum, nickel, copper, silver, gold, tin, and zinc, are pure elements.

✔ **What are five properties of metals?**

Summary

Matter is made up of tiny particles called atoms. Atoms are made of smaller, subatomic particles called protons, neutrons, and electrons. Elements are substances made up of only one kind of atom. Metals have luster, are malleable and ductile, and conduct electricity and heat.

Review

1. If you were to add all the missing elements to the chart on page C43, how many would there be between silicon and chlorine? What would their atomic numbers be?

2. What subatomic particles make up the nucleus of an atom?

3. How do atoms with different atomic numbers differ from each other?

4. **Critical Thinking** Choose a metal you know, and list three uses that illustrate three properties of metals.

5. **Test Prep** Which are **NOT** a part of atoms?

   A protons   **C** neutrons

   B electrons   **D** elements

LINKS

MATH LINK

Relative Mass Units Twelve atomic mass units (abbreviated as *amu*) is equal to the mass of one carbon atom. Calculate how many amu there are in 20 atoms of carbon and in 200 atoms of carbon.

WRITING LINK

Informative Writing—Report The development of the atomic theory is central to the development of chemistry. Suppose you are a newspaper reporter, and John Dalton has just published his atomic theory. Research the history of the development of the atomic theory, and write an article for your school newspaper announcing John Dalton's new theory.

HEALTH LINK

Essential Minerals Many elements, such as iron, are minerals needed for human health. Find out which ones are in multivitamin tablets. How much of each element does a vitamin tablet contain? Report your findings to your class.

TECHNOLOGY LINK

Learn more about metals by viewing *Intermetallics* on the **Harcourt Science Newsroom Video** in your classroom video library.

What Are Compounds?

In this lesson, you can . . .

INVESTIGATE how elements are grouped.

LEARN ABOUT the periodic table and compounds.

LINK to math, writing, language arts, and technology.

Mixing chemicals often produces unexpected results. ▼

INVESTIGATE

Grouping Elements

Activity Purpose Suppose you have 100 baseball cards, and you want to know whether the players at certain positions have anything in common. If you group the cards by player position, you will be able to **infer** common characteristics about each group more quickly. Scientists have grouped elements by their properties. In this investigation you will learn how elements can be grouped.

Materials

- aluminum foil
- copper wire
- steel (iron) paper clip
- sulfur
- graphite pencil "lead"
- lead solder
- helium-filled balloon

CAUTION

Activity Procedure

1. Copy the chart on page C47. You will use it to **record** the properties of the elements you **observe**.

2. What elements do the objects represent? **Record** your answers in the second column of the chart.

3. **Observe** each element. Is it a solid, a liquid, or a gas at room temperature? **Record** your observations in the column of the chart labeled "Phase."

4. What is the color of each element? (Carefully release some of the helium from the balloon.) **Record** what you **observe** in the chart. (Picture A)

5. Which elements have luster? (Which are shiny?) **Record** what you **observe** in the fifth column of the chart.

Picture A

Picture B

Object	Element	Phase	Color	Luster	Malleability
foil					
wire					
paper clip					
sulfur					
graphite					
solder					
balloon					

6. Which elements bend easily? **Record** what you **observe** in the column labeled "Malleability." **CAUTION** Wash your hands after handling the objects in this investigation. (Picture B)

Draw Conclusions

1. What similar properties did you **observe** in different elements?

2. Consider the properties you **observed**. Which elements do you **infer** could be grouped together? Explain.

3. **Scientists at Work** Scientists have made a periodic table, in which elements are classified, or grouped, by their properties. Using your observations, **predict** which elements from the activity are near each other in the periodic table.

Investigate Further Think of other properties that could be used to **classify** elements. **Plan and conduct a simple investigation** of some properties that would help you classify elements. Write instructions that others can follow to carry out the procedure.

Process Skill Tip

Using your observations of different elements, you can **predict** relationships among those elements.

Elements and Compounds

The Periodic Table

FIND OUT

- how elements are grouped in the periodic table

- how compounds form

VOCABULARY

periodic table
compound

As you learned in the investigation, some elements can be grouped together because they have similar properties. In 1869 a Russian chemist named Dmitri Mendeleev (duh•MEE•tree men•duh•LAY•uhf) organized elements by their atomic masses. Mendeleev noticed that if elements were put in order of atomic mass, some properties appeared in predictable patterns.

Scientists later found that using an order based on the number of protons in one atom of an element—atomic number—is better than one based on atomic mass.

THE INSIDE STORY

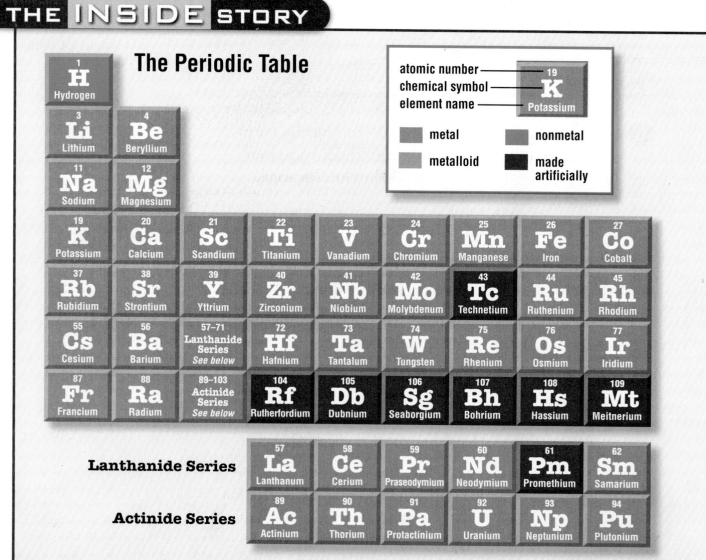

The Periodic Table

In the modern **periodic table**, elements are arranged in order of atomic number. They are also arranged so that elements with similar properties are in the same column. The elements in a column are part of a *group*. Elements in the same group often have the same number of electrons in the outer energy levels of their atoms. The arrangement of electrons gives elements their chemical properties.

All the elements on the left side of the periodic table, except hydrogen, are metals. All the elements on the far right are non-metals. A change of color separates metals from nonmetals. Some elements have properties of both metals and nonmetals. These elements are called *metalloids*.

Notice that every element in the table has an abbreviation, called a *chemical symbol*.

When the periodic table was first set up, it had empty spaces. The spaces were for elements that had not yet been discovered. As new elements were found, scientists filled in the spaces. Using the periodic table, Mendeleev correctly predicted that three new elements with certain properties would be discovered. Even today, new elements are being added to the table. However, now most new elements are made artificially.

✔ **Which two things determine the arrangement of elements in the periodic table?**

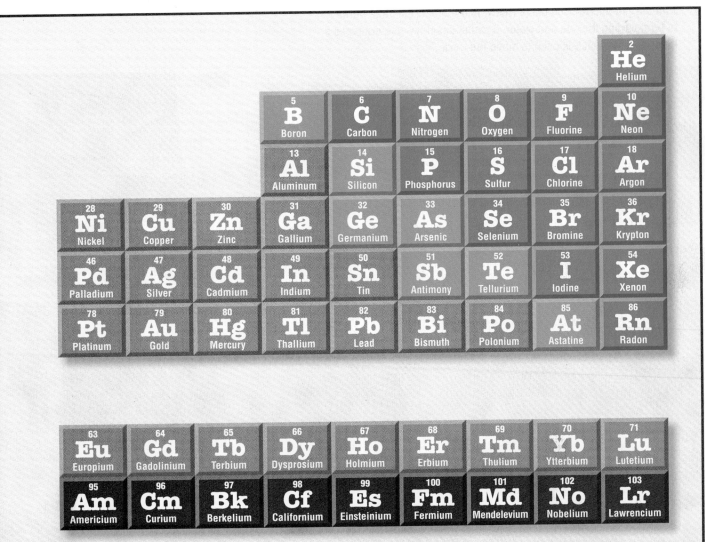

Compounds

In nature most elements are joined with other elements in compounds. A **compound** is a substance made of the atoms of two or more elements. Water is one of the most common compounds. It contains hydrogen and oxygen atoms. Table salt, sodium chloride, contains sodium and chlorine atoms.

A *chemical formula* shows which elements and how many atoms of each are in a compound. The chemical formula for water is H_2O. The small 2 next to the H means that there are 2 hydrogen atoms in every water molecule. Each water molecule also has 1 atom of oxygen. The chemical formula for table salt is NaCl. A salt molecule has 1 sodium atom and 1 chlorine atom. The chemical formula for glucose, a simple sugar, is $C_6H_{12}O_6$. In each molecule of glucose, there are 6 carbon atoms, 12 hydrogen atoms, and 6 oxygen atoms.

When atoms join to form a compound, they undergo a chemical change. The properties of the compound are different from those of the elements in it. Hydrogen and oxygen, both gases, combine to form water, a liquid compound. Compounds can also react with each other. When compounds react, they change, and form new products. For example, hydrochloric acid contains hydrogen and chlorine atoms. It reacts with

Two chemical reactions are happening here. In one, iron combines with oxygen to form iron oxide (rust). In the other, gasoline burns to form carbon dioxide and water. Burning gasoline also produces a lot of energy, which is used to move the truck. ▼

Combustion

Gasoline + Oxygen → Carbon Dioxide + Water + energy

Oxidation

Iron + Oxygen → Iron Oxide (rust)

sodium hydroxide (a base), which contains sodium, oxygen, and hydrogen atoms. The products are sodium chloride, which contains sodium and chlorine atoms, and water, which contains hydrogen and oxygen atoms. Water and salts are often the products of reactions between acids and bases.

✔ **What does a chemical formula show?**

Summary

In the periodic table, elements are arranged by atomic number and properties. The table shows names, chemical symbols, and atomic numbers for all the known elements. A compound is a combination of two or more different elements. A chemical formula shows the number of atoms of each element in one molecule of a compound.

Review

1. Using the periodic table on pages C48 and C49, find the name of the element that has 36 protons.

2. In what form are most elements in nature? What does this mean?

3. What information is shown in a chemical formula?

4. **Critical Thinking** Using their placement in the periodic table, classify these elements as metals or nonmetals: iron, cobalt, sodium, oxygen, chlorine, and helium.

5. **Test Prep** Which of these is **NOT** found in the periodic table?

   A name   **C** luster

   B atomic number   **D** chemical symbol

LINKS

MATH LINK

Ratios and Fractions Chemical formulas give the ratios of atoms in compounds. From this information you can calculate what fraction of the atoms in a compound are atoms of one element. For example, the chemical formula for ammonia is NH_3. What is the ratio of nitrogen atoms to hydrogen atoms? What fraction of the atoms in ammonia are nitrogen atoms?

WRITING LINK

Informative Writing—Description From the periodic table, choose an element. Research the element, and write a description for your teacher. Include the element's properties and uses.

LANGUAGE ARTS LINK

Word Origins The chemical symbols for some elements don't seem to make sense. Many, such as Au for gold, are based on the Latin name of the element. Use a dictionary of word origins to look up other elements with strange symbols. Make a list of these elements and the origins of their symbols.

TECHNOLOGY LINK

Learn more about molecules and compounds by visiting the National Museum of American History Internet site.
www.si.edu/harcourt/science

Discovering Elements

Ancient cultures believed that matter was made up of just four or five elements. The Greeks believed these elements were water, fire, earth, and air. The Chinese added wood as a fifth element. These beliefs continued to be held for many centuries.

About 2000 years ago, the practice of alchemy (AL•kuh•mee) began in Egypt. Although the goal of alchemy—changing one substance into another—was not possible, it led to the discovery of new chemical substances. It also marked the beginning of a new science—chemistry.

Atoms and Elements

Alchemy continued for the next 1600 years. Then in 1661, Robert Boyle, a British scientist, stated that matter is made up of tiny particles. He later proposed that all matter could be broken down into elements but that elements could not be broken down into simpler substances. Within the next century, oxygen and hydrogen were both identified as elements. Scientists also discovered that elements could combine to form compounds, such as water.

In 1808 John Dalton published his atomic theory, in which he stated that every element is made up of atoms and that each element has a unique arrangement of atoms. Dalton also showed that each element has a specific mass.

The Periodic Table

After the First International Chemical Congress met in 1860, chemists began grouping elements by atomic mass. Dmitri Mendeleev was the first to publish his

The History of Elements

350 B.C.
Aristotle suggests that all substances are made of fire, water, wind, or earth.

400
The term *chemistry* is first used by Egyptian alchemists to describe the practice of changing matter.

1808 —
Dalton states his atomic theory.

400 B.C. | A.D. 500 | A.D. 1000 | A.D. 1600 | A.D. 1700 | A.D. 1800

100 —
Gold, silver, copper, lead, iron, tin, and mercury are known.

880 —
A Muslim chemist, al-Razi, classifies chemical substances into mineral, vegetable, animal, and derivative.

1661 —
Boyle's book, *The Sceptical Chymist*, proves the ancient "four elements" theory wrong.

1869 —
The periodic table of the elements is published.

groupings. The chart, known as the periodic table of the elements, showed each element's symbol and atomic mass in a clear, orderly arrangement.

More Elements

In 1911 the atomic nucleus was discovered. Protons and neutrons were discovered soon after. These discoveries led scientists to define elements not only by atomic mass but also by atomic number—the number of protons in each atom. Grouping atoms by atomic number became a feature of the periodic table.

During the rest of the 1900s, many elements were added to the periodic table. Scientists continue to find new elements.

Knowledge of chemistry and atomic structure has even allowed scientists to make elements that don't occur in nature. And equipment such as the scanning tunneling microscope has made it possible to photograph the structure of some elements, revealing their ordered arrays of atoms.

THINK ABOUT IT

1. How were alchemists different from chemists?
2. Why is the number of elements in the periodic table not fixed?

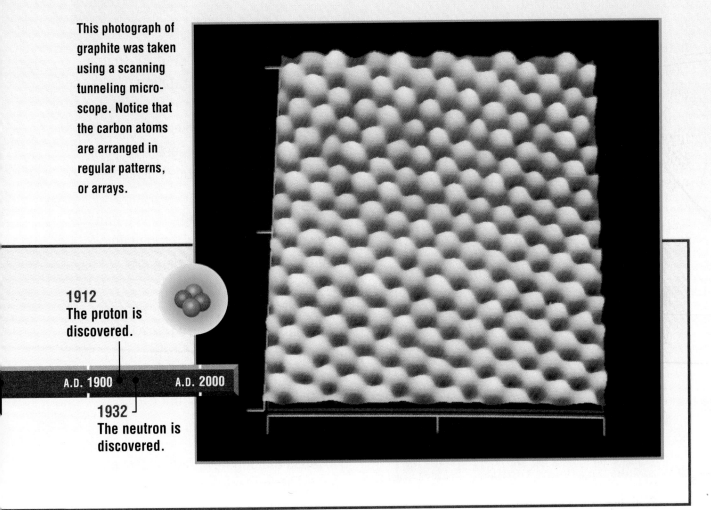

This photograph of graphite was taken using a scanning tunneling microscope. Notice that the carbon atoms are arranged in regular patterns, or arrays.

1912
The proton is discovered.

A.D. 1900   A.D. 2000

1932
The neutron is discovered.

Glenn T. Seaborg

NUCLEAR CHEMIST

". . . we almost made a . . . terrible mistake, because we thought we'd reached the very top of the periodic table, that nobody would ever go higher than atomic number 94."

Before Glenn Seaborg and his colleagues at the University of California began experimenting in 1940, uranium was the heaviest element in the periodic table. By bombarding uranium with atomic particles in a particle accelerator, they were able to make a new element, one not found in nature. Its nucleus contained 94 protons. Dr. Seaborg proposed that they name the new element *plutonium*.

In 1944 Dr. Seaborg proposed changing the periodic table to account for the way the new *transuranium* ("beyond uranium") elements fit into it. His fellow scientists advised him that suggesting such a radical change could ruin his scientific reputation.

Like uranium, plutonium is a radioactive element, which means it gives off particles, releasing energy in the process. This new element was used to produce nuclear energy and nuclear weapons.

Today, nuclear energy produces about 17 percent of the world's electricity. In addition, many radioactive elements are used to treat cancerous tumors.

In 1951 Dr. Seaborg was awarded the Nobel prize in chemistry for making plutonium. In 1997 the last element that he helped produce—atomic number 106—was named Seaborgium in his honor.

THINK ABOUT IT

- How has making new, radioactive elements affected society?

▲ **Dr. Seaborg in his laboratory**

Speedy Reactions

How can you speed up a reaction?

Materials

- 250-mL beaker
- 200 mL carbonated soft drink
- 1 teaspoon sugar

Procedure

1. Pour the carbonated drink into the beaker.
2. Add the sugar.
3. Observe what happens.

4. Repeat the procedure with different brands of soft drinks.

Draw Conclusions

Carbonated soft drinks contain flavorings, color-ings, water, and dissolved carbon dioxide gas. You probably heard some of the gas escape when you opened the can or bottle the soft drink came in. The remainder of the carbon dioxide comes out of the soft drink slowly over time. What happened when you added sugar to the drink? What do you think the foam is made of? Did different carbonated drinks behave differ-ently when the sugar was added? Explain.

Periodic Table

Where are various elements found?

Materials

- a copy of the periodic table
- poster board
- tape
- string
- various objects, such as a helium-filled balloon, a piece of charcoal, an aluminum can, a glass bottle, garden fertilizer, an eggshell, a steel nail, an old penny, a fishing weight

Procedure

1. Mount the periodic table on the poster board.
2. Tape one end of a piece of string to the bal-loon, and the other end to *He* (helium) on the periodic table.
3. Tape string to all the objects.
4. Tape the other end of each string to the cor-rect element on the periodic table.

Draw Conclusions

Which elements are found in these common objects? Why can't you find objects for all the elements on the periodic table?

Rusty Wool

What factors affect the rate at which steel rusts?

Materials

- 5 test tubes
- tablespoon
- salt
- container of water
- measuring cup
- marker
- steel wool pad
- 2 test-tube stoppers

Procedure

1 Make a saltwater solution by dissolving a tablespoon of salt in one cup of water.

2 After numbering the test tubes 1–5, prepare them as follows:

- Leave the first tube empty.
- Fill the second tube with plain water.
- Half-fill the third tube with plain water.
- Fill the fourth tube with salt water.
- Half-fill the fifth tube with salt water.

3 Break the steel wool pad into small pieces. Put a piece of steel wool into each test tube. The water will overflow the second and fourth tubes. Stopper these test tubes so that no air can get into them. Leave the other test tubes unstoppered.

4 Observe the test tubes for five days, noting any changes you see in the color of the steel wool. Record your observations in a chart.

Draw Conclusions

In which test tube was the steel wool the most rusted? In which test tube was the steel wool the least rusted? From your results, what seems to be the most important factor for speeding up the rusting of steel wool? Explain.

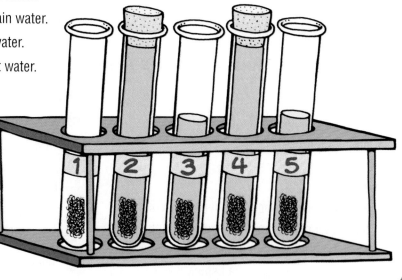

Floating Eggs

How can you change the density of a substance?

Materials

- plastic cup half-full of water
- 1 fresh egg in shell, uncooked
- table salt
- water
- spoon

Procedure

1. Carefully place the egg in the cup of water, and observe whether or not it floats.

2. Remove the egg, and stir several spoonfuls of salt into the water.

3. Carefully replace the egg in the water, and observe whether or not it floats.

Draw Conclusions

Why did the egg sink to the bottom of the cup at first? Did the egg ever float? If so, when and why? What physical property of the water changed?

Splitting Water

How can you break down water into its two substances?

Materials

- knife
- 2 copper wires, each about 30 cm (1 ft) long
- 2 metal paper clips
- 2 pieces of lead (actually graphite) from a mechanical pencil, each about 7.5 cm (3 in.) long
- clear plastic cup of water
- electrical or duct tape
- 9-volt battery

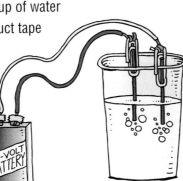

Procedure

1. Have an adult use the knife to remove about 3.5 cm (1.5 in.) of insulation from both ends of the wires.

2. Attach a paper clip to one end of each wire.

3. Use the paper clips to hold the pencil lead pieces to the inside of the cup of water. Let the pieces extend into the water, as shown.

4. Tape the other end of each wire to one of the electrodes on the battery. Don't let the wires touch each other.

Draw Conclusions

What happened after you attached the wires to the electrodes? What do you think caused this?

Chapter 2 Review and Test Preparation

Vocabulary Review

Use the terms below to complete the following paragraph. The page numbers in ( ) tell you where to look in the chapter if you need help.

nucleus (C41) **atom** (C42)

proton (C41) **molecule** (C42)

neutron (C41) **periodic table** (C49)

electron (C41) **compound** (C50)

element (C42)

The atomic theory states that matter is made up of tiny particles. One of these particles is called a(n) __1.__ . At the center of an atom is a tiny __2.__ . A(n) __3.__ , a positively charged subatomic particle, and a(n) __4.__ , a subatomic particle with no charge, are in the nucleus. A(n) __5.__ is a subatomic particle with a negative charge. It is found outside the nucleus. If an atom has a different number of protons from another atom, it is an atom of a different __6.__ . The elements are arranged in the __7.__ by atomic number. In nature, most elements are joined together in a(n) __8.__ . Two or more atoms joined together form a(n) __9.__ .

Connect Concepts

Using the periodic table, complete the table below.

Some Common Elements

Element	Chemical Symbol	Atomic Number	Number of Protons	Number of Electrons	Metal or Nonmetal	Example Compound
oxygen	(10)	8	(11)	(12)	(13)	(14), water
(15)	Ba	56	56	(16)	metal	BaSO$_4$, barium sulfate
(17)	S	16	(18)	(19)	nonmetal	(20), sulfur dioxide
sodium	(21)	(22)	(23)	11	(24)	(25), sodium chloride
(26)	C	(27)	(28)	(29)	nonmetal	CH$_4$, methane
iron	Fe	(30)	26	(31)	metal	FeO, iron oxide
(32)	(33)	(34)	1	(35)	nonmetal	(36), water
nitrogen	N	7	7	7	(37)	NH$_3$, ammonia
(38)	(39)	(40)	17	(41)	(42)	NaCl, sodium chloride
lead	(43)	82	(44)	82	metal	PbSO$_4$, lead sulfate

Check Understanding

Write the letter of the best choice.

45. Theories in science —

   A are based on philosophy

   B are based on experimental evidence

   C are never proved wrong

   D never change

46. The atomic theory states that matter is made up of —

   F atoms

   G earth and air

   H elements

   J earth, air, fire, and water

47. If an element has a gray luster and can be drawn into a wire, it is probably a —

   A nonmetal   **C** metal

   B gas   **D** alloy

48. What elements does the compound $MgCl_2$, magnesium chloride, contain?

   F chloride only

   G magnesium only

   H magnesium and calcium

   J magnesium and chlorine

Process Skills Review

49. What did you **observe** about the sealed box in the Lesson 1 investigation?

50. What did you **infer** about the contents and the inside shape of the sealed box?

51. What properties of elements can you **observe**?

Critical Thinking

Use the following information to answer the questions below.

- Fluorine is a pale yellow, poisonous gas. It does not conduct electricity. It has an atomic number of 9.

- Oxygen is a colorless gas. It does not conduct electricity. It has an atomic number of 8.

- Iron is a solid with a gray luster at room temperature. It is malleable and conducts electricity. It reacts with oxygen. It has an atomic number of 26.

- Sulfur is a bright yellow solid at room temperature. It is brittle and does not conduct electricity. It reacts with oxygen. It has an atomic number of 16.

- Gold is a yellow solid with a luster. It is malleable and conducts electricity. It has an atomic number of 79.

- Phosphorus can be a white solid at room temperature. It does not conduct electricity. It reacts with oxygen. It has an atomic number of 15.

52. Divide the elements into groups based on their properties. Explain how you grouped them.

53. Which of the elements are metals?

54. Which of the elements are nonmetals?

Performance Assessment

Element Detective

   Divide into teams of five. Your teacher will give each student an element clue card. Using your clue, decide the name of your element. Discuss your reasoning with other members of your team. Then line up in order of atomic number.

Energy

LESSON 1
What Are Kinetic and Potential Energy? C62

LESSON 2
What Is Electric Energy? C68

LESSON 3
What Are Light and Sound Energy? C76

LESSON 4
What Are Thermal and Chemical Energy? C84

SCIENCE THROUGH TIME   C90

PEOPLE IN SCIENCE   C92

ACTIVITIES FOR HOME OR SCHOOL   C93

CHAPTER REVIEW AND TEST PREPARATION   C94

What do a flashlight battery, snow on a mountainside, and a match have in common? Each has a form of stored energy. What do a beam of light, an avalanche, and a fire have in common? Each is energy in action.

Vocabulary Preview

energy
kinetic energy
potential energy
electric charge
electric force
electric current
conductor
electric circuit
insulator
resistor
electromagnet
reflection
refraction
lens
pitch
volume
temperature
heat
conduction
convection
radiation

⚡FAST FACT

An avalanche is a mass of snow that breaks loose and falls rapidly down a mountainside. Wind, skiers, or even loud noises can start an avalanche. Some avalanches reach speeds of 160 km/hr (about 100 mi/hr).

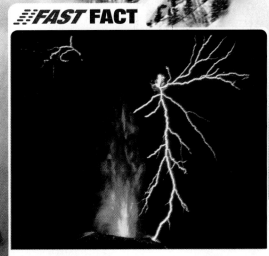

What Are Kinetic and Potential Energy?

In this lesson, you can . . .

INVESTIGATE how energy is changed from one form to another.

LEARN ABOUT kinetic and potential energy.

LINK to math, writing, social studies, and technology.

◀ This "balanced" rock has a lot of potential energy.

INVESTIGATE

Changing Energy Forms

Activity Purpose There are two major kinds of energy. For example, a bowling ball rolling down an alley has one kind of energy, and a diver standing on the edge of a platform has another kind of energy. In this investigation you will **experiment** with these two kinds of energy and **observe** how one kind can be changed into the other.

Materials

- graph paper, 8 sheets
- tape
- meterstick
- tennis ball
- colored markers
- computer (optional)

Activity Procedure

1. Tape four sheets of graph paper vertically to a wall as shown. Starting at the floor, use a meterstick to mark off 10-cm intervals on the left edge of the paper to a height of 100 cm. (Picture A)

2. Work with a partner. One person sits on the floor about 0.5 m from the graph paper. The other person holds the tennis ball a few centimeters from the wall at the 50-cm mark. Then he or she drops the ball.

3. The seated person **observes** the ball as it bounces, and uses a colored marker to **record** the height of each bounce on the graph paper. **Count** and record the number of times the ball bounces. (Picture B)

4 Repeat Steps 2 and 3 several times. Use a different-colored marker to **record** each trial.

5 Replace the paper and repeat Steps 1–4, but this time drop the ball from a height of 100 cm.

Draw Conclusions

1. **Compare** the drop height to the bounce height for each trial in the experiment. How are the heights related?

2. When you hold the ball in the air before dropping it, it has *potential energy* because of its position and because of gravitation. When you let go of the ball, it has *kinetic energy* because of its movement. **Infer** the point at which the ball has the most kinetic energy.

3. **Draw a conclusion** about how potential energy and kinetic energy are related in the bouncing ball.

4. **Scientists at Work** Scientists often use computers to help them **interpret data** and **communicate** the results of an experiment. Use a computer to write a report of your investigation. Be sure to describe the tests you conducted, include the data you collected, and summarize your conclusions.

Investigate Further Analyze the data you collected, and **predict** how high and how many times a ball dropped from a height of 200 cm will bounce. Then **experiment**, and **compare** your results to your predictions.

Picture A

Picture B

Process Skill Tip

Using a computer to help you **compare** and **interpret data** is one way to **communicate** the results of an experiment to others.

C63

Energy

Kinetic and Potential Energy

FIND OUT

- **what kinetic and potential energy are**
- **about different forms of energy**

VOCABULARY

energy
kinetic energy
potential energy

Have you ever heard someone say that a person has a lot of energy? What is energy? **Energy** is the ability to cause changes in matter. In the investigation energy caused matter (the tennis ball) to move. Energy can also change matter in other ways. For example, heat, which is a form of energy, can change solid ice into liquid water—a change in state.

There are two basic kinds of energy—the energy of motion and the energy of position or condition. The energy of motion, or energy in use, is **kinetic energy**. Any matter in motion has kinetic energy. When you let go of the tennis ball, it gained kinetic energy as it moved faster and faster toward the floor. It also had kinetic energy after it bounced back up from the floor. When the ball reached the top of each bounce, it stopped for an instant between rising and falling again. At this point its kinetic energy was zero.

While bouncing up, the ball gained energy of position. When the ball stopped at the top of a bounce, it had potential energy. **Potential energy** is the energy an object has because of where it is or because of its condition. Once the ball reached the top of its bounce, it fell again, changing more and more of its potential energy back into kinetic energy. If you caught the ball at the top of a bounce, it would keep that potential energy until you dropped it again.

❶ The potential energy of food is changed into kinetic energy by the pole vaulter's muscles as he runs toward the bar.

❷ When the vaulter sticks his pole in the ground, much of this kinetic energy is changed to potential energy in the bent pole.

❸ As the pole straightens, it releases that potential energy as kinetic energy to lift him up toward the bar.

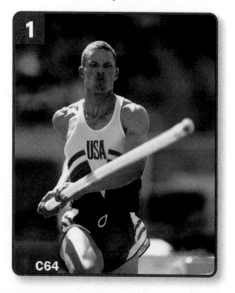

C64

The snow that has fallen high in the mountains has a lot of potential energy. During an avalanche, that potential energy is suddenly changed to kinetic energy, and the fast-moving snow can cause a lot of damage.

The change of the ball's energy back and forth between kinetic energy and potential energy is called the *transformation of energy.* Although energy often is transformed, or changed, from one form to another, the total amount of energy doesn't change. Energy can't be created or destroyed. This is the *law of conservation of energy.*

Energy can change forms several times during one activity. Look at the series of photographs of the pole vaulter. According to the law of conservation of energy, the amount of energy is always the same, but its form keeps changing.

Both the tennis ball in the investigation and the pole vaulter eventually stopped. However, it wasn't because energy was destroyed. With each bounce some of the ball's energy was lost as sound and heat. The heat caused by the friction of the ball hitting the floor warmed the air and the floor slightly. Eventually, the results of bouncing turned all of the ball's energy into other forms.

✔ **At what point in the process does the pole vaulter have his greatest kinetic energy?**

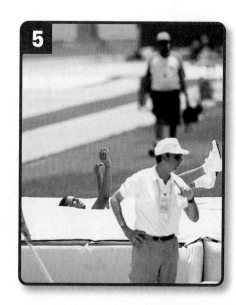

❹ At the instant the vaulter goes over the bar, kinetic energy is changed back to potential energy.

❺ As he falls, potential energy becomes kinetic energy until he hits the ground. At that instant he has neither kinetic energy nor potential energy.

C65

Forms of Energy

The kinetic energy that moving objects have is also called *mechanical energy*. A spinning top, a rolling bicycle, a flying airplane, and flowing water all have mechanical energy. But mechanical energy isn't the only form of kinetic energy. Kinetic energy can have many different forms.

Thermal energy is another form of kinetic energy. The movement of molecules of matter produces heat. Another form of kinetic energy, *electric energy*, is caused by the movement of the electrons in matter. Electric energy can be felt in an electric shock. It also produces the picture and sound on a television. *Light energy* from the picture moves to your eyes in waves. Your ears receive vibrations produced by the television speakers as *sound energy*.

Potential energy also takes several forms. *Elastic potential energy* is the energy stored in matter, such as in compressed springs, stretched rubber bands, and bent vaulting poles. In fact, any matter that can be forced into a shape that's different from its natural shape can store elastic potential energy—if it has the ability to return to its natural shape.

Gravitational potential energy is the energy matter has when it's in an elevated position. The tennis ball in the investigation had gravitational potential energy at the top of its bounce and elastic potential energy at the bottom of its bounce. Water behind a dam, a "balanced" rock, or any matter that can fall has gravitational potential energy.

Most of Earth's energy comes from the sun. Plants absorb light energy and store it as *chemical energy* in the food they make. When a pole vaulter starts running, chemical energy stored in his muscles is changed into *thermal energy* and *mechanical energy*.

✔ **Name three forms of energy.**

Energy is the ability to do work. In a water-powered mill, the mechanical energy of falling water turns the mill wheel. This mechanical energy is carried throughout the mill and is used by machines to do work.

The flashlight's dry cells (also called batteries) store chemical energy. When you flip the switch, chemical energy is changed to electric energy that moves through the light bulb. In the light bulb's filament, electric energy becomes thermal energy and light energy.

Summary

Energy is the ability to cause changes in matter. There are two basic types of energy—kinetic energy and potential energy. Electric energy, thermal energy, mechanical energy, light energy, and sound energy are all forms of kinetic energy. Chemical energy, gravitational potential energy, and elastic potential energy are forms of potential energy. The law of conservation of energy says energy can change form, but it can't be created or destroyed.

Review

1. What is energy?
2. What is kinetic energy?
3. You use mechanical energy to walk around. What form did this energy have before your body changed it to mechanical energy?
4. **Critical Thinking** If you toss a ball in the air, at what point does it have the most potential energy?
5. **Test Prep** Which law states that energy can't be created or destroyed?
   A the law of mechanical energy
   B the law of conservation of energy
   C the law of kinetic energy
   D the law of potential energy

LINKS

MATH LINK

Energy To calculate kinetic energy, you can use the following formula:

Energy = (mass × speed × speed) ÷ 2

Suppose a 1-kg object is moving at 10 m/sec. If the object speeds up to 20 m/sec, does its energy double?

WRITING LINK

Expressive Writing—Poem Brainstorm a list of words related to forms of kinetic and potential energy, such as *rush, shining,* and *loud.* Then use your favorite words to write a poem about using energy, such as in pole vaulting. Read your poem to a classmate.

SOCIAL STUDIES LINK

Energy Crisis In the 1970s the United States had an "energy crisis." There were fears that there would not be enough energy to run our cars, light and heat our homes, and meet other needs. Learn more about what caused this energy crisis. Report on your findings to your classmates.

TECHNOLOGY LINK

Learn more about kinetic and potential energy by visiting this Internet site.
www.scilinks.org/harcourt

What Is Electric Energy?

In this lesson, you can . . .

INVESTIGATE electric circuits.

LEARN ABOUT electric charges, currents, and circuits and electromagnets.

LINK to math, writing, art, and technology.

INVESTIGATE

Electric Circuits

Activity Purpose Electricity is one form of energy. It results from the force of electrons being attracted or repelled. To use this energy, you need to make an *electric circuit*—a path of wires and devices that electrons can follow back to their source. In this investigation you will **make a model** of two different electric circuits and **compare** them.

Materials

- 4 lengths of insulated wire with bare ends
- 2 light-bulb holders
- battery holder
- 2 light bulbs
- battery

Activity Procedure

1. To make electricity flow between the terminals, or charged ends, of a dry cell or battery, you need to connect the terminals in some way, such as with a wire. Electricity will then flow through any device you put along this path. Connect the wires, bulb holders, and battery holder as shown. (Picture A)

2. Insert the light bulbs and batteries. **Observe** what happens and **record** your observations.

3. Remove one of the bulbs from its holder. **Observe** and **record** what happens to the other bulb.

4. Now reconnect the wires, bulb holders, and battery holder as shown. **Observe** what happens and **record** your observations. (Picture B)

◀ Van de Graaff generators use friction to rub off electrons and build up electric charges on the spheres. These are the "lightning machines" used in old science-fiction movies.

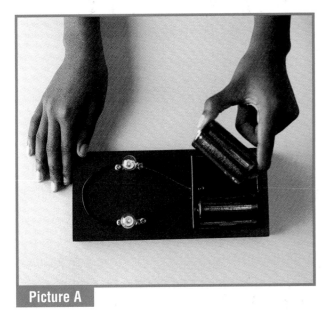

Picture A

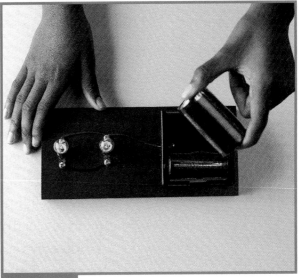

Picture B

5. Again remove one of the bulbs from its holder. **Observe** and **record** what happens to the other bulb.

6. Draw diagrams of both of the circuits you built. Use arrows to **compare** the path of the electric current in each circuit.

Draw Conclusions

1. What happened to the other bulb when one bulb was removed from the first circuit?

2. What happened to the other bulb when one bulb was removed from the second circuit?

3. **Scientists at Work** Scientists often **compare** results before they **draw a conclusion**. Cross out one bulb in each of your drawings. Then diagram the path the electric current must take if it can't pass through the bulb you crossed out. Compare your diagrams, and then draw a conclusion about which type of circuit would be better to use for a string of lights.

Investigate Further In the investigation you demonstrated that electricity flowing through a circuit produces light and heat (the glowing bulbs were warm). Now **plan and conduct a simple investigation** to answer any questions you have about other effects that electricity flowing through a circuit can produce. Select the equipment you will need to use and decide what data you will need to collect.

> **Process Skill Tip**
>
> If you **compare** the results of different experiments before you **draw a conclusion**, you will have more information on which to base your conclusion.

Electric Energy

Electric Charges

Electric energy runs computers, televisions, radios, and appliances, and it lights homes and streets. It is also the energy that produces lightning. Electric energy is produced by the movement of electrons.

You may recall that within an atom, electrons have a negative charge and protons have a positive charge. So the two types of particles attract each other. Most objects have equal numbers of protons and electrons. Sometimes, however, electrons are attracted to the protons of another object and rub off. When an object gains or loses electrons, it has an **electric charge**. An object that has gained electrons has a negative electric charge. An object that has lost electrons has a positive electric charge.

For example, when you drag your feet across a carpet on a dry day, electrons rub off your shoes and onto the carpet. The loss of these electrons produces a positive charge on your body, which makes it attract more electrons. When you reach for an object such as a doorknob, your body attracts electrons from that object. When this attraction is great enough, the electrons jump from the doorknob to your hand. You feel a shock and may even see a small spark.

✔ **What causes an electric charge?**

FIND OUT

• what electric energy is

• how static electricity differs from current electricity

• what an electric circuit is

• how electromagnets work

VOCABULARY

electric charge
electric force
electric current
conductor
electric circuit
insulator
resistor
electromagnet

When the boy rubs the balloon on his hair, electrons rub off the balloon and it becomes positively charged. Opposite charges on the balloon and the boy's sweater make the two objects attract each other.

Electric Force

Most objects have no charge because most objects have about the same numbers of protons and electrons. If an object has a charge, it attracts objects with the opposite charge. Similar to magnetic force, unlike charges attract each other, and like charges repel each other. This attraction or repulsion is called **electric force**. If two objects have large electric charges, they produce a large electric force. Like gravitational force, electric force depends on distance. Two charged objects produce a larger electric force when they are close together.

Charged objects have potential electric energy. This is sometimes called *static electricity,* because the electrons aren't moving. When charged objects are close to each other, potential energy can become kinetic energy. If the charges on the objects are the same, the objects repel each other. If the charges are opposite, the objects are drawn together. If the objects touch or come very close to each other, electrons may flow from one object to the other.

Electrons flow from negatively charged objects to positively charged objects. The

The Van de Graaff generator produces a large static charge by building up electrons on the sphere. The girl touching the sphere is also charged. You can see the effect of this charge in her hair. Since electrons all have the same charge, they repel each other, causing the girl's hairs to separate.

flow of electrons is called **electric current**. Once electrons have moved from one object to the other, the attraction between the objects is gone. The charges are balanced, and there is no electric force.

✔ **How do charges interact?**

◄ As updrafts in a thunderstorm carry rain along, friction rubs electrons off the drops. The bottom of the thundercloud has extra electrons. The top has extra protons. There is potential electric energy between the top and bottom of the cloud.

When the attraction between positive and negative charges becomes great enough, electrons move rapidly through the air between these areas. The potential electric energy becomes electric current. The cloud then gives off its energy in a flash of lightning. ►

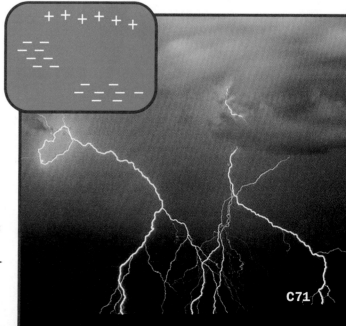

◀ A wall socket is an extension of the terminals of a generator.

Electric Current

Unlike static electricity, which does not move, an electric current is a flow of electrons. The shock you get by touching a doorknob is a small electric current. A lightning bolt is a brief but strong electric current.

To light a light bulb or run a computer, a continuous electric current must be produced. This requires a constant electric force, so a source of electrons is needed. A dry cell, a battery, or a generator can be the source of electrons.

In a dry cell or a battery, two different metals in a chemical bath build up opposite charges. In a generator, some outside force turns coils of wires between two magnets to produce opposite charges. Opposite charges build up on the terminals of a battery or generator.

Electrons are attracted from one terminal to the other. Connecting the two terminals allows an electric current to flow between them. Electric current flows through many kinds of matter if the electric force is strong enough. But some kinds of matter—especially metals—conduct, or carry, electrons more easily than others. Material that conducts electrons easily is called a **conductor**.

✔ **What is a conductor?**

THE INSIDE STORY

Comparing Circuits

For electrons to flow, a circuit has to complete a path between two terminals of opposite charges. Strings of lights can be wired between these terminals in series circuits or in parallel circuits.

In a *series circuit*, there is only one path for the electrons. If one of the bulbs burns out, all the other bulbs go out because the circuit is broken, and the electric current stops flowing.

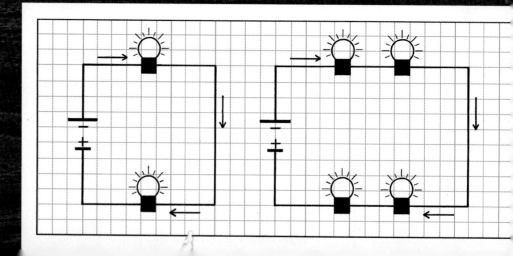

Electric Circuits

A conductor is used in the wire that makes an electric circuit. An **electric circuit** is any path along which electrons can flow. Copper and aluminum are often used as conductors. Metals are good conductors of electric current because their atoms don't hold electrons tightly. This allows electrons to move along from one atom to the next. An electric current flows through good conductors with little resistance.

The conductor in a circuit is wrapped with a material called an insulator (IN•suh•layt•er). An **insulator** is a material that doesn't carry electrons. Rubber, plastic, glass, and air are good insulators. They resist the flow of electrons through them. Insulation keeps wires from touching each other and completing an electrical circuit before the electrons can reach a device. When this happens, it is called a *short circuit*.

Some materials are neither conductors nor insulators. Inside many appliances are materials that don't completely stop the flow of electrons. However, they resist the flow in some way. These materials are called **resistors** (rih•ZIS•terz). Materials that resist electric current are important because they allow electric energy to be changed into other forms.

The filament in a light bulb, for example, resists the flow of electrons. This resistance produces heat. The filament gets hot enough to glow. Electrons flowing in an electric circuit can produce heat, light, sound, or movement. People use all these results in electric devices.

✔ **What materials make good conductors?**

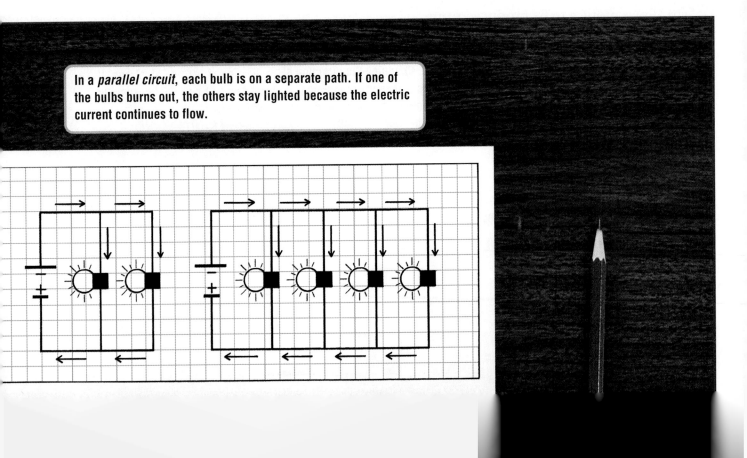

In a *parallel circuit*, each bulb is on a separate path. If one of the bulbs burns out, the others stay lighted because the electric current continues to flow.

Magnets and Electricity

Magnets are used to generate, or produce, electricity. Spinning a coil of wire inside a magnetic field produces an electric force between the ends of the coil. In a similar way, an electric current produces a magnetic field around it. A compass placed next to a wire carrying an electric current will point to the wire.

A current-carrying wire wrapped in a coil of more wire makes a strong magnet. A coil of current-conducting wire wrapped around an iron bar makes an even stronger magnet. Around the coil is a magnetic field much like the one around a bar magnet. But a bar magnet is always magnetized, while a coil wrapped around an iron bar is a magnet only when electric current flows through the coil. For this reason it is called an **electromagnet** (ee•LEK•troh•MAG•nit).

This link between electricity and magnetism allows motion to be produced from

▲ A junkyard is one place to see an electromagnet in action. This huge one picks up scrap metal when current flows through it. When the crane operator wants to drop the scrap, he or she will simply shut off current to the electromagnet.

Current moving through coils of wire inside a fan motor makes the coils electromagnets. Changing the direction of the current at just the right times makes the magnetic poles switch back and forth. Magnetic attraction and repulsion work together to turn the motor's shaft, to which the fan's blades are attached.

electric energy. An electric motor uses electromagnets. By changing the direction of the electric current, these electromagnets alternately attract and repel each other. This causes the motor to turn.

✔ **What forms around a wire carrying an electric current?**

Summary

Electric energy is the movement of electrons between areas that have opposite charges. When objects with opposite charges are close enough together, or when the charges are very large, electrons move between the objects. Electric current moves through an electric circuit. When electric current flows through a conductor, it produces a magnetic field, turning the conductor into an electromagnet.

Review

1. How do like electric charges react to each other?

2. Why are insulators placed around electric conductors?

3. What are resistors, and why are they important?

4. **Critical Thinking** Are the lights in your school connected in series circuits or parallel circuits? Explain.

5. **Test Prep** A coil that is magnetized only when an electric current flows through it is —
   A a battery
   B a generator
   C a conductor
   D an electromagnet

LINKS

MATH LINK

Power Power is measured in *watts*. A 60-watt light bulb uses 60 watts of power every second. Use a calculator to determine how much power a 60-watt light bulb would use in a year if it were never turned off.

WRITING LINK

Informative Writing—Narration
Alessandro Volta, Michael Faraday, Georg Simon Ohm, Charles Coulomb, Joseph Henry, and Nikola Tesla all added to our understanding of electricity and magnetism. Learn more about one of these scientists, and write a short biography to share with your class.

ART LINK

Wiring Diagrams Electrical engineers use a set of symbols to stand for electric devices when they draw circuits. Learn more about these symbols, including the symbols for a battery, a light bulb, a resistor, and a switch. Use these symbols to redraw the circuit diagrams you did in the investigation.

TECHNOLOGY LINK

Learn more about electricity by visiting the Smithsonian Institution Internet site. **www.si.edu/harcourt/science**

What Are Light and Sound Energy?

In this lesson, you can . . .

INVESTIGATE how light is reflected.

LEARN ABOUT light waves and sound waves and how they travel.

LINK to math, writing, social studies, and technology.

◀ This one-person band can send both sound energy and light energy your way. Your ears and eyes receive this energy, and your brain turns it into an image and sound.

INVESTIGATE

The Path of Reflected Light

Activity Purpose You probably use a mirror every day. But looking at a reflection as a scientist would can help you learn something about light. In this investigation you will **observe** and **measure** the angle at which light is reflected by a mirror.

Materials
- piece of corrugated cardboard, 10 cm × 10 cm
- small mirror
- masking tape
- ruler
- 3 pushpins of different colors
- protractor

Activity Procedure

1. Lay the cardboard flat. Use tape to attach the mirror vertically to one end of the cardboard. Push two of the pins into the cardboard, about 5 cm from the mirror. (Picture A)

2. Position yourself at eye level with the mirror. Align yourself so that your view of one pin lines up with the reflection of the other pin. Push a third pin into the cardboard at the edge of the mirror, right in front of where you see the reflection of the second pin. The first pin, the third pin, and the reflection of the second pin should appear to be in a straight line.

3. Draw lines on the cardboard to connect the three pins. These lines show how the reflected light from the first pin traveled to your eye. (Picture B)

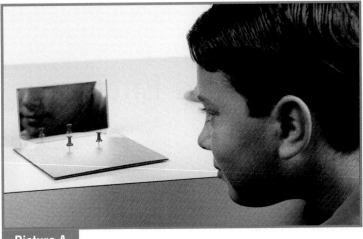

Picture A

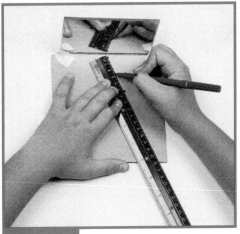

Picture B

4 Using the protractor, **measure** the angle between each line and the edge of the mirror. You will probably have to trace the edge of the mirror and then move it out of your way to make this measurement. **Record** your results.

5 Now remove the original pins and place two of them 10 cm from the mirror. Repeat Steps 2–4 with this new arrangement of pins. **Measure** the angles of the new lines, and **record** your results.

6 Now draw diagrams to **communicate** the results of the two experiments. Each diagram should show the locations of the pins and the mirror and the path of the reflected light.

Draw Conclusions

1. **Compare** the two angles you **measured** in each experiment.

2. The angle at which light strikes a mirror is the *angle of incidence.* The angle at which it reflects from the mirror is the *angle of reflection.* **Draw a conclusion** about the angle of incidence and the angle of reflection from a flat surface.

3. **Scientists at Work** When scientists **observe** a pattern that seems to always be true, it helps them **predict** what will happen in the future. Predict what the angles of incidence and reflection would be if the pins were 20 cm from the mirror.

Investigate Further **Hypothesize** or develop a testable question about how light would be reflected from a mirror that was not flat. Then **plan and conduct a simple investigation** to test your hypothesis or answer your question.

Process Skill Tip

If you **observe** that something always happens the same way under the same conditions, you will be able to **predict** what will happen in the future if the conditions are the same.

Light and Sound Energy

Light Energy

FIND OUT

- the characteristics of light energy and sound energy

- the wave characteristics of light and sound

VOCABULARY

reflection
refraction
lens
pitch
volume

We usually think about light as rays that start at a source, such as the sun, and travel in a straight line until they strike something, such as Earth. Light rays are a form of energy that can travel through empty space or through some kinds of matter. For example, light passes easily through gases in the atmosphere and through clear glass windows.

Sometimes light energy is absorbed when it strikes matter. Most objects absorb some colors of light. Other colors bounce off objects as a **reflection**. The colors of light that objects reflect are the colors we see.

A green leaf, for example, absorbs much of the sunlight that strikes it. The rest of the light—the green part—reflects off the leaf. That's why a leaf looks green to us. A mirror, however, reflects all colors.

In space, light energy from the sun travels at about 300,000 km/sec (186,000 mi/sec). When light passes through a glass window, it slows down. This change in speed causes light rays to bend. This bending of light rays is called **refraction**.

Light often refracts when it moves from one substance to another. For example, a pencil in a glass of water appears to bend at the water's surface. This is because light rays traveling from the pencil to your eyes bend as they move from the water, through the glass, and into the air.

✔ **What is reflection?**

A mirror reflects all the light that strikes it. ▼

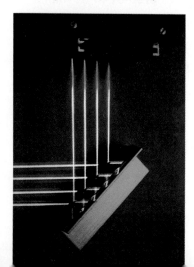

Light rays bend when passing through clear objects. ▼

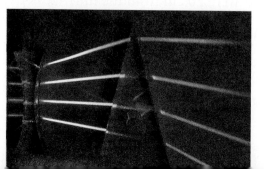

Some objects absorb all colors of light, producing a shadow. ▼

Lenses

Many people wear corrective lenses—glasses or contacts—to improve their vision. A **lens** is a piece of clear material that bends, or refracts, light rays passing through it. There are two kinds of lenses. A *convex lens* is thicker in the middle than at the edges. When light passes through a convex lens, the rays bend toward each other. The hand lens you use for investigations is a convex lens. It makes nearby objects look larger.

People who are farsighted have trouble seeing things that are close to them, like print on a page. Glasses or contacts with convex lenses magnify the print, allowing these people to read more easily.

Movie projectors and slide projectors also use convex lenses. As light from the bulb shines through the film, light rays spread apart. As these rays pass through the projector lens, they bend toward each other again.

The other type of lens is a *concave lens*. This lens is thicker around the edges than in the middle. When light rays pass through a concave lens, they bend away from each other. This makes distant objects seem nearer and smaller. Some cameras have a concave lens in their viewfinders. When you look through the viewfinder, you see a small version of what the final photograph will look like.

Concave lenses help people who are nearsighted. These people have trouble seeing distant objects. Concave lenses bend light rays outward just enough to make distant objects seem closer.

✔ **Compare the shapes of convex lenses and concave lenses.**

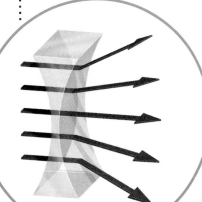

◄ The concave lens in a camera viewfinder bends light rays outward. The rays then appear to be coming from an image that is smaller and closer to the camera than it really is.

◄ The light rays bent by a convex lens all meet at one point and then cross, making the image on the screen appear upside-down. So slides or movie film must be put into a projector upside down.

Light Waves

When waves move across the ocean, the water doesn't actually move with the wave. Only the energy of the wave form moves. Light energy also moves as waves. These waves, called *electromagnetic waves*, are produced when vibrating electrons inside atoms give off energy.

Visible light waves—those we can see—are just a small part of the electromagnetic waves produced in the universe. Radio waves, microwaves, infrared waves, ultraviolet waves, and X rays are also types of electromagnetic waves. Unlike water waves, electromagnetic waves don't need a substance to move through. They move fastest, in fact, when there is no matter to slow them down, such as in space.

Within the range of visible light waves are different wave patterns that humans sense as different colors of light. We sense long wave patterns as red, and short wave patterns as violet. Between red and violet are all the colors of the rainbow.

✔ **How are electromagnetic waves produced?**

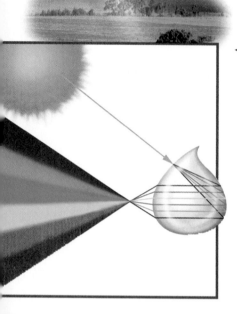

◀ When sunlight passes through a raindrop, the different waves that make up visible light move at slightly different speeds. This separates the white light into different colors.

THE INSIDE STORY

Light and Sound

Your eyes gather light waves, and your ears gather sound waves. In these organs the energy waves are changed into nerve impulses. Your brain interprets these impulses, and you see images and hear sounds.

Lens Light passes through the clear *lens*, which can thicken to help focus light from nearby objects.

Iris The colored *iris* widens in darkness and narrows in bright light to control the amount of light that enters through the *pupil*.

Cornea Light enters through the clear *cornea*, which acts as a convex lens and bends light rays.

Retina An upside-down image falls on the *retina*, where cells change light energy to electrical and chemical energy in the form of nerve impulses.

Sound Waves

Sound also moves as waves. However, in the case of sound, these waves are carried by vibrating matter.

Most of the sound waves we hear travel through air. But sound waves also travel through liquids, such as water, and even through solids. If you click two stones together while underwater, you can hear the sound more clearly than you can in air.

As a sound wave travels through matter, molecules in the matter move back and forth in the direction the sound wave is moving. As the sound moves forward, the molecules are squeezed together. This is called *compression*. After the first compression passes, pressure on the molecules drops. This is called *rarefaction* (rer•uh•FAK•shuhn). If a sound is continuous, both compression and rarefaction are repeated again and again.

The speed with which sound waves move determines the **pitch** of the sound. The

As the harp string vibrates, it moves quickly from side to side. When the string moves to the right, air to the right is compressed. When the string moves to the left, air to the right is rarefied.

faster the waves, the higher the pitch. In music, pitch is labeled with letters called notes. As you move from left to right on a piano keyboard, pitch increases.

Another way of measuring sound waves is to measure their strength. The more the molecules are squeezed during compression, the louder the sound is. The loudness of a sound is called **volume**.

✔ **How are sound waves carried?**

Hair cells When hair cells in the cochlea move, they change their mechanical energy to electrical energy—nerve impulses that are sent along the *cochlear nerve* to the brain.

Hammer, anvil, and stirrup The vibrating eardrum starts these three tiny bones—the *hammer*, *anvil*, and *stirrup*—moving.

Cochlea The stirrup transfers vibrations to the fluid in the *cochlea*, a coiled canal. The vibrating fluid moves hair cells that line the cochlea.

Eardrum The air pressure changes cause the *eardrum* to vibrate in and out at the same rate as the pitch of the sound.

Ear canal Sound waves enter the *ear canal* as air pressure changes.

Sound Energy

Like water waves, sound waves are waves of energy moving through matter. And like water waves, sound waves move molecules back and forth without carrying them along with the wave.

Because sound waves are vibrations of molecules, matter must be present for sound to travel. Where there is no matter, such as in outer space, sound cannot travel.

The sounds we hear travel mostly as vibrations of the gas molecules in the air around us. When sound waves move through air, they travel about 340 m/sec (1100 ft/sec). When sound waves move through denser materials, such as liquids and solids, they move faster. You can compare some of these speeds by using the table below.

Denser objects carry sound energy farther as well as faster than less dense objects. Whales, for example, produce sounds that travel underwater for hundreds of kilometers. Only very loud sounds can travel that far through air.

Sound energy travels even better through most solids. The rich sounds made by a cello or a guitar are due partly to the vibrations of the wood in the instruments. Try putting a ticking watch on one end of a table and

Humans see objects when light waves reflect off them. Animals such as dolphins and bats can use the reflection of sound waves to form "pictures" of objects around them. This sense is similar to humans using sonar to "see" objects on the ocean floor.

observing how clearly you can hear the ticking if you put your ear against the other end of the table.

However, not all solids carry sound vibrations. Materials that carry sound waves are called sound *conductors*. Materials that don't carry sound are called sound *insulators*. Materials with a lot of air spaces in them, such as fabrics and plastic foam, are good sound insulators.

✔ **About how fast does sound travel through air?**

Speed of Sound Waves Through Different Materials

Material	Speed of Sound in Material
Air	340 m/sec (about 1100 ft/sec)
Water	1500 m/sec (about 4900 ft/sec)
Steel	5000 m/sec (about 16,400 ft/sec)
Silver	2650 m/sec (about 8700 ft/sec)
Granite	3950 m/sec (about 13,000 ft/sec)

Summary

Light energy is electromagnetic energy that travels through space and through certain materials. When light waves strike an obstacle, they are absorbed, reflected, or refracted. Lenses are curved pieces of transparent matter that refract light rays. Sound energy is vibrations that travel through matter. Solids and liquids conduct sound better than gases.

Review

1. What is refraction?
2. What type of lens would you use to magnify your view of a butterfly?
3. What is a sound wave?
4. **Critical Thinking** If a bright, loud explosion took place in space, would it be seen or heard on Earth?
5. **Test Prep** Which part of the eye has cells that change light energy to nerve impulses?

   A the iris

   B the blind spot

   C the lens

   D the retina

LINKS

MATH LINK

Lightning and Thunder Suppose a thunderstorm is coming. First you see a flash of lightning. You hear the thunder 22 seconds later. Knowing the speed of sound in air, estimate how far away the storm is.

WRITING LINK

Informative Writing—Classification Make a list of all the uses of lenses you can think of. Classify the lens in each case as *concave* or *convex*. Exchange lists with a classmate, and talk about any differences between your lists.

SOCIAL STUDIES LINK

Law of Refraction The Egyptian astronomer Ptolemy stated the first law of refraction. But it was Willebord Snell who finalized the law now known as Snell's law. Research these men, and write a short report about Snell's law of refraction.

TECHNOLOGY LINK

Learn more about light energy by viewing *Psycholograms* on the **Harcourt Science Newsroom Video** in your classroom video library.

Learn more about light reflection by investigating *A Reflecting Story* on the **Harcourt Science Explorations CD-ROM.**

What Are Thermal and Chemical Energy?

In this lesson, you can . . .

INVESTIGATE the way heat moves through different materials.

LEARN ABOUT how thermal energy is transferred and how chemical energy is stored.

LINK to math, writing, social studies, and technology.

◄ This is a *thermogram*, a photo that records thermal energy. The purple, red, and orange areas are warmer than the blue and green areas.

INVESTIGATE

Heat Flow

Activity Purpose In this lesson you will learn about thermal energy, or heat. In this investigation you will **experiment** to help you understand the ways heat moves through different materials.

Materials
- margarine
- metal butter knife
- Styrofoam cup
- hot water
- clock
- plastic knife

CAUTION

Activity Procedure

1 Place a dab of cold margarine near the middle of the metal knife. Place another dab of margarine the same size near the tip of the knife's blade.

2 **CAUTION** **Be careful when pouring the hot water.** Half-fill the cup with hot water. Put the metal knife's handle into the water. The dabs of margarine should be above the level of the water. (Picture A)

3 **Predict** which dab of margarine will melt first—the one near the middle of the knife or the one near the end of the knife.

Picture A

Picture B

4 **Observe** the metal knife for ten minutes, and **record** your observations.

5 Repeat Steps 1–4, using the plastic knife. (Picture B)

6 **Experiment** to find out which material transfers heat faster—metal or plastic. Be sure to **identify and control variables** that might affect the results.

Draw Conclusions

1. **Draw conclusions** about how heat moves through the metal knife.

2. **Draw conclusions** about which material transfers heat faster.

3. **Scientists at Work** Scientists **identify and control variables** in an experiment to see how changing one variable affects the results. What variables did you control in your experiment? What variable did you test? What was the dependent variable?

Investigate Further **Experiment** to find out which knife cools faster. Decide what equipment you will need.

Process Skill Tip

To be sure that the results of an experiment are valid, you must **identify and control** all **variables** that might affect the results.

C85

Thermal Energy and Chemical Energy

Thermal Energy

FIND OUT

- what thermal energy is and how it moves
- what chemical energy is

VOCABULARY

temperature
heat
conduction
convection
radiation

You may recall that kinetic energy is the energy of motion. Kinetic energy is present in the movement of molecules. In liquids and gases, molecules bounce off one another at high speeds. Even in solid matter, molecules vibrate constantly. This kinetic energy of molecules is *thermal energy*.

The average kinetic energy of all the molecules in an object is the object's **temperature**. The higher the average kinetic energy, or the faster the molecules move, the higher the temperature. It's important to note that temperature and thermal energy aren't the same. For example, a large pot of boiling water and a small pot of boiling water have the same temperature, but the large pot has more thermal energy because it has more molecules.

When rapidly moving molecules (those in a hot substance) bump into slowly moving molecules (those in a cold substance), they transfer, or give off, some of their thermal energy to the slower molecules. The transfer of thermal energy from one substance to another is called **heat**. Heat always flows in the same direction—from the warmer substance to the cooler substance. As you observed in the investigation, heat warms the cooler substance, raising its temperature. Heat can also change the state of a substance, making a solid melt or a liquid evaporate.

✔ **What is heat?**

The molecules in the milk are moving slowly. Their thermal energy is low, so the liquid feels cold. ▼

The molecules in the hot cocoa are moving quickly. Their thermal energy is high, so the liquid feels hot. ▼

The foods in this hot breakfast were cooked by three methods of transferring heat.

▲ Radiation from the glowing coils in the toaster transfers heat to the surface of the bread.

Conduction transfers heat from the stove burner through the metal frying pan to the ham. ▼

◀ Convection currents transfer heat from the bottom of the pan all through the boiling water to the egg.

Transferring Thermal Energy

Thermal energy can be transferred, or moved, between objects in three ways: conduction, convection, and radiation.

Conduction (kuhn•DUHK•shuhn) is the direct transfer of heat between objects that touch. A frying pan in direct contact with an electric-stove burner gets hot because the burner is hot.

When solids transfer heat to other solids, it is usually by conduction. Materials that conduct heat easily are called *conductors*. Metals are good heat conductors. Materials that do a poor job of conducting heat are called *insulators*. Air is a good heat insulator. For example, double-paned windows have a layer of air between two layers of glass. This air slows down the rate at which heat can be conducted into or out of a building.

Convection (kuhn•VEK•shuhn) is heat transfer as a result of the mixing of a liquid or a gas. When you heat a pan of water on a stove, the water at the bottom of the pan heats up first. The hot water becomes less dense, and cold water from the top of the pan sinks below it. As the hot water rises, it cools and sinks. This movement of hot water rising, cooling, sinking, being reheated, and rising again transfers thermal energy throughout the pan.

Radiation (ray•dee•AY•shuhn) is the transfer of thermal energy by electromagnetic waves. Energy from the sun is transferred to Earth by electromagnetic waves. Some of that energy is thermal energy. Conduction and convection can transfer heat through matter, but only radiation can transfer heat through space.

✔ **What are the three ways thermal energy can be transferred?**

Chemical Energy

Chemical energy is the energy stored in the bonds between atoms when they join together to form molecules. Some chemical reactions give off thermal energy. Others take in thermal energy. This thermal energy is stored as a form of potential energy called *chemical energy*. Chemical energy can be released as kinetic energy when molecules break apart.

Chemical energy can be released as several forms of kinetic energy. Batteries, for example, contain chemical energy that can be used to produce electricity. During cellular respiration, your body changes chemical energy stored in the food you eat into mechanical energy that allows you to carry on your daily activities.

Other body processes change chemical energy into thermal energy. Some of that thermal energy is used to keep your body temperature at about 37°C (98.6°F). The table shows the amount of chemical energy stored in some of the foods you eat. The potential energy of foods is measured in units called Calories (C). A Calorie is the amount of heat needed to raise the temperature of 1000 g of water by 1°C.

Chemical energy can also be released as light and heat when wood and other fuels are burned. You can learn more about the release of chemical energy from fuels in Extension Chapter 2.

✔ **What is chemical energy?**

Potential Energy in Foods

Food (1 serving)	Energy (in Calories)	Food (1 serving)	Energy (in Calories)
Fruits		**Dairy Products**	
Apple	80	Ice cream	270
Banana	105	Cheese	110
Orange	80	Yogurt	230
Meats		**Vegetables**	
Chicken, roasted	140	Carrots	30
Hot dog	145	Corn	85
Pork chop	275	French fries	220
Roast beef, lean	175	Green beans	35
Salmon, baked	140	Lettuce	5
Shrimp, fried	240	Tomato	25
Bread and Cereal		**Snacks**	
Bread, white	65	Peanut butter	95
Macaroni and cheese	430	Pizza, cheese	290
Oatmeal	105	Popcorn, plain	30
Rice, white	180	Pretzel sticks	10

Grass stores energy from sunlight as chemical energy. By eating grass, the cow takes in this stored energy. Some of it becomes thermal energy, and some becomes mechanical energy. Some of it is stored as chemical energy in the cow's milk. ▼

Summary

Thermal energy is the kinetic energy of molecules. The average kinetic energy of the molecules in an object is the object's temperature. Heat is the transfer of thermal energy from one object to another. Conduction is the direct transfer of heat between objects that touch. Convection is the transfer of heat through currents in a gas or a liquid. Radiation is the transfer of energy by electromagnetic waves. When atoms join to form molecules, thermal energy can be stored as chemical energy. Chemical energy can be released as kinetic energy.

Review

1. What is convection?

2. What type of heat transfer takes place when you burn your hand on a stove?

3. Two atoms absorb thermal energy when joining together to form a molecule. What happens to that thermal energy?

4. **Critical Thinking** Suppose you drop an ice cube into a warm drink, and it melts. How is thermal energy transferred?

5. **Test Prep** Which form of energy transfer allows you to feel the warmth of the sun on your face?

     A radiation

     B conduction

     C convection

     D chemical energy

LINKS

MATH LINK

Thermal Energy Which has a higher temperature, a 100-g ice cube or 10 g of water at 1°C? Which has more thermal energy?

WRITING LINK

Informative Writing—Explanation Write two or three paragraphs for your teacher explaining how the transfer of energy from the sun provides most of Earth's energy.

SOCIAL STUDIES LINK

History of Calories Scientists once thought of heat as a fluid, called *caloric*, that flowed from one object to another. Benjamin Thompson, also known as Count Rumford, came up with the idea that, because heat could be caused by motion, heat and motion must be different forms of the same thing (energy). Research Count Rumford's experiments and his ideas about heat, and report to your class.

TECHNOLOGY LINK

Learn more about thermal and chemical energy by visiting the Harcourt Learning Site. **www.harcourtschool.com/ca**

Developing Sources of ENERGY

Archaeologists estimate that humans burned wood as a fuel as much as 14,000 years ago. For thousands of years, wood was just about the only source of fuel people had.

Fossil Fuels and Steam

During the Middle Ages, Europeans began mining coal. As centuries passed, coal was used more and more, since the growing population was rapidly cutting down the few remaining forests. In areas along rivers or streams, mills for grinding grain were powered by flowing water, and in Spain and Holland, wind power was used. In the mid-1600s, machines were invented that were powered by steam. Many of these machines were used to pump water out of coal mines.

In 1765 James Watt, a pioneer in the development of steam engines, was repairing a broken engine when he discovered a way to improve it. By 1800 Watt had made a condenser steam engine. It was more efficient than the old engines because it changed water vapor back into liquid water, which could be reheated to make more steam.

By 1830 a steam-powered train was running regularly in the United States. And by 1838 a steam-powered ship had crossed the Atlantic Ocean. Coal was the most widely used fuel for steam engines, especially in Europe. In the United States, many early steam engines used wood for fuel because the supply there seemed endless.

The History of Energy Sources

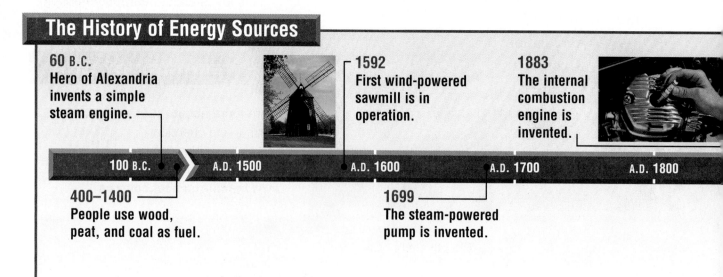

60 B.C.
Hero of Alexandria invents a simple steam engine.

400–1400
People use wood, peat, and coal as fuel.

1592
First wind-powered sawmill is in operation.

1699
The steam-powered pump is invented.

1883
The internal combustion engine is invented.

100 B.C.   A.D. 1500   A.D. 1600   A.D. 1700   A.D. 1800

Internal Combustion and Electricity

In 1883 a high-speed engine was invented that ignited gasoline mixed with air inside metal cylinders. Improvements in this internal combustion engine, as it was called, led to the development of the automobile. Gasoline, kerosene, and other petroleum products are still used as fuel for most forms of transportation.

In 1888 the first turbine-powered electric energy station was built. In the turbine, large blades, driven by steam, turned a shaft connected to an electric generator. Later, flowing water from hydroelectric dams was used as a source of energy to drive the turbines. Today coal is the most commonly used fuel for generating electricity.

New Fuels

Obtaining and using fossil fuels often harms the environment. For this reason, scientists and engineers have begun developing alternative energy sources, including solar energy, wind, and geothermal energy. Solar cells can capture the sun's energy and change it directly into electricity. In some desert areas, huge solar panels generate large amounts of electricity for use in homes and businesses. In California, Britain, the Netherlands, and other places, high-tech windmills generate electricity for many homes. In Hawai'i and Iceland, intense heat from inside of Earth, called geothermal energy, is used to heat buildings and to generate electricity.

THINK ABOUT IT

1. Why did coal replace wood as a fuel source in Europe?
2. Today's electric generating stations use turbines that are similar to what older devices?

In the 1960s, nuclear energy stations were built in many countries.

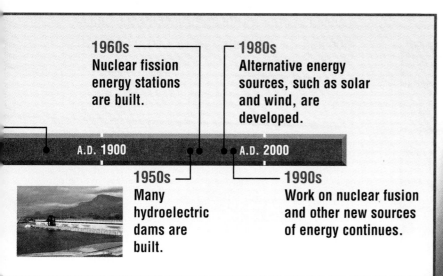

1960s
Nuclear fission energy stations are built.

1980s
Alternative energy sources, such as solar and wind, are developed.

A.D. 1900

A.D. 2000

1950s
Many hydroelectric dams are built.

1990s
Work on nuclear fusion and other new sources of energy continues.

Jean M. Bennett

PHYSICIST

Jean M. Bennett is a physicist who has done a great deal of work in the study of light scattering. Light scattering occurs when a beam of light strikes an uneven surface and is reflected in many different directions. This scattering is not at all like the parallel rays of light that are reflected by a smooth surface.

Dr. Bennett's work has many real-life uses, especially for optical equipment such as lenses. Most lenses used in optical equipment are polished to a very smooth finish. Then the lenses are treated with a thin coating to help prevent "ghost" reflections. If you have ever seen a faint double image on a television screen instead of one sharp image, you have an idea of what a ghost reflection is. However, the thin coating also gives a lens a surface that is not perfectly smooth, which causes the light to scatter. Dr. Bennett has worked with lens manufacturers to make lenses with smoother surfaces and coatings that scatter less light. This research helps people who wear glasses to be able to see better, especially at night.

In addition to working on light scattering, Dr. Bennett has also done research on the physics of Earth's atmosphere. She is currently an important member of the research department of the Naval Air Warfare Center at China Lake, California.

THINK ABOUT IT

1. Why is it important to develop better coatings as lenses also get better?

2. Can you think of another situation in which doing something to solve one problem caused another problem? Describe the situation and the problem.

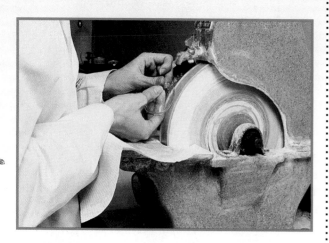

Grinding lenses

Sound Waves

How do sound waves travel?

Materials

- glass pie pan with 200 mL water
- overhead projector
- tin can
- tuning fork
- uncooked rice
- balloon
- spring toy

Procedure

1. Put the pie pan with water on the projector. Turn the projector on.

2. Tap the tuning fork on a solid object. Place the end of the fork in the water. Observe the waves on the screen.

3. Now stretch the balloon over the tin can.

4. Sprinkle rice on top of the stretched balloon.

5. Tap the tuning fork, and gently touch the end of the fork to the balloon. Observe the action of the rice.

6. Stretch the spring toy out on a smooth surface. Gather some coils at one end. Then let them go. Observe how the compression waves travel.

Draw Conclusions

In Step 2, how did the sound waves travel from the tuning fork? How did Step 5 show that sound waves are energy waves? Sound waves travel as compression waves, like those you made with the spring toy. Describe the movement of compression waves.

The Eyes Have It

How does the brain receive images?

Materials

- flashlight
- small, round fishbowl
- small toy car
- sheet of white paper
- hand lens

Procedure

1. Line up the materials in the order shown.

2. Darken the room. Turn on the flashlight.

3. Shine the light on the toy car.

4. Focus the shadow through the lens and the fishbowl, and onto the white paper. Observe the image formed on the paper.

Draw Conclusions

What organ does this model represent? What part of that organ does each part of the model represent? What happens to the shadow of the toy car projected onto the paper? When an image is received on the retina and sent to the brain, what does the brain do with this image?

Chapter 3 Review and Test Preparation

Vocabulary Review

Use the terms below to answer Questions 1 through 12. The page numbers in ( ) tell you where to look in the chapter if you need help.

energy (C64)　　　　**reflection** (C78)
kinetic energy (C64)　**refraction** (C78)
potential energy (C64)　**lens** (C79)
electric charge C70)　**pitch** (C81)
electric force (C71)　　**volume** (C81)
electric current (C71)　**temperature** (C86)
conductor (C72)　　　**heat** (C86)
electric circuit (C73)　**conduction** (C87)
insulator (C73)　　　**convection** (C87)
resistor (C73)　　　　**radiation** (C87)
electromagnet (C74)

1. The three ways in which heat is transferred are ____, ____, and ____.

2. A ____ is a clear material that bends light rays.

3. ____ causes changes in matter.

4. A ____ carries electric current easily, while an ____ does not.

5. A sound's ____ is determined by the speed of its energy waves, while ____ is determined by the strength of the waves.

6. When an ____ flows through a coil of wire wrapped around a bar of iron, it makes an ____.

7. When a piece of wood burns, it releases ____.

8. The energy of motion is called ____, while the energy of position is called ____.

9. The bouncing of light rays off an object is called ____. The bending of light rays by an object is called ____.

10. A path for electricity, called an ____, may include a ____ that changes electric energy into other forms of energy.

11. The attraction or repulsion of an ____ is called an ____.

12. The average kinetic energy of all the molecules in an object is the object's ____.

Connect Concepts

Write the terms from the Word Bank that belong in the concept map.

potential　kinetic　static　thermal
radiation　sound　light　convection
chemical　electric　current　conduction

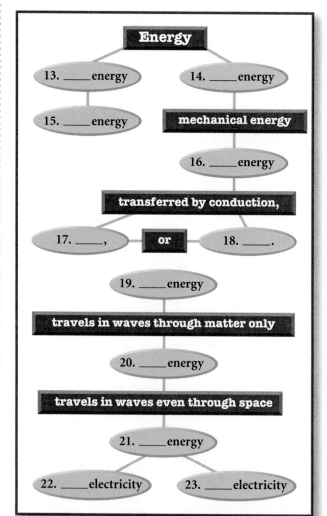

Check Understanding

Write the letter of the best choice.

24. Metals and other materials that transfer heat and electricity easily are called —

A insulators   **C** radiators

B resistors   **D** conductors

25. The color you see in an object is the color of light the object —

F absorbs   **H** refracts

G reflects   **J** conducts

26. Because there is no matter in space, thermal energy moves from the sun to Earth by —

A radiation   **C** insulation

B convection **D** conduction

27. Lightning and the spark you may see when you touch a doorknob on a dry day are both caused by —

F thermal energy

G static electricity

H electromagnetism

J resistors

28. An object with a positive charge will attract another object with —

A a negative charge

B a positive charge

C a positive or a negative charge

D no charge

Critical Thinking

29. Suppose you throw a ball high into the air and then it falls to the ground. Describe where the ball has the greatest potential energy and where it has the greatest kinetic energy.

30. If energy can be neither created nor destroyed, what happens to the sunlight that falls on Earth?

Process Skills Review

31. You touch a lamp cord and get a shock. **Draw a conclusion** about the insulation on the cord.

32. You record the temperature in a pan of water as it heats. You want to **make a graph** to display your results. What type of graph should you use?

33. You conduct an experiment with parallel and series electric circuits. What is one way you could **communicate** about the circuits you built?

34. You want to **compare** two materials to see which is the better conductor of thermal energy. Name two quantities you will measure.

35. You want to **plan and conduct an experiment** to show convection. Name two items you could use in your experiment.

36. You experiment to compare the colors of light reflected by different substances. Name one **variable** you must **control**.

Performance Assessment

Energy Audit

Take ten minutes to identify as many forms of energy around you right now as possible. Make a list of these forms and of how they are being transferred or changed from one form to another during those ten minutes.

Unit Project Wrap Up

Here are some ideas for ways to wrap up your unit project.

Make a Chart
Use a computer and word processing software to make a chart comparing cereals. Which do you think is most healthful? Which do you think is the best buy?

Write an Ad
Write and illustrate an ad for a real food product. Tell how you are sure the claims you make for the product are true.

Make a Scrapbook
Cut pictures from newspapers and magazines that show changes in matter. Mount the pictures on sheets of paper and put the paper together to make a book. Write on the pages how matter changed in each picture.

Investigate Further
How could you make your project better? What other questions do you have about matter? Plan ways to find answers to your questions. Use the Science Handbook on pages R2-R9 for help.

Extension Chapters

California Science Standards

Extension Chapters

CALIFORNIA SCIENCE STANDARDS

Chapter 1 Renewable and
Nonrenewable Resources   E2

Chapter 2 How People Use Energy   E30

Chapter 1

LESSON **1**
What Are Natural Resources? E4

LESSON **2**
How Do Fossil Fuels Form? E10

LESSON **3**
How Are Natural Resources Conserved? E18

SCIENCE AND TECHNOLOGY   E24

PEOPLE IN SCIENCE   E26

ACTIVITIES FOR HOME OR SCHOOL   E27

CHAPTER REVIEW AND TEST PREPARATION   E28

Renewable and Nonrenewable Resources

Can you picture what life would be like if there were no oil or coal? How would people drive their cars or make electricity? Coal and oil are natural resources that people use for energy.

Vocabulary Preview

natural resource
nonrenewable resource
renewable resource
reusable resource
fossil fuels
natural gas
peat
lignite
bitumen
anthracite
recycling

⠿*FAST* FACT

More than three-fourths of the energy we use comes from fossil fuels (natural gas, coal, and petroleum). Less than four percent comes from inexhaustible energy sources, such as the sun, the wind, or the ocean tides.

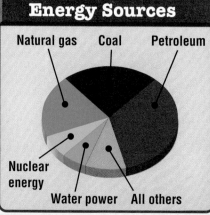

Energy Sources

Natural gas   Coal   Petroleum

Nuclear energy

Water power   All others

What Are Natural Resources?

In this lesson, you can . . .

INVESTIGATE the properties of minerals.

LEARN ABOUT Earth's natural resources.

LINK to math, writing, technology, and other areas.

Color is just one of the physical properties of minerals. ▼

▲ Quartz
▼ Pyrite

INVESTIGATE

Properties of Minerals

Activity Purpose Minerals have physical properties, or characteristics. Minerals can be hard or soft. Some are magnetic. Minerals such as quartz can form beautiful crystals. The properties of minerals make them useful to people for various purposes. In this investigation you will **observe** minerals. Then you will **make predictions** about their properties.

Materials
- 6 mineral samples (talc, pyrite, quartz, fluorite, magnetite, graphite)
- tile
- magnet

Activity Procedure

1. Make a copy of the chart below. List the names of the minerals your teacher gives you.

2. **Observe** each mineral. **Predict** which one will be the hardest. Then rub the minerals against each other to test their hardness. A harder mineral will scratch a softer one. Under *Hardness* on the chart, write a number from 1 to 6 for the hardness of each mineral. Use 1 for the softest mineral and 6 for the hardest mineral.

Mineral	Hardness	Shine	Streak	Magnetic
talc				
pyrite				
quartz				
fluorite				
magnetite				
graphite				

Picture A

Picture B

3 **Observe** each mineral, and decide whether or not it is shiny. Write *yes* next to the name of the mineral if it is shiny. Write *no* if it is not.

4 Now **predict** the color of the streak each mineral will make. A streak is the colored line a mineral makes when it is rubbed on a tile. Then rub each mineral on the tile. If the mineral makes a streak, write the color of the streak next to the mineral's name. Write *none* if the mineral does not make a streak. (Picture A)

5 Finally, **predict** which minerals will be attracted to a magnet. Test each mineral with a magnet. Write *yes* next to the names of minerals that stick to the magnet. Write *no* next to the names of those that do not. (Picture B)

Draw Conclusions

1. Which mineral is the softest? **Compare** your test results with your predictions.

2. Which minerals make streaks? **Compare** your test results with your color predictions.

3. Which minerals are magnetic? **Compare** your test results with your predictions.

4. **Scientists at Work** Scientists often **predict** what might happen. How did careful observations of the mineral samples help you make better predictions about their properties?

Investigate Further Use the data you recorded on each mineral's properties to **infer** its uses.

Process Skill Tip

Before you **predict,** make careful observations. This makes your prediction better than a simple guess.

LEARN ABOUT

Natural Resources

Nonrenewable Resources

In the investigation you learned that minerals have many physical properties. Properties such as hardness and shine make minerals useful for different purposes. Useful minerals and other materials that people take from the Earth are called **natural resources**.

In the past hundred years, people have been using natural resources at a faster rate than ever before. That has made scientists wonder whether some natural resources may one day be completely used up. A resource that cannot be replaced once it is used up is called a **nonrenewable resource**. Nonrenewable resources take thousands of years to form. Once they are used up, they are, as a practical matter, gone.

Rock and mineral resources are nonrenewable. We use rock resources to construct buildings and roads. The silicon chips that make a computer work come from minerals. So does the "lead," or graphite, in a pencil. Other mineral resources are

FIND OUT

- **what natural resources are**
- **why some natural resources might get used up**

VOCABULARY

natural resource
nonrenewable resource
renewable resource
reusable resource

The aluminum in the basketball backboard comes from the mineral bauxite. ▶

Our bodies need mineral resources. Foods such as fruits and vegetables take minerals from the soil.

E6

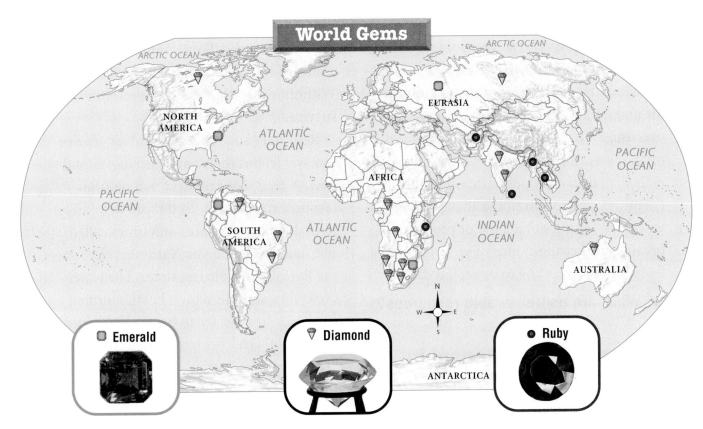

ARCTIC OCEAN

ARCTIC OCEAN

EURASIA

NORTH AMERICA

ATLANTIC OCEAN

PACIFIC OCEAN

PACIFIC OCEAN

AFRICA

SOUTH AMERICA

ATLANTIC OCEAN

INDIAN OCEAN

AUSTRALIA

N
W E
S

▢ Emerald

▽ Diamond

● Ruby

ANTARCTICA

▲ Gems are rare and valuable minerals. Some parts of the world have large deposits of certain gems.

▲ Many buildings are made of granite. Granite is used for buildings because it is hard, and its surface can be polished.

▲ Limestone is also an important building material. It is used to make the concrete for this basketball court.

necessary for the production of metals such as aluminum, iron, copper, silver, and gold. And gems—such as diamonds, rubies, and emeralds—are minerals, too.

Any rock containing a large amount of a mineral is called a *mineral deposit*. Mineral deposits form in several ways. Some minerals dissolve in hot water. As the hot mineral solution flows through cracks in cooler rocks, some minerals fall out of solution and form deposits called *veins*. Gold, copper, and silver are found in veins.

Mineral deposits can also form in magma. As magma cools, heavy minerals sink, forming deposits rich in metals such as iron and nickel.

Mineral deposits are distributed unevenly in the Earth. Some nations have many mineral resources, while other nations have few. Nations usually trade with each other to get the resources they need.

Soil is another nonrenewable resource. All the Earth's forests and food crops take minerals out of the soil as they grow. Minerals go back into the soil when plants and animals die and decay. But people can destroy soil by overusing it or by putting certain chemicals on it. Overusing soil removes more minerals than decay can put back. And some chemicals can poison soil so that nothing will grow. Losing soil is a major problem, because it takes thousands of years for even a few centimeters of soil to be replaced.

✔ **What are nonrenewable resources?**

Renewable and Reusable Resources

The Earth produces new amounts of some natural resources at the same rate as they are used. A **renewable resource** is a resource that is replaced as it is used.

Most forests, for example, are renewable resources, but only if enough new trees are allowed to grow. Important products, such as lumber, paper, cardboard, tar, and turpentine, come from forests. When humans cut down trees, new ones can grow in their place. If large areas of an old forest are cut at one time, however, the new forest may have different kinds of plants and animals than the old forest did. Some animals need the plants of the old forest for food or shelter. Without those plants the animals might not survive.

Resources such as water and air are not renewable, but they can be used over and over. A **reusable resource** is a natural resource that can be used more than once. Reusable resources are sometimes called *inexhaustible resources*. Natural cycles renew the Earth's reusable resources. The water cycle, for example, allows Earth's limited supply of fresh water to be used over and over again. Heat from the sun evaporates water from the Earth's surface—mainly from the oceans—into the atmosphere. As air cools, water vapor condenses, forming clouds. Water then falls back to Earth from clouds as rain or snow.

Although reusable resources cannot be used up, they can be polluted. During evaporation, water loses any pollution it may have picked up. However, rain and snow pick up any pollution in the air. Acid rain, for example, falls where cloud drops mix with certain chemical pollutants in the air.

✔ **What is a renewable resource?**

Some resources—air, forests, and water—can last forever if they are used carefully.

Summary

Natural resources are useful materials that people take from the Earth. Resources such as soil, rocks, and minerals are nonrenewable. Once they are used up, they cannot be replaced. Some resources—such as forests, water, and air—are renewable or reusable.

Review

1. What is a renewable resource?
2. What is a reusable resource?
3. List two types of nonrenewable resources.
4. **Critical Thinking** What would happen if resources such as air and water could not be reused?
5. **Test Prep** Which of the following is a reusable resource?
   A quartz
   B water
   C a tree
   D iron

LINKS

MATH LINK

Recycling It takes about 100 recycled aluminum cans to make 90 new cans. If your school has a party, and 375 aluminum cans are returned for recycling, how many new cans can be made?

WRITING LINK

Informative Writing—Compare and Contrast Write a paragraph for a younger student explaining the differences between renewable, nonrenewable, and inexhaustible resources. Use examples in your explanation.

SOCIAL STUDIES LINK

Resource Map Choose a mineral resource that is found in the United States, such as copper or iron. Make a map of the United States showing where this resource is found.

PHYSICAL EDUCATION LINK

PE Resources How many products made from natural resources are used during PE class? Look around during the class, and then make a list.

TECHNOLOGY LINK

Learn more about mineral resources by viewing *River of Gold* on the **Harcourt Science Newsroom Video** in your classroom video library.

How Do Fossil Fuels Form?

In this lesson, you can . . .

INVESTIGATE storage rocks.

LEARN ABOUT how fossil fuels form.

LINK to math, writing, social studies, and technology.

This tower separates petroleum into products such as asphalt, heating oil, and gasoline. ▼

INVESTIGATE

What Kinds of Rocks Store Petroleum

Activity Purpose Petroleum is one of the most important fuel resources in the United States. The petroleum that people use today came from the decay of ancient sea life. The remains of microscopic organisms settled to the sea floor and became part of the ocean sediments. In time, the sediments changed to rock. It was within this *source rock* that the decaying organisms slowly changed into petroleum. The pressure of additional sediments squeezed the petroleum out of the source rock and into layers called *storage rock*. In this investigation you will **use numbers** to **compare** rocks and determine which is the best storage rock.

Materials

- limestone
- sandstone
- shale
- paper plates
- dropper
- mineral oil
- clock

Activity Procedure

1. Place the rock samples on separate paper plates. **Observe** each rock. **Predict** which will be the best storage rock.

2. Fill the dropper with mineral oil. Put 5 drops of oil on the limestone sample. (Picture A)

Picture A

Picture B

3. **Observe** and **record** the time it takes for the 5 drops of oil to soak into the limestone.

4. Continue adding oil, counting the drops, until the limestone will hold no more oil. **Record** the number of drops it takes. (Picture B)

5. Repeat Steps 2–4 with the other rock samples.

Draw Conclusions

1. Which rock soaked up the oil the fastest? What was the time?

2. Which rock soaked up the most oil? What was the number of drops?

3. Which rock is the best storage rock? Explain how you came to this conclusion. What other information do you need to support this conclusion?

4. **Scientists at Work** Scientists often **use numbers** to **compare** things. How did you use numbers to compare the oil-storing ability of the rocks?

Investigate Further Develop a testable question about which of the rocks might be a source rock for petroleum. Decide what equipment you will need, and then make quantitative observations about each rock.

Process Skill Tip

You can **use numbers** to do many things. You can solve math problems, count objects, put things in order, or **compare** one thing with another. In this activity you compared the oil-storing ability of certain rocks.

How Fossil Fuels Form

Fossil Fuels

FIND OUT

• the types of fossil fuels

• how fossil fuels form

VOCABULARY

fossil fuels
natural gas
peat
lignite
bitumen
anthracite

Coal, natural gas, and petroleum are valuable resources known as **fossil fuels**. They are called *fossil* fuels because they formed from the remains of once-living organisms. Fossil fuels are nonrenewable resources.

Burning a fossil fuel releases large amounts of energy. That's one reason why people use fossil fuels more than any other energy source on Earth. Another reason is that fossil fuels are found in many places. In the last hundred years, the technology for finding fossil fuels has improved. This has increased the use of fossil fuels.

Fossil fuels are also important resources for making other products. For example, coal is used to make steel. And many chemicals, called petrochemicals, are made from petroleum. Petrochemicals are used to produce medicines, makeup, paints, and plastics.

✔ **What are fossil fuels?**

Many energy stations burn coal to produce electricity. ▼

A lot of the items you use every day are made of chemicals that come from petroleum. ▼

Almost all cars, trucks, and buses run on fuel made from petroleum. ▼

Energy from the Sun

Burning fossil fuels releases energy that came from the sun. The energy was stored in the bodies of ancient organisms that were buried in sediments millions of years ago. So coal, natural gas, and petroleum are found in layers of sedimentary rock.

Petroleum is the world's most widely used fossil fuel. It produces a lot of heat when it is burned. Petroleum is used mainly for transportation, because it is easier to store and transport than coal and natural gas.

The petroleum used today formed when microorganisms died and fell to the bottoms of ancient seas. Over many years, layer upon layer of sediment covered them. Deep within the Earth, where there is a lot of heat and pressure, the organic matter of their decayed bodies slowly turned into petroleum and natural gas.

Natural gas is mostly a gas called *methane.* It is usually found with petroleum. Natural gas is used mostly for heating and cooking.

Coal is the most common fossil fuel. Much of the coal used today comes from

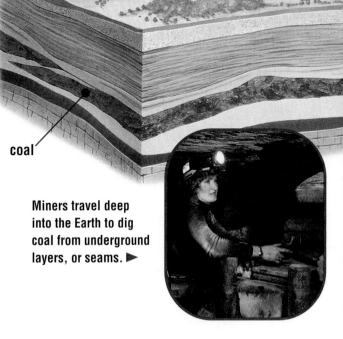

coal

Miners travel deep into the Earth to dig coal from underground layers, or seams. ▶

plants that lived in swamps millions of years ago. As these plants died, they sank to the bottoms of the swamps. Mud and other sediments covered their remains, and slowly the plants changed into coal.

The United States has large deposits of fossil fuels, especially coal and natural gas. But the United States uses so much petroleum that some is imported from places such as Saudi Arabia and Nigeria.

Electric energy stations use most of the coal mined in the United States. Years ago, burning coal produced clouds of black smoke. Today, stations that burn coal have ways to control pollution.

The world is slowly running out of fossil fuels. To conserve fuel resources, many nations are trying to cut down on their use of these fuels. They are beginning to use energy sources that are inexhaustible— wind, solar, and hydroelectric energy.

✔ **Where did the energy in fossil fuels come from originally?**

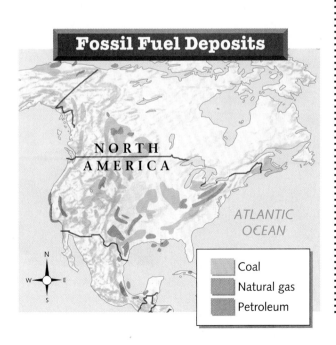

Fossil Fuel Deposits

NORTH AMERICA

ATLANTIC OCEAN

N
W E
S

- Coal
- Natural gas
- Petroleum

Coal Formation

As coal forms, it goes through four steps, or stages. At each stage the amount of carbon it contains increases. The first stage is the formation of peat. **Peat** is a soft, brown material made up of partly decayed plants. It forms as dead plants build up in swamps. Today some swamps and bogs, which are areas of wet and spongy ground, have deep layers of peat.

The second stage of coal formation produces lignite. **Lignite** (LIG•nyt) is a soft, brown rock. It forms as layers of sand and mud cover peat. As the layers build up, the pressure of their weight squeezes moisture out of the peat, turning it into a soft rock.

THE INSIDE STORY

Coal Formation

Peat can be found in marshy areas in Great Britain, Russia, and Ukraine. Some people dig out the peat and use it for heating and cooking. Burning peat produces a lot of smoke and pollutants. ▼

Most lignite mines are in eastern European countries. Lignite produces a lot of smoke when it is burned, but it doesn't provide much heat. ▼

Peat

Lignite

Over millions of years, this pressure, along with heat from inside the Earth, turns peat into lignite.

Bitumen is the third stage of coal formation. **Bitumen** (bih•TOO•muhn) is a fairly hard, dark brown or black rock. Millions of years of heat and the weight of even more layers of sediment turn lignite into bitumen.

Bitumen is the most common type of coal mined and used today.

In the fourth stage, bitumen becomes anthracite. **Anthracite** (AN•thruh•syt) is a hard, black rock. Anthracite forms under great heat and pressure. It is almost pure carbon.

✔ **What are the four stages of coal formation?**

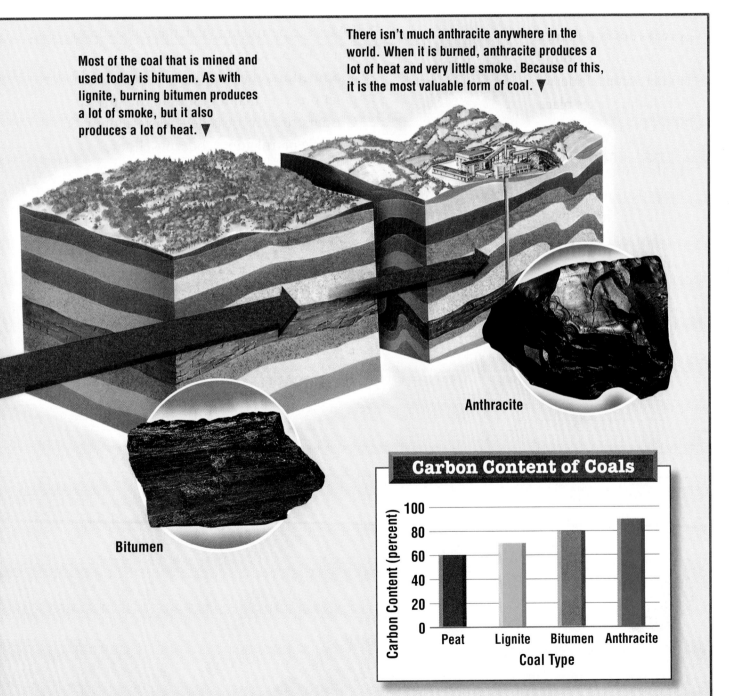

Most of the coal that is mined and used today is bitumen. As with lignite, burning bitumen produces a lot of smoke, but it also produces a lot of heat. ▼

There isn't much anthracite anywhere in the world. When it is burned, anthracite produces a lot of heat and very little smoke. Because of this, it is the most valuable form of coal. ▼

Anthracite

Bitumen

Carbon Content of Coals

Carbon Content (percent)

100	
80	
60	
40	
20	
0	

Peat   Lignite   Bitumen   Anthracite

Coal Type

Petroleum and Natural Gas

Petroleum and natural gas are found only in sedimentary rock. Almost 60 percent of the world's supply is in sandstone. The rest is in limestone and other porous rocks. Geologists can identify rock structures that are likely to hold petroleum and natural gas, so they know where to look for these resources.

Since the microorganisms that formed them lived in seas, many petroleum and natural gas deposits are found under water. Underwater drilling takes place from huge platforms built over the water. In the United States these platforms are located in the Gulf of Mexico and off the California coast.

Some deposits of petroleum and natural gas are under land, in places that were once shallow seas. Drilling for these deposits occurs in California, Texas, Alaska, and other states.

When a drill locates a deposit of petroleum or natural gas, the petroleum has to be pumped from the ground. Natural gas comes out by itself. If there is not enough petroleum in one area to be pumped out directly, hot water or steam is forced into the deposit through a nearby well. This forces the petroleum, which is lighter than water, to the surface.

Sometimes the petroleum is under such great pressure that it gushes to the surface. Gushers, as they are called, waste a lot of valuable petroleum. Modern wells are capped to keep this from happening.

✔ **How are petroleum and natural gas taken from the ground?**

◀ Drills sink deep into a pocket of petroleum. The petroleum is then pumped to the surface.

not to scale

Summary

Coal, oil, and natural gas are fossil fuels. Fossil fuels formed over millions of years from the decayed remains of organisms. Coal formation occurs in four stages, producing peat, lignite, bitumen, and anthracite. Petroleum and natural gas formed from microorganisms buried under ancient seas.

Review

1. List two products that contain petro-chemicals made from petroleum.

2. What is most coal used for in the United States?

3. How did Earth's deposits of coal form?

4. **Critical Thinking** As coal forms, how does its carbon content change? How might this change affect its ability to heat?

5. **Test Prep** Which of these is **NOT** a stage in the formation of petroleum?

   A Microorganisms sink to the bottom of shallow seas.

   B Layers of mud pile on top of the remains.

   C Organisms in mud produce new microorganisms.

   D The remains slowly turn into petroleum.

LINKS

MATH LINK

Petroleum Reserves Use a computer and a graphing program such as *Graph Links* to make a graph showing the world's top five producers of petroleum. How does the amount of petroleum the United States produces compare to that of other nations?

WRITING LINK

Informative Writing—Report As you watch TV commercials, look for those that show fossil fuels being used. Then write a commercial that shows ways fossil fuels could be conserved. Present your commercial to your class.

SOCIAL STUDIES LINK

History of Petroleum When was petroleum first discovered? How was it first used? Write a short report on the early history of petroleum.

TECHNOLOGY LINK

Learn more about the formation of fossil fuels by visiting this Internet site. **www.scilinks.org/harcourt**

How Are Natural Resources Conserved?

In this lesson, you can . . .

INVESTIGATE how people use natural resources.

LEARN ABOUT how people can conserve natural resources.

LINK to math, writing, social studies, and technology.

This Earth Day costume is made of old cans, paper, and bottles. ▼

How People Use Natural Resources

Activity Purpose Suppose you're on a hike. You started out with three pieces of fruit and you have one piece left. You want to eat it, but you're not sure how long it will be before you can get more food. So you decide to save the fruit. You have reached an important conclusion—it is not always best to use everything right away, because the supply may run out. In this investigation you will **hypothesize** about how people can use resources without using them up too quickly.

Materials

- small bowl of paper clips
- 3 generation cards (parents, children, grandchildren)

Activity Procedure

1 Work in a group of three. Place your group's generation cards face down on a table. The bowl of paper clips stands for Earth's supply of a certain resource, such as iron.

2 Each person in the group now takes a generation card. Hold up your card so the other people in your group can see it. The card tells you your generation. It also tells you how many people are in your generation. (Picture A)

Picture A

3 Each generation will now get paper clips from the bowl. The person from the parents' generation goes first. He or she takes five clips from the bowl for each person in his or her generation. (Picture B)

4 Next, the person from the children's generation takes five clips for each person in his or her generation.

5 Finally, the person from the grandchildren's generation takes five clips for each person in his or her generation.

Draw Conclusions

1. Did everyone get the same number of clips?

2. Where did a problem occur?

3. What could be done to avoid the problem?

Picture B

4. **Scientists at Work** Scientists **hypothesize** what the results of an investigation might be. Hypothesize what will happen if each person from a generation gets only three or four clips, instead of five.

Investigate Further With the members of your group, list the products people use that are made from a natural resource, such as a certain metal. Describe several things people could do to make sure that in the future there will be enough of this resource. Then select and use appropriate tools and technology to simulate your plan.

Process Skill Tip

When you **hypothesize,** you make a sensible guess about what might happen under certain conditions. You should base your hypothesis on observations, the results of previous experiments, or what you already know.

Conserving Natural Resources

FIND OUT

- why conserving natural resources is necessary

- how reusing and recycling can conserve resources

VOCABULARY

recycling

Making Choices

What would happen if one day there were no iron or petroleum or lumber? In the investigation you found out that using too much of a resource quickly can cause it to run out. The choices people make today about using natural resources can make the difference between having them in the future or not.

Earth's human population is growing, but the amounts of most natural resources are not. More people will demand more iron, oil, lumber, and other resources. Thinking about future demands for resources helps people plan ways to conserve them now. Conserving natural resources often involves choices. When you pour a glass of lemonade, do you use a disposable paper cup or a washable glass? Using a glass saves paper, but using a paper cup saves water.

Each decision has only a small effect on natural resources. But the choices of many people over time have a big effect. The photograph below shows land that was once a strip mine. The choices for this mined land were to leave it as it was after the coal was removed or to try to restore it to the way it had been before the coal was mined. Because people chose to restore the land, many will enjoy it in the future.

✔ **What does conserving resources often involve?**

The top layers of soil and rock were removed to mine coal. Soil, plants, and wildlife were destroyed. ▼

This mined land was partially restored by replacing the soil and planting grass and trees. Reclaimed land is a future resource.

▲ Instead of cutting down all the trees, people can do selective cutting, taking some trees and leaving others. The trees that are left help replace the cut trees by producing seeds.

◄ People can replant trees where they have been cut down.

Changing Behaviors

The simplest way to conserve natural resources is to use fewer resources. Using fewer aluminum cans, for example, means that less bauxite—aluminum ore—will have to be mined. Driving less or driving cars that are more fuel-efficient means that less petroleum will be needed. This works for nonrenewable resources. However, conserving renewable and reusable resources means saving them from damage and protecting them from overuse.

Saving resources from damage includes keeping them free of pollution. For many years, few people realized how dangerous pollution was to natural resources. Many people thought the supply of Earth's reusable resources was so large that nothing could damage it.

Now people realize that water pollution can kill fish and oxygen-producing microorganisms. People also know that air pollution can kill trees and make people sick. And garbage and rusting cars are just plain ugly. Most scientists agree that preventing pollution is an important part of conserving natural resources.

Renewable resources need protection from overuse. For example, in the early 1900s the hunting of whales was a big business. So many countries hunted whales that the population of blue whales, the largest whale species, was almost completely destroyed. In 1965 it became illegal to hunt blue whales in the Southern Hemisphere. This allowed the population to increase to the point that blue whales are now unlikely to become extinct. Today only Japan, Norway, and Russia hunt blue whales.

Forests are another renewable resource that needs protection from overuse. Forests are not just trees. They also provide habitats for many kinds of animals. Loss of habitat is the biggest threat to wildlife. Reasonable limits on the number of trees that can be cut allow forests to renew themselves. Selective cutting helps protect habitats for wildlife.

✔ **How can reusable and renewable resources be conserved?**

Reduce, Reuse, Recycle

People in the United States use more resources per person than most other people in the world. It takes 500,000 trees each week just to make the paper for Sunday newspapers. Every year, Americans throw away 28 billion glass bottles and jars. The average American uses about 90 kg (200 lb) of plastic each year—most of it in packaging that is thrown away.

One way to conserve resources is to reduce the amounts that are used. Using less energy conserves fossil fuels. Using less paper conserves forests. And using fewer bottles and cans conserves minerals.

Another way to conserve resources is to reuse things. Paper or plastic grocery bags can be reused by taking them back to the store, or they can be used as garbage bags or lunch bags.

Many things that can't be reused can be recycled. **Recycling** is the process of taking back a resource used to make a product. That resource is then made into a new product. Many communities have programs for collecting newspaper, glass, aluminum, and plastic. Trucks carry these materials to recycling centers where they are broken down into raw materials to make new products. In some states or communities, recycling is not just a good idea—it's the law.

Sometimes people choose disposable items because they are less expensive or easier to use. But if the materials can't be reused or recycled, the resources used in them will be lost. Recycling saves other resources, too. Recycling aluminum cans, for example, saves both minerals and fuel. The process of making new cans from recycled aluminum uses much less energy than making cans from bauxite does.

✔ **What is recycling?**

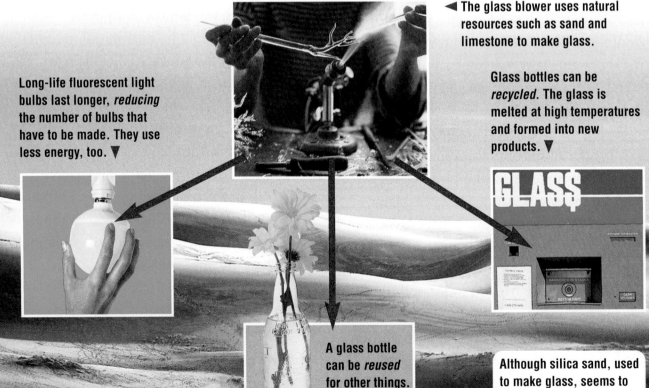

◀ The glass blower uses natural resources such as sand and limestone to make glass.

Long-life fluorescent light bulbs last longer, *reducing* the number of bulbs that have to be made. They use less energy, too. ▼

Glass bottles can be *recycled*. The glass is melted at high temperatures and formed into new products. ▼

GLASS

A glass bottle can be *reused* for other things.

Although silica sand, used to make glass, seems to be inexhaustible, it is a nonrenewable resource.

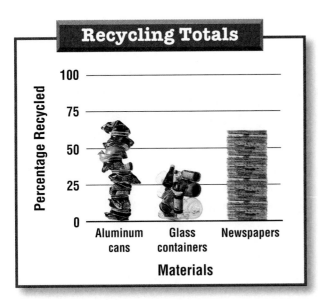

Recycling Totals

Percentage Recycled (y-axis): 0, 25, 50, 75, 100

Materials (x-axis): Aluminum cans, Glass containers, Newspapers

▲ Americans recycle almost 67 percent of their aluminum cans, 63 percent of their newspapers, and 38 percent of their glass containers.

Summary

Earth has a limited supply of natural resources. They must be conserved so that they will last as long as possible. Protecting resources from damage and overuse is a part of conservation. Reusing and recycling products saves resources needed to make new products.

Review

1. How does pollution harm natural resources?

2. What changes result from cutting down an old forest?

3. How does reusing products help conserve natural resources?

4. **Critical Thinking** How does using less electricity save natural resources?

5. **Test Prep** Which resource is **NOT** a type of natural resource?

   A reusable resource

   B renewable resource

   C remarkable resource

   D nonrenewable resource

LINKS

MATH LINK

Recycled Content Look for packaging that has *recycled* or *post-consumer content* on the label. Make a list of all the items you find, what each is made of, and how much of the material in each is recycled. Then make a circle graph for all the recycled packaging. The parts of the graph should show the percentages of recycled paper, plastic, aluminum, and glass in the packaging you find.

WRITING LINK

Informative Writing—How-To Make a poster for a school recycling program. Explain the recycling laws or policies in your community.

SOCIAL STUDIES LINK

Conservation Make a list of everything you used this morning. Did you use any recycled or reusable products? How did you conserve resources? How could you have conserved more? Share your ideas with a classmate.

TECHNOLOGY LINK

Learn more about conserving natural resources by visiting this Smithsonian Institution Internet site.

www.si.edu/harcourt/science

E23

Getting More Oil from Wells

Scientists and petroleum engineers are using water, gas, heat, and soap to help keep oil flowing from thousands of old oil wells.

Pumped Up

The petroleum, or oil, that people use is deposited in layers of rock. In some deposits, the oil forms large, flat pools between rock layers. In others it fills a network of tiny cracks within the rock. In still others, the oil is mixed with sand, the way sea water is mixed with sand at the beach.

If an oil deposit is deep below the surface, the weight of the rock above produces pressure on it. This makes it easy to get the oil out. Companies drill down to the deposit, and the oil rushes up to the surface. This pressure also keeps the oil flowing out of the well. When the pressure is too low to push the oil up through the well pipe, a pump can often pull it up. The use of this combination of natural pressure and pumping is known as primary oil production.

This photograph from the early 1900s shows an oil gusher in a California oil field. Gushers waste a lot of valuable oil.

Natural gas is burned off so the oil can be pumped from this offshore well.

However, primary production doesn't work on shallow deposits, and it won't get all the oil out of deep deposits. In fact, most deep wells are abandoned when only about one-third of the oil has been removed. Getting the rest of the oil out is too difficult or too expensive.

Wishing for Better Wells

Oil companies have usually looked for new places to drill for oil that is easy to recover. However, oil company geologists and engineers are now also working on ways to get the oil that primary production can't recover. The use of these new methods of getting more oil out of old wells is called secondary recovery or enhanced recovery.

One method used in secondary recovery is injection. Water or gas is pumped down into the ground near an oil well. This produces pressure that forces the oil into the well pipe. In some wells this method makes it possible to pump out about half the oil left after primary production. Injection can also be used to get oil from some shallow deposits.

Scientists at the U. S. Department of Energy are working on other secondary recovery methods, too. One, called thermal extraction, uses heat. Steam is pumped into the deposit. Heat from the steam makes the oil thinner, so it flows more easily. The steam also increases pressure.

Scientists are also mixing detergents with the water injected into wells. The soapy liquid makes the oil flow more easily. Other scientists are experimenting with microorganisms that "eat" oil. When these organisms digest some of the oil in a deposit, they produce gas (like millions of little burps!) that increases pressure in the well.

THINK ABOUT IT

1. What is a name for the use of methods of getting more oil out of old wells?
2. How does thermal extraction work?

WEB LINK:
For science and technology updates, visit The Learning Site.
www.harcourtschool.com/ca

Careers   Oil Rig Worker

What They Do Oil rig workers help drill new wells and help keep old wells productive.

Education and Training Most oil rig workers train on the job. They start by handling pipe and learn to work with complicated drilling machinery.

Paul D. MacCready

ENGINEER

"If you have the enthusiasm to charge ahead, you can do all sorts of things. People can do so much more than they realize."

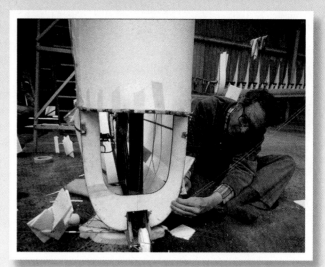

Paul MacCready is best known as the inventor of the *Gossamer Condor,* the world's first successful human-powered flying machine. Yet this remarkable invention is only one of many accomplishments of this creative engineer. Dr. MacCready has won the U.S. soaring championship four times in his gliders, which are aircraft without engines. He was also the first American to win the world soaring championship. His second human-powered vehicle, the *Gossamer Albatross,* was the first human-powered aircraft to cross the English Channel. A third invention, the *Bionic Bat,* set a record for human-powered speed.

Dr. MacCready has done more than invent human-powered aircraft. He has also worked to develop environmentally friendly forms of transportation. In 1987 he built a solar-powered car, the Sunraycer, which competed in a race across Australia. In 1990 he worked with General Motors to develop the Impact, an electric car.

Today Dr. MacCready is working for AeroVironment, a company he founded in 1971 in Monrovia, California. He and his partners help businesses learn about environmental issues and wind power. They also design remote-controlled electric airplanes, which are used by the Department of Defense to gather information.

THINK ABOUT IT

1. How has Dr. MacCready combined his interests in soaring, engineering, and business?
2. How might the use of Dr. MacCready's vehicles help the environment?

The *Centurion,* an atmospheric research aircraft

Minerals

How can you identify minerals from their crystals?

Materials

- talcum powder
- table salt
- chalk
- black construction paper
- hand lens
- microscope slides
- microscope

Procedure

1 Put a little talcum powder, chalk, and table salt on a sheet of black construction paper. Observe each substance with the hand lens.

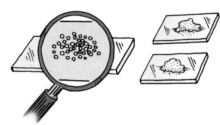

2 Put a little of each substance on a micro-scope slide. Observe under low power of the microscope.

3 Now mix the three substances together on a microscope slide. Observe the mixture under low power.

4 Try to identify each substance in the mixture.

Draw Conclusions

Talc, salt, and chalk are all minerals. Some minerals form crystals with regular shapes. What shape are the salt crystals? How are the talc and chalk different from the salt? How could you separate a mixture of the three minerals?

The 3 Rs

What objects could be reduced, reused, or recycled?

Materials

- paper
- pencil

Procedure

1 Fold the paper into three columns.

2 Label the columns "Reduce," "Reuse," and "Recycle."

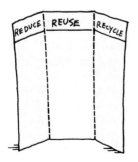

3 As you go through your day at school, write in the appropriate column each object you use that could be reduced in amount, reused in another way, or recycled to make a new object.

Draw Conclusions

How many objects did you list in each column? Compare your lists with those of your class-mates. Then every day for a week, choose an object from one column and for that day, reduce the amount you use, reuse the object in a different way, or recycle the object.

Chapter ① Review and Test Preparation

Vocabulary Review

Use the terms below to complete the sentences. The page numbers in ( ) tell you where to look in the chapter if you need help.

natural resource (E6)
nonrenewable resource (E6)
renewable resource (E8)
reusable resource (E8)
fossil fuel (E12)
natural gas (E13)
peat (E14)
lignite (E14)
bitumen (E15)
anthracite (E15)
recycling (E22)

1. A ____ is a resource that can be replaced as it is used.

2. A hard, black form of coal is ____.

3. A soft, brown material made up of partly decayed plants is ____.

4. ____ is the process of taking a resource back from a product.

5. A ____ is a useful mineral or other material that people take from the Earth.

6. ____ is a gas made up mostly of methane.

7. A soft, brown form of coal is ____.

8. A ____ is a resource that cannot be replaced once it is used.

9. A ____ is a resource that can be used more than once.

10. ____ is a fairly hard, dark brown or black form of coal.

11. A ____ is a fuel such as coal, petroleum, and natural gas that formed in the Earth from decayed organisms.

Connect Concepts

Use the Word Bank to complete the chart. List the three main categories of natural resources on the top lines. Then list an example of each type of resource on the lines below.

minerals/rocks	soil	forests
nonrenewable	coal	fossil
renewable	water	reusable
natural gas	air	petroleum

Three Categories of Natural Resources

12. _____	19. ____	21. ____
13. _____		22. ____
14. ____ fuels		
Three types of the resource in #14:	20. ____	23. ____
15. _____		
16. _____		
17. _____		
18. _____		

Check Understanding

Write the letter of the best choice.

24. All natural resources are —

    A useful materials that can be replaced

    B useful materials that cannot be replaced

    C useful materials that are used for fuel

    D useful materials that people take from the Earth

25. Fossil fuels are important to us because —

    F they produce heat when burned

    G they are reusable resources

    H they are the only fuels used to make electricity

    J they are renewable resources

26. Conservation of natural resources could include —

    A the use of more renewable sources of energy

    B cutting down on the use of fossil fuels

    C replacing soil and planting trees

    D all of the above

27. Fossil fuels include —

    F jet fuel, graphite, and lead

    G bauxite, oil, and coal

    H natural gas, oil, and coal

    J coal, oil, and peat

28. The stages of coal formation, in order, are —

    A peat, lignite, bitumen, anthracite

    B bitumen, anthracite, peat, lignite

    C anthracite, peat, lignite, bitumen

    D lignite, bitumen, anthracite, peat

Critical Thinking

29. How would your life be different if water were a nonrenewable resource?

30. Most electricity is produced using fossil fuels. Some people think electricity should be produced using resources such as wind, water, and solar energy. Why might people have this opinion?

31. How does recycling plastic conserve fossil fuels?

Process Skills Review

32. **Predict** what might happen to non-renewable resources as the population increases.

33. Assume that the recycling rate for aluminum cans is 66 percent and that the recycling rate for all other aluminum is 38 percent. **Use numbers** to **infer** the recycling rate of aluminum foil and building materials.

34. Wildlife is a renewable resource. **Predict** what would happen if the number of animals born to a species were less than the number killed by hunters. How could conservation change this?

Performance Assessment

Identifying Resources

Classify the resources needed for each of the following objects or activities as *non-renewable, renewable, or reusable:* a cotton T-shirt; water used to bathe; a ride on a school bus; a pencil; this book; a glass bottle; and electricity produced by wind energy.

LESSON **1**
How Do People Use
Fossil Fuels?   E32

LESSON **2**
How Can Moving
Water Generate
Electricity?   E38

LESSON **3**
What Other Sources
of Energy Do People
Use?   E44

SCIENCE AND TECHNOLOGY   E50

PEOPLE IN SCIENCE   E52

ACTIVITIES FOR HOME
OR SCHOOL   E53

CHAPTER REVIEW AND
TEST PREPARATION   E54

Vocabulary Preview

chemical bonds
hydroelectric energy
tidal energy
biomass
nuclear energy
geothermal energy
solar energy
fusion energy

How People Use Energy

Early humans used energy mostly for heating and for cooking. When they learned how to work with metal, their energy use increased. Each new technology led them to use more energy. This is still true today. Every year people use about two percent more energy than they did the year before.

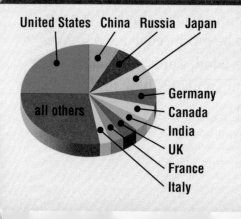

≡FAST FACT

Most of the world's energy is used by a small number of countries. The United States, for example, uses one-fourth of all the energy in the world.

Energy Use

United States China Russia Japan

Germany
Canada
India
UK
France
Italy

all others

FAST FACT

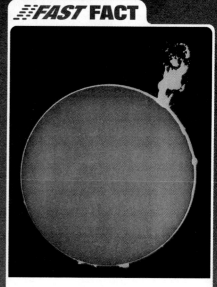

Less than one-billionth of the sun's energy reaches the surface of Earth. Yet one hour's worth of solar energy is more energy than everyone on Earth uses in an entire year.

FAST FACT

ENIAC, the first electronic digital computer, required huge amounts of electricity. Fifty years later, some hand-held computers use less energy than a portable radio.

How Do People Use Fossil Fuels?

In this lesson, you can . . .

INVESTIGATE
how stored energy is released from chemical compounds.

LEARN ABOUT
how fossil fuels are used.

LINK to math, writing, health, and technology.

INVESTIGATE

How Stored Energy Is Released

Activity Purpose In a previous chapter you learned about the law of conservation of energy. It states that energy can change forms but cannot be created or destroyed. One of the forms that potential energy takes is the chemical energy stored in fossil fuels and other compounds. In this investigation you will release chemical energy stored in a compound called calcium chloride. You will **observe** and **compare** liquids to determine what form of energy is released.

Materials
- water
- measuring cup
- Styrofoam cup
- thermometer
- clock with second hand
- safety goggles
- calcium chloride
- spoon

Activity Procedure

1. Make a table like the one on page E33. Measure 50 mL of water in the measuring cup, and pour it into the Styrofoam cup. Put the thermometer in the water. After 30 seconds, **measure** the temperature of the water and **record** it in the table.

2. **CAUTION** **Put on the safety goggles.** Add 2 spoonfuls of calcium chloride to the cup of water. Stir the water with the spoon until the calcium chloride dissolves. Wait 30 seconds. Then **measure** and **record** the temperature. (Picture A)

◄ In 1859 E. L. Drake drilled the first producing oil well, at Oil Creek in Titusville, Pennsylvania. Most of the oil was used to produce kerosene for lamps.

Substance	Temperature
Water without chemical	
Water with chemical after 30 seconds	
Water with chemical after 60 seconds	
Water with chemical after 120 seconds	

3 **Measure** and **record** the temperature of the water two more times, after 60 seconds and again after 120 seconds. Then **compare** the temperature of the water before and after you added calcium chloride. (Picture B)

Draw Conclusions

1. How did the temperature of the water change when you added calcium chloride?

2. **Infer** whether the calcium chloride gives off heat or absorbs heat as it dissolves in water.

3. What do you **infer** might have caused the water temperature to change?

4. **Scientists at Work** Scientists **observe** and **measure** to gather as much data as they can from an experiment. What did you learn from this experiment about how the chemical energy in some compounds can be released?

Investigate Further **Hypothesize** what will happen when different chemicals, such as sodium chloride (table salt) or magnesium sulfate (Epsom salts), are placed in water. **Plan and conduct a simple investigation** to test your hypothesis. Be sure to write instructions others can follow to carry out the procedure. Then **classify** the reactions as *exothermic* (giving off heat), *endothermic* (taking in heat), or *no reaction*.

Picture A

Picture B

Process Skill Tip

When you **observe** and **measure** carefully, the data you gather will be more useful.

Fossil Fuel Use

FIND OUT

- how people use fossil fuels

VOCABULARY

chemical bonds

Burning Fuels Produce Thermal Energy

As a tree grows, it uses energy from sunlight to build the chemical compounds it needs. Solar energy is stored in the tree's molecules. If molecules are broken apart, energy is released. In the investigation you observed that much of that energy is thermal energy, or heat. Burning wood or fossil fuels also breaks apart molecules and releases heat.

Stored solar energy, or chemical energy, exists in all living organisms. Most of it is stored in the **chemical bonds** that join atoms of carbon to each other and to atoms of other elements, such as hydrogen. When living matter from forests, swamps, and shallow seas is buried under sediments for long periods of time, the chemical energy is buried as well. When fossil fuels are taken from the ground, their chemical energy can be converted to thermal energy by burning.

✔ **How is the chemical energy stored in fossil fuels released?**

Solar energy is stored as chemical energy in living organisms. This energy can be released by burning. Wood was used as a fuel for heating and for cooking during much of America's history, but it doesn't really release much heat. The table shows the amount of thermal energy released by burning different fuels.

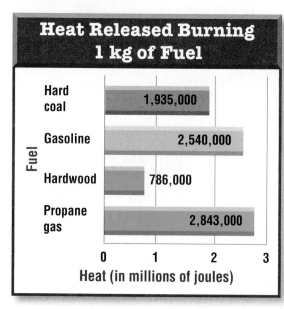

Heat Released Burning 1 kg of Fuel

Fuel	Heat (in millions of joules)
Hard coal	1,935,000
Gasoline	2,540,000
Hardwood	786,000
Propane gas	2,843,000

Using Fossil Fuels

Fossil fuels are the main source of energy for industrial nations like the United States. Coal is taken from Earth's crust by strip mining or by deep mining. Wells are drilled into the crust to obtain natural gas or petroleum.

As the graph on page E34 shows, fossil fuels release large amounts of thermal energy when they're burned. People use this energy in many ways. In homes, offices, and schools, thermal energy is used to heat water or the air. On cold days the heat that comes from your classroom's radiators or air vents was probably produced by burning coal, oil, or natural gas.

In a gas stove, natural gas or bottled gas, such as propane, is burned to provide heat for cooking food. Natural gas is usually distributed through underground pipelines. Bottled gas is brought in by truck to fill local storage tanks.

Petroleum is the main source of energy for transportation. Cars, trucks, buses, trains, and planes have engines that burn fuel made from petroleum, such as gasoline or diesel fuel. As gasoline burns, it expands rapidly. The resulting force turns the engine's crankshaft. Through a series of gears, this movement turns the wheels that push the vehicle.

Similar engines are used in electric energy stations. As you learned in an earlier chapter, when these engines run, they turn electric generators.

Much of the energy for generating electricity in the United States comes from burning fossil fuels, especially coal. Fossil fuels are also used for purposes other than thermal energy production. Plastics, fertilizers, chemicals, and some medicines are made partly from petroleum and coal. Even your shoes and clothes may be made partly from petroleum.

✔ **Name four uses of fossil fuels.**

Fossil fuels are used for plastics, such as the ones in this kayak, paddle, and helmet. ▼

Alternatives to Fossil Fuels

Experts disagree about how much fossil fuel is still buried in the Earth, but the supply is limited. The remains of living organisms take millions of years to become petroleum or coal. However, in just a few years, a geologist can find a fossil-fuel deposit, a company can sell the fuel, and users can burn it. Since fossil fuels form so slowly but are used so quickly, they are *nonrenewable resources.*

Scientists don't know how small the supplies of fossil fuels are, but there are good reasons to use other sources of energy. One reason is that fossil fuels are needed more and more to make things, such as new types of plastics. Fossil fuels may also turn out to have uses not yet discovered.

Another reason for using other sources of energy is that burning fossil fuels releases large amounts of carbon dioxide into the air. Some scientists are concerned that the carbon dioxide may trap heat in Earth's

▲ This playground equipment is made of recycled soft-drink bottles and other plastic items. Recycling plastics can reduce the use of fossil fuels.

An electric car produces no carbon dioxide itself. But the electricity to charge the car's battery may be produced by burning fossil fuels. ▼

atmosphere and cause environmental changes such as global warming.

To reduce the use of fossil fuels, many companies are developing alternative sources of energy. These include wind energy and geothermal energy (heat from within the Earth). In California and other places, some utility companies generate large amounts of electricity from these inexhaustible energy sources. Another method of using less fossil fuels is to recycle plastics and oils, such as the oil from car engines.

✔ **Why are fossil fuels considered nonrenewable resources?**

Summary

Coal, natural gas, and petroleum are fossil fuels formed from once-living matter that has been buried for millions of years. Fossil fuels are used to heat homes, move vehicles, and generate electricity. Because fossil fuels take millions of years to form, they are nonrenewable.

Review

1. Name three types of fossil fuels.
2. How is the chemical energy in fossil fuels changed to electric energy?
3. In what way does the energy in fossil fuels come from sunlight?
4. **Critical Thinking** Why isn't it correct to say that fossil fuels *make* thermal energy?
5. **Test Prep** Gasoline is produced from —

   A coal   C kerosene
   B natural gas   D petroleum

LINKS

MATH LINK

Calories A *calorie* is a unit of heat. One calorie is the amount of heat needed to raise the temperature of 1 g of water by 1°C. Suppose you fill a kettle with 1000 g of water at 20°C. Then you heat the water until it reaches 100°C. How many calories are needed to do this?

WRITING LINK

Expressive Writing—Friendly Letter Send e-mail to a friend. In the e-mail, describe all the energy changes that have occurred over millions of years to produce the electricity to send the e-mail.

HEALTH LINK

Comparing Calorie Content When you read on a food label that a snack has a certain number of Calories, you are learning about the chemical energy stored in that food. Each food Calorie (*Calorie* with a capital *C*) is the amount of energy needed to raise the temperature of 1 kg of water 1°C. Make a table that compares the energy stored in equal amounts of different foods.

TECHNOLOGY LINK

Learn more about generating electricity by visiting the National Museum of American History Internet site.
www.si.edu/harcourt/science

2

How Can Moving Water Generate Electricity?

In this lesson, you can . . .

INVESTIGATE the power of falling water.

LEARN ABOUT how the energy of falling water is changed to electric energy.

LINK to math, writing, social studies, and technology.

◄ The water behind Hoover Dam has a lot of potential energy. The dam's hydroelectric plant changes this potential energy to kinetic energy and then to electric energy.

INVESTIGATE

Water Power

Activity Purpose To produce electricity, an energy station must change some other form of energy. In some cases, the mechanical energy of falling water is used. In this investigation you will **make a model** of a water wheel. Then you will **plan and conduct an investigation** to determine the amount of energy in falling water.

Materials

- two 10-cm plastic disks
- stapler
- scissors
- pencil sharpened at both ends
- 0.5-m length of string
- 30-g mass
- basin
- 1-L plastic bottle filled with water
- meterstick
- stopwatch

Activity Procedure

1. **CAUTION** Be careful when using scissors. Staple the plastic disks together near their centers. Using the scissors, cut four 3-cm slits into the disks as shown. At each slit, fold the disks in opposite directions to form a vane. (Picture A)

2. Again using the scissors, punch a 0.5-cm hole at the center of the disks. Insert the pencil. It will serve as the axle on which the water wheel rotates.

3. Use the scissors to make a smaller hole next to the pencil hole. Insert one end of the string into the hole, and tie a knot in the string to keep it in place. Tie the mass to the other end of the string.

4 Place the basin near the edge of the desk. Hold your water wheel over the basin. Your fingertips should hold the pencil points so the pencil can turn. The mass on the string should hang over the edge of the desk. (Picture B)

5 Have a partner slowly pour water over the wheel from a height of about 10 cm. Using the stopwatch, **measure** and **record** the time it takes for the mass to reach the level of the desk. Repeat this step several times.

6 Now repeat Steps 4 and 5, but have your partner pour the water from a height of about 20 cm. Again, **measure** and **record** the time it takes for the mass to reach the level of the desk.

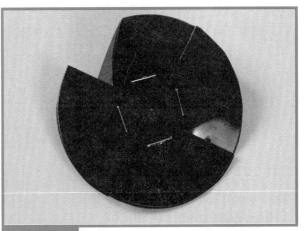
Picture A

Picture B

Draw Conclusions

1. What **variables** did you **control** in your investigation? What variable did you change?

2. Recall that the greater the power, the more quickly work is done. Which of your trials produced more power? Why?

3. **Scientists at Work** Scientists often look beyond the results of an investigation. For example, how does the height from which the water is poured affect the speed at which the water wheel turns? **Plan and conduct a simple investigation** to find out. Be sure to **identify and control variables,** so that you have only a single, independent variable to test.

Investigate Further **Hypothesize** about the rate of flow and the speed at which the water wheel turns. Then **plan and conduct a simple investigation** to test your hypothesis. Be sure to **identify and control variables**. Write instructions others can follow to carry out the procedure.

> **Process Skill Tip**
>
> Scientists **plan and conduct simple investigations** to gather data. To gather accurate data, **identify and control variables,** allowing only one to change.

Electricity and Moving Water

Hydroelectric Energy

Recall that energy cannot be created or destroyed, but that it can change forms. An electric generator works by changing mechanical energy into electric energy. Generators can be connected to any source of mechanical energy that makes their parts spin. One of these sources is falling water. Electricity generated from the force of falling water is called **hydroelectric energy**. *Hydro* means "water."

For thousands of years, people have used the energy of falling water to turn wheels along streams and rivers. The first water wheels probably powered mills that ground grain. During the

FIND OUT

• how electric energy is produced from the mechanical energy of moving water

• how tidal energy stations work

VOCABULARY

hydroelectric energy
tidal energy

Hydroelectric dams often produce large lakes, which can be used for recreation. ▼

Fish swimming upstream can't get past a hydroelectric dam, so many dams have small rivers around them. Other dams have "fish ladders"—stepped waterfalls that fish can jump up, step by step, to get past the dam. ▶

The water that moves through the dam (above) flows through turbines (at the right), setting them spinning. The turbines turn the electric generators.

▲ High-tension lines carry electricity produced at the energy station to places where it is needed.

Industrial Revolution of the 1700s and 1800s, water wheels provided the energy that turned the machines in many factories. Today about one-fifth of the world's energy is hydroelectric energy.

Hydroelectric energy stations use the energy of falling water to spin turbines. A *turbine* is an improved form of the water wheel you made in the investigation. Water strikes the blades of a turbine and makes it spin. The rotating turbine then spins the shaft of an electric generator. The electricity produced by the generator is then sent over power lines to homes, schools, and factories.

The energy that spins a hydroelectric turbine comes from the potential energy of water under pressure. Water near the surface of a lake exerts a force on the water below it. The greater the depth of the water, the greater the energy the water has due to this pressure. So people build dams across rivers to increase the depth of the water. The dam has openings, or gates, at the bottom that allow water to flow through. As water flows through a gate, it spins the vanes of the turbine.

Like almost all energy on Earth, hydroelectric energy can be traced back to the sun. The sun provides the energy that evaporates water from lakes and oceans and carries water vapor high into the air. When this water vapor condenses, it falls back to Earth as rain or snow. As runoff water flows into lakes, it compresses the water beneath it, passing on its potential energy. Rivers below the turbines carry the water back to the oceans. The water cycle is complete, and people have an inexhaustible source of energy.

✔ **What form of energy goes into a hydroelectric energy station? What form comes out?**

Tidal Energy

Along much of Earth's coastlines, tides rise and fall twice a day. In some places these changes in water level are especially large. There the mechanical energy of the moving water can be used to produce electricity. This is a form of hydroelectric energy called **tidal energy**.

Tidal energy plants depend on the difference in water height between high tide and low tide. They produce electricity by holding back water at high tide and letting it fall through turbines at low tide. For a tidal energy station to be efficient, the difference between water level at high tide and low tide must be large.

One place that is famous for its tides—sometimes called *supertides*—is the Bay of Fundy, in Canada. Supertides occur where

The world's first commercial tidal energy station was built at the mouth of the Rance River in Brittany, France. The station produces enough electricity for a city of 300,000 people. ▼

THE INSIDE STORY

A Tidal Energy Station

Tidal energy stations have turbines that are turned by tidal currents. The turbines are usually reversible so that they can operate on both incoming and outgoing tides.

When the tide comes in, water levels rise on one side of the station. Once the difference in water level is 3 m (about 10 ft) or more, the force of the water is great enough to spin turbines connected to electric generators.

When water is at the same level on both sides of the station, the gates are closed. The tide goes out, leaving higher water behind the station. Then the gates are opened and water again flows through the turbines, this time spinning them in the opposite direction.

an incoming tide is funneled into a narrow bay or river channel. As the bay narrows, the water level rises. Tides in the Bay of Fundy can rise and fall more than 15 m (50 ft). Several tidal energy plants have been proposed for this bay, and one is already working.

✔ **Why are tidal energy plants most efficient in places with supertides?**

Summary

An electric generator changes mechanical energy to electric energy. One source of this mechanical energy is moving water. Hydroelectric energy stations use the energy of falling water to spin turbines that generate electricity. The mechanical energy present in ocean tides can also generate electric energy.

Review

1. What is hydroelectric energy?
2. What is the name of a device that turns mechanical energy into electricity?
3. Why do tidal energy stations depend on large differences in water height between high tide and low tide?
4. **Critical Thinking** Compare tidal energy with the hydroelectric energy generated by a dam.
5. **Test Prep** Raising the level of water behind a dam improves the efficiency of a hydroelectric plant by increasing —

   A the water's weight

   B the water's potential energy

   C the water's temperature

   D the water's mass

LINKS

MATH LINK

Estimation In 1990, hydroelectric stations in the United States generated about 264 billion kilowatt hours of energy. This was less than $\frac{1}{10}$ of the total electric energy produced in the United States that year. Estimate the total electric energy production in the United States in 1990.

WRITING LINK

Informative Writing—Report You flip a switch and light floods the room. Electric energy produces that light. Write a short report for your teacher describing the source of electricity in your area. Where is the generator that produces the electric energy? What sort of energy station produces it? What kind of energy is changed to produce the electric energy?

SOCIAL STUDIES LINK

History of Water Wheels Learn more about the early history and uses of water wheels in other parts of the world. Report your findings to your class.

TECHNOLOGY LINK

Learn more about hydroelectric and other forms of energy by investigating *Energy and You* on the **Harcourt Science Explorations CD-ROM.**

What Other Sources of Energy Do People Use?

In this lesson, you can . . .

 INVESTIGATE how steam can turn a turbine.

LEARN ABOUT alternative energy sources.

LINK to math, writing, literature, and technology.

People have used windmills for hundreds of years to capture the energy of the wind. ▶

INVESTIGATE

A Steam-Powered Turbine

Activity Purpose A turbine is a type of rotating engine powered by water, wind, or steam. It is often part of an electric energy station. In Lesson 2 you saw how water can turn a turbine. But wind or steam can also turn a turbine. In this investigation you will **make a model** of a steam-powered turbine.

Materials

- two 10-cm plastic disks
- stapler
- scissors
- pencil
- ring stand
- 2 paper clips
- flask
- water
- one-hole stopper with bent-glass tube
- hot plate
- safety goggles

 CAUTION

Activity Procedure

1. You can modify the water wheel you made in the last investigation by adding 12 more vanes to the wheel and enlarging the hole. Or you can follow Steps 2 and 3 to make your turbine.

2. **CAUTION** Be careful when using the scissors. Staple the plastic disks together near their centers. Using the scissors, cut sixteen 3-cm slits into the disks as shown. At each slit, fold the disks in opposite directions to form a vane. (Picture A)

3. Again using the scissors, cut a 0.5-cm round hole in the center of the disks. Make the hole as round as possible. Insert the pencil. It will serve as the axle on which the turbine rotates. The turbine should

spin freely on its axle. Now suspend the axle and turbine from the ring stand arm with two bent paper clips.

4 Fill the flask with water. Put the stopper with the bent glass tube in the flask. Set the flask on the hot plate. Point the open end of the glass tube toward the vanes on the bottom of the turbine.

5 **CAUTION** **Put on the safety goggles, and use caution around the steam.** Turn on the hot plate. **Observe** and **record** your observations of the turbine as the water begins to boil. Draw a diagram of your turbine to **communicate** your results. Be sure to include labels and arrows to show what happens. (Picture B)

Picture A

Draw Conclusions

1. **Infer** the source of energy for turning the turbine.

2. **Communicate** in several paragraphs how the energy from the source was changed to turn the turbine. Include tests you conducted, data you collected, and your conclusions.

3. **Scientists at Work** When scientists **communicate,** they try to show clearly or describe what is happening. In what two ways did you communicate the results of this investigation? Which way was clearer?

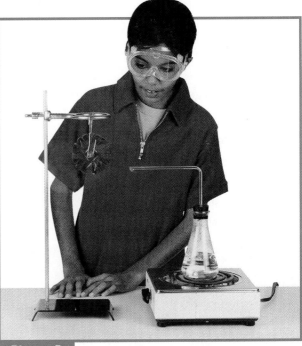

Picture B

Investigate Further **Plan and conduct a simple investigation** to determine how much work your turbine can do. Decide what questions you will need to answer and what equipment you will need to use. Write instructions others can follow to carry out the procedure.

> ### Process Skill Tip
> Including arrows on a diagram can be a clear way to **communicate** information about motion and direction.

Other Energy Sources

FIND OUT

• what other energy sources are used in the United States

• what energy sources we may rely on in the future

VOCABULARY

biomass
nuclear energy
geothermal energy
solar energy
fusion energy

Energy for Today

Fossil fuels and hydroelectric energy are major energy sources in much of the world. Other energy sources may be less common, but they are still important. These include biomass, nuclear, wind, geothermal, and solar energy.

Biomass In some parts of the world, biomass is an important source of energy. **Biomass** is organic matter, such as wood, that is living or was recently alive. Biomass is often burned directly. However, as you saw in the graph on page E34, burning wood doesn't release much energy. In the United States, a major source of biomass is garbage. Burning garbage doesn't release much energy either, but it is basically a free energy source. Heat from burning biomass is used to boil water. The steam then turns turbines that run electric generators.

Biomass can also be made into liquid fuels. Alcohol made from wood or corn is mixed with gasoline to produce a fuel called gasohol. Other plants produce oils that can be burned in modified gasoline or diesel engines.

Nuclear Energy Energy is released when the nucleus of an atom is split apart. This energy is called **nuclear energy**. Splitting nuclei releases a large amount of thermal energy. A nuclear energy station uses this thermal energy to boil water. The resulting steam is directed through turbines and electric generators.

A nuclear energy station produces a large amount of energy from a small amount of fuel. However, the fuel and the waste products of the nuclear reactions are very dangerous to living organisms.

Wind Energy Wind energy is one of the oldest forms of energy used by people. Wind is still used all over the world. In the United States, for example, many farmers use windmills to pump

Wood, a type of biomass, is still used as a source of energy in some places. ▼

Nuclear energy is released in a pool of water. This helps keep dangerous materials from getting too hot. ▼

water from below the ground for irrigation. Some windmills on farms also generate small amounts of electricity.

A different kind of farm—a wind farm—uses modern windmills, or wind turbines, connected to electric generators. A wind farm can produce electricity wherever there is a steady wind. To get as much energy from the wind as possible, the blades of some wind turbines are 100 m (about 330 ft) across.

The advantage of using windmills or wind turbines to generate electricity is that the fuel—the wind—is free, nonpolluting, and inexhaustible. However, wind turbines are expensive, and the strength of the wind usually isn't constant.

Geothermal Energy In some parts of the world, people use heat from inside the Earth, called **geothermal energy**, to heat homes and produce electricity. Geothermal energy occurs where underground water lies close to hot magma. The water boils, and the steam forces its way to the surface. There it is used to turn turbines to generate electric energy. Sometimes steam or very hot water is piped directly to buildings to provide heat. In the United States, there are several geothermal energy stations near San Francisco, California.

▲ At The Geysers, north of San Francisco, underground water is heated by nearby magma. The escaping steam is directed to turbines to generate electricity.

▲ Solar panels change light energy directly into electricity.

Solar Energy The energy of sunlight is called **solar energy**. There are several ways to use solar energy. Solar collectors absorb and focus the sun's energy to heat water. Solar-heated water is often used to heat

This wind farm at Altmont Pass in California relies on a strong, steady wind to drive a set of 300 wind turbines.

swimming pools. In some homes and businesses, the hot water is piped to faucets throughout the building.

Some solar energy stations heat water until it boils. The steam is then used to spin turbines connected to electric generators.

Solar energy can also be changed directly into electricity by *solar cells*. These cells, arranged in flat panels, are made in layers. Sunlight frees electrons from one layer. They are attracted to the other layer. This produces an electric potential that can turn on lights or run motors. Large panels of solar cells are used to power satellites and space stations. Strips containing just a few cells provide the small amount of electricity needed to run a calculator.

Although solar energy is free, solar collectors and cells can be expensive. And many places do not have enough sunny days to make it possible to use solar energy.

✔ **What are the advantages and disadvantages of each source of energy?**

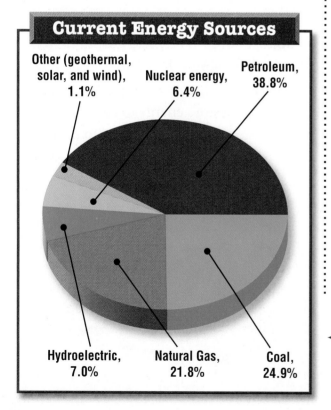

Current Energy Sources

Other (geothermal, solar, and wind), 1.1%

Nuclear energy, 6.4%

Petroleum, 38.8%

Hydroelectric, 7.0%

Natural Gas, 21.8%

Coal, 24.9%

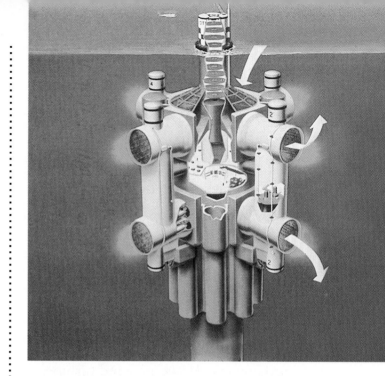

▲ Ocean thermal energy conversion (OTEC) uses thermal energy from the ocean to produce electricity. This experimental system uses differences in temperature between warm upper layers and cold lower layers of ocean water.

Energy for Tomorrow

New sources of energy are always being developed. Scientists look for sources low in cost and low in risk to humans and to the environment.

One of these future sources is fusion. **Fusion energy** is released when the nuclei of two small atoms are forced together to form a larger nucleus. This is the same process that happens in the core of the sun. The heat you feel on a sunny day has fusion energy as its source.

Unfortunately, the heat needed to start fusion is so high that no known material can contain it. Success with fusion has so far been limited to small experiments using force fields to hold the atoms.

◄ Energy sources such as wind, geothermal, and solar make up a larger percent of world energy production today than in the past. In the future they will probably be even more important.

Another promising source of energy for the future is hydrogen, which can be burned like fossil fuels. Ocean water could provide an almost limitless source of hydrogen. Today the best way to separate hydrogen from water is by using electricity. However, using electricity to produce another energy source is expensive.

Scientists are also working on ways to release thermal energy from water to produce electricity. This process is called ocean thermal energy conversion, or OTEC.

✔ **What is the biggest problem with developing fusion power?**

Summary

In addition to fossil fuels and hydroelectric energy, the United States uses small amounts of energy from other sources. These sources include biomass, nuclear energy, wind, geothermal energy, and solar energy. Researchers continue to work on new sources of energy, such as fusion.

Review

1. What is the disadvantage of nuclear energy?
2. Why is geothermal energy not an energy source that can be used in all areas?
3. In what ways are wind and solar energy similar?
4. **Critical Thinking** How is the nuclear energy now in use different from fusion energy?
5. **Test Prep** Many forms of energy are used to heat water, producing —

   A fuel   **C** hydrogen
   B wind   **D** steam

LINKS

MATH LINK

Comparing Wind Speeds For a windmill to produce electric energy, the wind speed should be a constant 13 km/hr. Research the wind conditions in your area by using the weather station from an earlier chapter or by looking at the weather page of a local newspaper. Decide whether wind energy is a possible source for producing electricity where you live.

WRITING LINK

Persuasive Writing—Business Letter Write a letter to your electric company. Ask for information on your area's use of alternative sources of energy, such as biomass, nuclear energy, wind energy, geothermal energy, or solar energy. Be sure to ask clearly, to explain why you are asking, and to thank the person for his or her time.

LITERATURE LINK

Poem: "The Wind" Read "The Wind," a poem by Robert Louis Stevenson. What words does the poet use to describe the wind's energy?

TECHNOLOGY LINK

Learn more about alternatives to using fossil fuels by viewing *Wind Power and Electric Cars* on the **Harcourt Science Newsroom Video** in your classroom video library.

Canola Motor Oil

What can you do with vegetable oil, besides making a salad or frying something for supper? Soon you can put it in your family's car! At least that's the hope of the scientists developing vegetable motor oil.

Did You Say Vegetable Oil?

The engine of a car has many moving parts. To reduce the friction produced when those parts rub together, oil lubricates them, or keeps them slippery. Motor oil helps a car work by keeping the engine running smoothly. The oil now used for this purpose is a petroleum product. Petroleum oil works well in engines. Why replace it with something different? Why use vegetable oil?

Duane Johnson, an agronomist, or crop scientist, wanted to help Colorado farmers. He was looking for a crop they could grow to make money for themselves and their communities. He realized that canola might be that crop. For years people had grown canola plants, crushed their seeds to extract the oil, and used it for cooking. Colorado farmers could raise canola, and the oil could be processed in nearby towns.

But all the canola needed for cooking oil was already being grown. Growing more

A field of canola

Canola oil can be used in place of petroleum-based oil in most vehicles.

canola would simply drive down the price. So Johnson started thinking about other ways to use canola oil. For example, would it work in an engine?

The Advantages of Canola Motor Oil

After several years of research, he developed a canola-based motor oil and tested it in various cars. It worked! As word of his invention spread, mechanics from as far away as New Zealand wanted to buy canola motor oil.

People were eager to try it because they recognized its advantages. One advantage is that it helps protect the environment. Engines using petroleum-based motor oils make a lot of pollution. Switching to canola motor oil reduces the amount of pollution from car engines by up to 40 percent. Also, canola oil spills aren't harmful to organisms as petroleum spills are. Still another advantage is that after the oil has been used in car engines, drivers can dispose of it easily, since it isn't a hazardous waste. Like recycled petroleum oils, it can be made into chain oils and other lubricants, or it can be burned as a low-grade fuel oil. But unlike recycled

petroleum oil, recycled canola oil doesn't cause pollution.

Perhaps the biggest advantage is that canola is a renewable resource. It can be grown year after year. Scientists hope that growing canola and other renewable energy sources will help meet future needs now filled by petroleum products. Some European buses have been using seed-oil fuels. Think about exhaust fumes that smell like popping corn!

THINK ABOUT IT

1. What are some advantages of using canola motor oil?

2. Why are crop fuels renewable resources, but fossil fuels are not?

WEB LINK:
For science and technology updates, visit The Learning Site.
www.harcourtschool.com/ca

Careers   Auto Mechanic

What They Do   Auto mechanics repair and maintain cars, buses, and trucks. They work at service stations, garages, auto centers, and public transportation agencies.

Education and Training   Many mechanics get their start by taking old cars apart and putting them back together. High schools, community colleges, and automobile manufacturers have auto-mechanic classes and training seminars. On-the-job training at a service station is also possible.

Meredith Gourdine
PHYSICIST, ENGINEER

"We believe there are many uses for this discovery in everyday life—an improved source of power for heat and light in homes, making sea water drinkable by taking the salt out of it, making painting and coating processes easier, and reducing the amount of pollutants in smoke."

As an undergraduate at Cornell University, Meredith Gourdine majored in engineering physics and served as captain of the track team. His performance as an athlete was so outstanding that he won a silver medal at the 1952 Olympic Games. Then he went on to earn a doctorate at the California Institute of Technology.

Over the next 30 years, Dr. Gourdine developed a career as a pioneer researcher and inventor in the field known as electrogasdynamics.

Electrogasdynamics is the generation of energy from the motion of gas molecules that have been electrically charged under high pressure. Dr. Gourdine holds about 30 patents for inventions, such as a system for removing smoke from burning buildings and a method for removing fog from airport runways. Both of these inventions work by giving particles in the air a negative charge. The charged particles are then attracted to the ground by electromagnets.

Currently, Dr. Gourdine is working to perfect a generator that uses moving gas particles to convert low-voltage electricity into high-voltage electricity. Dr. Gourdine's generator may provide a much-needed new source of energy.

THINK ABOUT IT

1. Why is it important to give airborne particles such as smoke and fog a negative charge?
2. Why do you think Dr. Gourdine's generator might be important in the future?

A smoky fire

Saving Energy

What materials make good heat insulators?

Materials

- 4 tin cans
- 4 thermometers
- cotton batting
- newspaper
- Styrofoam peanuts

Procedure

1 Put a thermometer in each can. Record the temperature of each can.

2 Pack cotton batting around one thermometer, shredded newspaper around another,

and Styrofoam peanuts around a third. The control can will have a thermometer only.

3 Predict which item will be the best heat insulator.

4 Put all four cans in a sunny window.

5 Record the temperature of each can every minute for 10 min.

Draw Conclusions

In this experiment you tested three items that could help conserve energy. Which material was the best insulator? Home builders try to build energy-efficient homes. Design an energy-efficient house for an outdoor pet. Remember that the house may need to protect the pet from cold weather as well as hot weather.

Clean It Up

What materials can be used to contain and clean up an oil spill?

Materials

- small bowl of water
- 20 mL vegetable oil
- rubber bands
- string
- cotton batting
- paper towels

Procedure

1 Carefully pour a small amount of oil on top of the water in the bowl.

2 Brainstorm different ways to use the materials to contain the spill or clean up the oil.

3 Try out your ideas.

Draw Conclusions

To protect the environment from damage, an oil spill must be contained quickly. Then the oil must be removed from the water. Which of the items you tested were most helpful in containing the oil spill? Which of the items were most helpful in cleaning up the oil spill? Research to find out what materials are actually used.

Chapter 2 Review and Test Preparation

Vocabulary Review

Use the terms below to complete the sentences. The page numbers in ( ) tell you where to look in the chapter if you need help.

chemical bonds (E34)

hydroelectric energy (E40)

tidal energy (E42)

biomass (E46)

nuclear energy (E46)

geothermal energy (E47)

solar energy (E47)

fusion energy (E48)

1. One alternative energy source is ____, organic matter that is burned or may be turned into liquid fuel.

2. One future energy source is ____, which is the same process the sun uses.

3. One of the biggest disadvantages of ____ is that the fuel used and the waste produced are dangerous to organisms.

4. The energy in fossil fuels is stored in ____ that join atoms of carbon together.

5. A ____ station produces energy by holding water at high tide and releasing it through turbines at low tide.

6. In some areas people use ____ from water heated by hot magma.

7. A solar cell turns ____ directly into electricity.

8. A ____ station produces electricity from the energy of falling water.

Connect Concepts

Write the terms from the Word Bank below in the correct column of the concept map.

nuclear energy   wind   fossil fuels

geothermal   hydroelectric   ocean thermal
 energy   energy   energy conversion

tidal energy   solar energy   (OTEC)

fusion energy   biomass

Energy Sources			
Energy from Sunlight	**Energy from Atoms**	**Energy from Earth**	**Energy from Forces in Space**
9. _____	15. _____	17. _____	18. _____
10. _____	16. _____		
11. _____			
12. _____			
13. _____			
14. _____			

Check Understanding

Write the letter of the best choice.

19. The energy in fossil fuels that is turned into thermal energy when it burns is —

  A chemical   **C** heat

  B electric   **D** mechanical

20. The energy at the bottom of a waterfall is the same energy that is turned into electric energy in a —

  F hydroelectric energy station

  G nuclear energy station

  H solar energy station

  J coal energy station

21. Solar cells are dependent on the weather from day to day, as are —

  A hydroelectric energy stations

  B nuclear energy stations

  C geothermal energy stations

  D wind farms

22. The thermal energy from many sources is turned into —

  F chemical energy

  G electric energy

  H solar energy

  J mechanical energy

Critical Thinking

23. Fossil fuels form from once-living matter. Why are they considered *nonrenewable* sources of energy?

24. Suppose you are an engineer designing a hydroelectric energy station. You can build the dam 10 m high or 25 m high. Which would you choose? Explain.

25. Suppose you are going to build a wind farm. What decisions will you need to make about its location? Explain.

Process Skills Review

26. Your family is going to build a new house. What three features might you **compare** in choosing an energy source for heating the house?

27. You plan to **measure** the thermal energy released during a chemical reaction. What tool would you use?

28. You decide to **plan and carry out a simple investigation** to decide the best place for a solar collector at your home. What are two factors you should test for in each area you investigate?

29. You want to **compare** the amounts of heat released by gasoline and kerosene. What **variables** should you **identify and control** when you experiment?

30. For a report on fossil fuels, you plan to **communicate** the steps necessary to produce electricity from coal. Choose a type of display—a table, a chart, a diagram, or a graph. Explain why this is the best way to communicate the steps.

Performance Assessment

Producing Light Energy

Draw a diagram that traces the energy in the light bulb the student is drawing back through the steps it took in getting to you. Show the different forms the energy took on its journey.

References

Science Handbook

Planning an Investigation   **R2**

Using Science Tools   **R4**

Using a Hand Lens   R4

Using a Thermometer   R4

Caring for and Using a Microscope   R5

Using a Balance   R6

Using a Spring Scale   R6

Measuring Liquids   R7

Using a Ruler or Meterstick   R7

Using a Timing Device   R7

Using a Computer   R8

Table of Measurements   R10

Health Handbook   R11

Glossary   R42

Index   R52

Planning an Investigation

When scientists observe something they want to study, they use the method of scientific inquiry to plan and conduct their study. They use science process skills as tools to help them gather, organize, analyze, and present their information. This plan will help you use scientific inquiry and process skills to work like a scientist.

Step 1—Observe and ask questions.

I wonder which design of paper airplane will fly the greatest distance?

- Use your senses to make observations.
- Record a question you would like to answer.

Step 2—Make a hypothesis.

My hypothesis: This airplane with the narrow wings will fly the greatest distance.

- Choose one possible answer, or hypothesis, to your question.
- Write your hypothesis in a complete sentence.
- Think about what investigation you can do to test your answer.

Step 3—Plan your test.

I'll launch each airplane three times from the same spot, with the same amount of force.

- Write down the steps you will follow to do your test. Decide how to conduct a fair test by controlling variables.
- Decide what equipment you will need.
- Decide how you will gather and record your data.

Step 4 — Conduct your test.

I'll record each distance and then find the average distance each airplane traveled.

- Follow the steps you wrote.
- Observe and measure carefully.
- Record everything that happens.
- Organize your data so that you can study it carefully.

Step 5 — Draw conclusions and share results.

My hypothesis was correct. The airplane with the narrow wings flew the greatest distance.

- Analyze the data you gathered.
- Make charts, graphs, or tables to show your data.
- Write a conclusion. Describe the evidence you used to determine whether the results of your test supported your hypothesis.
- Decide whether your hypothesis was true.

Investigate Further

I wonder which airplane will fly for the longest time?

Using Science Tools

Using a Hand Lens

A hand lens magnifies objects, or makes them look larger than they are.

1. Hold the hand lens about 12 centimeters (5 in.) from your eye.

2. Bring the object toward you until it comes into focus.

Using a Thermometer

A thermometer measures the temperature of air and most liquids.

1. Place the thermometer in the liquid. Don't touch the thermometer any more than you need to. Never stir the liquid with the thermometer. If you are measuring the temperature of the air, make sure that the thermometer is not in line with a direct light source.

2. Move so that your eyes are even with the liquid in the thermometer.

3. If you are measuring a material that is not being heated or cooled, wait about two minutes for the reading to become stable. Find the scale line that meets the top of the liquid in the thermometer, and read the temperature.

4. If the material you are measuring is being heated or cooled, you will not be able to wait before taking your measurements. Measure as quickly as you can.

Caring for and Using a Microscope

A microscope is another tool that magnifies objects. A microscope can increase the detail you see by increasing the number of times an object is magnified.

Caring for a Microscope

- Always use two hands when you carry a microscope.
- Never touch any of the lenses of a microscope with your fingers.

Using a Microscope

1. Raise the eyepiece as far as you can using the coarse-adjustment knob. Place your slide on the stage.

2. Always start by using the lowest power. The lowest-power lens is usually the shortest. Start with the lens in the lowest position it can go without touching the slide.

3. Look through the eyepiece, and begin adjusting it upward with the coarse-adjustment knob. When the slide is close to being in focus, use the fine-adjustment knob.

4. When you want to use a higher-power lens, first focus the slide under low power. Then, watching carefully to make sure that the lens will not hit the slide, turn the higher-power lens into place. Use only the fine-adjustment knob when looking through the higher-power lens.

You may use a Brock microscope. This is a sturdy microscope that has only one lens.

1. Place the object to be viewed on the stage.

2. Look through the eyepiece, and begin raising the tube until the object comes into focus.

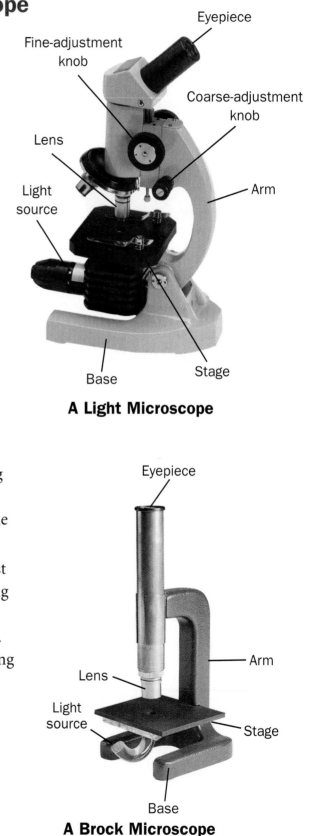

A Light Microscope

A Brock Microscope

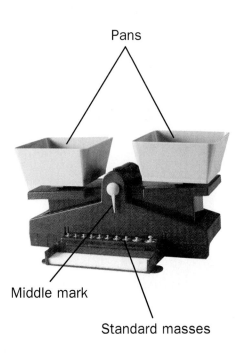

Pans

Middle mark

Standard masses

Using a Balance

Use a balance to measure an object's mass. Mass is the amount of matter an object has.

1. Look at the pointer on the base to make sure the empty pans are balanced.

2. Place the object you wish to measure in the left pan.

3. Add the standard masses to the other pan. As you add masses, you should see the pointer move. When the pointer is at the middle mark, the pans are balanced.

4. Add the numbers on the masses you used. The total is the mass in grams of the object you measured.

Using a Spring Scale

Use a spring scale to measure forces such as the pull of gravity on objects. You measure weight and other forces in units called newtons (N).

Measuring the Weight of an Object

1. Hook the spring scale to the object.

2. Lift the scale and object with a smooth motion. Do not jerk them upward.

3. Wait until any motion of the spring comes to a stop. Then read the number of newtons from the scale.

Measuring the Force to Move an Object

1. With the object resting on a table, hook the spring scale to it.

2. Pull the object smoothly across the table. Do not jerk the object.

3. As you pull, read the number of newtons you are using to pull the object.

Beaker   **Graduate**

Measuring Liquids

Use a beaker, a measuring cup, or a graduate to measure liquids accurately.

1. Pour the liquid you want to measure into a measuring container. Put your measuring container on a flat surface, with the measuring scale facing you.

2. Look at the liquid through the container. Move so that your eyes are even with the surface of the liquid in the container.

3. To read the volume of the liquid, find the scale line that is even with the surface of the liquid.

4. If the surface of the liquid is not exactly even with a line, estimate the volume of the liquid. Decide which line the liquid is closer to, and use that number.

Using a Ruler or Meterstick

Use a ruler or meterstick to measure distances and to find lengths of objects.

1. Place the zero mark or end of the ruler or meterstick next to one end of the distance or object you want to measure.

2. On the ruler or meterstick, find the place next to the other end of the distance or object.

3. Look at the scale on the ruler or meterstick. This will show the distance you want or the length of the object.

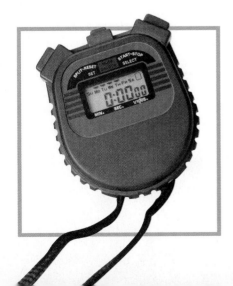

Using a Timing Device

Use a timing device such as a stopwatch to measure time.

1. Reset the stopwatch to zero.

2. When you are ready to begin timing, press start.

3. As soon as you are ready to stop timing, press stop.

4. The numbers on the dial or display show how many minutes, seconds, and parts of seconds have passed.

Using a Computer

A computer can help you communicate with others and can help you get information. It is a tool you can use to write reports, make graphs and charts, and do research.

Writing Reports

To write a report with a computer, use a word processing software program. After you are in the program, type your report. By using certain keys and the mouse, you can control how the words look, move words, delete or add words and copy them, check your spelling, and print your report.

Save your work to the desktop or hard disk of the computer, or to a floppy disk. You can go back to your saved work later if you want to revise it.

There are many reasons for revising your work. You may find new information to add or mistakes you want to correct. You may want to change the way you report your information because of who will read it. Computers make revising easy. You delete what you don't want, add the new parts, and then save. You can save different versions of your work if you want to.

For a science lab report, it is important to show the same kinds of information each time. With a computer, you can make a general format for a lab report, save the format, and then use it again and again.

Making Graphs and Charts

You can make a graph or chart with most word processing software programs. Or, you can use special software programs such as Data ToolKit or Graph Links. With Graph Links you can make pictographs and circle, bar, line, and double-line graphs.

First, decide what kind of graph or chart will best communicate your data. Sometimes it's easiest to do this by sketching your ideas on paper. Then you can decide what format and categories you need for your graph or chart. Choose that format for the program. Then type your information. Most software programs include a tutor that gives you step-by-step directions for making a graph or chart.

Doing Research

Computers can help you find current information from all over the world through the Internet. The Internet connects thousands of computer sites that have been set up by schools, libraries, museums, and many other organizations.

Get permission from an adult before you log on to the Internet. Find out the rules for Internet use at school or at home. Then log on and go to a search engine, which will help you find what you need. Type in keywords, words that tell the subject of your search. If you get too much information that isn't exactly about the topic, make your keywords more specific. When you find the information you need, save it or print it.

Harcourt Science tells you about many Internet sites related to what you are studying. To find out about these sites, called Web sites, look for Technology Links in the lessons in this book.

If you need to contact other people to help in your research, you can use e-mail. Log into your e-mail program, type the address of the person you want to reach, type your message, and send it. Be sure to have adult permission before sending or receiving e-mail.

Another way to use a computer for research is to access CD-ROMs. These are discs that look like music CDs. CD-ROMs can hold huge amounts of data, including words, still pictures, audio, and video. Encyclopedias, dictionaries, almanacs, and other sources of information are available on CD-ROMs. These computer discs are valuable resources for your research.

Measurement Systems

SI Measures (Metric)

Temperature
Ice melts at 0 degrees Celsius (°C).
Water freezes at 0°C.
Water boils at 100°C.

Length and Distance
1000 meters (m) = 1 kilometer (km)
100 centimeters (cm) = 1 m
10 millimeters (mm) = 1 cm

Force
1 newton (N) = 1 kilogram ×
    meter/second/second (kg-m/s^2)

Volume
1 cubic meter (m^3) = 1m × 1m × 1m
1 cubic centimeter (cm^3) =
    1 cm × 1 cm × 1 cm
1 liter (L) = 1000 milliliters (mL)
1 cm^3 = 1 mL

Area
1 square kilometer (km^2) =
    1 km × 1 km
1 hectare = 10,000 m^2

Mass
1000 grams (g) = 1 kilogram (kg)
1000 milligrams (mg) = 1 g

Rates (Metric and Customary)
kmh = kilometers per hour
m/s = meters per second
mph = miles per hour

Customary Measures

Volume of Fluids
8 fluid ounces (fl oz) = 1 cup (c)
2 c = 1 pint (pt)
2 pt = 1 quart (qt)
4 qt = 1 gallon (gal)

Temperature
Ice melts at 32 degrees
    Fahrenheit (°F).
Water freezes at 32°F.
Water boils at 212°F.

Length and Distance
12 inches (in.) = 1 foot (ft)
3 ft = 1 yard (yd)
5280 ft = 1 mile (mi)

Weight
16 ounces (oz) = 1 pound (lb)
2000 pounds = 1 ton (T)

Health Handbook

Nutrition and Food Safety

The Food Guide Pyramid   R12
Understanding Serving Size   R13
Fight Bacteria   R14
Food Safety Tips   R15

Being Physically Active

Planning Your Weekly Activities   R16
Guidelines for a Good Workout   R17
Warm-Up and Cool-Down Stretches   R18
Building a Strong Heart and Lungs   R20

Safety and First Aid

Fire Safety   R22
Earthquake and Thunderstorm Safety   R23
First Aid for Choking and Bleeding   R24

Caring for Your Body Systems

The Food Guide Pyramid

No one food or food group supplies all the nutrients you need. That's why it's important to eat a variety of foods from all the food groups. The Food Guide Pyramid can help you choose healthful foods in the right amounts. By choosing more foods from the groups at the bottom of the pyramid, and few foods from the group at the top, you will eat nutrient-rich foods that provide your body with energy to grow and develop.

Fats, oils, and sweets
Eat sparingly.

Meat, poultry, fish, dried beans, eggs, and nuts
2–3 servings

Milk, yogurt, and cheese **2–3 servings**

**Fruits
2–4 servings**

**Vegetables
3–5 servings**

Breads, cereals, rice, and pasta 6–11 servings

Understanding Serving Size

The Food Guide Pyramid suggests a number of servings to eat each day from each group. But a serving isn't necessarily the amount you eat at a meal. A plate full of macaroni and cheese may contain three or four servings of pasta (macaroni) and three servings of cheese. That's about half your bread group servings and all your milk servings at one sitting! The table below can help you estimate the number of servings you are eating.

Food Group	Amount of Food in One Serving	Easy Ways to Estimate Serving Size
Bread, Cereal, Rice, and Pasta Group	$\frac{1}{2}$ cup cooked pasta, rice, or cereal 1 ounce ready-to-eat (dry) cereal 1 slice bread, $\frac{1}{2}$ bagel	ice-cream scoop large handful of plain cereal or a small handful of cereal with raisins and nuts
Vegetable Group	1 cup of raw, leafy vegetables $\frac{1}{2}$ cup other vegetables, cooked or chopped raw $\frac{3}{4}$ cup vegetable juice $\frac{1}{2}$ cup tomato sauce	about the size of a fist ice-cream scoop
Fruit Group	medium apple, pear, or orange $\frac{1}{2}$ large banana, or one medium banana $\frac{1}{2}$ cup chopped or cooked fruit $\frac{3}{4}$ cup of fruit juice	about the size of a baseball
Milk, Yogurt, and Cheese Group	$1\frac{1}{2}$ ounces of natural cheese 2 ounces of processed cheese 1 cup of milk or yogurt	about the size of two dominoes $1\frac{1}{2}$ slices of packaged cheese
Meat, Poultry, Fish, Dried Beans, Eggs, and Nuts Group	3 ounces of lean meat, chicken, or fish 2 tablespoons peanut butter $\frac{1}{2}$ cup of cooked dried beans	about the size of your palm
Fats, Oils, and Sweets Group	1 teaspoon of margarine or butter	about the size of the tip of your thumb

Fight Bacteria

You probably already know to throw away food that smells bad or looks moldy. But food doesn't have to look or smell bad to make you ill. To keep your food safe and yourself from becoming ill, follow the procedures shown in the picture below. And remember—when in doubt, throw it out!

FIGHT BAC!

Keep Food Safe From Bacteria

CLEAN Wash hands and surfaces often.

SEPARATE Don't cross-contaminate.

CHILL Refrigerate promptly.

COOK Cook to proper temperatures.

BAC

™

Food Safety Tips

Tips for Preparing Food

- Wash hands in hot, soapy water before preparing food. It's also a good idea to wash hands after preparing each dish.
- Defrost meat in the microwave or the refrigerator. Do NOT defrost meat on the kitchen counter.
- Keep raw meat, poultry, fish, and their juices away from other food.
- Wash cutting boards, knives, and countertops immediately after cutting up meat, poultry, or fish. Never use the same cutting board for meats and vegetables without thoroughly washing the board first.

Tips for Cooking Food

- Cook all food thoroughly, especially meat. Cooking food completely kills bacteria that can make you ill.
- Red meats should be cooked to a temperature of 160°F. Poultry should be cooked to 180°F. When done, fish flakes easily with a fork.
- Eggs should be cooked until the yolks are firm. Never eat food that contains raw eggs. Never eat cookie dough made with raw eggs.

Tips for Cleaning Up the Kitchen

- Wash all dishes, utensils, and countertops with hot, soapy water. Use a disinfectant soap, if possible.
- Store leftovers in small containers that will cool quickly in the refrigerator. Don't leave leftovers on the counter to cool.

Being Physically Active

Planning Your Weekly Activities

Being active every day is important for your overall health. Physical activity strengthens your body systems and helps you manage stress and maintain a healthful weight. The Activity Pyramid, like the Food Guide Pyramid, can help you choose a variety of activities in the right amounts to keep your body strong and healthy.

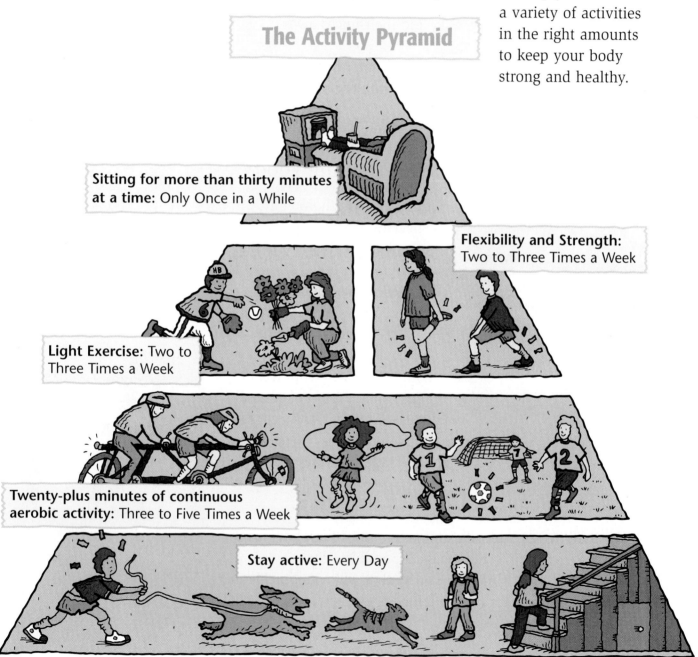

The Activity Pyramid

Sitting for more than thirty minutes at a time: Only Once in a While

Flexibility and Strength: Two to Three Times a Week

Light Exercise: Two to Three Times a Week

Twenty-plus minutes of continuous aerobic activity: Three to Five Times a Week

Stay active: Every Day

Guidelines for a Good Workout

There are three things you should do every time you are going to exercise—warm up, work out, and cool down.

Warm-Up When you warm up, your heart rate, respiration rate, and body temperature gradually increase and more blood begins to flow to your muscles. As your body warms up, your flexibility increases, helping you avoid muscle stiffness after exercising. People who warm up are also less prone to exercise-related injuries. Your warm-up should include five minutes of stretching and five minutes of a low-level form of your workout exercise. For example, if you are going to run for your primary exercise, you should spend five minutes stretching, concentrating on your legs and lower back, and five minutes walking before you start running.

Workout The main part of your exercise routine should be an aerobic exercise that lasts twenty to thirty minutes. Some common aerobic exercises include walking, bicycling, jogging, swimming, cross-country skiing, jumping rope, dancing, and playing racket sports. You should choose an activity that is fun for you and that you will enjoy doing over a long period of time. You may want to mix up the types of activities you do. This helps you work different muscle groups and provides a better overall workout.

Cool-Down When you finish your aerobic exercise, you need to give your body time to return to normal. You also need to stretch again. This portion of your workout is called a cool-down. Start your cool-down with three to five minutes of low-level activity. For example, if you have been running, you may want to jog and then walk during this time. Then do stretching exercises to prevent soreness and stiffness.

Warm-Up and Cool-Down Stretches

Before you exercise, you should always warm up your muscles. The warm-up stretches shown here should be held for at least fifteen to twenty seconds and repeated at least three times. At the end of your workout, spend about two minutes repeating some of these stretches.

► **Hurdler's Stretch** HINT—Keep the toes of your extended leg pointed up.

▲ **Shoulder and Chest Stretch** HINT—Pulling your hands slowly toward the floor makes this stretch more effective. Keep your elbows straight, but not locked!

▼ **Sit-and-Reach Stretch** HINT—Remember to bend at the waist. Keep your eyes on your toes!

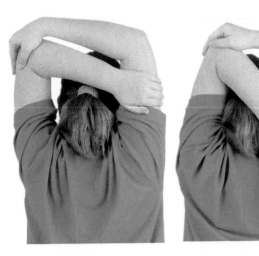

▲ **Upper Back and Shoulder Stretch**
HINT—Try to stretch your hand down
so that it lies flat against your back.

▼ **Thigh Stretch** HINT—Keep both
hands flat on the floor. Try to lean
as far forward as you can.

▲ **Calf Stretch** HINT—Remember to keep both
feet on the floor during this stretch. Try
changing the distance between your feet. Is
the stretch better for you when your legs
are closer together or farther apart?

Tips for Stretching

- Never bounce when stretching.
- Remember to hold each stretch for fifteen to twenty seconds.
- Breathe normally. This helps your body get the oxygen it needs.
- Stretch only until you feel a slight pull, NOT until it hurts.

Being Physically Active

Building a Strong Heart and Lungs

Aerobic activities, those that cause deep breathing and a fast heart rate for at least twenty minutes, help both your heart and your lungs. Because your heart is a muscle, it gets stronger with exercise. A strong heart doesn't have to work as hard to pump blood to the rest of your body. Exercise also allows your lungs to hold more air. With a strong heart and lungs, your cells get oxygen faster and your body works more efficiently.

◀ **Swimming** Swimming may provide the best overall body workout of any sport. It uses all the major muscle groups, and improves flexibility. The risk of injury is low, because the water supports your weight, greatly reducing stress on the joints. Just be sure to swim only when a lifeguard is present.

▶ **In-Line Skating** In-line skating gives your heart and lungs a great workout. Remember to always wear a helmet when skating. Always wear protective pads on your elbows and knees, and guards on your wrists, too. Learning how to skate, stop, and fall correctly will make you less prone to injuries.

▶ **Tennis** To get the best aerobic workout from tennis, you should run as fast, far, and hard as you can during the game. Move away from the ball so that you can step into it as you hit it. Finally, try to involve your entire body in every move.

▲ **Bicycling** Bicycling provides good aerobic activity that places little stress on the joints. It's also a great way to see the countryside. Be sure to use a bike that fits and to learn and follow the rules of the road. And *always* wear your helmet!

▶ **Walking** A fast-paced walk is a terrific way to build your endurance. The only equipment you need is a good pair of shoes and clothes appropriate for the weather. Walking with a friend can make this exercise a lot of fun.

Fire Safety

Fires cause more deaths than any other type of disaster. But a fire doesn't have to be deadly if you prepare your home and follow some basic safety rules.

- Install smoke detectors outside sleeping areas and on any additional floors of your home. Be sure to test the smoke detectors once a month and change the batteries in each detector twice a year.

- Keep a fire extinguisher on each floor of your home. Check monthly to make sure each is properly charged.

- Work with your family to make a fire escape plan for each room of your home. Ideally, there should be two routes out of each room. Sleeping areas are most important, because most fires happen at night. Plan to use stairs only; elevators can be dangerous in a fire.

- Pick a place outside for everyone to meet. Designate one person to call the fire department or 911 from a neighbor's home.

- Practice crawling low to avoid smoke. If your clothes catch fire, follow the three steps listed below.

1. STOP

2. DROP

3. ROLL

Earthquake Safety

An earthquake is a strong shaking of the ground. The tips below can help you and your family stay safe in an earthquake.

Before an Earthquake	During an Earthquake	After an Earthquake
• Secure tall, heavy furniture, such as bookcases, to the wall. Store the heaviest items on the lowest shelves. • Check for potential fire risks. Bolt down gas appliances, and use flexible hosing and connections for both gas and water utilities. • Reinforce and anchor overhead light fixtures to help keep them from falling.	• If you are outdoors, stay outdoors and move away from buildings and utility wires. • If you are indoors, take cover under a heavy desk or table or in a doorway. Stay away from glass doors and windows and heavy objects that might fall. • If you are in a car, drive to an open area away from buildings and overpasses.	• Continue to watch for falling objects as aftershocks shake the area. • Adults should have the building checked for hidden structural problems. • Check for broken gas, electric, and water lines. If you smell gas, an adult should shut off the gas main and you should leave the area. Report the leak.

Thunderstorm Safety

Thunderstorms are severe storms. Lightning associated with thunderstorms can injure or kill people, cause fires, and damage property. Here are some thunderstorm safety tips.

- **If you are inside, stay there.** The best place to take cover is inside a building.
- **If you are outside, try to take shelter.** If possible, get into a closed car or truck. If you can't take shelter, get into a ditch or low area, if possible.
- **If you are outside, stay away from tall objects.** Don't stand under a lone tree, in an open field, on a beach, or on a hilltop. Find a low place to stay.
- **Stay away from water.** Lightning is attracted to water, and water conducts electricity.
- **Listen for weather bulletins and updates.** The storms that produce lightning may also produce tornadoes. Be ready to take shelter in a basement or interior hallway away from windows and doors.

First Aid

The tips on the next few pages can help you provide simple first aid to others or yourself. Always tell an adult about any injuries that occur.

For Choking . . .

If someone else is choking . . .

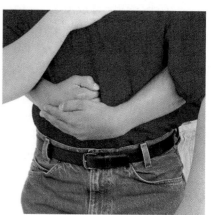

1. Recognize the Universal Choking Sign—grasping the throat with both hands. This sign means a person is choking and needs help.

2. Stand behind the choking person, and put your arms around his or her waist. Place your fist above the person's belly button. Grab your fist with your other hand.

3. Pull your hands toward yourself, and give five quick, hard, upward thrusts on the person's stomach.

If you are choking when alone . . .

1. Make a fist, and place it above your belly button. Grab your fist with your other hand. Pull your hands up with a quick, hard thrust.

2. Or, keep your hands on your belly, lean your body over the back of a chair or over a counter, and shove your fist in and up.

For Bleeding . . .

If someone else is bleeding . . .

Wash your hands with soap, if possible.

Put on protective gloves, if available.

Wash small wounds with soap and water. Do *not* wash serious wounds.

Place a clean gauze pad or cloth over the wound. Press firmly for ten minutes. Don't lift the gauze during this time.

If you don't have gloves, have the injured person hold the gauze or cloth in place with his or her hand for ten minutes.

If after ten minutes the bleeding has stopped, bandage the wound. If the bleeding has not stopped, continue pressing on the wound and get help.

If you are bleeding . . .

- Wash your wound if it is a small cut. If it is a serious wound, do *not* wash it.
- Place a gauze pad or clean cloth over the wound, and hold it firmly in place for ten minutes. Don't lift the gauze or cloth until ten minutes has passed.
- If you have no gauze or cloth, apply pressure with your hand.
- If after ten minutes the bleeding has stopped, bandage the wound. If the bleeding has not stopped, continue pressing on the wound and get help.

Sense Organs

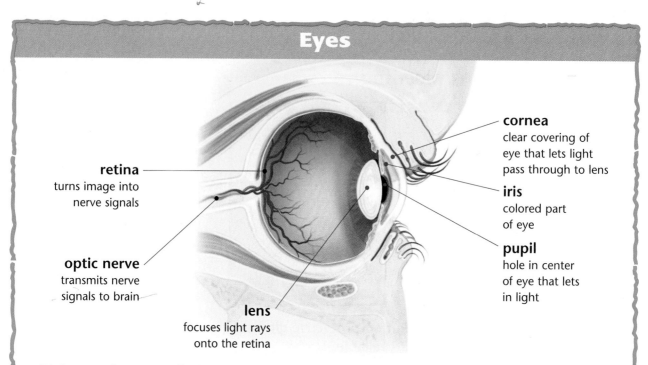

Eyes

retina
turns image into
nerve signals

optic nerve
transmits nerve
signals to brain

lens
focuses light rays
onto the retina

cornea
clear covering of
eye that lets light
pass through to lens

iris
colored part
of eye

pupil
hole in center
of eye that lets
in light

Light rays bounce off objects and enter your eye through your pupil. A lens inside your eye focuses the light rays, and the image of the object is projected onto the retina at the back of your eye. In the retina the image is turned into nerve signals. Your brain analyzes the signals to tell you what you're seeing.

Ears

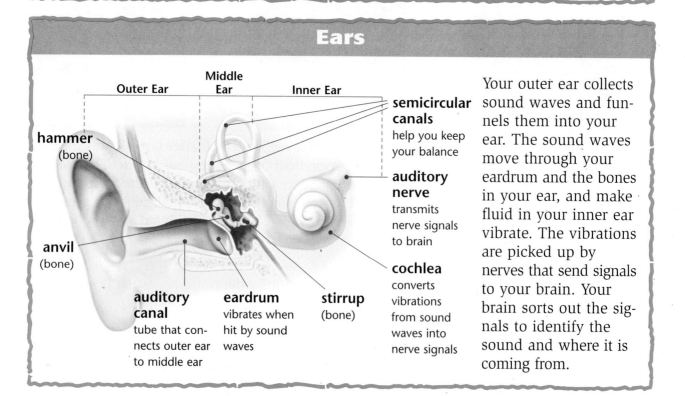

Outer Ear
Middle Ear
Inner Ear

hammer
(bone)

anvil
(bone)

auditory canal
tube that connects outer ear to middle ear

eardrum
vibrates when hit by sound waves

stirrup
(bone)

semicircular canals
help you keep your balance

auditory nerve
transmits nerve signals to brain

cochlea
converts vibrations from sound waves into nerve signals

Your outer ear collects sound waves and funnels them into your ear. The sound waves move through your eardrum and the bones in your ear, and make fluid in your inner ear vibrate. The vibrations are picked up by nerves that send signals to your brain. Your brain sorts out the signals to identify the sound and where it is coming from.

Nose

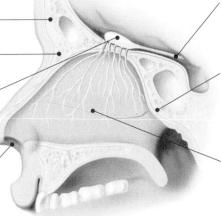

skull

nasal bone

olfactory (sense of smell) bulb
group of nerves that carry information to olfactory tract

nostrils
openings to nose

olfactory tract
carries information from olfactory bulb to brain

mucous membrane
warms and moistens air you breathe in

nasal cavity
main opening inside nose

When you breathe in, air is swept upward to nerve cells in your nasal cavity. Your nasal cavity is the upper part of your nose inside your skull. Different nerve cells respond to different odors in the air and send signals to your brain.

Skin

The skin is made of three layers, the outer epidermis, the middle dermis, and the lower subcutaneous layer. Nerve cells in your skin signal your brain about stimuli (conditions around you) that affect your skin.

Merkel's endings
respond to medium pressure

epidermis

dermis

subcutaneous layer

Krause's endings
cold and mechanoreceptors

Pacini's endings
react to heavy pressure

free nerve endings
react to painful stimuli

Meissner's endings
respond to light pressure and small, fast vibration

Ruffini's endings
sense changes in temperature and pressure

Caring for Your Senses

Injuries to your brain can affect your senses. Protect your brain by wearing safety belts in the car and helmets when playing sports or riding your bike.

Tongue

Your tongue is covered with about 10,000 tiny nerve cells, or taste buds, that pick out tastes in the things you eat and drink. Different taste buds respond to different tastes and send signals to your brain.

taste buds

Activity

With a partner, toss a table tennis ball back and forth 15 times. Then put a patch over one eye and toss the ball again. Was it easier to catch the ball when you had both eyes open or only one eye open?

Skeletal System

our bones fit together and attach to your muscles at your joints. Your bones and muscles work together at your joints to allow you to move in many directions. Each joint is designed to do a certain job.

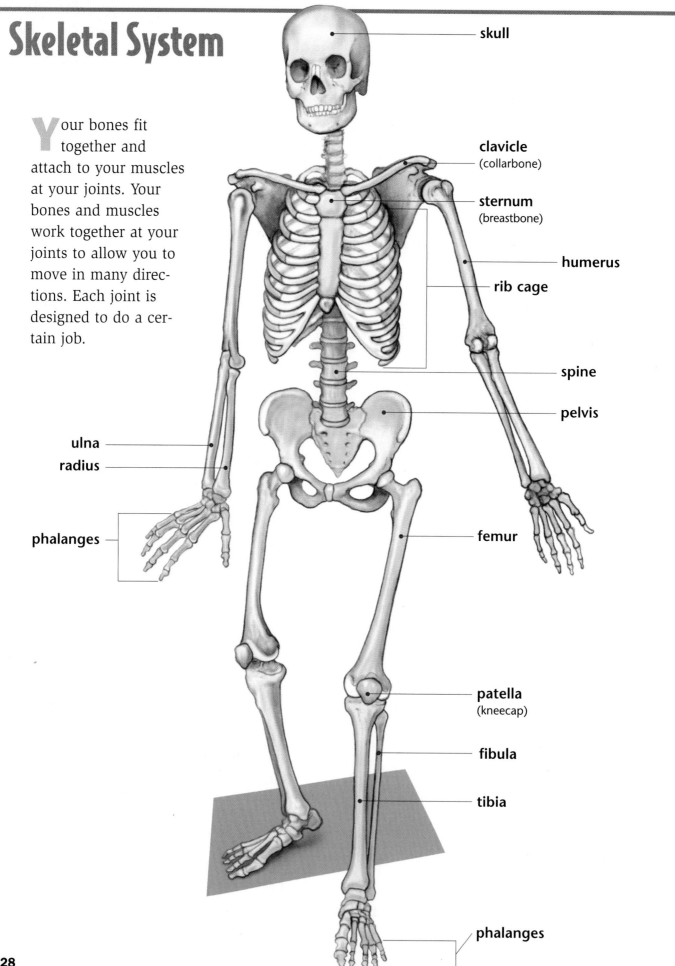

skull

clavicle
(collarbone)

sternum
(breastbone)

humerus

rib cage

spine

pelvis

ulna

radius

phalanges

femur

patella
(kneecap)

fibula

tibia

phalanges

Bones and Joints

flat bone (rib)

Kinds of Bones Bones come in four basic shapes: long, short, flat, and irregular. Long bones, such as those in your legs, arms, and fingers, are narrow with large ends and are slightly curved. These bones can support the most weight. Short bones, found in your wrists and ankles, are chunky and wide. These bones allow maximum movement around a joint. Flat bones, such as your skull and ribs, are platelike. They provide protection for especially delicate parts of your body. Irregular bones, such as those in your spine and your ears, have unique shapes that don't fit into any other category.

irregular bone (vertebra)

short bone (wrist)

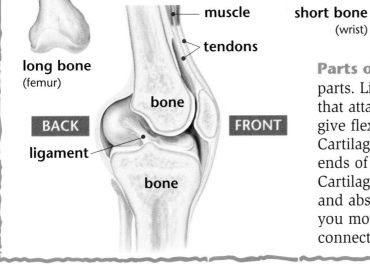

muscle
tendons
bone
BACK   FRONT
ligament
bone

long bone (femur)

Parts of a Joint A joint has several parts. Ligaments are tough, elastic bands that attach one bone to another. Ligaments give flexibility for bending and stretching. Cartilage is a cushioning material at the ends of bones that meet in a joint. Cartilage helps the bones move smoothly and absorbs some of the impact when you move. Tendons are dense cords that connect bones to muscles.

Caring for Your Skeletal System

- Move and flex your joints regularly through exercise. If you don't, they might get injured or become stiff and sore. Be sure to warm up and cool down whenever you exercise.

- You can injure a joint by using it too much or moving it in a way it is not designed to move.

- Calcium is necessary for healthy bones. You can get calcium from milk, dairy products like yogurt and cheese, or some dark green, leafy vegetables.

Activities

1. Build a model of a long bone and a short bone. Use a sheet of construction paper. Cut off a strip about 1 inch (2.5 cm) wide. Roll the strip and the remainder of the sheet into tight cylinders. Test their strength by putting objects on top of them.

2. Make a model of a joint. Cut out two strips of cardboard and join them together using a round metal fastener. What does the fastener represent?

Muscular System

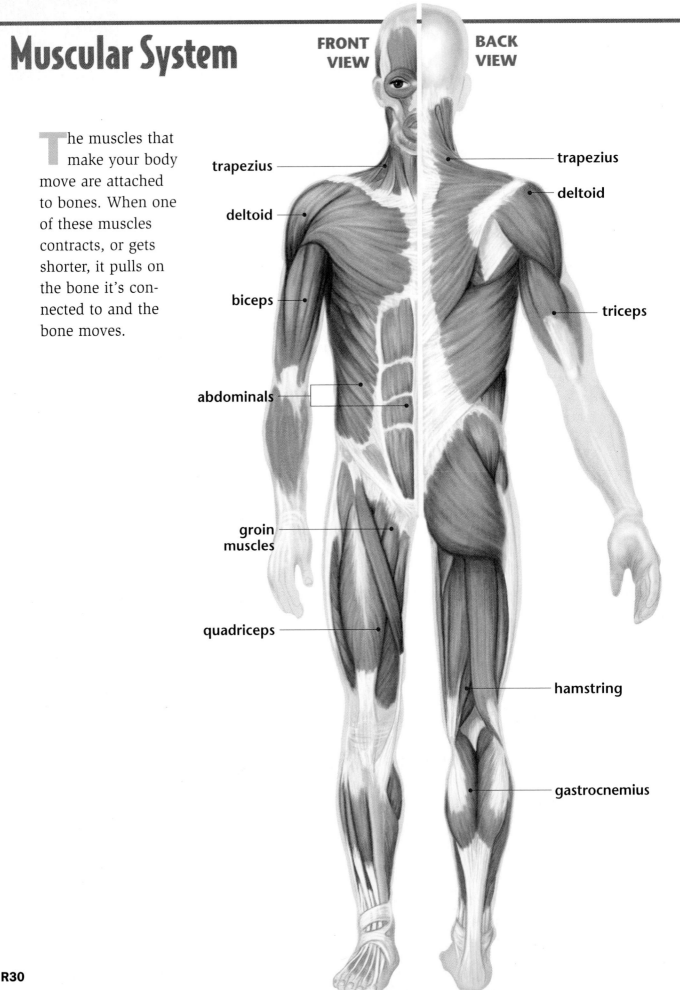

FRONT VIEW

BACK VIEW

The muscles that make your body move are attached to bones. When one of these muscles contracts, or gets shorter, it pulls on the bone it's connected to and the bone moves.

trapezius

deltoid

biceps

abdominals

groin muscles

quadriceps

trapezius

deltoid

triceps

hamstring

gastrocnemius

Muscles and Bones

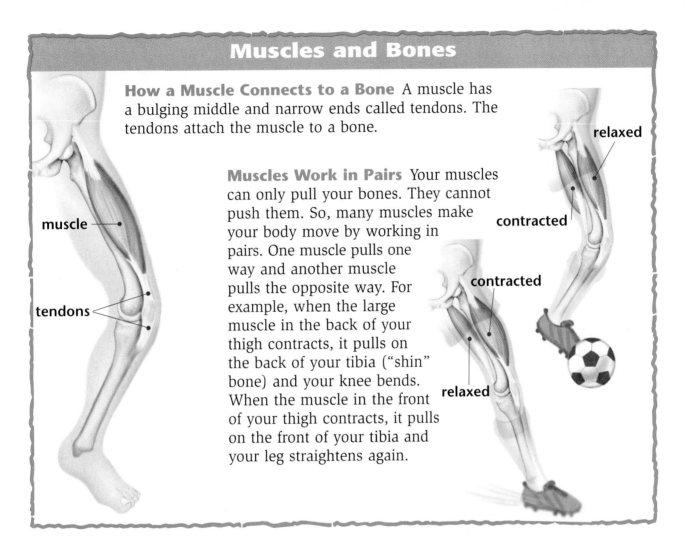

How a Muscle Connects to a Bone A muscle has a bulging middle and narrow ends called tendons. The tendons attach the muscle to a bone.

muscle

tendons

relaxed

contracted

contracted

relaxed

Muscles Work in Pairs Your muscles can only pull your bones. They cannot push them. So, many muscles make your body move by working in pairs. One muscle pulls one way and another muscle pulls the opposite way. For example, when the large muscle in the back of your thigh contracts, it pulls on the back of your tibia ("shin" bone) and your knee bends. When the muscle in the front of your thigh contracts, it pulls on the front of your tibia and your leg straightens again.

Caring for Your Muscular System

- Take a brisk five-minute walk and do gentle stretches before you start to play a sport to loosen your tendons, ligaments, and muscles and help prevent injuries.

- You should ease out of exercise too. Because your muscles contract during exercise, they need to be stretched when you finish.

Activities

1. Wrap your fingers around your upper arm, so you can feel both the top and bottom of your arm. Slowly bend and straighten your arm several times. Which muscles are working as a pair?

2. Write a paragraph about which muscles work in pairs when you play your favorite sport.

Digestive System

Digestion is the process of breaking food into tiny pieces that are absorbed by your blood and carried to all parts of your body. Each part of your digestive system does a different job.

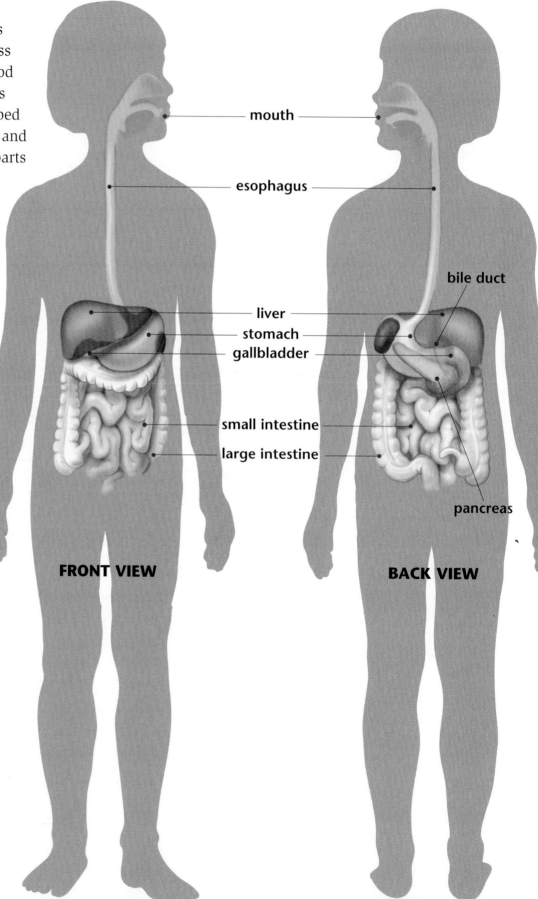

mouth

esophagus

bile duct

liver

stomach

gallbladder

small intestine

large intestine

pancreas

FRONT VIEW

BACK VIEW

Some Digestive Organs

Esophagus When you swallow, the chewed and moistened food goes down a tube to your stomach. This tube, called the esophagus, is about 10 inches (25.4 cm) long. The food is pushed down the esophagus by a squeezing muscle action, similar to squeezing a tube of toothpaste. When you swallow, your airway is protected by the epiglottis and your vocal cords. If you try to talk and swallow, you cough or choke.

— esophagus

Stomach The walls of your stomach are made of very strong muscles. Once food reaches the stomach, more chemicals are added that digest the food more thoroughly. At the same time, the stomach muscles squeeze the liquid food mixture.

stomach

Food leaves your stomach in two stages. First, the top of your stomach squeezes the liquid food mixture into the small intestine. Second, the solid particles are pushed into the small intestine by the muscles in the lower part of your stomach.

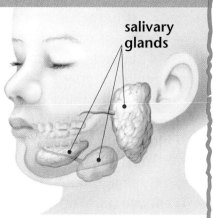

salivary glands

Salivary Glands When you chew your food, it is moistened with saliva. The saliva comes from three sets of glands: one set under your tongue, one on each side of your head in front of your ear, and one on each side of your head under your jaw.

Saliva is mostly water, but it does contain a chemical called *amylase* that helps digest starches. Saliva also helps keep your mouth clean and helps control infection.

Caring for Your Digestive System

- Try to drink at least six to eight glasses of water a day. Water helps food move through your digestive system.

- Chew your food thoroughly. Large pieces of food are more difficult to digest, and the large pieces might cause you to choke.

Activities

1. **Chew a cracker and then hold it in your mouth for about a minute. Move it around. How has the taste changed?**

2. **Record the amount of water you drink every day for three days. Are you drinking at least six glasses of water every day?**

Circulatory System

Blood is carried throughout your body by arteries, veins, and capillaries. Arteries deliver blood with needed materials, such as oxygen and nutrients, to parts of your body. Veins carry blood with waste or unused materials, such as carbon dioxide. Capillaries are microscopic blood vessels that allow needed substances to seep into your body's tissues.

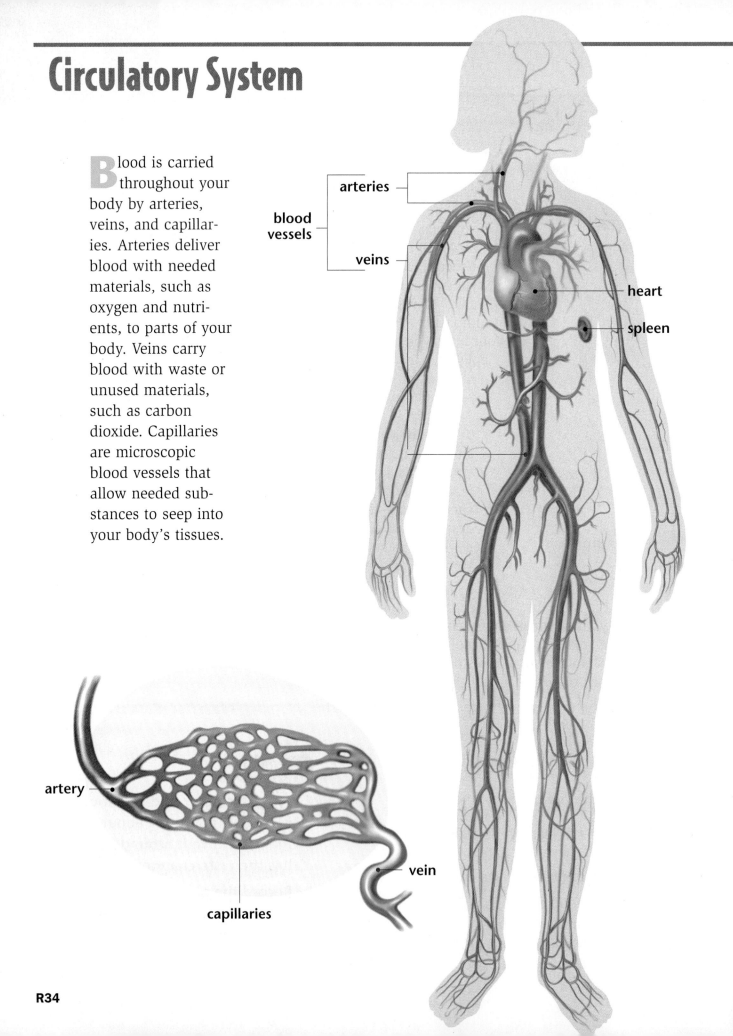

blood vessels

arteries

veins

heart

spleen

artery

capillaries

vein

How Blood Moves in Your Heart

Your heart has four chambers. The upper chambers are called atria. The lower chambers are called ventricles. Here is how blood moves through the heart.

1. Blood comes from your body into the right atrium. Blood comes from your lungs into the left atrium. The atria squeeze.

2. Two valves open, and the blood moves into the ventricles. When both ventricles have filled with blood, the valves shut. The ventricles squeeze.

3. Two different valves then open. The right ventricle sends blood through one valve to the lungs. The left ventricle sends blood through the other valve to the body. The "lub-dub" of your heartbeat is the sound of valves slamming shut.

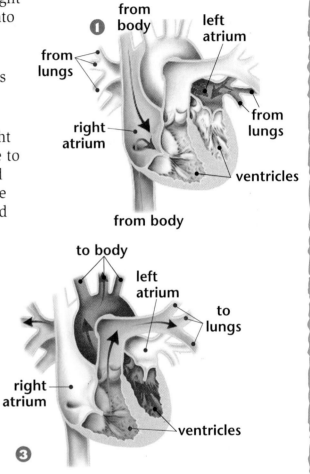

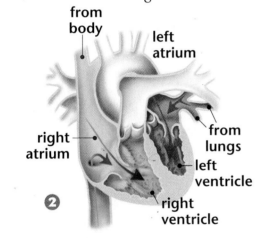

Caring for Your Circulatory System

- Don't ever smoke. Smoking narrows blood vessels and can cause high blood pressure.

- Remember, your heart is a constantly working muscle. Exercise strengthens your heart by making it beat harder, which makes the heart muscles larger and able to push more blood with each "squeeze" or "beat."

Activities

1. Take your pulse for ten seconds. Multiply that number by six to find how many times your heart beats in a minute. How many times does your heart beat in a day?

2. Feel your pulse in various places—your wrist, your neck, behind your knee. Where is it easiest to feel?

Respiratory System

Your lungs are filled with air tubes, air sacs, and blood vessels. The air tubes and blood vessels in your lungs divide until they are very small. At the ends of the tiny air tubes are air sacs called alveoli. The smallest blood vessels, capillaries, surround the alveoli.

Blood coming from your body (blue) delivers waste gases to your lungs. It then picks up oxygen (red) and takes it to your body.

nose

mouth

trachea
(windpipe)

air tubes

lungs

blood vessels

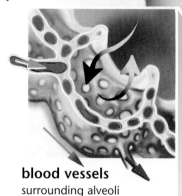

blood vessels
surrounding alveoli

alveoli
(air sacs)

How Oxygen Travels to Your Body Parts

Your heart and lungs are connected by veins and arteries. The blood your heart pumps out to the rest of your body comes directly from your lungs, where it is filled with oxygen. The blood delivers the oxygen and picks up carbon dioxide. When the blood returns to your heart, it needs oxygen. Your heart sends the blood to your lungs, where oxygen is added and carbon dioxide is removed.

Tiny blood vessels in your lungs release carbon dioxide into the alveoli and absorb oxygen from the air inside the alveoli. The replenished blood returns to the heart, and the process starts over.

It takes just one minute for blood to circulate around your entire body.

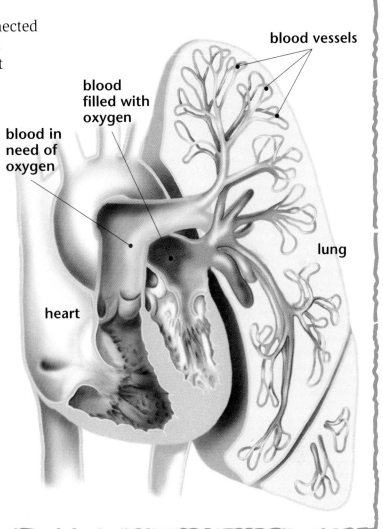

blood vessels

blood filled with oxygen

blood in need of oxygen

lung

heart

Caring for Your Respiratory System

- Don't ever smoke. The tar in cigarettes damages the lungs. Avoid environmental tobacco smoke too. Inhaling someone else's smoke can be as dangerous as smoking a cigarette yourself, especially for people with asthma.

- If you exercise so hard that you can't talk or you feel dizzy, your body is not getting enough oxygen. Slow down.

Activities

1. List three sports you think would exercise your respiratory system the most and three sports you think would exercise it the least.

2. Survey people you know about their thoughts on cigarettes and health. Record their answers.

3. Write the words to a jingle for an anti-smoking commercial.

Nervous System

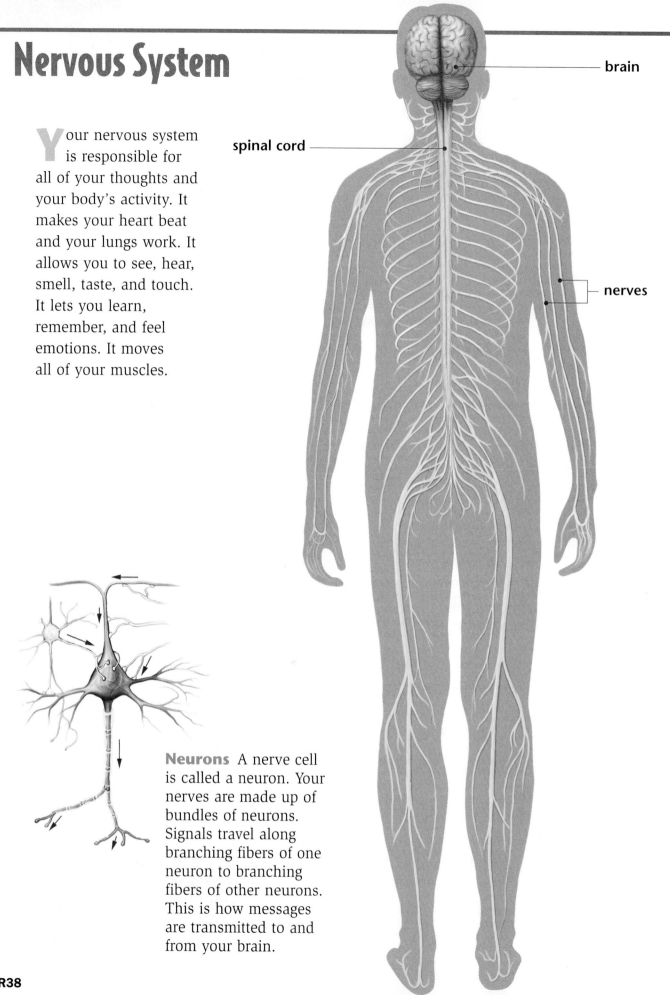

Your nervous system is responsible for all of your thoughts and your body's activity. It makes your heart beat and your lungs work. It allows you to see, hear, smell, taste, and touch. It lets you learn, remember, and feel emotions. It moves all of your muscles.

brain

spinal cord

nerves

Neurons A nerve cell is called a neuron. Your nerves are made up of bundles of neurons. Signals travel along branching fibers of one neuron to branching fibers of other neurons. This is how messages are transmitted to and from your brain.

Your Nervous System

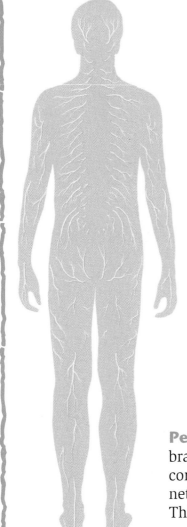

Autonomic Nervous System Your autonomic nervous system keeps your body's systems functioning and in balance. Masses of nerves called ganglia receive messages from your brain and relay those messages to organs like your heart, lungs, and kidneys.

ganglia

heart

spinal cord

Peripheral Nervous System Major nerves branch off your brain and spinal cord. They continue to branch and form a complicated network that spreads throughout your body. This is your peripheral nervous system.

Caring for Your Nervous System

- Do not take any drugs unless given by your parents or guardian or a doctor. Some drugs can affect your brain cells.

- Eat a well-balanced diet. Your nervous system cannot work properly without certain nutrients.

- Learning new skills builds new nerve connections in your brain.

Activities

1. Put one hand in a bowl of very warm water and one hand in a bowl of cold water. Then put both hands in a bowl of warm water. How does each hand feel?

2. Blindfold a friend. Touch your friend's back with two fingers and your friend's palm with two fingers. Can your friend tell how many fingers you used in each place?

Immune System and Endocrine System

Your immune system defends your body from harmful invaders, such as organisms that cause infection. White blood cells, which are your immune system's primary infection fighters, are produced in your bone marrow, thymus, lymph nodes, and spleen.

Tonsils Your tonsils are also lymph tissue. They produce white blood cells. When your body has an infection, lymph nodes can become infected. Infected lymph nodes become swollen and painful.

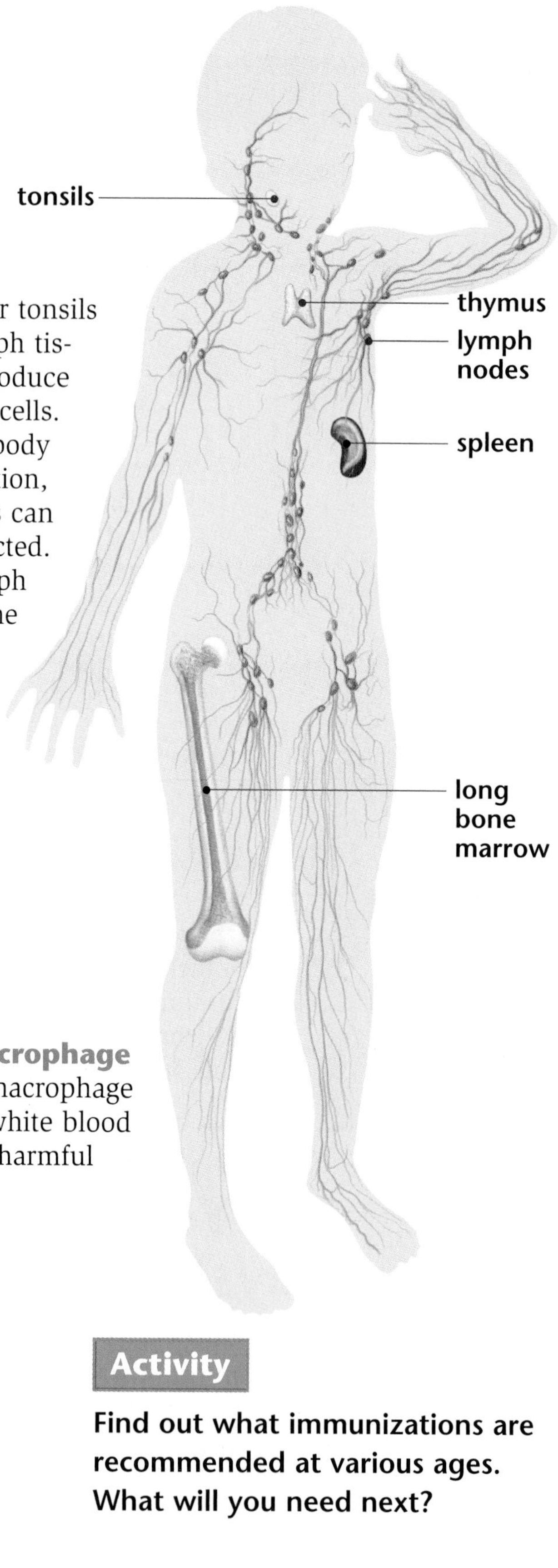

tonsils

thymus

lymph nodes

spleen

long bone marrow

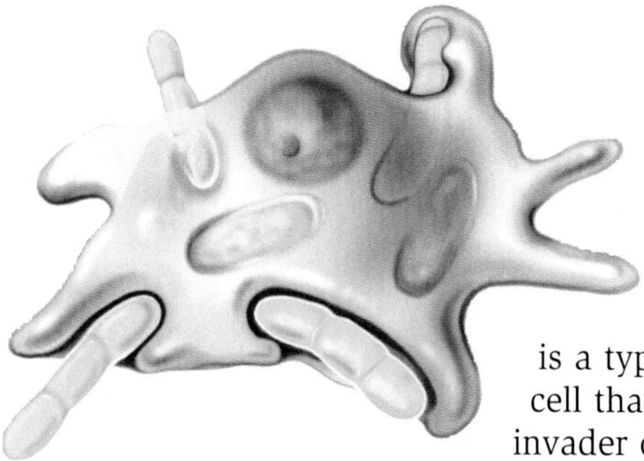

Macrophage A macrophage is a type of white blood cell that eats harmful invader cells.

Caring for Your Immune System

One way to help your body fight disease is through immunization (shots that protect you from certain diseases). You were required to have some immunizations as an infant and "boosters" before you started school.

Your endocrine system works with your nervous system to help your body grow normally and work and react as it should. The endocrine system does this by releasing hormones into your bloodstream. Hormones are chemicals that deliver instructions to various organs and tissues.

pituitary gland
controls body's day-to-day functioning, long-term growth, and reproduction

thyroid gland
helps set the pace at which your body functions

parathyroid glands
control level of calcium in your blood

thymus gland

adrenal glands
produce a sudden, remarkable burst of energy in response to stress or danger

pancreas
helps regulate the amount of sugar in your bloodstream

Caring for Your Endocrine System

Some drugs, such as steroids, can harm your endocrine system. Avoid these drugs.

Activity

The next time you are startled, feel your heartbeat. How is it different from normal?

Glossary

This Glossary contains important science words and their definitions. Each word is respelled as it would be in a dictionary. When you see the ′ mark after a syllable, pronounce that syllable with more force than the other syllables. The page number at the end of the definition tells where to find the word in your book. The boldfaced letters in the examples in the Pronunciation Key that follows show how these letters are pronounced in the respellings after each glossary word.

PRONUNCIATION KEY

a	add, map	m	move, seem	u	up, done
ā	ace, rate	n	nice, tin	û(r)	burn, term
â(r)	care, air	ng	ring, song	yōō	fuse, few
ä	palm, father	o	odd, hot	v	vain, eve
b	bat, rub	ō	open, so	w	win, away
ch	check, catch	ô	order, jaw	y	yet, yearn
d	dog, rod	oi	oil, boy	z	zest, muse
e	end, pet	ou	pout, now	zh	vision, pleasure
ē	equal, tree	ŏŏ	took, full	ə	the schwa, an
f	fit, half	ōō	pool, food		unstressed vowel
g	go, log	p	pit, stop		representing the sound
h	hope, hate	r	run, poor		spelled
i	it, give	s	see, pass		*a* in *above*
ī	ice, write	sh	sure, rush		*e* in *sicken*
j	joy, ledge	t	talk, sit		*i* in *possible*
k	cool, take	th	thin, both		*o* in *melon*
l	look, rule	t͟h	this, bathe		*u* in *circus*

Other symbols:
- • separates words into syllables
- ′ indicates heavier stress on a syllable
- ′ indicates light stress on a syllable

air mass [âr′mas′] A huge body of air which has the same general properties as the land or water over which it forms **(B46)**

air pressure [âr′presh′ər] The weight of particles of air pressing down on the Earth's surface **(B7)**

alveoli [al•vē′ə•lī] Tiny air sacs, located at the ends of bronchi in the lungs, through which gases are exchanged with the blood **(A18)**

amphibian [am•fib′ē•ən] An animal with moist skin and no scales **(A44)**

angiosperm [an′jē•ō•spûrm′] A flowering plant **(A83)**

anthracite [an′thrə•sīt′] A hard, black rock; fourth stage of coal formation **(E15)**

asteroid [as′tə•roid] Small rocky object that moves around the sun **(B127)**

atmosphere [at′məs•fir] Layer of air that surrounds Earth **(B6)**

atom [a′təm] The smallest unit of an element that has all the properties of that element **(C42)**

axis [ak′sis] An imaginary line that passes through Earth's center and its North and South poles **(B93)**

biomass [bī′ō•mas′] Organic matter, such as wood, that is living or was recently alive **(E46)**

bird [buhrd] A vertebrate with feathers **(A45)**

bitumen [bi•tōō′mən] A fairly hard, dark brown or black rock; third stage of coal formation **(E15)**

bone marrow [bōn′ mar′ō] Connective tissue that produces red and white blood cells **(A24)**

capillaries [kap′ə•ler′ēz] The smallest blood vessels **(A17)**

carbon dioxide–oxygen cycle [kär′bən di•ok′sīd′ ok′sə•jən sī′kəl] The process by which carbon and oxygen cycle among plants, animals, and the physical environment **(A74)**

cell [sel] The basic unit of structure and function in all living things **(A6)**

cell membrane [sel′ mem′brān′] Thin covering that encloses a cell and keeps its parts together **(A8)**

cellular respiration [sel′yōō•lər res′pə•rā′shən] Process by which cells release energy from food in order to carry on life processes **(A106)**

chemical bonds [kem′i•kəl bondz′] Forces that join atoms to each other **(E34)**

chlorophyll [klôr′ə•fil′] Pigment, or coloring matter, that helps plants use light energy to produce sugars **(A68)**

classification [klas′ə•fi•kā′shən] The grouping of things by using a set of rules **(A38)**

climate [klī′mit] The average of all weather conditions through all seasons over a period of time **(B76)**

combustibility [kəm•bus′tə•bil′ə•tē] The chemical property of being able to burn **(C24)**

comet [kom′it] A small mass of dust and ice that orbits the sun in a long, oval-shaped path **(B127)**

compound [kom′pound] A substance made up of the atoms of two or more different elements **(C50)**

condensation [kon′dən•sā′shən] Process by which a gas changes into a liquid **(B15, C17)**

conduction [kən•duk′shən] The direct transfer of heat between objects that touch **(C87)**

conductor [kən•duk′tər] Material that conducts electrons easily **(C72)**

convection [kən•vek′shən] The transfer of heat due to the mixing of a liquid or a gas **(C87)**

corona [kə•rō′nə] The sun's atmosphere **(B119)**

cotyledons [kot′ə•lēd′ənz] Structures where food is stored in seeds **(A122)**

cytoplasm [sīt′ō•plaz′əm] A jellylike substance containing chemicals that help keep a cell functioning **(A9)**

density [den′sə•tē] The concentration of matter in an object **(C9)**

diffusion [di•fyo͞o′zhən] The process by which many materials move in and out of cells **(A10)**

eclipse [i•klips′] The passing of one object through the shadow of another object **(B94)**

electric charge [i•lek′trik chärj′] The charge obtained by an object as it gains or loses electrons **(C70)**

electric circuit [i•lek′trik sûr′kit] The path along which electrons flow **(C73)**

electric current [i•lek′trik kûr′ənt] The flow of electrons from a negatively charged object to a positively charged object **(C71)**

electric force [i•lek′trik fôrs′] The attraction or repulsion of objects due to their electric charges **(C71)**

electromagnet [i•lek′trō•mag′nit] A temporary magnet made by passing an electric current through a wire coiled around an iron bar **(C74)**

electron [ē•lek′tron′] A subatomic particle with a negative charge **(C41)**

element [el′ə•mənt] A substance made up of only one kind of atom **(C42)**

El Niño [el nēn′yō] A short-term climate change that occurs every two to ten years **(B79)**

embryo [em′brē•ō] Tiny plant inside a seed **(A122)**

energy [en′ər•jē] The ability to cause changes in matter **(C64)**

epidermis [ep′ə•dûr′mis] The outer layer of cells of a leaf **(A102)**

evaporation [ē•vap′ə•rā′shən] The process by which a liquid changes into a gas **(B15, C16)**

F

fertilization [fûr′təl•i•zā′shən] The joining of a male reproductive cell with a female reproductive cell **(A116)**

fiber [fī′bər] Any material that can be separated into threads **(A90)**

fish [fihsh] A vertebrate that lives in water **(A45)**

forecast [for′kast′] A prediction of what the weather will be like in the future **(B68)**

fossil fuels [fos′əl fyoo′əlz] Fuels formed from the remains of once-living organisms **(E12)**

front [frunt] The border where two air masses meet **(B47)**

fungi [fun′ji′] Living things such as mushrooms that look like plants, but cannot make their own food **(A39)**

fusion energy [fyoo′zhən en′ər•jē] The energy released when the nuclei of two atoms are forced together to form a larger nucleus **(E48)**

gas [gas] State of matter without a definite shape or volume **(C14)**

genus [jē′nəs] The second smallest grouping used in classification **(A40)**

geothermal energy [jē′ō•thûr′məl en′ər•jē] Heat from inside the Earth **(E47)**

germinate [jûr′mə•nāt′] To sprout **(A124)**

global warming [glō′bəl wôrm′ing] A rise in Earth's average temperature due to an increase in carbon dioxide **(B80)**

grafting [graft′ing] A form of artificial reproduction that can produce desirable characteristics in woody plants **(A126)**

grain [grān] The seeds of certain plants that are used for food **(A88)**

gravitropism [grav′i•trō′piz•əm] A plant's response to gravity **(A111)**

greenhouse effect [grēn′hous′ i•fekt′] The process by which the Earth's atmosphere absorbs heat from the sun **(B80)**

gymnosperm [jim′nō•spûrm′] A plant with unprotected seeds; conifers or cone-bearing plants **(A82)**

heat [hēt] The transfer of thermal energy from one substance to another **(C86)**

humidity [hyoo·mid′ə·tē] A measure of the amount of water in the air **(B13)**

hurricane [hur′ə·kān′] A large, spiraling storm system with winds that exceed 119 km/hr (74 mi/hr) **(B54)**

hydroelectric energy [hī′drō·ē·lek′trik en′ər·jē] Electricity generated from the energy of moving water **(E40)**

insulator [in′sə·lāt′ər] Material that does not conduct electrons **(C73)**

invertebrate [in·vûr′tə·brit] An animal without a backbone **(A45)**

joints [joints] Places where bones meet and are attached to each other and to muscles **(A24)**

kinetic energy [ki·net′ik en′ər·jē] The energy of motion, or energy in use **(C64)**

kingdom [king′dəm] The largest group into which living things are classified **(A39)**

law of universal gravitation [lô′ uv yoon′ə·vûr′səl grav′i·tā′shən] Law that states that all objects in the universe are attracted to all other objects **(B133)**

lens [lenz] A piece of clear material that bends, or refracts, light rays passing through it **(C79)**

ligaments [lig′ə·mənts] Bands of connective tissue that hold a skeleton together **(A25)**

lignite [lig′nīt′] A soft, brown rock; the second stage of coal formation **(E14)**

liquid [lik′wid] State of matter with a definite volume but no definite shape **(C14)**

local winds [lō′kəl windz′] Winds dependent upon local changes in temperature **(B41)**

mammal [mam′əl] An animal that has hair and produces milk for its young **(A44)**

mass [mas] The amount of matter in an object **(C7)**

matter [mat′ər] Anything that has mass and takes up space **(C6)**

microclimate [mī′krō·klī′mit] The climate of a very small area **(B76)**

molecule [mol′ə·kyool′] A grouping of two or more atoms joined together **(C42)**

moneran [mō•ner′ən] The kingdom of organisms that have only one cell and no nucleus **(A39)**

natural gas [nach′ər•əl gas′] A gas, methane, usually found with petroleum **(E13)**

natural resource [nach′ər•əl rē′sôrs′] Any of the useful minerals and other materials that people take from the Earth **(E6)**

nephrons [nef′ronz′] Tubes inside the kidneys where urea and water diffuse from the blood **(A20)**

neuron [no͞or′on′] A specialized cell that can receive information and transmit it to other cells **(A26)**

neutron [no͞o′tron′] A subatomic particle with no charge **(C41)**

nitrogen cycle [nī′trə•jən sī′kəl] The cycle in which nitrogen gas is changed into forms of nitrogen that plants can use **(A73)**

nonrenewable resource [non′ri•no͞o′ə•bəl rē′sôrs′] A resource that cannot be readily replaced once it is used **(E6)**

nonvascular plant [non•vas′kyə•lər plant′] A plant that does not have tubes for transporting food and water **(A52)**

nuclear energy [no͞o′klē•ər en′ər•jē] The energy released when the nucleus of an atom is split apart **(E46)**

nucleus [no͞o′klē•əs] 1 *(cell)* Organelle that controls all of a cell's activities. 2 *(atom)* The center of an atom. **(A8, C41)**

orbit [ôr′bit] The path one body in space takes as it revolves around another body, such as Earth as it revolves around the sun **(B93, B132)**

organ [ôr′gən] Tissues that work together to perform a specific function **(A12)**

osmosis [os•mō′sis] The diffusion of water and dissolved materials through a cell membrane **(A10)**

ovary [ō′və•rē] The part of a flower that contains the eggs **(A117)**

palisade layer [pal′ə•sād′ lā′ər] The layer of cells in a leaf where most photosynthesis occurs **(A103)**

peat [pēt] A soft, brown material made up of partly decayed plants; first stage of coal formation **(E14)**

periodic table [pir′ē•od′ik tā′bəl] A table of elements arranged in order of increasing atomic number; elements grouped by similar properties **(C49)**

phloem [flō′em] Tubes that transport food in vascular plants **(A67)**

photosphere [fōt′ə•sfir′] The visible surface of the sun **(B119)**

photosynthesis [fōt′ō•sin′thə•sis] The process by which plants make food **(A102)**

phototropism [fō•tō•trō′piz•əm] A plant's response to light **(A110)**

physical properties [fiz′i•kəl prop′ər•tēz] Characteristics of a substance that can be observed or measured without changing the substance **(C6)**

pistil [pis′təl] The female part of a flower **(A116)**

pitch [pich] A characteristic of sound determined by the speed at which sound waves move **(C81)**

planet [plan′it] A large object that moves around a star **(B124)**

pollen [pol′ən] Flower structures that contain the male reproductive cells **(A82)**

potential energy [pō•ten′shəl en′ər•jē] The energy an object has because of its place or its condition **(C64)**

precipitation [pri•sip′ə•tā′shən] Any form of water that falls from clouds, such as rain, snow, sleet, or hail **(B13)**

prevailing winds [prē•vāl′ing windz′] Global winds that blow constantly from the same direction **(B41)**

protist [prō′tist] The kingdom of organisms that have only one cell and a nucleus, or cell control center **(A39)**

proton [prō′ton′] A subatomic particle with a positive charge **(C41)**

R

radiation [rā′dē•ā′shən] The transfer of thermal energy by electromagnetic waves **(C87)**

reactivity [rē′ak•tiv′ə•tē] The ability of a substance to go through a chemical change **(C23)**

receptors [ri•sep′tərz] Nerve cells that detect conditions in the body's environment **(A26)**

recycling [rē•sī′kling] The process of taking a resource from a product and making it into a new product **(E22)**

reflection [ri•flek′shən] Light energy that bounces off objects **(C78)**

refraction [ri•frak′shən] The bending of light rays as they pass through a substance **(C78)**

renewable resource [ri•nōō′ə•bəl rē′sôrs] A resource that is replaced as quickly as it is used **(E8)**

reptile [rep′tīl] An animal that has dry, scaly skin **(A44)**

resistor [ri•zis′tər] A material that resists the flow of electrons **(C73)**

reusable resource [rē•yōō′zə•bəl rē′sôrs] A natural resource that is renewed by natural cycles and, therefore, can be used more than once; an inexhaustible resource **(E8)**

revolve [ri•volv′] To travel in a closed path around an object **(B92)**

rotate [rō′tāt] The spinning of Earth or any object on its axis **(B93)**

satellite [sat′ə•līt′] A natural body, like the moon, or an artificial object that orbits another object **(B101)**

seedling [sēd′ling] Plant stage when a germinated seed begins growing and making its own food **(A124)**

solar energy [sō′lər en′ər•jē] The energy of sunlight **(E47)**

solar flare [sō′lər flâr′] A brief burst of energy from the sun's photosphere **(B120)**

solar system [sō′lər sis′təm] A group of objects in space that move around a central star **(B124)**

solar wind [sō′lər wind′] A fast-moving stream of particles thrown into space by a solar flare **(B120)**

solid [sol′id] State of matter with a definite shape and a definite volume **(C14)**

solubility [sol′yə•bil′ə•tē] The ability of one substance to be dissolved in another substance **(C10)**

space probe [spās′ prōb′] A robot vehicle used to explore deep space **(B102)**

species [spē′shēz] The smallest grouping used in classification **(A40)**

spore [spôr] A single reproductive cell that grows into a new plant **(A81)**

stamens [stā′mənz] The male parts of a flower **(A116)**

station model [stā′shən mod′əl] An arrangement of symbols and numbers that show the weather conditions recorded at a weather station **(B68)**

stratosphere [strat′ə•sfir′] Layer of the atmosphere that contains ozone; located above the troposphere **(B8)**

sunspot [sun′spot′] A dark (cooler) area on the photosphere of the sun **(B120)**

surface map [sûr′fis map′] A map that includes station model symbols and information about fronts and about centers of high pressure and low pressure **(B68)**

system [sis′təm] Organs that work together to perform a function **(A12)**

telescope [tel′ə•skōp′] An instrument that magnifies distant objects, or makes them appear larger **(B101)**

temperature [tem′pər•ə•chər] The average kinetic energy of all the molecules in an object **(C86)**

tendons [ten′dənz] Tough bands of connective tissue that attach muscles to bones **(A25)**

thunderstorm [thun′dər•stôrm′] A very strong storm with a lot of rain, thunder, lightning, and sometimes hail **(B52)**

tidal energy [tīd′əl en′ər•jē] A form of hydroelectric energy that produces electricity from the rise and fall of tides **(E42)**

tissue [tish′oo͞] Cells that work together to perform a specific function **(A12)**

tissue culture [tish′oo͞ kul′chər] Process of growing plants artificially in laboratories **(A126)**

tornado [tôr•nā′dō] An intense windstorm that often forms within a severe thunderstorm **(B56)**

transpiration [tran′spə•rā′shən] Process by which plants give off water through their stomata **(B27)**

tropical storm [trop′i•kəl stôrm′] The stage of hurricane development when the winds of a tropical depression reach a constant speed of 63 km/hr (39 mph) **(B54)**

tropism [trō′piz′əm] A plant's response to a stimulus **(A110)**

troposphere [trō′pō•sfir′] Layer of the atmosphere closest to Earth **(B8)**

vascular plant [vas′kyə•lər plant′] A plant that has tubes for transporting food and water **(A50)**

vegetative propagation [vej′ə•tāt′iv prop′ə•gā′shən] A form of asexual reproduction in plants; reproduction without seeds **(A125)**

vertebrate [vûr′tə•brit] An animal with a backbone **(A44)**

villi [vil′ī] Tiny tubes sticking into the small intestine that absorb nutrients into the blood **(A19)**

volume [vol′yəm] 1 *(measurement)* The amount of space that an object takes up. 2 *(sound)* The loudness of a sound **(C8, C81)**

water cycle [wôt′ər sī′kəl] The cycle in which Earth's water moves through the environment **(B15)**

weather [weth′ər] The condition of the atmosphere at any moment **(B12)**

weather balloon [weth′ər bə•loon′] A balloon released into the atmosphere that carries a package of instruments to record data about temperature, air pressure, and humidity **(B69)**

weather map [weᵗʰ′ər map′] A map that shows data about recent weather conditions across a large area **(B70)**

weight [wāt] A measure of the pull of gravity on an object **(C7)**

xylem [zi′ləm] Tubes that transport water and minerals in vascular plants **(A67)**

A

A4 rocket, B106
Abdominal muscles, R30
Acid rain, C25, E8
Acid(s), C24
Acorns, A123
Active transport, A11
Activity pyramid,
   weekly planning, R16
Adrenal glands, R41
Aerobic activities, R20–21
Agronomist, A129
Air
   properties of, B4–7
Air, gases in, C10
Air mass(es), B46, B48
   and weather, B46–49
   meeting of, B47
   movement of, B47–49
Air pollution, E21
Air pressure, B7, B14
   and wind, B41
Air tubes, lung, R36
Alchemy, C52
Aluminum, E6–7
Aluminum (element), C43
Alveoli (air sacs), A18, R36
Ammonia, A20
Amphibians, A44
Amylase, R33
Anemometer, B13, B69
Angiosperms, A83, A116–119,
   A122
Animal kingdom, A39
Animals, described, A44
Anther, A117
Anthracite, C42, E15
Anvil, C81, R26
Apollo 11, B107
Apollo, Project, B102
Aristotle, A54, B58, C40, C52
Armstrong, Neil, B106–107
Arrazi, C52

Arteries, A17, R34
Asexual reproduction, A125
Asphalt, self-healing, C28–29
Aspirin, A90
Asteroids, B127
Astronomical Unit (AU), B121
Astrophysicist, B137
Atmosphere, B6–9, B10–13
   layers of, B8
   of the sun, B118
Atmospheric conditions,
   measuring, B10–13
Atom, C40, C42, C52
   structure of, C41
Atomic mass, C53
Atomic number, C42, C53
Atomic theory, C40
Auditory canal, R26
Auditory nerve, R26
Auto mechanic, A121
Autonomic nervous system,
   R39
Avalanche, C60, C65
Axon, A26

B

B-protein, A92, A93
Bacteria, A7, A38–39
   fighting, R14
Balance, C7
   using, R6
Ball-and-socket joints, A24
Bark, A51, A67
Barometer, B13–14, B58, B69
Bases, C24
Bats, A119
Battery, C72
Bauxite, E6, E21
Bay of Fundy, Canada, E42
Behaviors, changing, E21
Bennett, Jean M., C92
Biceps, R30
Biomass, E46

Birds, A45
Bitumen, E15
Bjerknes, Jacob, B59
Bladder, A20
Blood, A16, A17
Blood vessels, A16, R34, R36
Body organization, A12
Body system, A12
Bohr, Niels, C41
Boiling, C16–17
Boiling point, C18
Bone marrow, A24, R40
Bone(s), A24–25, A47
   kinds of, R29
Botanical explorer, A56
Boyle, Robert, C52
Brain, A26, R38
Branches, A67
Breathing, A18
Brock microscope, R5
Bronchi, A18
Bud, A117
Buoys, B18, B70
Bur, A123
Burning
   fuels, E34
   garbage, E46
   heat released by (chart), E34
Butterfly, A114

C

Cactus, A68, A126
Calcium, A47
California Current, B78
Calories (C), C88
   use of (chart), C61
Canola motor oil, E50–51
Capillaries, A17, A18, R34
Carbon atoms, C42
Carbon dioxide, A10, A17, A18,
   A20, A68, A102–107, B6–7,
   B80, E36, R37

Carbon dioxide-oxygen cycle, A74–75

Cardiac muscles, A25

Cartilage, R29

Cell membrane, A8–9

Cell reproduction, A8

Cell theory, A28–29

Cell transport, A10–11

Cell wall, A8, A9

Cells, A28–29, A39
  animal, A9
  discovery of, A6
  history of, A28–29
  kinds of, A7
  leaf, A68
  plant, A7, A8, A50

Cellular respiration, A104–105, A106–107, C88

Central nervous system, A26

Chemical bonds, E34

Chemical energy, A102, C66, C88

Chemical formula, C50

Chemical reactions, C22

Chemical symbols, C49

Chemistry, beginning of, C52

Chlorine (element), C43

Chlorophyll, A68, A102, A104–105

Chloroplasts, A8–9, A68, A102–103, A104

Cholera, A92–93

Chromosomes, A8–9

Circulatory system, A16, A17, R34–35
  caring for, R35

Cirrus clouds, B16

Class, A40

Classification, A38–53
  animal, A44–47
  history of, A54–55
  plant, A50–53

Clavicle, R28

Climate Analysis Center (CAC), B32

Climate(s), B76–81
  and latitude, B77
  changes in, B79
  defined, B76
  effects of water on, B77
  human effect on, B80–81
  world, B78

Clouds, B15–17, B20

Coal, E13, E35
  carbon content of, E15
  formation of, E14–15

Cochlea, C81, R26

Cochlear nerve, C81

Cocklebur, A113

Coconut tree, A120

Cold front, B47, B49

Combustibility, C24

Combustion, C50

Comet, B127

Compound(s), C50–51, C52

Compression, C81

Computer, using, R8–9

Concave lens, C79

Condensation, B15, C17

Condenser steam engine, C90

Conduction, C87

Conductivity, C44–45

Conductor(s), C72, C82, C87

Cones, A82

Congreve, Sir William, B106

Conifers, A51, A82

Connective tissue, A12

Conservation of energy law, C65

Conservation of matter law, C26

Convection, C87

Convection zone, B119

Convex lens, C79

Copper, density of, C9

Core
  of sun, B118–119

Coriolis, Gustave, B58

Coriolis effect, B58

Corn, new products from, A128–129

Corn kernel, A122

Cornea, C80, R26

Cornfield, A102

Corona, B118

Cotyledons, A122, A124

Crab, A45

Craters, of moon, B95–96, formation of B98–99

Crocuses, A64

Cross-pollination, A118

Cumulonimbus clouds, B16

Cumulus clouds, B16

Currents, B23
  and weather, B78

Cuticle, leaf, A103

Cuttings, A126

Cytoplasm, A8, A9, A11

D

Dalton, John, C40, C52

Dandelions, A65

Day
  length of, B113

Day-neutral plants, A112

Dead Sea, B22

Decomposition, A128

Deimos, B128

Deltoid, R30

Democritus, C40

Dendrites, A26

Density, C9

Dermis, R27

Desert zone, B78

Diamond(s), C42
  density of, C9

Dicots, A122

Diesel fuel, E35

Diet, healthful, A88, R12–13

Diffusion, A10

Digestive system, A16, A19, R32–33

Digitalis, A90

Displacement, C8

Distillation, C25

DNA code, A28, A29

Doppler radar, B69, B72–73

Drake, E.L., E32

Drop of Water, A, (Wick), B29

Dry cell, C72

Ductility, C44

E. coli, A93

Ear canal, C81

Eardrum, C81, R26

Ears, C81, R26

Earth, B125
and moon compared, B96
and moon in space, B90–93
atmosphere of, B6–9
gravity of, C7
poles of, B23
rotation and revolution of, B92–93

Earth Day float, E18

Earth's surface, uneven heating of, B40–43

Earthquake safety, R23

Eastwood, Alice, A94

Eclipses, B94

Eggs, A116, A118

El Niño, B32, B59, B79
tracking of, B82–83

Elastic potential energy, C66

Electric charge, C70

Electric circuits, C73

Electric current, C71–72

Electric energy, C66, C70–75, E35

Electric energy station, C91

Electric force, C71

Electric generators, E35, E41

Electric motor, C75

Electricity, C91, E13
production of, E12

Electromagnet, C74

Electromagnetic waves, C80

Electrons, C41, C70

Elements, C42, C52–53
common (chart), C43
grouping, C48–49
history of, C52–53

Embryo, A84, A85
seed, A122

Endocrine system, R41

Energy, C60–67
developing sources of, C90–91
forms of, C66
kinetic, C64
potential, C64
transformation of, C65
worldwide use of (chart), E30

Energy levels, C41

Energy sources, E46–49
current (chart), E48
history of, C90–91

Epidermis, R27
leaf, A102

Epiglottis, R33

Epithelial tissue, A12

Equator, B42, B77

Esophagus, A19, R32, R33

Evaporation, A21, B15, B20, C16–17

Excretory system, A16, A20

Eyes,
human, C80, R26
of hurricanes, B54
potato, A125

Fahrenheit, G.D., B59

Family (classification), A40

Felis concolor, A57

Femur, R28

Ferns, A50, A81

Ferris, Roxanna S., A56

Fertilization, A116–117

Fiber, A90

Fibrous roots, A65

Fibula, R28

Fire safety, R22

Fish, A45

First aid
for bleeding, R25
for choking, R24

Fish ladder, E40

Florida, climate, B77

Flowering (chart), A112

Flowering plants, life cycle of, A118

Flowers, A48, A84, A114–119

Fog, B16

Food
and bacteria, R14
safety tips, R15

Food energy, A106–107

Food guide pyramid, A89, R12

Forecast, B68

Forests, as renewable resources, E8

Fossil fuels, C90
alternatives to, E36–37
deposits, worldwide, E13
formation of, E12–17
use of, E34–35

Foxglove, A90

Free nerve endings, R27

Freezing, C16

Freezing point, C18

Friction, C65

Frogs, A44
life cycle of, A84

Front, B47
Fruit, A83, A118
Fungi kingdom, A39
Fusion energy, E48

Galileo, B100–101
Gallbladder, A19, R32
Gallium, C12
Ganglia, R39
Gas exchange, in lungs, A18
Gas(es), C10, C14, C15
Gasoline, E35
Gastric juice, A19
Gastrocnemius, R30
Gems, worldwide sources for, E7
Generator, C72
Geneticists, A29, A93
Genus, A40, A54–55
Geologists, E25, E36
Geothermal energy, C91, E37, E47
Germ theory, A28–29
Germs, A28–29
Geysers, E47
Giant sequoia, A51
Glaciers, B79
Glass, use and reuse of, E22
Glenn, John, B106
Global warming, B80, E37
Global wind pattern, B41–42, B58
Glucose, A104–105
Goddard, Robert, B106
Gopher, A55
Gourdine, Meredith, E52
Graduated cylinder, C8
    how to use, R7
Grafting, A126
Grain, A88
Grana, A104

Granite, E7
Graphite, C42, E6
Grass(es), A118
Grasshopper, body parts of, A46
Gravitational force, C71
Gravitational potential energy, C66
Gravitropism, A111
Gravity, A111, B15, C7
Gray Herbarium, Harvard University, A56
Greenhouse effect, B80
Groin muscles, R30
Ground water, B15, B21, B27
Growth ring, A51, A67
Guard cells, leaf, A103
Gushers, oil, E16, E24
Gymnosperms, A82, A116

H

Hail, B13, B53
Hair cells, C81
Hammer, in ear, C81, R26
Hamstring, R30
Hand lens, C79
    using, R4
Harris, Bernard A., A30
Heart, A16, R34, R39
    aerobic activities for, R20–21
    and blood movement, R34
Heart chambers, A17
Heartwood, A51
Heat, C86
    and changes in states, C17
    effect of, on matter, C86
Heavy-machine operator, B31
Heredity factors, A29
Hero of Alexandria, C90
High-pressure area, B14
Highway engineer, C29
Hinge joints, A24

Hooke, Robert, A6, A28
Hoover Dam, E38
Horsetails, A81
Hubble Space Telescope. B102
Human body systems, A16–21, A24–27, R26–41
Humerous, R28
Humidity, B13
Humus, A128
Hurricane, B54–55
    categories, B37
    safety, B55
    tracking, B50–51
Hydroelectric dams, C91
Hydroelectric energy, E38, E40–41
Hydrogen energy, E49
Hydrosorb, A129
Hygrometer, B13

I

"I Wandered Lonely as a Cloud" (Wordsworth), A119
Ice Age, B79
Iguana, A7
Immovable joints, A24
Immune system, R40
Immunization ("shots"), R40
Indicators, C24
Industrial Revolution, E41
Infrared waves, C80
Inner ear, R26
Insects, A45, A118
Insulators, C44, C73, C82, C87
Internal combustion engine, C90–91
International Space Station, B104
Internet, R9
Invertebrates, A45

Io, B128
Iris, flower, A125
Iris, in eye, C80, R26
Iron (element), C43
Ithaca bog beetle, A35

J

Johnson, Duane, E50
Joints, A24
  kinds of, R29
Jumping frog, body parts of,
  A46
Jupiter, B126

K

Kalanchoe, A125
Kelp, A34
Kidneys, A20
Kinetic energy, C64, C86
Kingdoms, A39, A55–56
Kitchen, cleanliness, R15
Kloth, Carolyn, B60
Kooyman, Shirley Mah, A130
Krause's endings, R27

L

Large intestine, A19, R32
Latitude, B51
  and climate, B77
Lavoisier, Antoine, C26
Law of conservation of energy,
  C65
Law of conservation of matter,
  C26
Law of universal gravitation,
  B133
Leapheart, Theophilus, C30
Leaves, A68–69
structure of, A102–103

Left atrium, R35
Left ventricle, R35
Lens, C79
Lens, eye, C80, R26
Life cycles
  plants, A80–81
  animal/plant compared, A84
Ligaments, A25, R29
Light energy, A102, A104, C66
  speed of, C78
Light rays, C78–79
Light waves, C80
Lightning, B52,
  and electric charges, C71,
  frequency of, B36
Lignite, E14–15
Lima bean, A122
Limestone, E7
Linnaeus, A54
Liquid(s), C14, C15
  measuring, R7
Liver, A19, A20, R32
Liverworts, A52
Living things, grouping, A38–41
Lobes, A52
Loma Linda University, CA, A93
Long-day plants, A112
Lorenz, Edward, B84
Low-pressure area, B14
Lower epidermis, of leaf, A103
Lunar eclipse, B94
Lungs, A18, R36–37
  aerobic activities for,
  R20–21
Luster, C44
Lymph nodes, R40

M

MacCready, Paul D., E26
Macrophage, R40
Magellan spacecraft, B113
Magma, E7, E47

Magnetars, B136–137
Magnetic field, C74
Magnetic force, C71
Magnets, and electricity,
  C73–75
Magnification, A6
Maine, climate, B77
Malleability, C44
Mammals, A35, A44
Maple trees, A123
Maria, of moon, B95
Mars, B125
Mass, C7
Matter
  changes in states of, C16–19
  chemical changes, C22–23
  conservation of, C26
  defined, C6
  forms of, C14
  particles of, C15
  physical changes, C22–23
  states of, C14
Mayas, B100
Mechanical energy, C66
Meissner's endings, R27
Melting, C16
Melting point, C18
Mendel, Gregor, A28, A118
Mendeleev, Dmitri, C48–49,
  C52
Mercury, planet, B124–125
Mercury barometer, B14
Merkel's endings, R27
Mesosphere, B8
Metal(s), C44–45
Metalloids, C49
Meteorologica (Aristotle), B58
Meteorologists, B16
Meterstick, using, R7
Mexia, Ynes, A56
Microclimate(s), B76
Microscope, A4
  using and caring for, R5
Microwaves, C80
Middle ear, R26

Mimosa, A112
Mineral deposits, E7
Minerals, E6
    properties of E4–5
Mining, coal, E13
Mining industry, C25
Mirrors, C76
Mitochondria, A8, A9, A10
Mixture(s), C10
Molecular biologists, A28
Molecules, C42, C82, C88
    asphalt, C29
Moneran kingdom, A39
Mongoose, A44
Monocots, A122
Moon(s)
    and Earth compared, B96
    and Earth in space, B90–93
    gravity of, C7
    of other planets, B128
    orbit around Earth, B134
    phases of, B92–93
Moon's surface, B95
Mosses, A48, A52, A78
Mount Wheeler, NM, B76
Mountain zone, B78
Mouth, R32, R36
Mucous membrane, R27
Mudslides, B79
Multi-fruit tree, A127
Muscle cells, A7
Muscle tissue, A12
Muscle(s), A25
    and bones, R31
    in pairs, R31
Muscles, human, A26
Muscular system, R30–31
    caring for, R31

N

NASA, B32
Nasal bone, R27
Nasal cavity, R27
National Aeronautic and Space
    Administration. See NASA
National Oceanic and Atmos-
    pheric Administration
    (NOAA), B32
National Weather Service, B58
Natural cycles, A73–75
Natural gas, E13, E16, E35
Natural materials, recycled, A72
Natural resources, E6–17
    conserving, E20–23
    inexhaustible, E8
    nonrenewable, E6–7, E36
    renewable, E8
    reusable, E8
Navarro, Julio, B138
Nectaries, A118
Negative charge, C70
Nephrons, A20
Neptune, B127
Nerve cells, A7, A26, R38
Nerve impulses, C80
Nerves, A26, R38
Nervous system, A26, R38–39
    caring for, R39
Nervous tissue, A12
Neurons, A26, R38
Neutral atom, C41
Neutrons, C41, C53
Newton, Sir Isaac, B130, B133
Nitrogen cycle, A73
Nonrenewable resources, E6–7,
    E36
Nonvascular plants, A52–53,
    A80–81
    reproduction of, A80
North America, air masses of,
    B48

North Carolina, climate, B77
Nose, R27, R36
Nostril, R27
Nuclear energy, E46
Nuclear fission, C91
Nuclear fusion, C91
Nucleus,
    atomic, C41, C53
    cell, A8–9, A28, A39
Nucleus, cell, A8–9, A28, A39

O

Ocean thermal energy, E48
Ocean thermal energy
    conversion (OTEC), E48
Ocean water, B20–23
Oil, from wells, E24–25
Oil rig worker, E25
Olfactory bulb, R27
Olfactory tract, R27
Optic nerve, R26
Orbits
    of electrons, C41
    of planets and moons,
        B132–135
Order, A40
Ore, C25
Organelles, A8
Organs, A12
Orrery, B130, B135
Osmosis, A10–11
Outer ear, R26
Ovary, A117, A118
Ovules, A117
Oxidation, C50
Oxygen, A68, A102, A103,
    A104–105, R37
Oxygen (element), C43
Ozone layer, B8

P

Pacini's endings, R27
Palisade layer, of leaf, A103
Pancreas, A19, R41
Parallel circuits, C72–73
Parathyroid glands, R41
Particles,
> of air, B7
> of matter, C15

Passive transport, A11
Pasteur, Louis, A29
Patella (kneecap), R28
Pea plant, life cycle of, A84
Peat, E14–15
Pelvis, R28
Penicillin, A29
Periodic table, C48–49, C52–53
Peripheral nervous system, A26, R39
Petals, A117
Petrochemicals, E12
Petroleum, E13, E16, E35
Phalanges, R28
Phloem, A67, A102
Phobos, B129
Photosphere, B118–119
Photosynthesis, A102–107, B7
Phototropism, A110
Phylum, A40
Pigment, A68
Pintail Lake, AZ, B31
Pistil, A116, A117
Pitch, C81
Pituitary gland, R41
Planet(s), B124
> distances between, B122–123
> inner, B124–125
> outer, B126–127

Plant cell structures, A8
Plant kingdom, A39
Plants
> and carbon dioxide, B7

> and oxygen, B7
> as food, A88–89
> as medicines, A90
> food making by, A102–107
> growth of, A122–127
> parts of, A64–69
> sexual reproduction, A116–119
> soft-stemmed, A66–67
> uses of, A88–91
> woody, A66–67

Plasma, A17
Plastic, E36
> from plants, A128–129

Platelets, A17
Platypus, duckbill, A35
Pluto, B127
Pointillism, A27
Polar climate, B77
Polar zone, B78
Pollen, A82, A114, A116
Pollination, A83, A117
> methods of, A118

Pollution, E8, E21
Polylactic acid resin (PLA), A129
Positive charge, C70
Potato plant, A125
Potato vaccines, A92–93
Potential energy, in foods (chart), C88
> power of, B37

Precipitation, B13, B21, B27, B76–77
Prevailing winds, B41–42, B78
Primary oil production, E25
Principia Mathematica, **(Newton),** B133
Products, chemical, C23, C26
Project Apollo, B102
Propane, E35
Properties, C6
> chemical, C20–21
> of metals, C44
> physical, C6–11

> separating, C24, C25
Protist kingdom, A39
Protists, A34
Protons, C41, C53, C70
Ptolemy, C83
Pulmonary arteries, A18
Pulmonary veins, A18
Pupil, of eye, C80, R26
Pyrite, E4

Q

Quadriceps, R30
Quartz, E4
Quinine, A90

R

Radiation, C87
Radiation zone, B119
Radio telescope(s), B101, B136
Radio waves, C80
Radius, R28
Rain forest, Amazon, A123
Rain gauge, B13, B49
Rarefaction, C81
Reactants, C23, C26
Reactivity, C23
Receptors, A26
Recycling, E22–23, E36, E37
Red blood cells, A7, A17
Red maple, A116
Reduce, reuse, recycle, E22
Reflection, C78
Reflexes, A26
Reforesting, E21
Refraction, C78
Reproduction
> artificial, A126
> asexual, A125
> sexual, A116–119

Reptiles, A44

Resistors, C73
Respiratory system, A16, A18, R36–37
Retina, C80, R26
Rib cage, A25, R28
Right atrium, R35
Right ventricle, R35
Rings
growth, A51, A67
of planets, B128
Root hairs, A65
Roots, A65–66, A111
storage, A66
Ruffini's endings, R27
Runners, A125
Runoff, B15, B21
Rust, C50

S

Safety
and first aid, R24
earthquake, R23
fire, R22
food, R14–15
in science, xvi
thunderstorm, R23
Saffir-Simpson Hurricane Scale, B37
Saliva, A19, R33
Salivary glands, A19, R33
Sapwood, A51
Satellite, B101
weather, B59, B72
Saturn, B126
rings of, B113, B128
Scales, plant, A82
Scales, skin, A7
Scanning tunneling microscope, C53
Sceptical Chymist, The (Boyle), C52
Schleiden, Matthias, A6, A28

Schmitt, Harrison, B108
Schwann, Theodor, A6, A28
Sea sponge, A45
Secondary recovery, oil, E25
Sedimentary rock, E16
Seedling, A84, A85, A124
Seeds, A111, A118, A122
apple, A83
compared, A122
dispersal of, A123
germination, A124
Selective cutting, E21
Self-pollination, A118
Semicircular canals, R26
Sense organs, R26–27
caring for, R27
Sepals, A117
Series circuit, C72
Serving size, R13
Shadows, C78
"Shin" bone, R31
Short-day plants, A112
Show Low wetlands, AZ, B30–31
SI (International System of Units), C11
Sierra Club, A56
Silica, A81
Silicon (element), C43
Silicon chips, E6
Silver sword (plant), A62
Single-cell organism, A28
Skeletal system, A25, R28
Skeleton, A47, R28
snake, A44
Skin, R27
Skull, A25, R27, R28
Small intestine, A19, R32
Smallpox vaccine, A28
Smooth muscles, A25
Snail, A45
Snell, Willebord, C83
Sodium (element), C43
Sodium chloride, B22
Soil, as nonrenewable resource, E8

Solar cells, E48
Solar eclipse, B94
Solar energy, C91, E31, E34, E47–48
Solar features, B120–121
Solar flares, B120
Solar panels, E47
Solar prominence, B121
Solar system,
exploration of, B100–104
Solar wind, B118, B120
Solids, C14, C15
Solubility, C10
Solutions, C10
Sonar, C82
Sound energy, C66, C82
Sound waves, C81
speed of, C82
Space exploration, B100–104
Space shuttle, B102
orbit of, B132–133
Space Station,
International, B104
Mir, B107
Spacesuits, B103
Species, A40, A54–55
number of, A35
Sperm, A116, A117, A118
Spider plants, A125
Spiders, A45
Spinal cord, A26, A43, R38–39
Spine, human, R28
Spines, plant, A68
Spleen, R34, R40
Spongy layer, of leaf, A103
Spore capsules, A80
Spores, A81
Spring scale, C7
using, R6
Spruce tree, A116
Sputnik, B101

Stamen, A116, A117

Standard masses, R6

Starch, A104, A106

Static electricity, C71

Station model, B68

making a, B66–67

Stationary front, B47

Steam engine, C90

Steam power, C90–91

Stem, A66–67

Stephenson-Hawk, Denise, B32

Sternum, R28

Stigma, A117

Stimulus, A110

Stirrup, in ear, C81, R26

Stomach, A19, R32, R33

Stomata, A68, A103

Storage rock, E10

Storm front, B46–47

Stratosphere, B8

Stratus clouds, B16

Strawberry plant, A125

Stretching, R18–19

Strip mining, E20

Style, A117

Subatomic particles, C41

Subcutaneous layer, R27

Sublimation, C17

Substances, use of, and properties, C24–25

Sugar beet root, A66

Sugar cane stems, A66

Sugaring Time (Lasky), A53

Sulfur, states of, C16–17

Sun, B114–121

energy from, B116–117, E13

features of, B114–121

heating of Earth by, B40

structure of, B118–119

Sun bear, A36

Sundew plant, A112

Sunspots, B114–115, B118, B120

Supertides, E42–43

Surface map, B68

Sweating, A21

Synapse, A26

Tadpole, A84

Taproots, A65

Taste buds, R27

Telescope, B101

Temperate climate, B77

Temperate zone, B78

Temperature, B13, B48, C86

and climate, B76

atmospheric, B9

Tendons, A25

Tendrils, A68

Thermal energy, C86–88, E34, E46

Thermal extraction, oil, E25

Thermogram, C84

Thermometer, B13

using a, R4

Thermosphere, B8

Thompson, Benjamin (Count Rumford), C89

Thunderheads, B16

and fronts, B47

Thunderstorms, B52–53, C71

and tornadoes, B56

frequency of, B36

safety, B53, R23

Thymus, R40, R41

Thyroid, R41

Tibia, R28

Tidal energy, E42–43

Tidal energy station, E42

Timing device, using, R7

Tissue, A12–13

Tissue culture, A126

Titan, B128

Titusville, PA, E32

Tongue, R27

Tonsils, R40

Tornado, B56

chasers, B83

safety, B56

Tortoiseshell beetle, A45

Trachea (windpipe), A18, R36

Trade winds, B42

Traits, plant, A118

Transpiration, B27

Trapezius, R30

Trees, A51

Triceps, R30

Tropical climate, B77

Tropical depression, B54

Tropical storm, B54

Tropical zone, B78

Tropisms, A110–111

Troposphere, B8, B12

Trunk, tree, A51, A67

Tuberculosis, A29

Tubers, A125

Tubes. *See* Vascular plants

Turbines, C91, E41

U

Ulna, R28

Ultraviolet waves, C80

Universal choking sign, R24

University of Nebraska, A129

Updrafts, B41

Uranus, B127

Urea, A20

Ureters, A20

Urethra, A20

U.S. Department of Agriculture, A129

U.S. Department of Energy, E25

V

Vacuoles, A8, A9, A11

Van de Graaff generators, C68, C71

Vascular plants, A50–51, A80–81

cone-bearing, A82

flowering, A83

reproduction of, A81

Vegetative propagation, A125

Veins, human, A17, R34

Veins, mineral, E7

Veins, plant, A68, A102

Venus, B124–125

Venus' flytrap, A68, A112

Vertebrae, A42–43

Vibrations, C81

Viking spacecraft, B102

Villi, A19

Visible light waves, C80

Vocal cords, R33

Volume, of matter, C8

Volume, sound, C81

Voluntary muscles, A25

W

Warm front, B47–48

Water

and living organisms, B27

and weather, B15–16, B20–21

daily gain and loss, A20

on the moon, B96

use, B28–29

Water cycle, B15–16, B20–21

and humans, B28

and weather, B26–27

Water pollution, B28, E21

Water strider, A38

Water treatment, B28, B31

Water vapor, B6, B15, B20, E41

Watt, James, C90

Waves

electromagnetic, C80

sound, C81

visible light, C80

Weather, B12

and air, B46–49

forecasting, B58–59, B68–69

local conditions, B74–75

Weather balloon, B69

Weather map, B70–71

Weather satellites, B59

Weather stations, B68, B72

using a, B10-11

Weather symbols, B66–67

Weather vane, B42

Weight, C7

Wells, E35

Westerlies, B42

Wetlands

artificial, B30–31

importance of, B30–31

White blood cells, A17, A29

Wind

causes of, B40–43

defined, B41

global, B42

local, B41

prevailing, B41–42

speed, estimating, B44–45

"Wind, The" (Stevenson), E49

Wind energy, C91, E37, E46–47

Wind farm, E47

Wind turbine, E47

Wind vane, B13, B58, B69

Windmills, E44

Windsock, B44, B45

Woodchuck, A55

Workout, guidelines for, R17–19

Worms, A45

X

X-1, B106

X rays, C80

Xylem, A67, A102

Z

Zygote, A81, A82, A117

Photography Credits: Page placement key: (t) top, (c) center, (b) bottom, (l)-left, (r) right, (bg) background, (i) inset

Cover: (bg)Eduardo Garcia/FPG International; Gail Shumway/FPG International

Table of Contents: Page v Sp. Bob Gatkany/Dorling Kindersley; v (bg) Telegraph Colour Library/FPGInternational; vi (bg)Tim Crosby/Liaison International; vi Alvis Upitis/The Image Bank; vii Eric & David Hosking/Photo Researchers; vii Telegraph Colour Library/FPGInternational

Unit A: A1 Anup & Manoj Shah/Animals Animals; A1 (bg) Grant V. Faint/The Image Bank; A2-A3 Image Shop/Phototake; A3 (l) Lawrence Migdale/Photo Researchers; A3 (c) Quest/SPL/Photo Researchers; A4 Charles D. Winters/Timeframe Photography, Inc./Photo Researchers; A6 (l) The Granger Collection, New York; A6 (c), A6 (r) Courtesy of Hunt Institute for Botanical Documentation, Carnegie Mellon University, Pittsburg, PA; A7 (tl) Ed Reschke/Peter Arnold, Inc.; A7 (tr) Michel Viard/Peter Arnold, Inc.; A7 (bl) Courtesy of Dr. Sam Harbo D.V.M., and Dr. Jurgen Schumacher D.V.M., Veterinary Hospital, University of Tennessee; A7 (br) A. B. Sheldon/Dembinsky Photo Associates; A8 Dwight R. Kuhn; A9 Courtesy of Dr. Sam Harbo D.V.M., and Dr. Jurgen Schumacher D.V.M., Veterinary Hospital, University of Tennessee; A10 Biophoto Associates/Science Source/Photo Researchers; A11 (l) J. Barry OíRourke/The Stock Market; A11 (r) Jim Brown/The Stock Market; A14 Michael Newman/PhotoEdit; A16 (l) Dr. Tony Brain/SPL/Photo Researchers; A16 (r) Prof. P. Motta/Dept. of Anatomy/University ìLa Sapienzaî, Rome/SPL/Photo Researchers; A22 Gary Holscher/Tony Stone Images; A28 (l) Kevin Collins/Visuals Unlimited; A28 (r) Alferd Pasieka/Peter Arnold, Inc.; A29 (l) Barbara Wright/Animals Animals; A29 (r) Dr. Dennis Kunkel/Phototake; A30 NASA; A33 Charles D. Winters/Timeframe Photography, Inc./Photo Researchers; A34-A35 Gregory Ochocki/Photo Researchers; A35 (t) Dave Watts/Tom Stack & Associates; A35 (b) Frances Fawcett/Cornell University/American Indian Programs; A36 Christian Grzimek/Okapia/Photo Researchers; A38-A39 Bill Lea/Dembinsky Photo Associates; A39 (t) Bill Lea/Dembinsky Photo Associates; A39 (c) S. Nielsen/Bruce Coleman, Inc.; A39 (b) Andrew Syred/SPL/Photo Researchers; A39 (tc) Dr. E. R. Degginger/Color-Pic; A39 (bc) Robert Brons/BPS/Tony Stone Images; A41 Daniel Cox/Tony Stone Images; A42 Arthur C. Smith, III/Grant Heilman Photography; A44-A45 (b) Runk/Schoenberger/Grant Heilman Photography; A44 (tl) Ana Laura Gonzalez/Animals Animals; A44 (bl) Tom Brakefield/The Stock Market; A45 (tl) Leonard Lee Rue, III/Bruce Coleman, Inc.; A45 (tc) Hans Pfletschinger/Peter Arnold, Inc.; A45 (tr) Mark Moffett/Minden Pictures; A45 (br) Larry Lipsky/DRK; A46 (t) James Balog/Tony Stone Images; A46 (b) Stephen Dalton/Photo Researchers; A48 Darrell Gulin/Tony Stone Images; A50 (l) Dr. E. R. Degginger, FPSA/Color-Pic; A51 Phil A. Dotson/Photo Researchers; A52 (t) Heather Angel/Biofotos; A52-A53 Runk Schoenberger/Grant Heilman Photography; A54 (tl) Art Resource, NY; A54 (tr) The Granger Collection, New York; A54 (bl) SuperStock; A54 (br) E. R. Degginger/Photo Researchers; A55 (i) Leonard Lee Rue III/Photo Researchers; A55 S. J. Krasemann/Peter Arnold, Inc.; A56 (t) Courtesy of Hunt Institute for Botanical Documentation, Carnegie Mellon University, Pittsburg, PA; A56 (b) Grant Heilman Photography; A60-A61 Tom Bean/Tony Stone Images; A61 (t) Inga Spence/Visuals Unlimited; A61 (b) Ned Therrien/ Visuals Unlimited; A62 James Randklev/Tony Stone Images; A64 (l) Matt Meadows/Peter Arnold, Inc.; A64 (c) Richard Choy/Peter Arnold, Inc.; A64 (r) Reinhard Siegel/Tony Stone Images; A65 Norman Myers/Bruce Coleman, Inc.; A65 (li) Dr. E. R. Degginger/Color-Pic; A65 (ri) John Kaprielian/Photo Researchers; A67 Jane Grushow/Grant Heilman Photography; A68-A69 (t), A68 (ti) Runk/Schoenberger/Grant Heilman Photography; A68-A69 (b) Alan Levenson/Tony Stone Images; A70 Wolfgang Kaehler Photography; A72 Randy Ury/The Stock Market; A73 Thomas Hovland from Grant Heilman Photograpy; A76 Wolfgang Kaehler Photography; A78 Darrell Gulin/Dembinsky Photo Associates; A80 Kim Taylor/Bruce Coleman, Inc.; A81, A82 (t) Runk/Schoenberger/Grant Heilman Photography; A82 (b) S.J. Krasemann/Peter Arnold, Inc.; A83 (t) Dr. E. R. Degginger/Color-Pic; A83 (b) Robert Maier/Earth Scenes; A84 (animal life cycle) (t) Gregory K. Scott/Photo Researchers; A84 (r) Harry Rogers/National Audubon Society; A84 (b) David M. Dennis/Tom Stack & Associates; A84 (l) Jen & Des Bartlett/Bruce Coleman, Inc.; A84 (plant life cycle) (t) Dr. E. R. Degginger/Color-Pic; A84 (r) Barry L. Runk/Grant Heilman Photography; A84 (b) Jane Grushow/Grant Heilman Photogra-

phy; A84 (l) Dwight R. Kuhn; A90 (l) Alan & Linda Detrick/Photo Researchers; A90 (r) Angelina Lax/Photo Researchers; A91 Grant Heilman Photography; A91 (i) Will & Deni McIntyre/Photo Researchers; A92 D. Cavagnaro/DRK; A93 (t) Dr. Dennis Kunkel/PhotoEdit; A93 (r) Mark Richards/PhotoEdit; A94 (t), A94 (b), Special Collections, California Academy of Science; A96 (l) Runk/Schoenberger/Grant Heilman Photography; A96 (r) Dr. E. R. Degginger/Color-Pic; A97 James Randklev/Tony Stone Images; A98-A99 Tony Craddock/Tony Stone Images; A99 (t) R. & E. Thane/Earth Scenes; A99 (b) Nuridsany et Perennou/Photo Researchers; A100 Steven Ogilvy/Picture It; A102 Wendell Metzen/Bruce Coleman, Inc.; A104 Dr. Kenneth R. Miller/SPL/Photo Researchers; A105 Dr. E. R. Degginger/Color-Pic; A106 B. W. Hoffmann/AGStock USA; A106 (i) Bachmann/Photo Researchers; A108 Peter Steiner/The Stock Market; A110 Cathlyn Melloan/Tony Stone Images; A111 (l) Runk/Schoenberger/Grant Heilman Photography; A111 (r) Lee Rentz/Bruce Coleman, Inc.; A112 (t) Michael Hubrich/Dembinsky Photo Associates; A112 (c) John Shaw/Bruce Coleman, Inc.; A112 (b) Phyllis A. Betow/Bruce Coleman, Inc.; A114 Gay Bumgarner/Tony Stone Images; A116 (l) Leonard Lee Rue, III/Photo Researchers; A116 (r) Dwight R. Kuhn; A116 (tli) Dick Scott/Dembinsky Photo Associates; A116 (bli) Michael P. Gadomski/Photo Researchers; A116 (ri) Dr. E. R. Degginger/Color-Pic; A118 (l) Pal Hermansen/Tony Stone Images; A118 (r) Hans Pfletschinger/Peter Arnold, Inc.; A119 Merlin Tuttle/Photo Researchers; A120 Frans Lanting/Minden Pictures; A123 (t) David Cavagnaro/Peter Arnold, Inc.; A123 (b) Kevin Schafer Photography; A123 (tc) E. R. Degginger/Bruce Coleman, Inc.; A123 (bc) Gregory K. Scott/Photo Researchers; A123 (bg) Jeff Lepore/Photo Researchers; A124 Runk/Schoenberger/Grant Heilman Photography; A125 (l) Kenneth W. Fink/Photo Researchers; A125 (tr) Jerome Wexler/National Audubon Society/Photo Researchers; A125 (b) G. I. Bernard/Earth Scenes; A126-A127 (t) G. R. Roberts Photo Library; A126 (bl) Dr. E. R. Degginger/Color-Pic; A126 (br) Rosenfeld Images, Ltd./SPL/Photo Researchers; A127 (i) Holt studios, Int./Photo Researchers; A128 Dana Downie/AGStock USA; A129 (b) Mark Richards/PhotoEdit; A130 Dennis Carlyle Darling/HRW; A132 ; A134 Wendy W. Cortesi; A135 Gay Bumgarner/Tony Stone Images

Unit B: B1 Dorling Kindersley; B1 (bg) Telegraph Colour Library/FPG International; B2-B3 SuperStock; B3 (t) Clyde H. Smith/Peter Arnold, Inc. B3 (b) Earl Roberge/Photo Researchers; B4 Keren Su/Stock, Boston; B6 Space Frontiers-TCL/Masterfile; B10, B12 (r) Warren Faidley/International Stock Photography; B12 (l) Everett Johnson/Tony Stone Images; B13 (bg) Orion/International Stock Photography; B13 (bli) M. Antman/The Image Works; B13 (bri) Dr. E. R. Degginger/Color-Pic; B14 (t) David M. Grossman/Photo Researchers; B14 (b) Mark Stephenson/Westlight; B16 (l) Dan Sudia/Photo Researchers; B16 (tr) Kent Wood/Photo Researchers; B16 (cr) Kevin Schafer/Peter Arnold, Inc.; B16 (br) Gary Meszaros/Dembinsky Photo Associates; B18 Michael Giannechini/Photo Researchers; B20-B21 Greg Vaughn/Tony Stone Images; B22 (t) C. Vincent/Natural Selection Stock Photography; B22 (b) Bob Daemmrich Photography, Inc.; B22 (bi) SuperStock; B24 Philip A. Savoie/Bruce Coleman, Inc.; B28 (r) A. Ramey/Stock, Boston; B28 (bl) Richard Gaul/FPG International; B30-B31 Lee Rentz/Bruce Coleman, Inc.; B31 (t) John Shaw/Bruce Coleman, Inc.; B31 (b) Ken Graham/Bruce Coleman, Inc.; B32 (t) Clark Atlanta University; B32 (b) NASA/SPL/Photo Researchers; B36-B37 Warren Faidley/International Stock Photography; B37 (t) Bob Abraham/The Stock Market; B37 (b) NRSC Ltd/SPL/Photo Researchers; B44 Bruce Watkins/Earth Scenes; B47 C. OíRear/Westlight; B48 (b) Bill Binzen/The Stock Market; B50 NASA/Science Photo Library/Photo Researchers; B56 (tl), (bl), B56-B57 (b) Larry Miller/Science Source/Photo Researchers; B58 Brad Gaber/The Stock Market; B59 (tr) Phil Degginger/Bruce Coleman, Inc.; B59 (bg) A. Ramsey/Woodfin Camp & Associates; B59 (b) NASA; B60 (t) Eli Reichman/HRW; B60 (b) NASA/Goddard Space Flight Center/JPL/Harcourt; B62 NASA/Science Photo Library/Photo Researchers; B63 Larry Miller/Science Source/Photo Researchers; B64-B65 Bob Abraham/The Stock Market; B66 George Hall/Check Six; B68 (l) Bruno P. Zehnder/Peter Arnold, Inc.; B68 (br) NASA; B68-B69 (bg) T Chinami/The Image Bank; B69 (l) Bob Daemmrich/The Image Works; B69 (c) Brownie Harris/The Stock Market; B71 (t) Phillip H. Coblentz/Tony Stone Images; B71 (b) C. Aurness/Corbis; B72 (bg), (li), (ri) Warren Faidley/International Stock Photography; B74 Richard Brown/Tony Stone Images; B76 (l) Tom Till; B76 (r) Coco McCoy/Rainbow; B76 (c); B77 (t) Randy Ury/The Stock Market; B77 (c) Larry

Cameron/Photo Researchers; B77 (b) Jeff Greenberg/Photo Researchers; B78 (l) Ron Sefton/Bruce Coleman, Inc.; B78 (r) Jose Fuste Raga/The Stock Market; B78 (c) John Lawrence/Tony Stone Images; B78 (cl) Fritz Prenzel/Peter Arnold, Inc.; B78 (cr) Marcello Pertinetti/Photo Researchers; B79 Paul Sequeira/Photo Researchers; B79 (i) Joe Sohm/Chromosomm/Photo Researchers; B80-B81 J. Richardson/Westlight; B82-B83 G. Jacobs, Stennis Space Center/Geosphere Project/Science Photo Library/Photo Researchers; B83 Howard Bluestein/Photo Researchers; B84 (t) Massachusetts Institute of Technology; B84 (b) Scott Camazine/Photo Researchers; B88-B89 Guodo Cozzi/Bruce Coleman, Inc.; B89 (l) Ray Pfortner/Peter Arnold, Inc.; B89 (r) Painting by Helmut Wimmer; B90 NASA; B92, B93 StockTrek; B94 (t) Dennis Di Cico/Peter Arnold, Inc.; B94 (b) Frank Rossotto/StockTrek; B95. B96 (tl), B96 (tr), B96 (br), B96 (ctr), B96 (cbr), B98 NASA; B96 (bl) Paul Stepan/Photo Researchers; B96 (ctl) Francois Gohier/Photo Researchers; B100-B101 (b) SPL/Photo Researchers; B100 (t), B100 (br) The Granger Collection, New York; B100 (bl) Martha Cooper/Peter Arnold, Inc.; B101 (tl) Sovfoto/Eastfoto; B101 (tr), B101 (br) NASA; B101 (bl) Courtesy of AT&T Archives; B102, B103, B104-B105, B106, B107, B108, B110, B111 NASA; B112-B113 Jerry Schad/Photo Researchers; B113 NASA; B114 StockTrek; B117 (t) Warren Faidley/International Stock Photography; B117 (c) Pekka Parviainen/SPL/Photo Researchers; B117 (b) Brian Atkinson/Tony Stone Images; B118 (t) Rev. Ronald Royer/SPL/Photo Researchers; B118 (c) NASA; B118 (b) Hale Observatory/SS/Photo Researchers; B120 Wards Sci/Science Source/Photo Researchers; B122 NASA; B125 (t) U.S. Geological Survey/SPL/Photo Researchers; B125 (b) David Crisp and the WFPC2 Science Team (Jet Propulsion Laboratory/California Institute of Technology); B125 (ct) NASA; B125 (cb) National Oceanic and Atmospheric Administration; B126 NASA; B126-B127 Erich Karkoschka (University of Arizona Lunar & Planetary Lab) and NASA; B127 (r) Dr. R. Albrecht, ESA/ESO Space Telescope European Coordinating Facility, NASA; B127 (c) Lawrence Sromovsky (University of Wisconsin-Madison), NASA; B128, B129 NASA; B130 Tom McHugh/Photo Researchers; B133 Erich Lesing/Art Resource, NY; B135 Scala/Art Resource, NY; B136 Chris Cheadle/Tony Stone Images; B137 (t) Dr. Robert Mallozzi of University of alabama/Huntsville & NASA; B137 (b) Tony Freeman/PhotoEdit; B138 Courtesy of Julio Navarro; B143 StockTrek

Unit C: C1 Alvis Upitis/The Image Bank; C1 (bg) Tim Crosby/Liaison International; C2-C3 Charles Krebs/The Stock Market; C3 (l) H. Armstrong Roberts; C3 (r) Jim Steinberg/Photo Researchers; C7 (b) NASA; C10 Ron Chapple/FPG International; C10 (bi) Dr. E. R. Degginger/Color-Pic; C12 Charles D. Winters/Photo Researchers; C14 Spencer Swanger/Tom Stack & Associates; C15 (c) Phil Degginger/Color-Pic; C16 Dr. E. R. Degginger/Color-Pic; C17 (bl), C17 (br) Tom Pantages; C18, C19 Yoav Levy/Phototake; C20 NASA; C23 (t), C23 (b) Tom Pantages; C23 (c) Yoav Levy/Phototake; C24 Horst Desterwinter/International Stock Photography; C25 (t) Dr. E. R. Degginger/Color-Pic; C25 (b) Norman O. Tomalin/Bruce Coleman, Inc.; C28 Joe Sohm/Photo Researchers; C29 (t) Doug Martin/Photo Researchers; C29 (b) Gary A. Conner/PhotoEdit; C30 (t) Glenn Photography; C30 (b) Geoff Tompkinson/SPL/Photo Researchers; C36-C37 Pete Saloutos/Tony Stone Images; C37 (t) Jan Taylor/Bruce Coleman, Inc.; C37 (b) Dr. E. R. Degginger/Color-Pic; C38 SuperStock; C40 Lee Snider Photo Images; C42 (t) J. & L. Weber/Peter Arnold, Inc.; C42 (b) Dr. E. R. Degginger/Color-Pic; C43 top to bottom (1) Joe Towers/The Stock Market; (2) Christopher S. Johnson/Stock, Boston; (4) Telegraph Colour Library/FPG International; (6) George Haling/Photo Researchers; C44 Wesley Hitt/Tony Stone Images; C44 (li) Richard Laird/FPG International; C46 Yoav Levy/Phototake; C50 Michael Monello/Julie A. Smith Photography; C52 (l) Mel Fisher Maritime Heritage Society, Inc.; C53 Michigan Molecular Institute; C54 AP Photo/Wide World; C60-C61 Scott Warren; C61 (b) M. Zhilin/M. Newman/Photo Researchers; C62 Jan Butchofsky-Houser/Dave G. Houser; C64 (l) Duomo Photography; C64 (c) William R. Sallaz/Duomo Photography; C64 (r) Steven E. Sutton/Duomo Photography; C65 (t) Gary Bigham/International Stock Photography; C65 (ti) Ken Gallard Photographics; C65 (bl) Steven E. Sutton/Duomo Photography; C65 (br) Duomo Photography; C66 Greg L. Ryan/Sally Beyer/AllStock/PNI; C68 Peter Menzel Photography; C70-C71, C71 (br) Phil Degginger/Bruce Coleman, Inc.; C71 (t) Ontario Science Centre; C74 (l) Michael J. Schimpf; C76 Tony Stone Images; C78 (l), C78 (c) E. R. Degginger/Bruce Coleman, Inc.; C78 (r) Tony Freeman/PhotoEdit; C80 (t) Tim Beddow/Tony Stone Images; C81 (t) Danila G. Donadoni/Bruce Coleman, Inc.; C82-C83 Norbert Wu/Tony Stone

Images; C84 Chuck OíRear/H. Armstrong Roberts, Inc.; C88-C89 Peter Cade/Tony Stone Images; C90 (l) David Overcash/Bruce Coleman, Inc.; C90 (r) David Young-Wolff/Photo Edit; C91 (l) Keith Gunnar/Bruce Coleman, Inc.; C91 (r) John Elk, III/Bruce Coleman, Inc.; C92 (t) Dr. Jean M. Bennett; C92 (b) Diane Schiumo/Fundamental Photographs; C96 (bg) Tim Crosby/Liaison International; E1 Alvis Upitis/The Image Bank

Extension Chapters: E1 (bg) Bios (klein-Hubert/Peter Arnold, Inc.; E1 Eric & David Hosking/Photo Researchers; E2-E3 Terry Vine/Tony Stone Images; E3 (t) Bruce Hands/Tony Stone Images; E3 (b) Joe Sohm/Chromosohm/Stock, Boston; E4 (t) Arnold Fisher/SPL/Photo Researchers; E4 (b) Runk/Schoenberger/Grant Heilman Photography; E6-E7 (b) Debra P. Hershkowitz/Bruce Coleman, Inc.; E6 (l), E7 (tl), E7 (tr), E7 (c), E7 (br) Dr. E. R. Degginger/Color-Pic; E7 (tc) Vanessa Vick/Photo Researchers; E8-E9 Michael P. gadomski/Photo Researchers; E10 J. C. Carton/Bruce Coleman, Inc.; E12 (l) Larry Lefever from Grant Heilman Photograpy; E12 (r) Thomas Kitchin/Tom Stack & Associates; E13 Kenneth Murray/Photo Researchers; E14 (l) Dr. E. R. Degginger/Color-Pic; E14 (r), E15 (l) Breck P. Kent/Earth Scenes; E15 (r) Dr. E. R. Degginger/Color-Pic; E18 Richard B. Levine; E20, E20 (i) Matt Meadows/Peter Arnold, Inc.; E21 Jack W. Dykinga/Bruce Coleman, Inc.; E21 (i) David Aronson/Stock, Boston; E22 (bg) Dick Rowan/Photo Researchers; E22 (t) Henneghien/Bruce Coleman, Inc. E22 (cr) Michele Burgess/Stock, Boston; E24 Shell Photo Service; E25 (t) Jeremy Hardie/Tony Stone Images; E25 (b) David R. Frazier; E26 (t) Otis Imbodenngs/NGS Image Collection; E26 (b) AP Photo/Damian Dovarganes/Wide World Photos; E29 David Young-Wollf/Tony Stone Images; E30-E31 Jeff Hunter/The Image Bank; E31 (t) SPL/Photo Researchers; E31 (bl) James King-Holmes/SPL/Photo Researchers; E31 (br) Ron Chapple/FPG International; E32 Cary Wolinsky/Stock, Boston/PNI; E34 Billy E. Barnes/PhotoEdit; E35 (t) Gary Conner/PhotoEdit; E35 (c) Bill Aron/PhotoEdit; E35 (b) Myrleen Ferguson/PhotoEdit; E36 (t) Tony Freeman/PhotoEdit; E36 (b) David Young-Wolff; E38 Jim McCrary/Tony Stone Images; E40 Wendell Metzen/Bruce Coleman, Inc.; E40 (i) Mark E. Gibson; E41 (l) Keith Gunnar/Bruce Coleman, Inc.; E41 (c) Tony Freeman/PhotoEdit; E41 (r) Mark Newman/Bruce Coleman, Inc.; E42 Claus Militz/Okapia/Photo Researchers; E44 Myrleen Ferguson/PhotoEdit; E46 (t) Alan L. Detrick/Photo Researchers; E46 (b) Cameramann International; E47 (t) Nicholas de Vore III/Bruce Coleman, Inc.; E47 (c) Andrew Rakoczy/Bruce Coleman, Inc.; E47 (b) Glen Allison/Tony Stone Images; E48 Lockheed Space and Missile Co., Inc.; E50 Mark E. Gibson; E51 (t) M. E. Rzucidlo/H. Armstrong Roberts; E51 (b) Andy Sacks/Tony Stone Images; E52 (t) Drew Donovan Photography; E52 (b) Stan Ries/International Stock Photography

Health Handbook: R20 (t) Tony Freeman/PhotoEdit; R20 (b) David Young-Wolff/PhotoEdit; R21 (t) Myrleen Ferguson Cate/PhotoEdit; R21 (b) David Young-Wolff/PhotoEdit; R23 Tony Freeman/PhotoEdit

All other photographs by Harcourt photographers listed below, ©**Harcourt:** Weronica Ankarorn, Bartlett Digital Photography, Victoria Bowen, Eric Camden, Digital Imaging Group, Charles Hodges, Ken Karp, Ken Kinzie, Ed McDonald, Sheri OiNeal, Terry Sinclair

Illustration Credits: Tim Alt B20-21, C15, C16-17, C32, C34, C41, C42, C43, C58; Art Staff B14; Paul Breeden A66; Lewis Calver A8, A9, A10, A11, A12, C80-81; Mike Dammer A57, A131, B61, B85 B109, B140, B141, C55, C57, E53; Eldon Doty A31, A95, B109, C33, C55, C57, E53; Pat Foss A131, A132, A133, B139, C31, C32, C56, C93, E27; Geosystems B42, B47, B48, B49, B55, B70, B71, B77, B78, B79, E7, E13; Patrick Gnan C67, C79, C80; Pedro Julio Gonzalez A46; Dale Gustafson A73, C66, C72-73, E42; Tim Hayward A40; Jackie Heda A16, A17, A18, A19, A20, A25, A26; Roger Kent A67, A80, A81, A102-103, A104-105, A117, A118, A122, A125; Mike Lamble B92-93, B94, B95, B111, B132-133, B134; Ruth Lindsay A74-75; Lee MacLeod A27; Janos Marffy B52-53, B54-55; Sebastian Quigley B12-13, B15, B40, B41, B116-117, B118-119, B124, B125, B126-127; Rosie Sanders A82, A83; Mike Saunders A50, A51, B7, B8-9, B26-27, B110, E13, E14-15, E16-17; Steve Seymour B46-47; Andrew Shiff A31, A95, A133, B33, B139, B140, B141, C31, C93; Beth Willert A24.

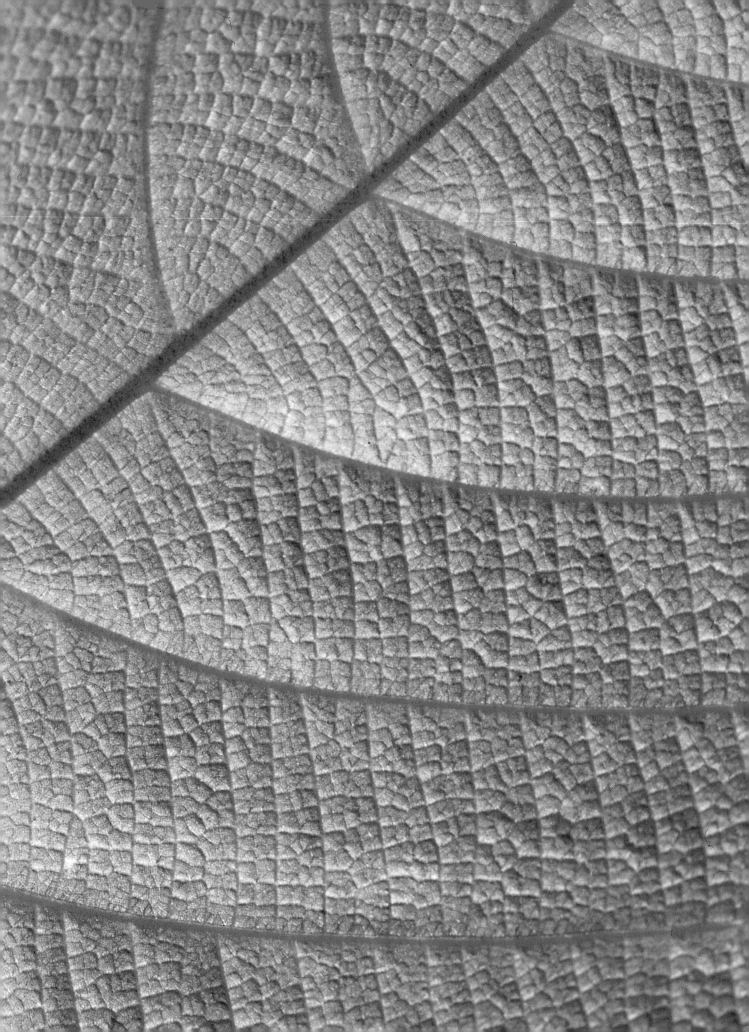

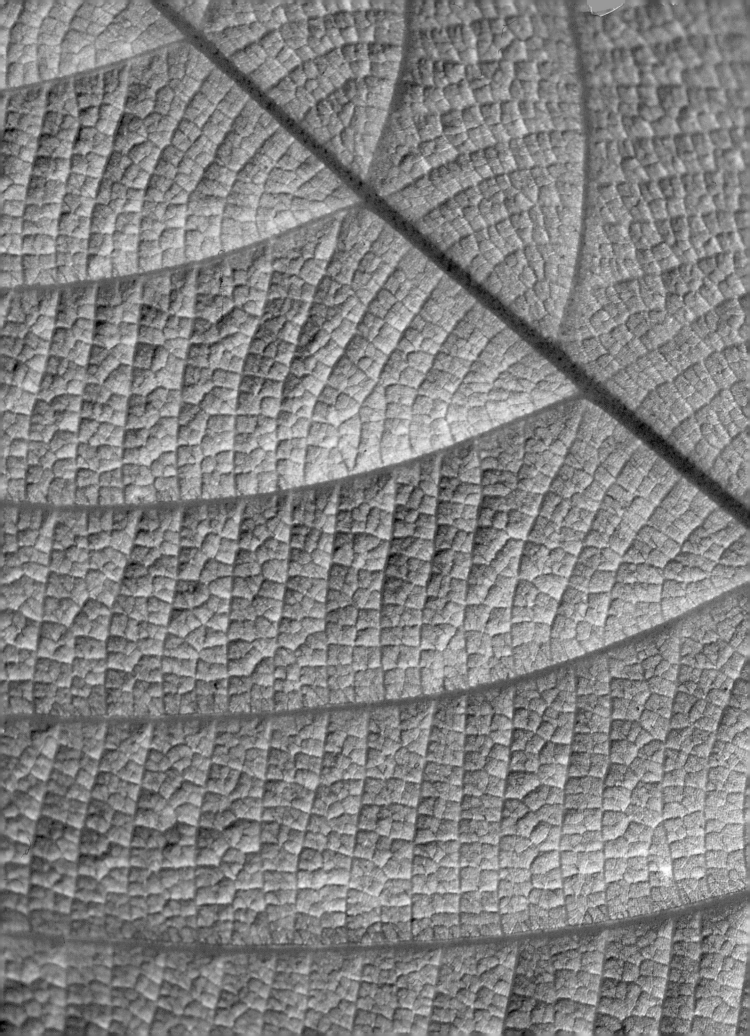